URASAWA X TEZUKA

A NEW VISION BASED ON ASTRO BOY – *'THE GREATEST ROBOT ON EARTH'*
BY NAOKI URASAWA AND OSAMU TEZUKA

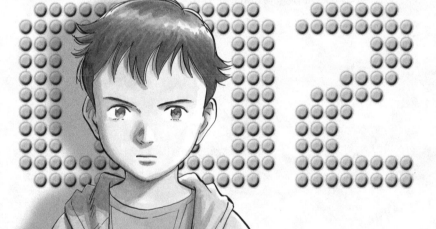

002

CO-AUTHORED WITH TAKASHI NAGASAKI
SUPERVISED BY MACOTO TEZKA
WITH THE COOPERATION OF TEZUKA PRODUCTIONS

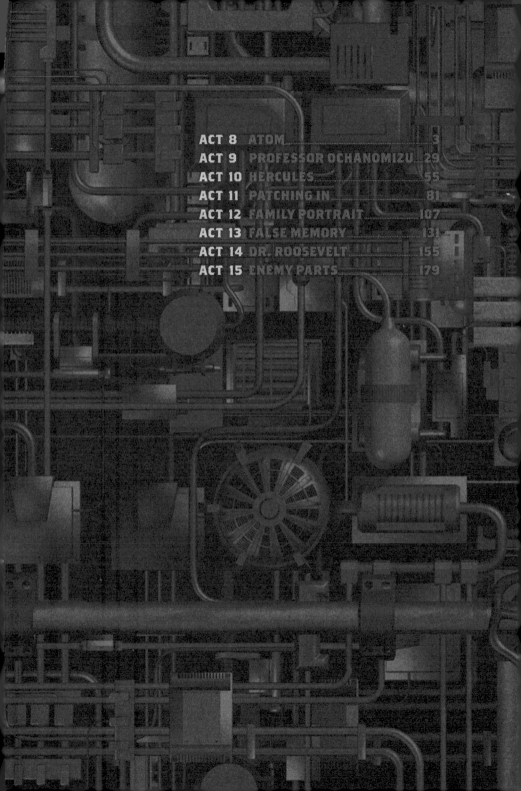

Act 8 ATOM

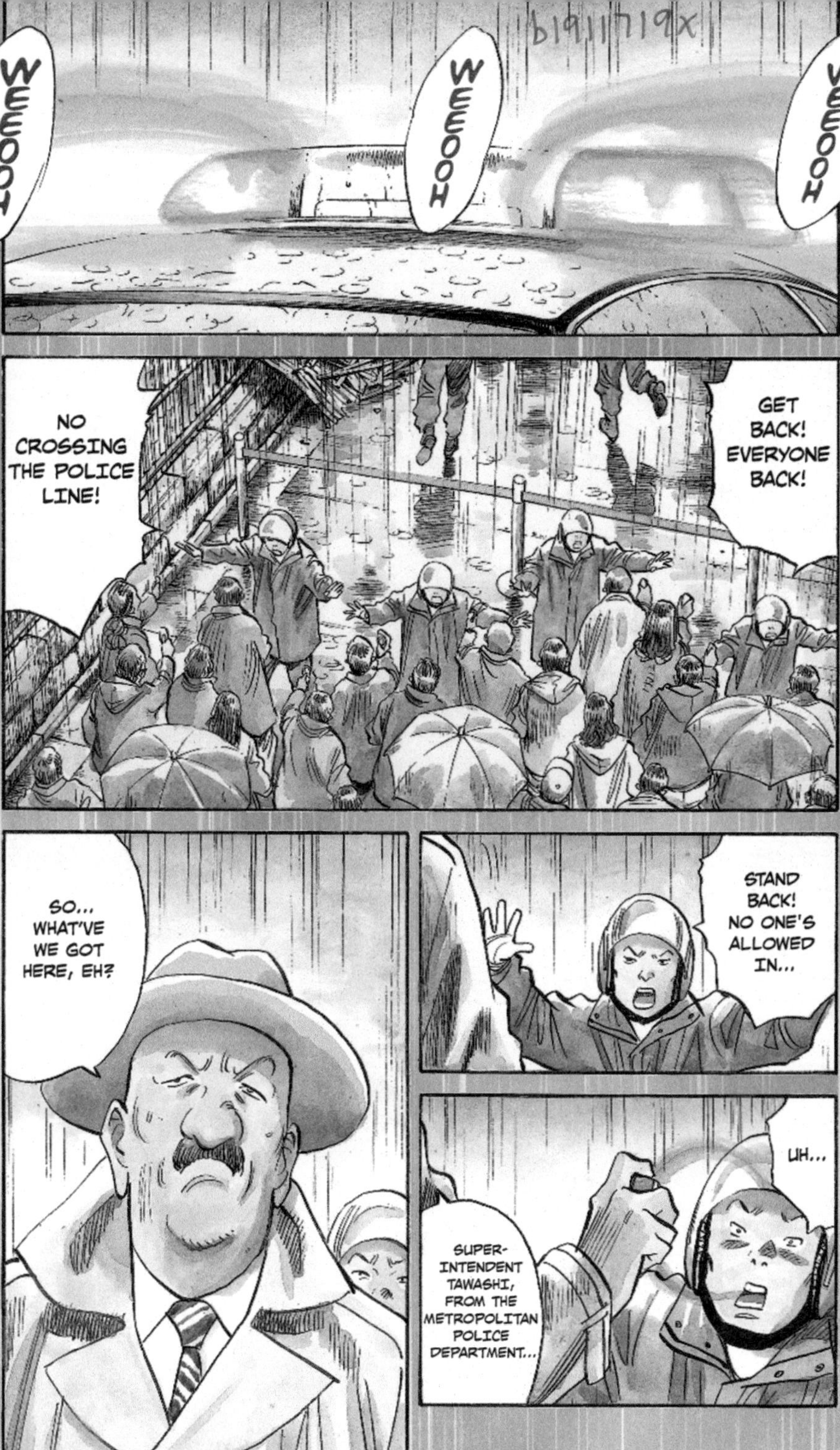
WEEEOOOH
WEEEOOOH
WEEEOOOH
GET BACK! EVERYONE BACK!
NO CROSSING THE POLICE LINE!
STAND BACK! NO ONE'S ALLOWED IN...
UH...
SUPER-INTENDENT TAWASHI, FROM THE METROPOLITAN POLICE DEPARTMENT...
SO... WHAT'VE WE GOT HERE, EH?

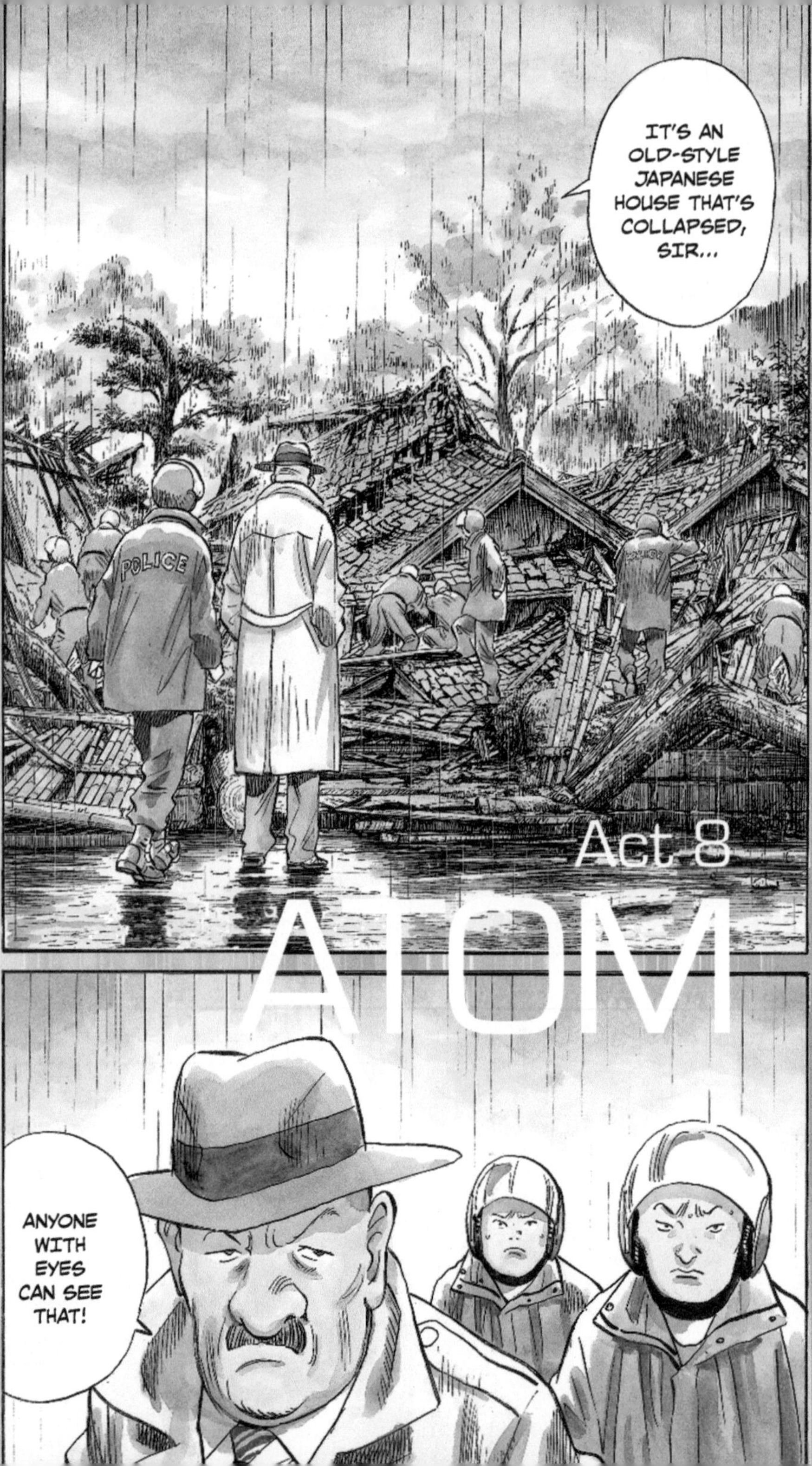
IT'S AN OLD-STYLE JAPANESE HOUSE THAT'S COLLAPSED, SIR...
Act 8
ATOM
ANYONE WITH EYES CAN SEE THAT!

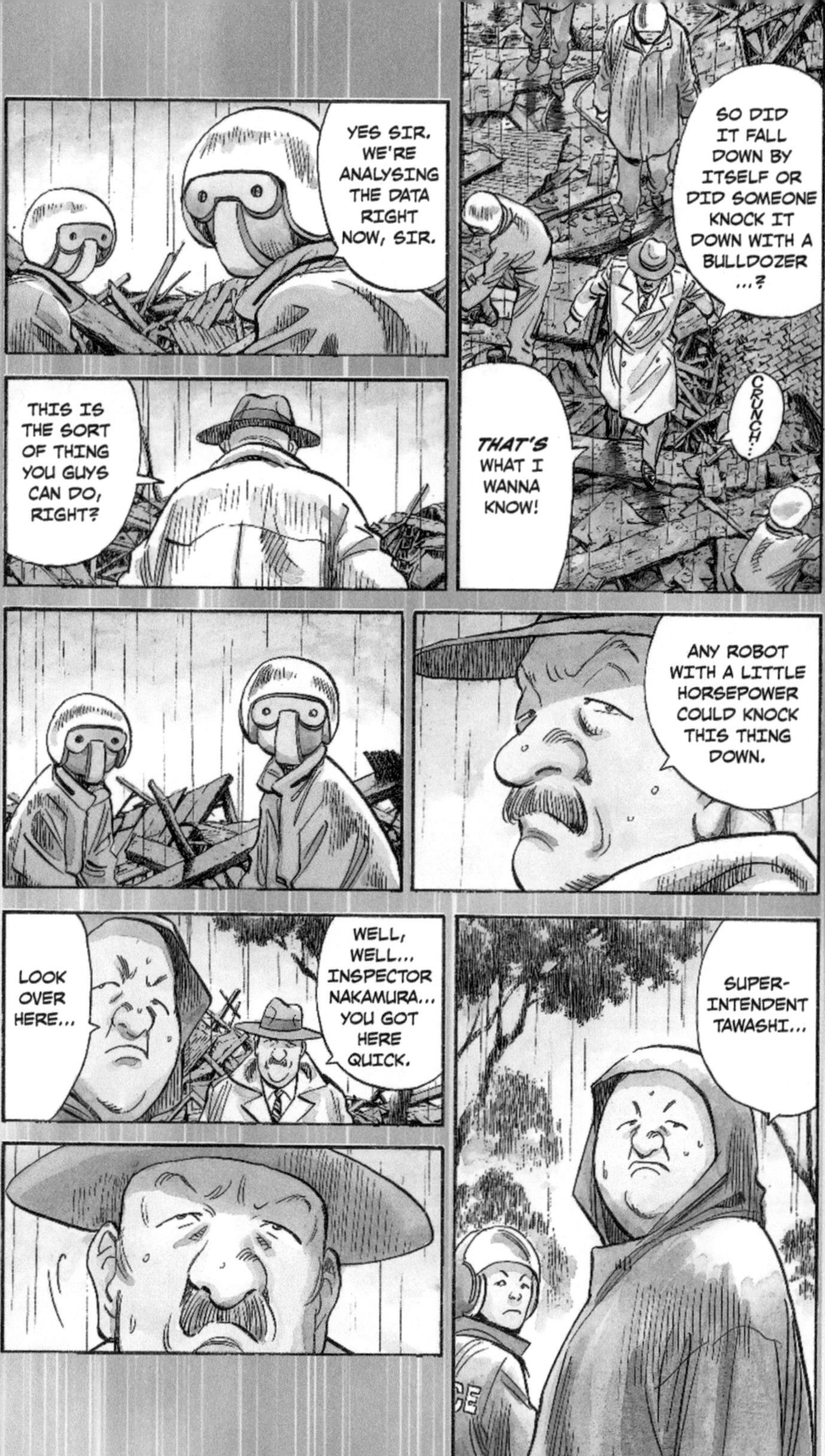
SO DID IT FALL DOWN BY ITSELF OR DID SOMEONE KNOCK IT DOWN WITH A BULLDOZER ...?
CRUNCH...
THAT'S WHAT I WANNA KNOW!
YES SIR. WE'RE ANALYSING THE DATA RIGHT NOW, SIR.
THIS IS THE SORT OF THING YOU GUYS CAN DO, RIGHT?
ANY ROBOT WITH A LITTLE HORSEPOWER COULD KNOCK THIS THING DOWN.
SUPER-INTENDENT TAWASHI...
WELL, WELL... INSPECTOR NAKAMURA... YOU GOT HERE QUICK.
LOOK OVER HERE...

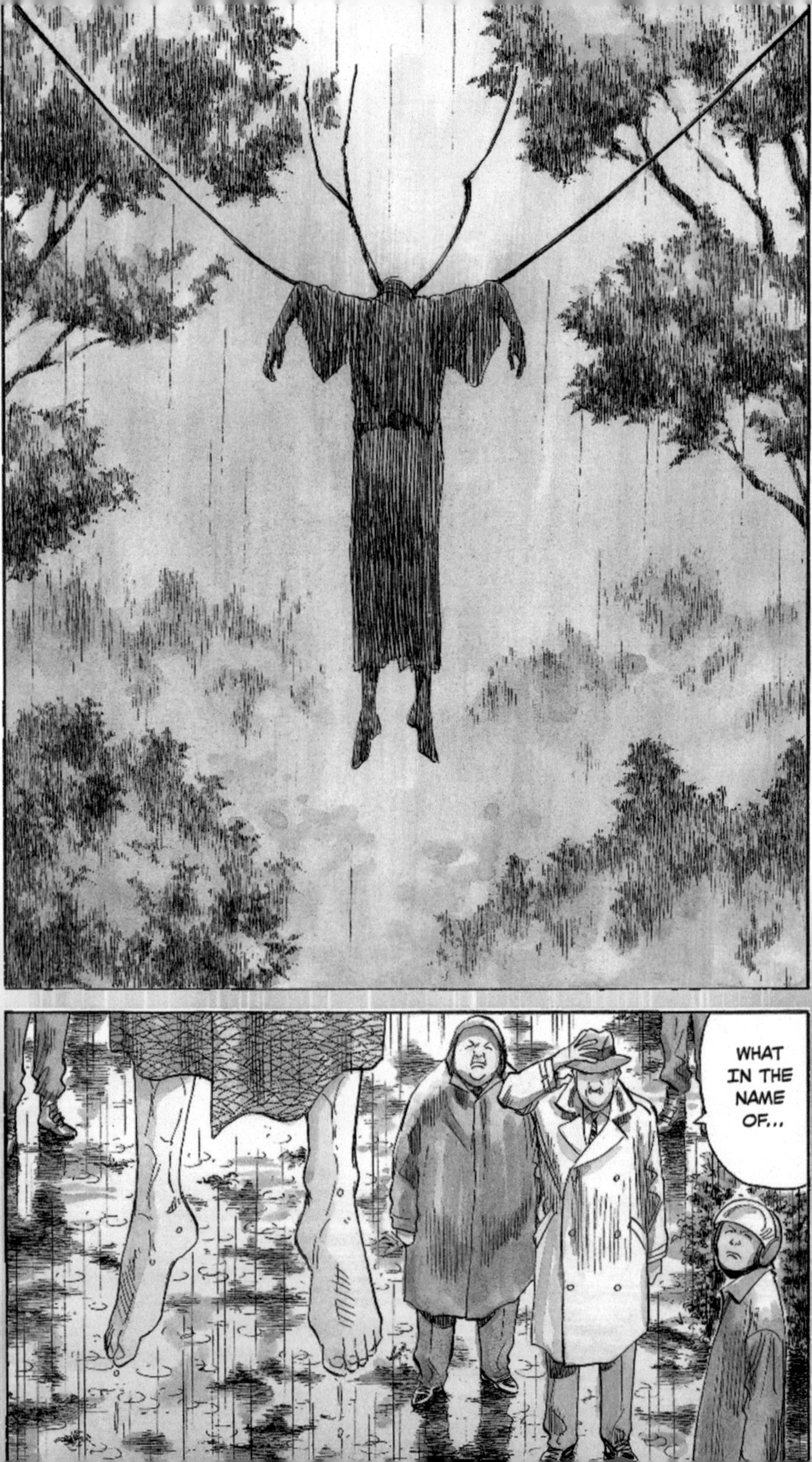
WHAT IN THE NAME OF...

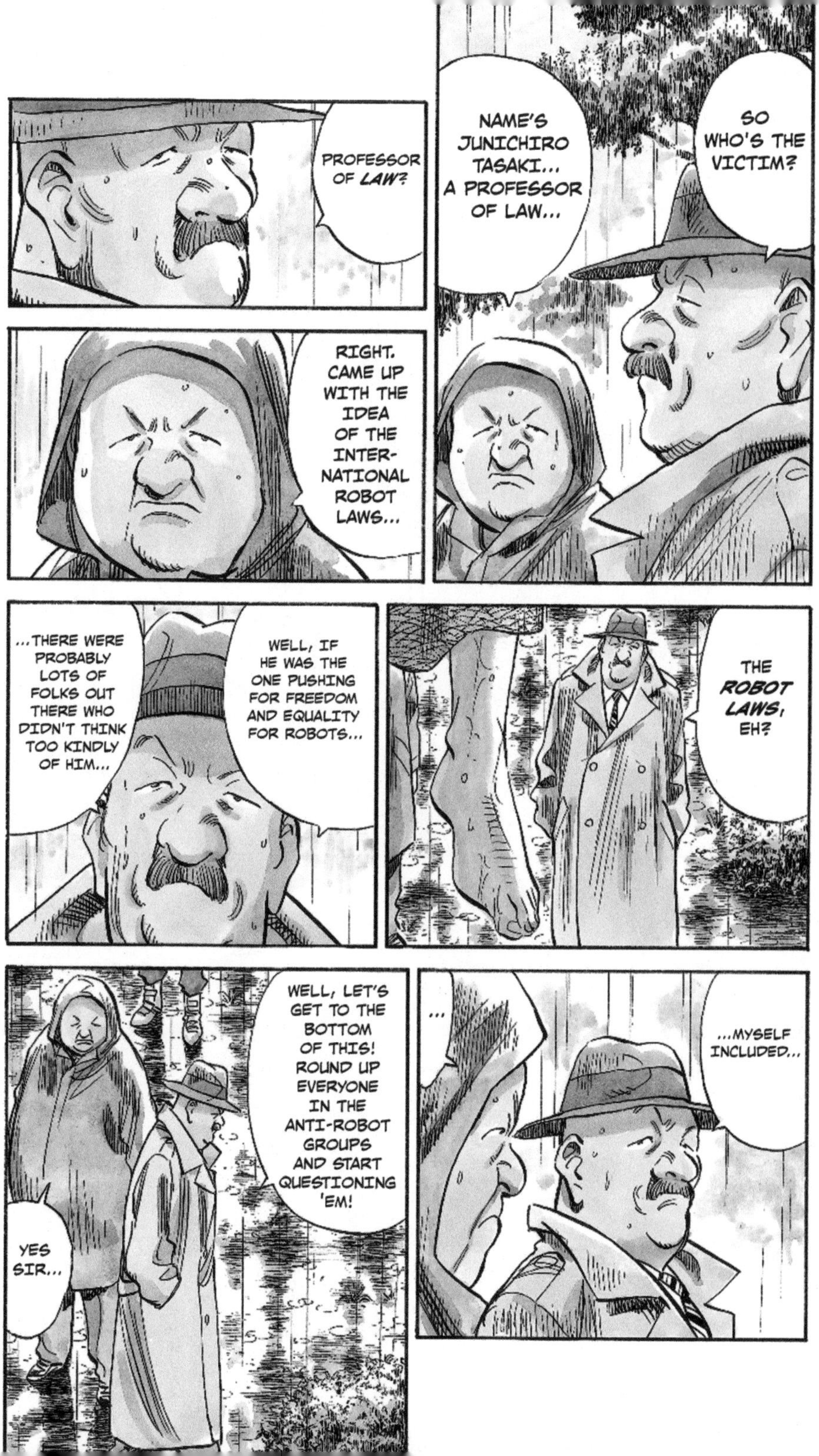
SO WHO'S THE VICTIM?
NAME'S JUNICHIRO TASAKI... A PROFESSOR OF LAW...
PROFESSOR OF *LAW*?
RIGHT. CAME UP WITH THE IDEA OF THE INTER-NATIONAL ROBOT LAWS...
THE *ROBOT LAWS*, EH?
WELL, IF HE WAS THE ONE PUSHING FOR FREEDOM AND EQUALITY FOR ROBOTS...
...THERE WERE PROBABLY LOTS OF FOLKS OUT THERE WHO DIDN'T THINK TOO KINDLY OF HIM...
...MYSELF INCLUDED...
...
WELL, LET'S GET TO THE BOTTOM OF THIS! ROUND UP EVERYONE IN THE ANTI-ROBOT GROUPS AND START QUESTIONING 'EM!
YES SIR...

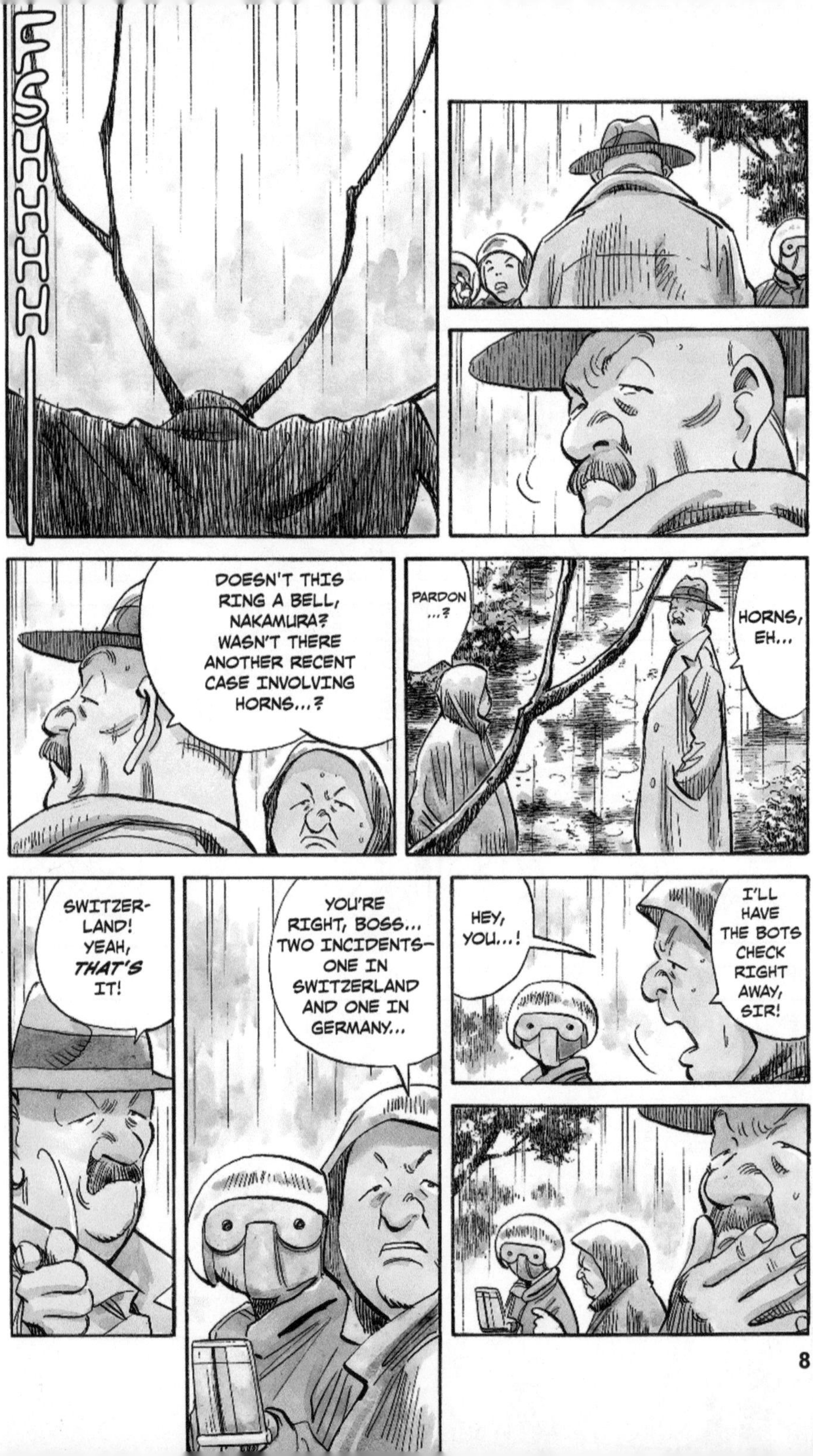
FSHHHHHH
HORNS, EH...
PARDON ...?
DOESN'T THIS RING A BELL, NAKAMURA? WASN'T THERE ANOTHER RECENT CASE INVOLVING HORNS...?
I'LL HAVE THE BOTS CHECK RIGHT AWAY, SIR!
HEY, YOU...!
YOU'RE RIGHT, BOSS... TWO INCIDENTS— ONE IN SWITZERLAND AND ONE IN GERMANY...
SWITZER-LAND! YEAH, THAT'S IT!

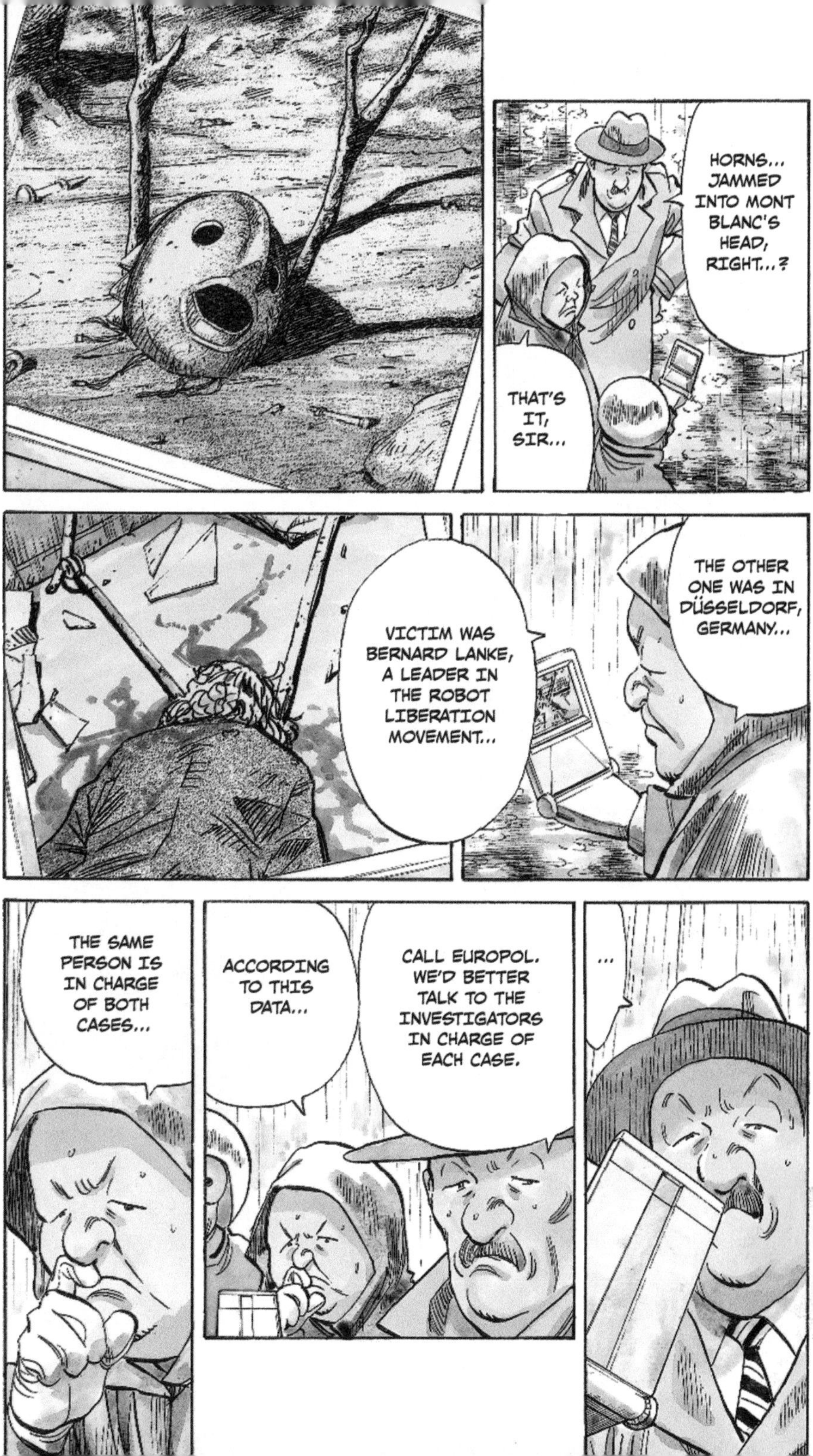
HORNS... JAMMED INTO MONT BLANC'S HEAD, RIGHT...?
THAT'S IT, SIR...
THE OTHER ONE WAS IN DÜSSELDORF, GERMANY...
VICTIM WAS BERNARD LANKE, A LEADER IN THE ROBOT LIBERATION MOVEMENT...
...
CALL EUROPOL. WE'D BETTER TALK TO THE INVESTIGATORS IN CHARGE OF EACH CASE.
ACCORDING TO THIS DATA...
THE SAME PERSON IS IN CHARGE OF BOTH CASES...

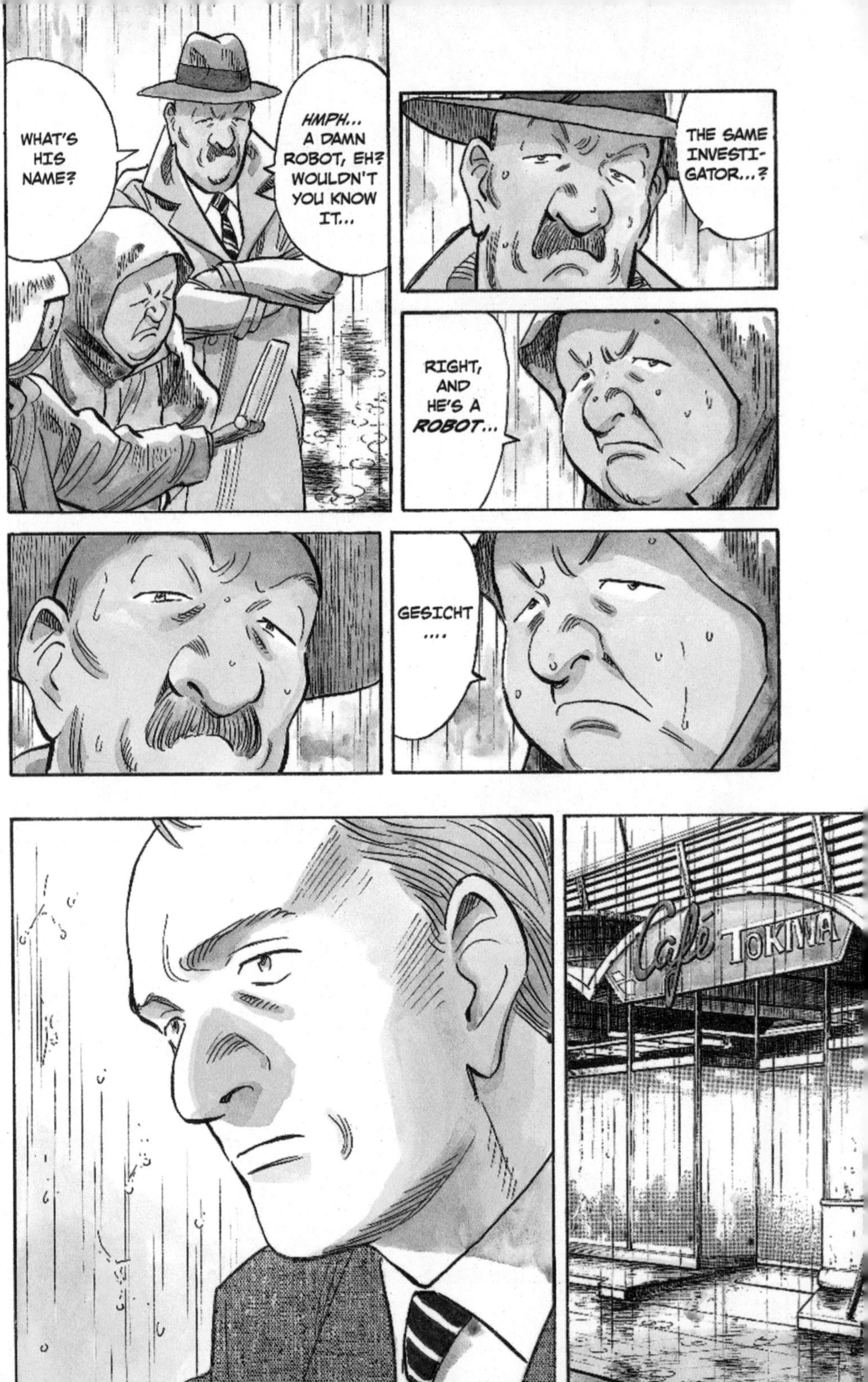
THE SAME INVESTI-GATOR...?
RIGHT, AND HE'S A ROBOT...
HMPH... A DAMN ROBOT, EH? WOULDN'T YOU KNOW IT...
WHAT'S HIS NAME?
GESICHT ....
Café TOKIWA

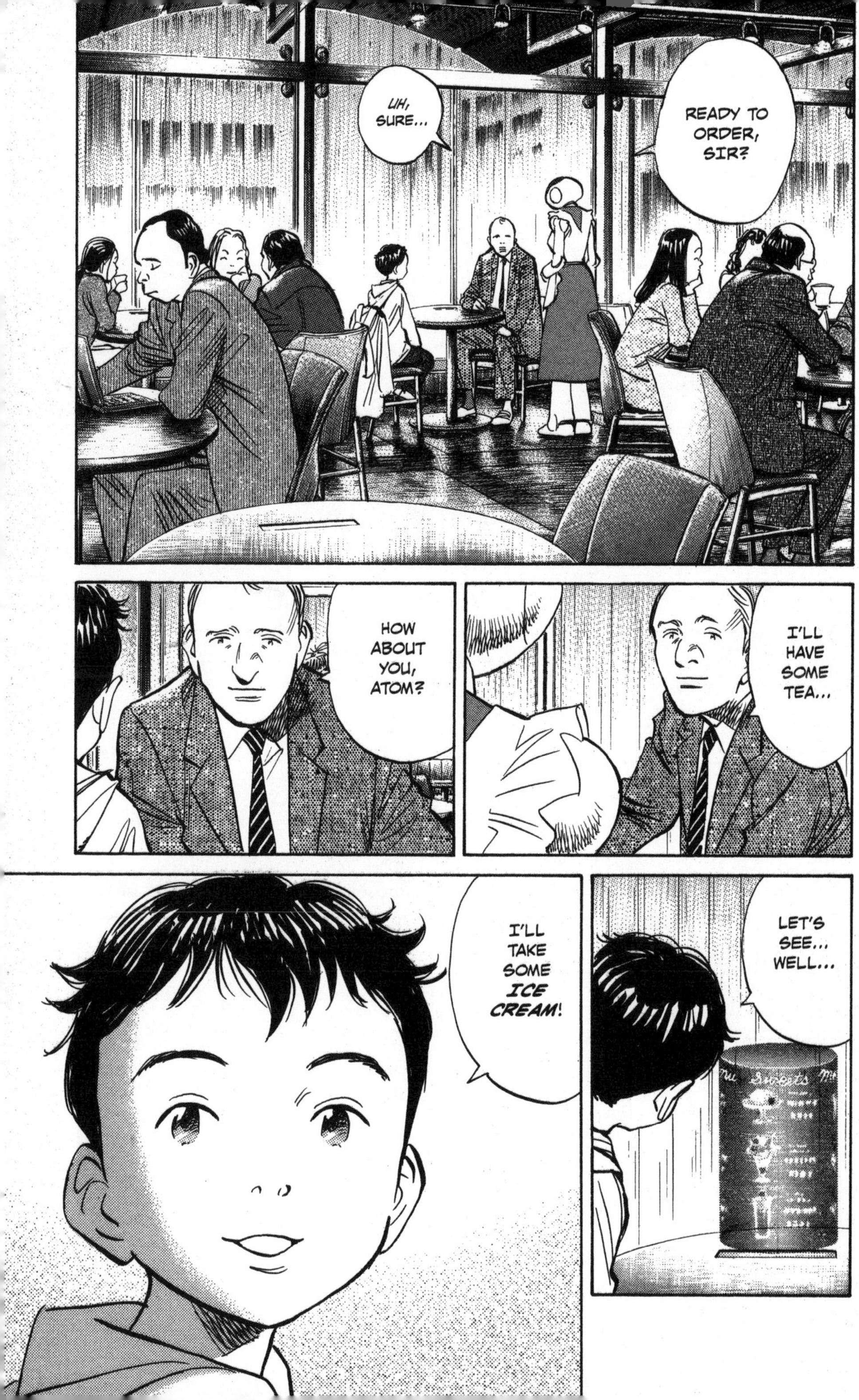
READY TO ORDER, SIR?
UH, SURE...
I'LL HAVE SOME TEA...
HOW ABOUT YOU, ATOM?
LET'S SEE... WELL...
I'LL TAKE SOME *ICE CREAM*!

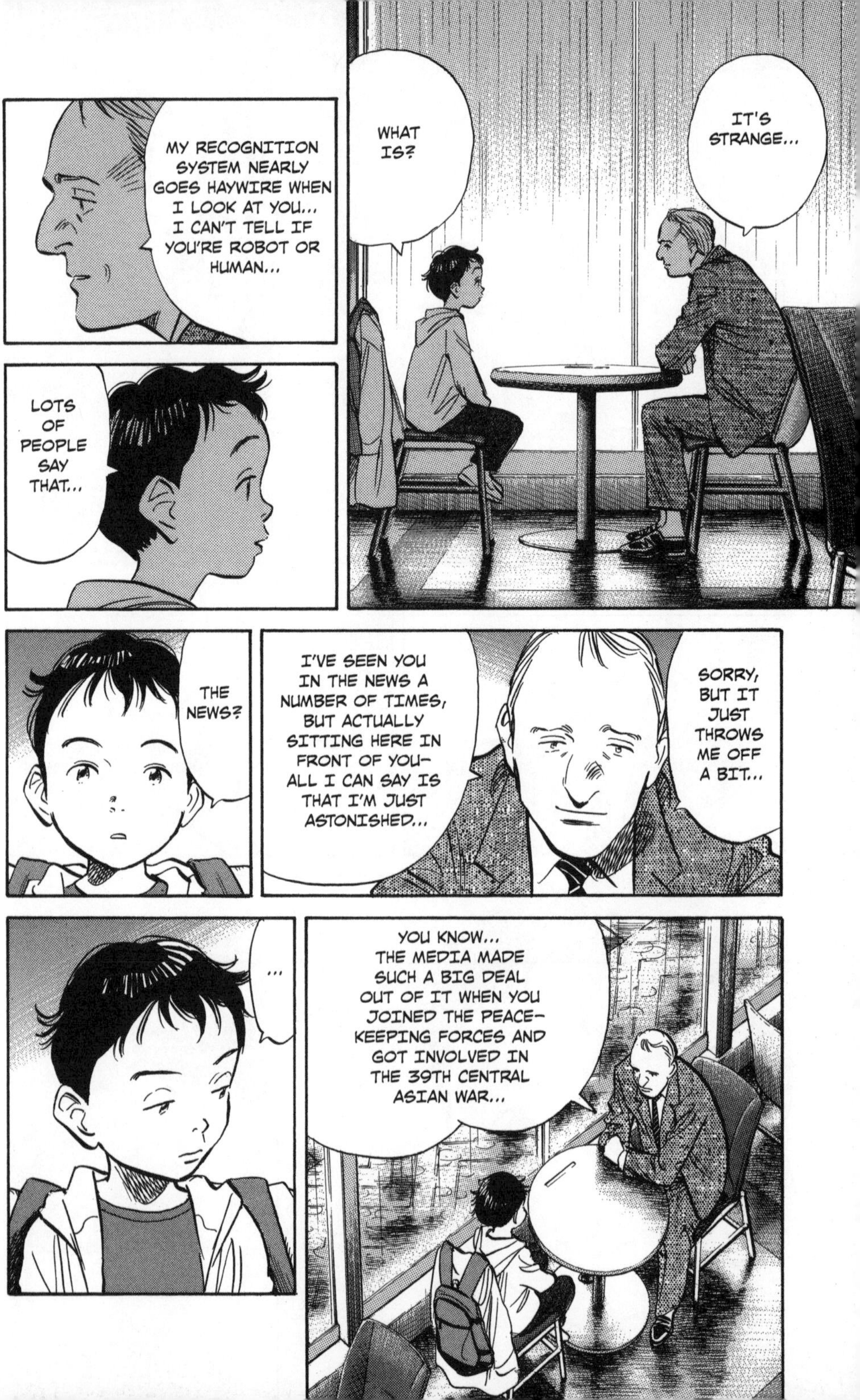
IT'S STRANGE...
WHAT IS?
MY RECOGNITION SYSTEM NEARLY GOES HAYWIRE WHEN I LOOK AT YOU... I CAN'T TELL IF YOU'RE ROBOT OR HUMAN...
LOTS OF PEOPLE SAY THAT...
SORRY, BUT IT JUST THROWS ME OFF A BIT...
I'VE SEEN YOU IN THE NEWS A NUMBER OF TIMES, BUT ACTUALLY SITTING HERE IN FRONT OF YOU–ALL I CAN SAY IS THAT I'M JUST ASTONISHED...
THE NEWS?
YOU KNOW... THE MEDIA MADE SUCH A BIG DEAL OUT OF IT WHEN YOU JOINED THE PEACE-KEEPING FORCES AND GOT INVOLVED IN THE 39TH CENTRAL ASIAN WAR...
...

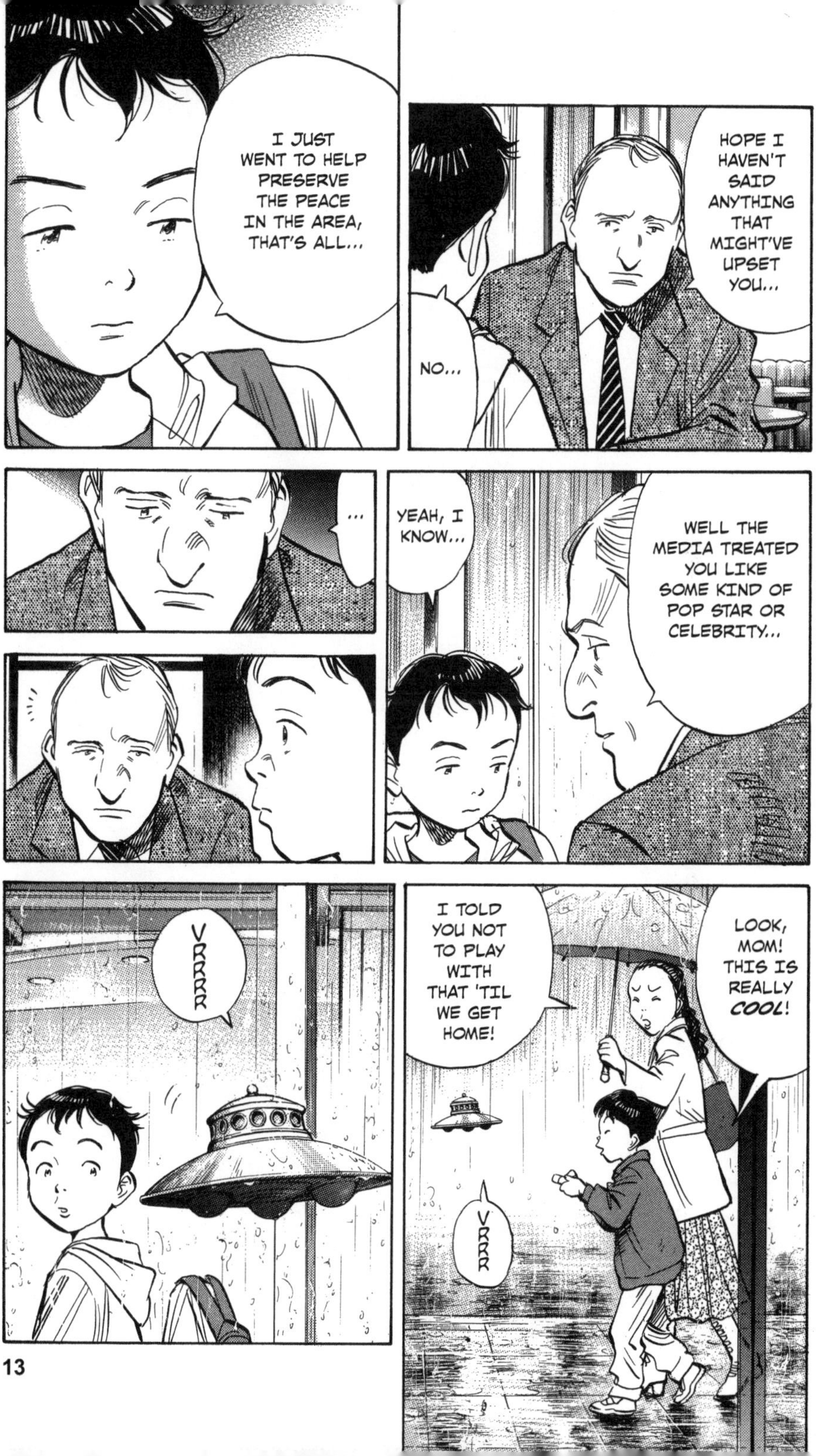
HOPE I HAVEN'T SAID ANYTHING THAT MIGHT'VE UPSET YOU...
NO...
I JUST WENT TO HELP PRESERVE THE PEACE IN THE AREA, THAT'S ALL...
WELL THE MEDIA TREATED YOU LIKE SOME KIND OF POP STAR OR CELEBRITY...
YEAH, I KNOW...
...
LOOK, MOM! THIS IS REALLY **COOL**!
I TOLD YOU NOT TO PLAY WITH THAT 'TIL WE GET HOME!
VRRR
VRRRR

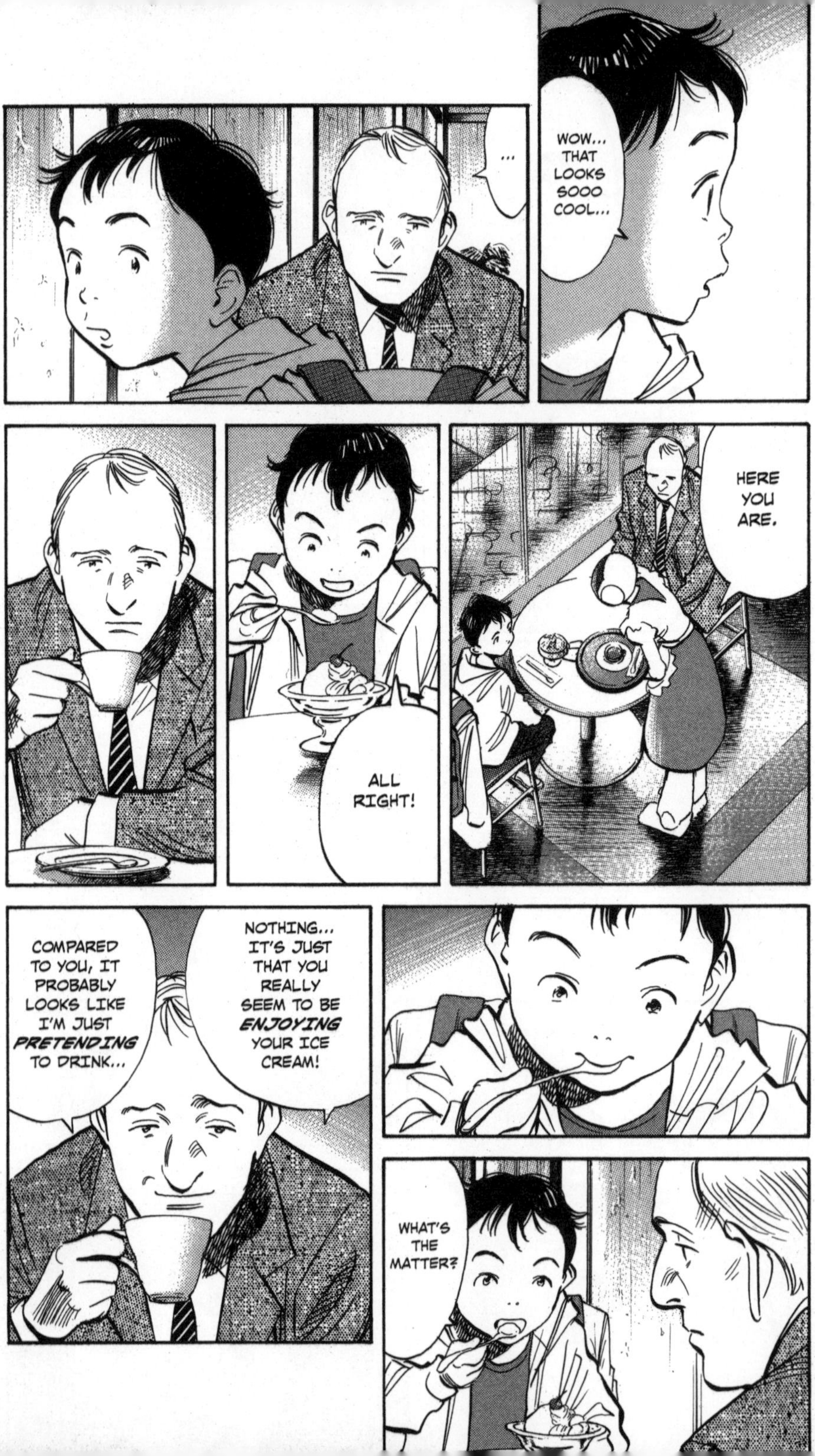
WOW... THAT LOOKS SOOO COOL...
...
HERE YOU ARE.
ALL RIGHT!
WHAT'S THE MATTER?
NOTHING... IT'S JUST THAT YOU REALLY SEEM TO BE *ENJOYING* YOUR ICE CREAM!
COMPARED TO YOU, IT PROBABLY LOOKS LIKE I'M JUST *PRETENDING* TO DRINK...

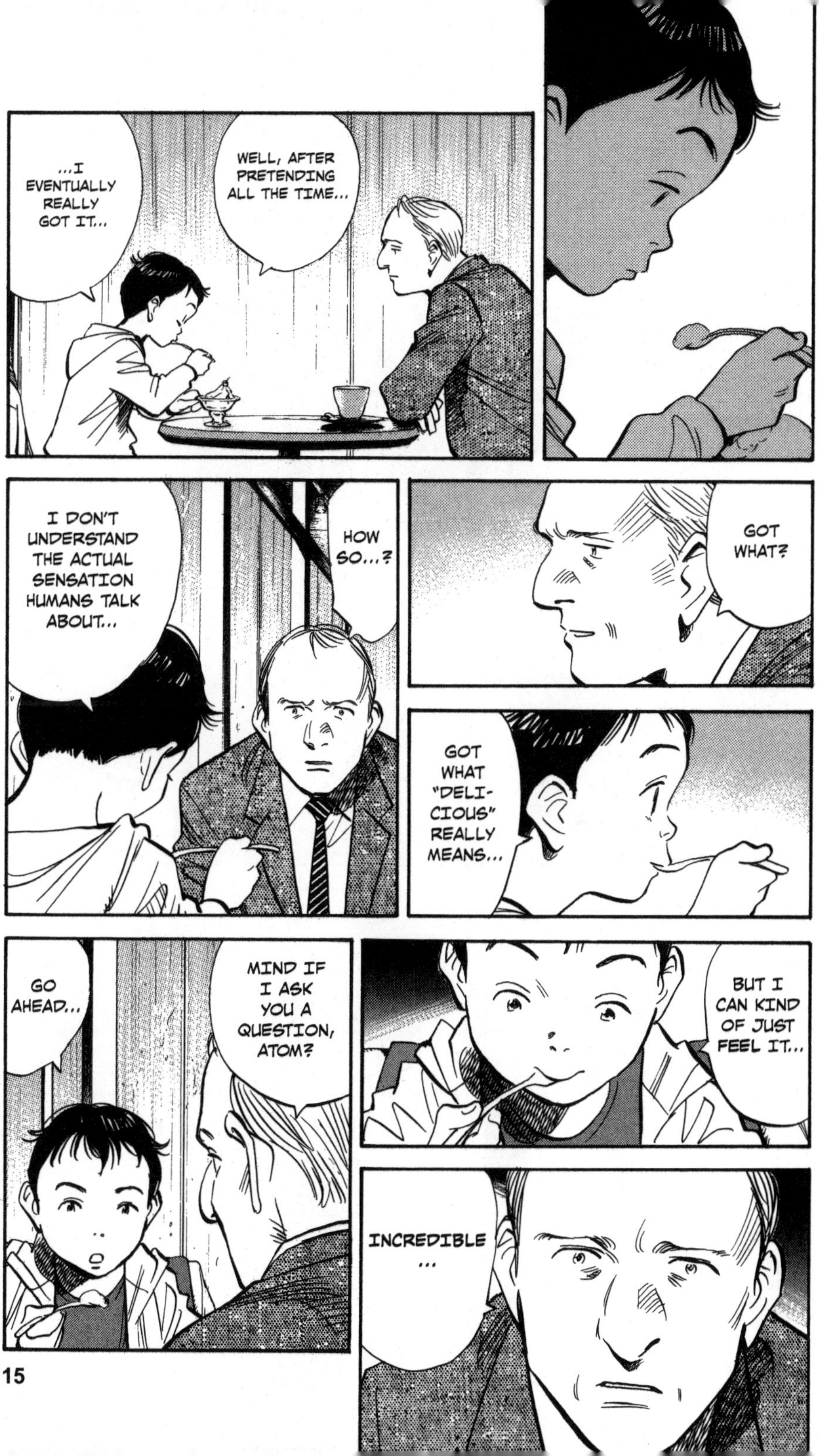
WELL, AFTER PRETENDING ALL THE TIME...
...I EVENTUALLY REALLY GOT IT...
GOT WHAT?
GOT WHAT "DELICIOUS" REALLY MEANS...
HOW SO...?
I DON'T UNDERSTAND THE ACTUAL SENSATION HUMANS TALK ABOUT...
BUT I CAN KIND OF JUST FEEL IT...
INCREDIBLE ...
MIND IF I ASK YOU A QUESTION, ATOM?
GO AHEAD...

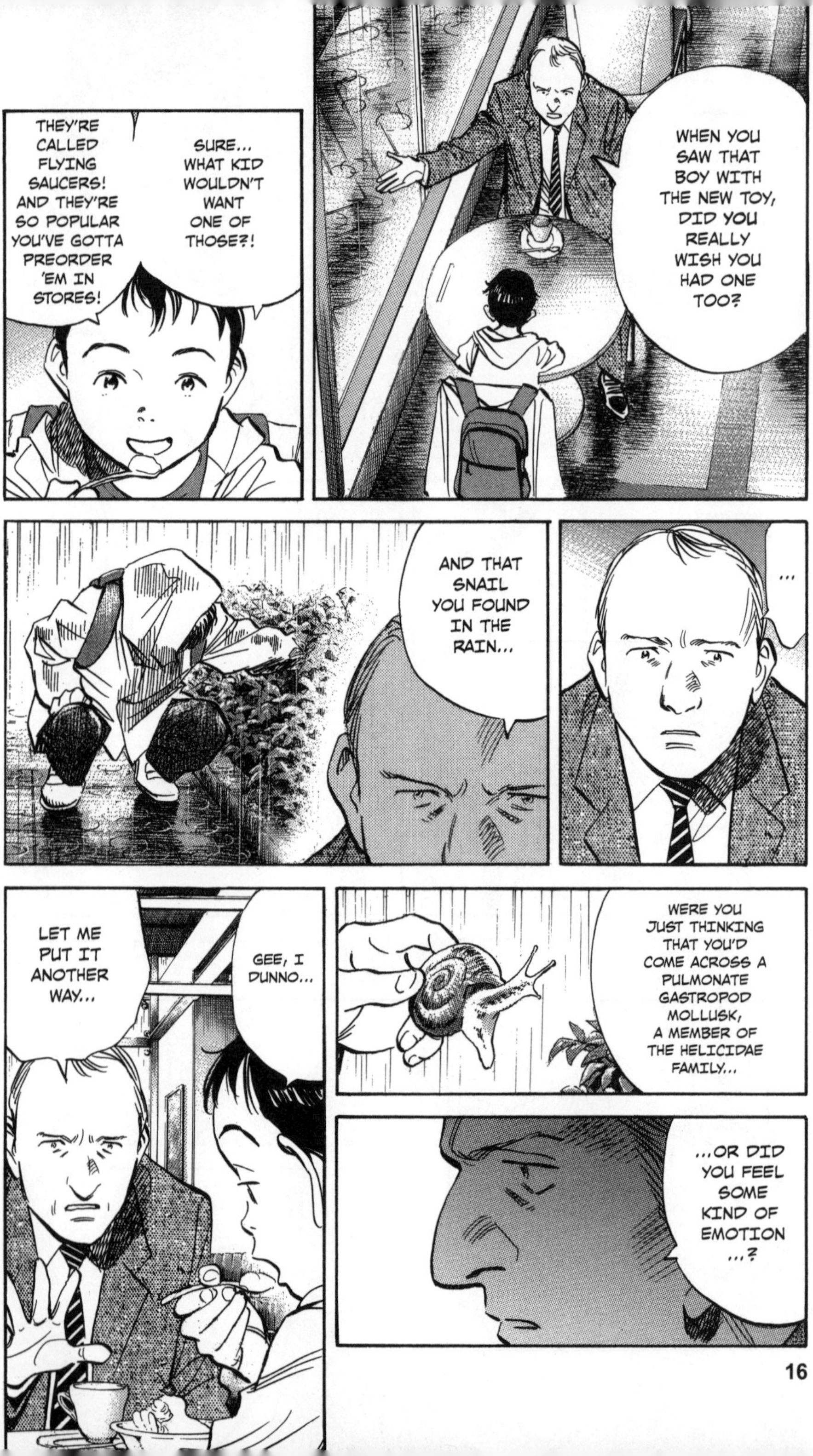
WHEN YOU SAW THAT BOY WITH THE NEW TOY, DID YOU REALLY WISH YOU HAD ONE TOO?
SURE... WHAT KID WOULDN'T WANT ONE OF THOSE?!
THEY'RE CALLED FLYING SAUCERS! AND THEY'RE SO POPULAR YOU'VE GOTTA PREORDER 'EM IN STORES!
...
AND THAT SNAIL YOU FOUND IN THE RAIN...
WERE YOU JUST THINKING THAT YOU'D COME ACROSS A PULMONATE GASTROPOD MOLLUSK, A MEMBER OF THE HELICIDAE FAMILY...
...OR DID YOU FEEL SOME KIND OF EMOTION ...?
GEE, I DUNNO...
LET ME PUT IT ANOTHER WAY...

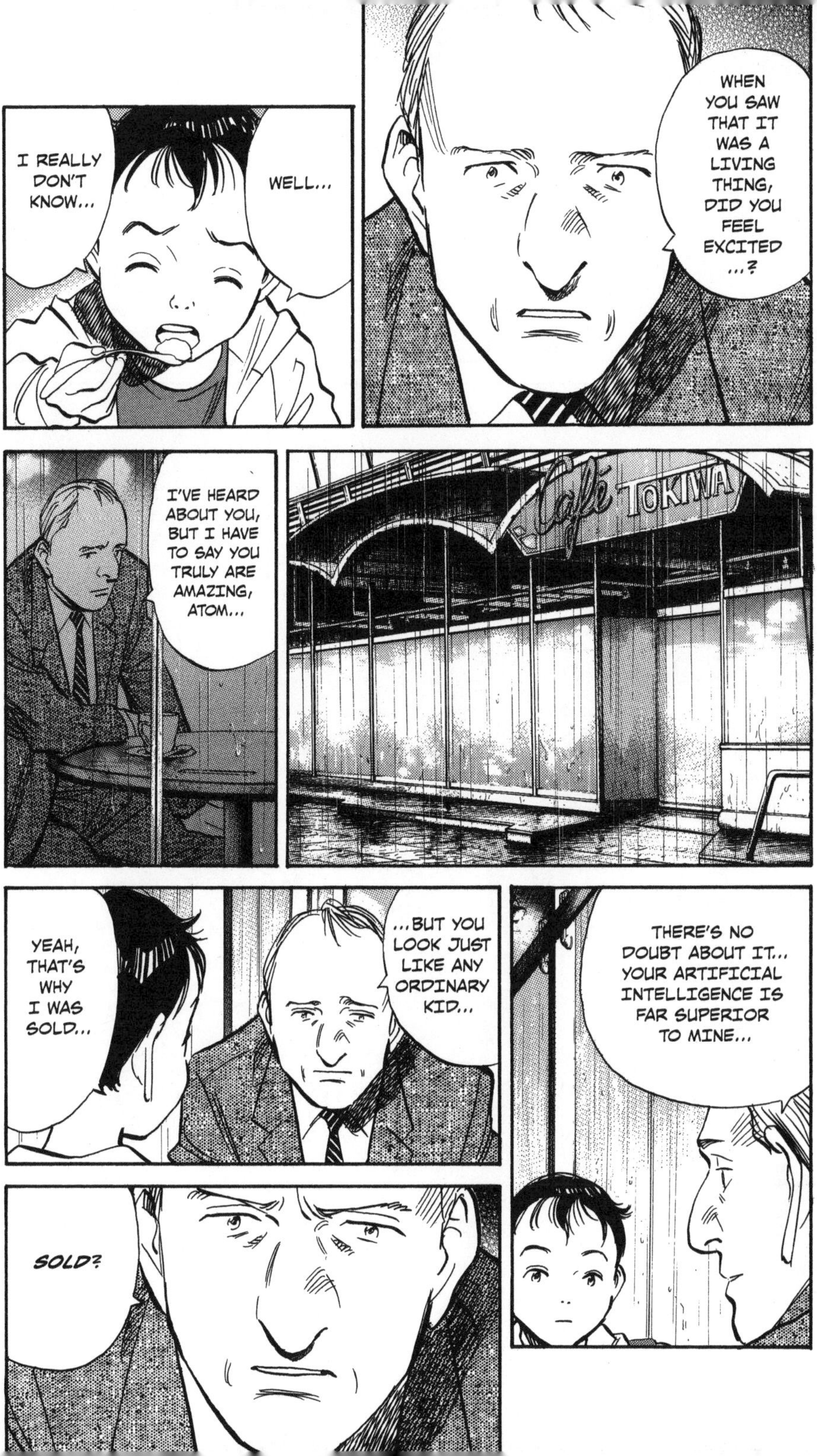
WHEN YOU SAW THAT IT WAS A LIVING THING, DID YOU FEEL EXCITED ...?
WELL...
I REALLY DON'T KNOW...
Café TOKIWA
I'VE HEARD ABOUT YOU, BUT I HAVE TO SAY YOU TRULY ARE AMAZING, ATOM...
THERE'S NO DOUBT ABOUT IT... YOUR ARTIFICIAL INTELLIGENCE IS FAR SUPERIOR TO MINE...
...BUT YOU LOOK JUST LIKE ANY ORDINARY KID...
YEAH, THAT'S WHY I WAS SOLD...
SOLD?

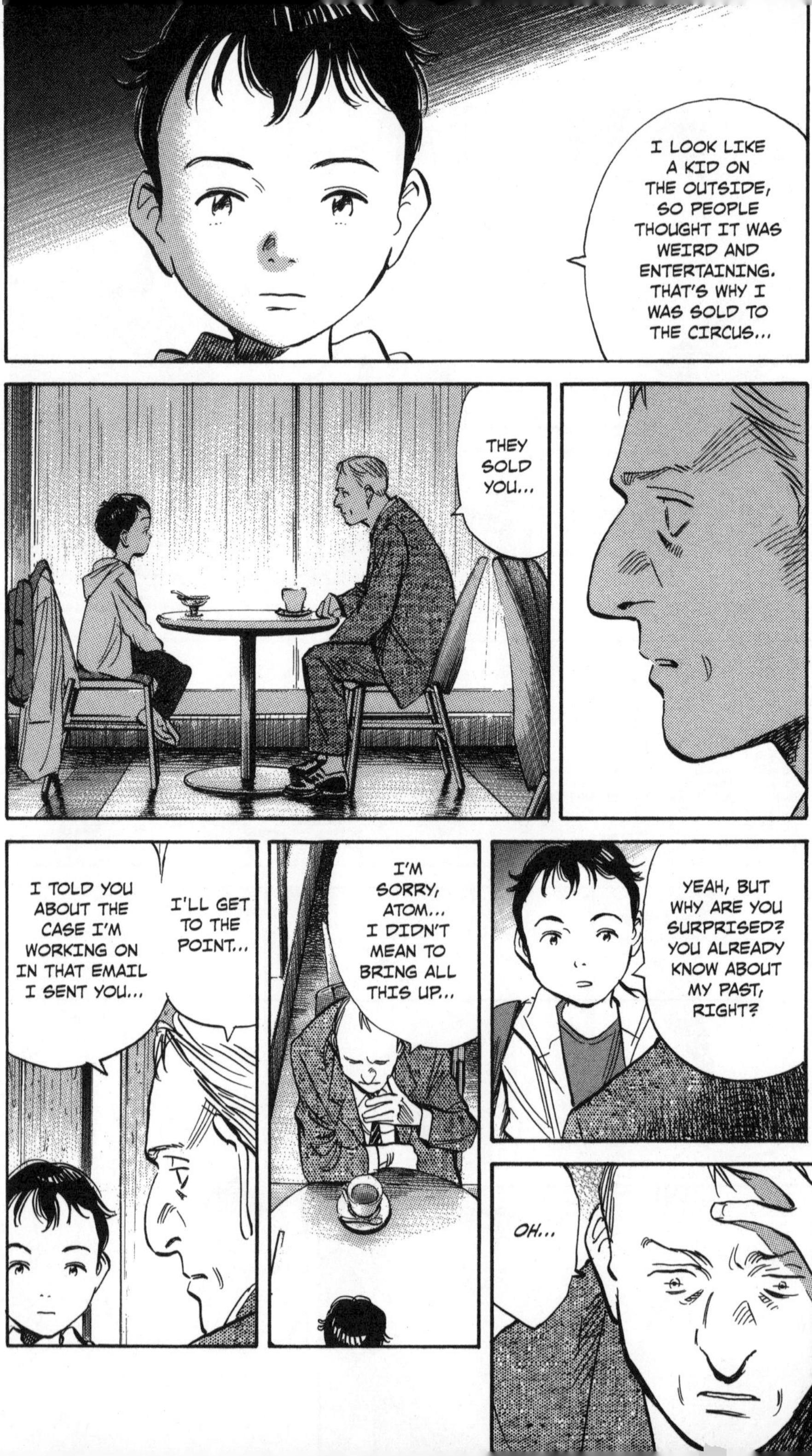
I LOOK LIKE A KID ON THE OUTSIDE, SO PEOPLE THOUGHT IT WAS WEIRD AND ENTERTAINING. THAT'S WHY I WAS SOLD TO THE CIRCUS...
THEY SOLD YOU...
YEAH, BUT WHY ARE YOU SURPRISED? YOU ALREADY KNOW ABOUT MY PAST, RIGHT?
OH...
I'M SORRY, ATOM... I DIDN'T MEAN TO BRING ALL THIS UP...
I'LL GET TO THE POINT...
I TOLD YOU ABOUT THE CASE I'M WORKING ON IN THAT EMAIL I SENT YOU...

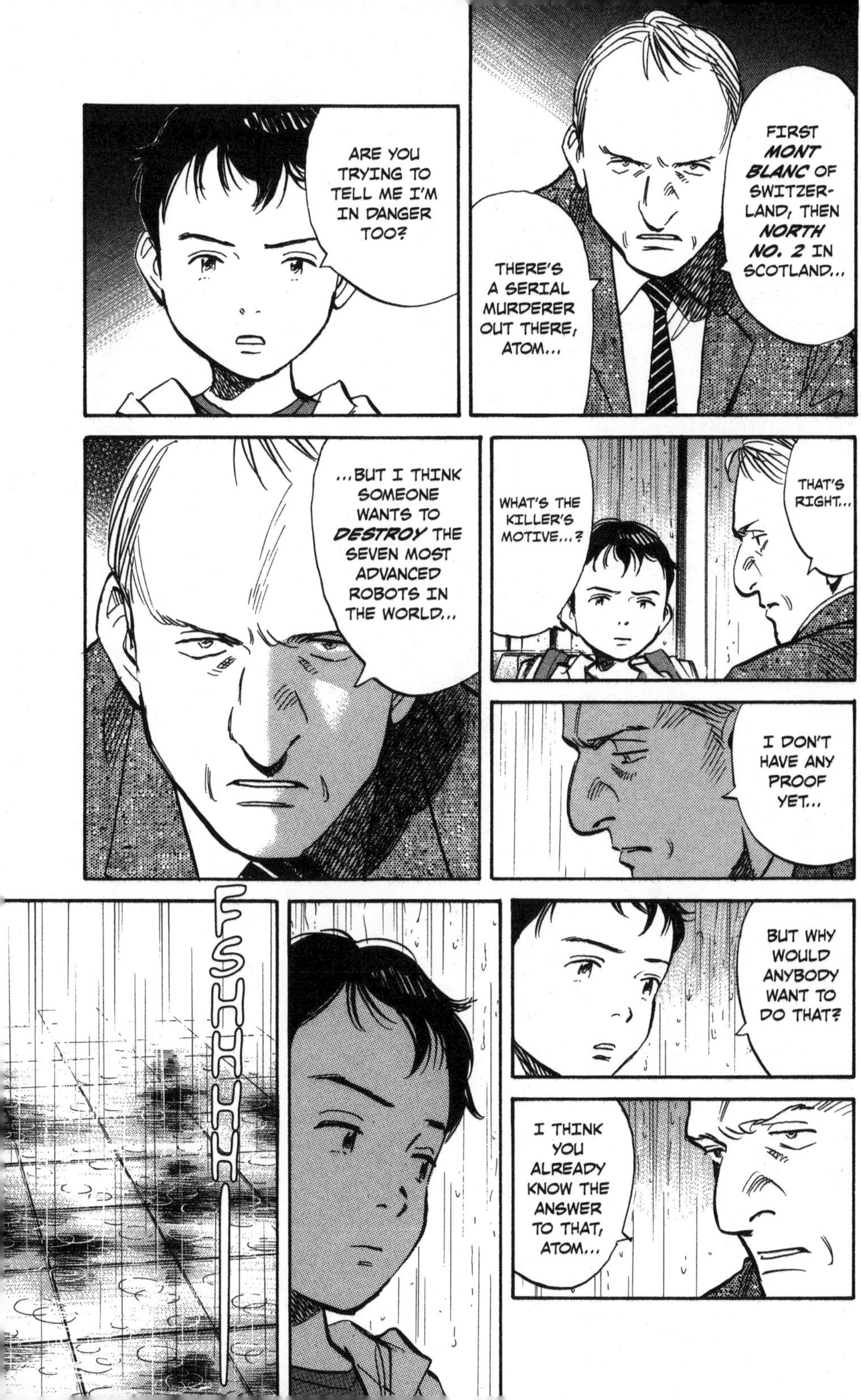
FIRST MONT BLANC OF SWITZERLAND, THEN NORTH NO. 2 IN SCOTLAND...
THERE'S A SERIAL MURDERER OUT THERE, ATOM...
ARE YOU TRYING TO TELL ME I'M IN DANGER TOO?
THAT'S RIGHT...
WHAT'S THE KILLER'S MOTIVE...?
I DON'T HAVE ANY PROOF YET...
...BUT I THINK SOMEONE WANTS TO DESTROY THE SEVEN MOST ADVANCED ROBOTS IN THE WORLD...
BUT WHY WOULD ANYBODY WANT TO DO THAT?
I THINK YOU ALREADY KNOW THE ANSWER TO THAT, ATOM...
FSHHHHH

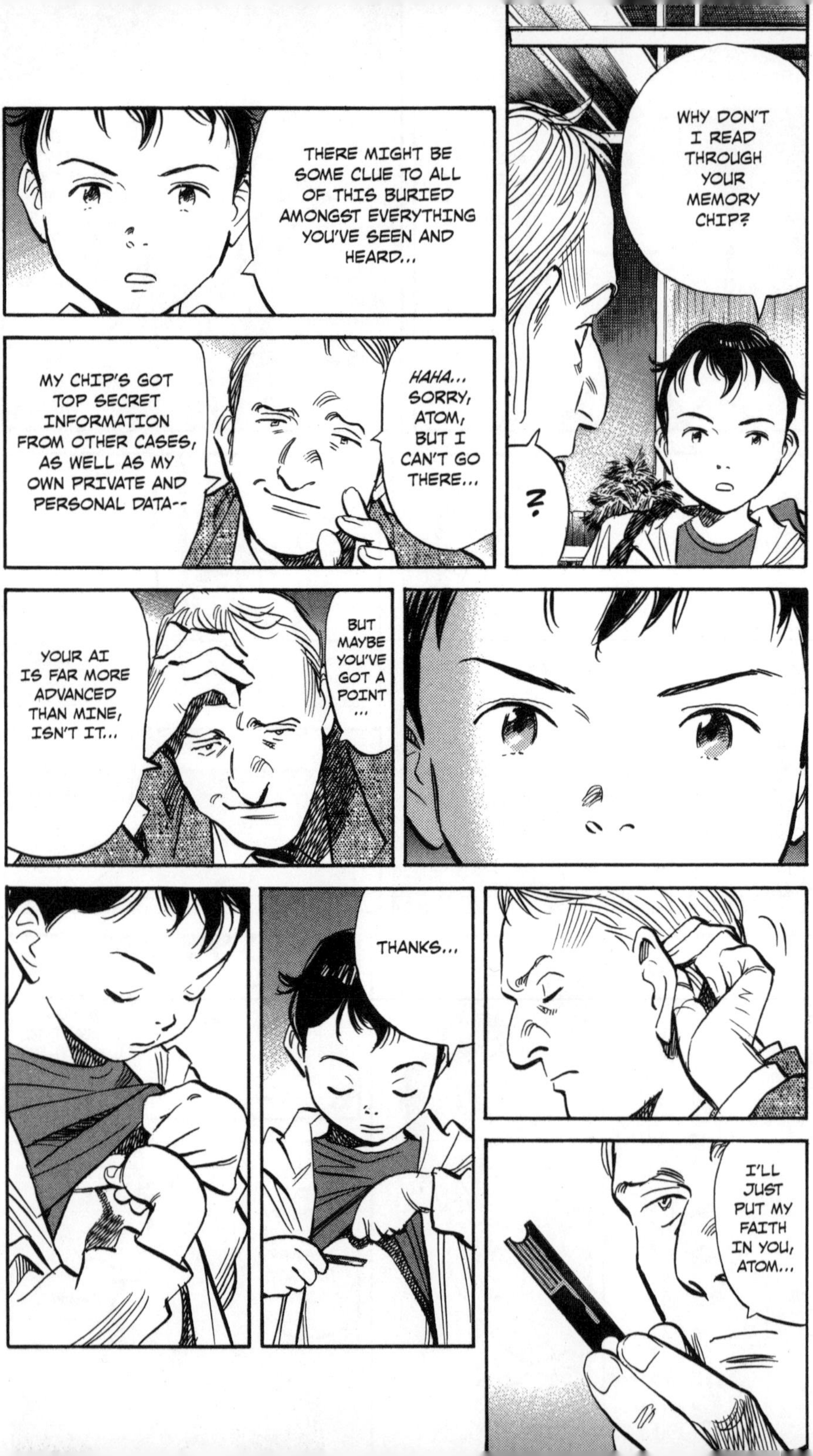
WHY DON'T I READ THROUGH YOUR MEMORY CHIP?
?
THERE MIGHT BE SOME CLUE TO ALL OF THIS BURIED AMONGST EVERYTHING YOU'VE SEEN AND HEARD...
HAHA... SORRY, ATOM, BUT I CAN'T GO THERE...
MY CHIP'S GOT TOP SECRET INFORMATION FROM OTHER CASES, AS WELL AS MY OWN PRIVATE AND PERSONAL DATA--
BUT MAYBE YOU'VE GOT A POINT ...
YOUR AI IS FAR MORE ADVANCED THAN MINE, ISN'T IT...
I'LL JUST PUT MY FAITH IN YOU, ATOM...
THANKS...

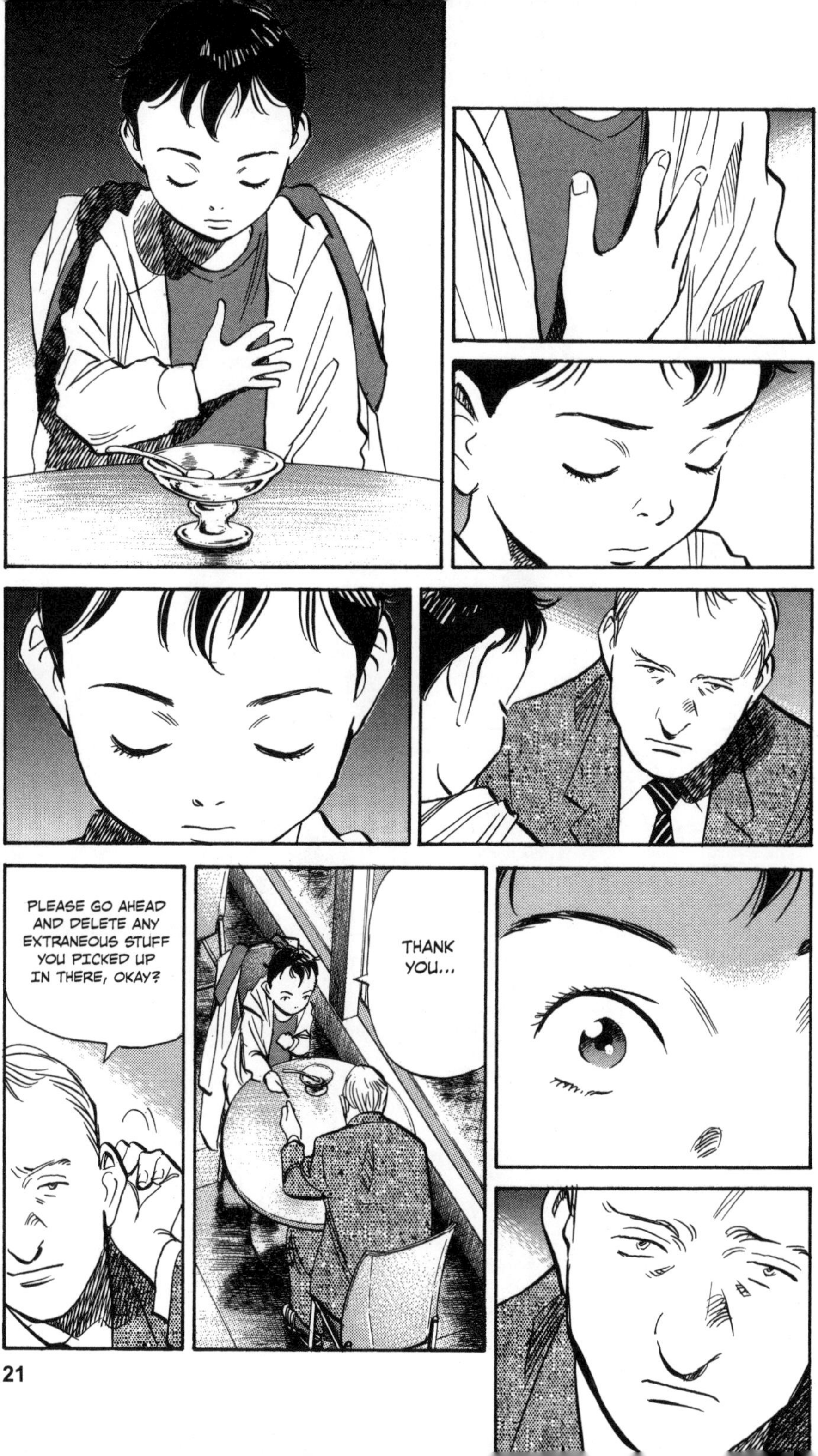
THANK YOU...
PLEASE GO AHEAD AND DELETE ANY EXTRANEOUS STUFF YOU PICKED UP IN THERE, OKAY?

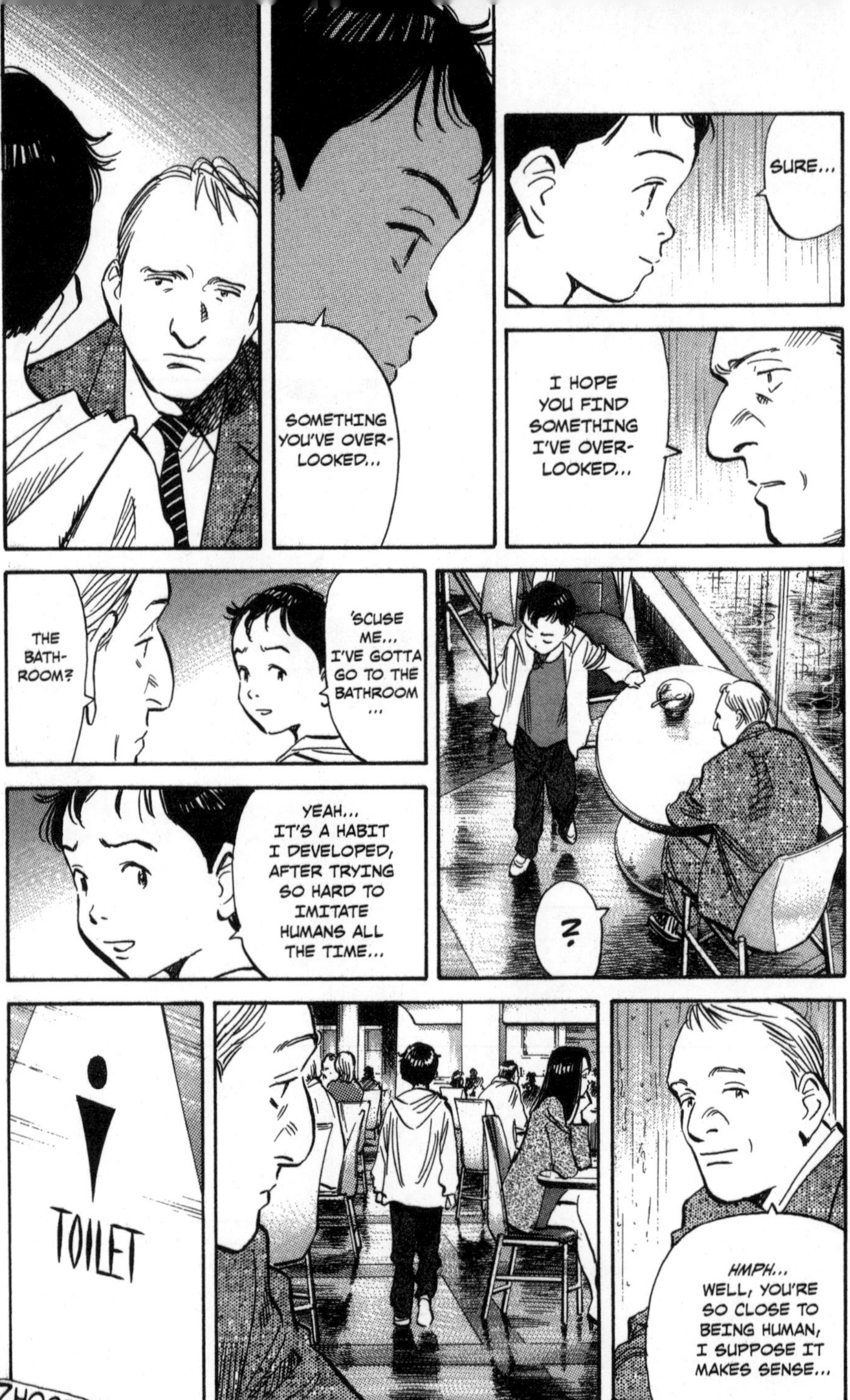
SURE...
I HOPE YOU FIND SOMETHING I'VE OVER-LOOKED...
SOMETHING YOU'VE OVER-LOOKED...
?
'SCUSE ME... I'VE GOTTA GO TO THE BATHROOM ...
THE BATH-ROOM?
YEAH... IT'S A HABIT I DEVELOPED, AFTER TRYING SO HARD TO IMITATE HUMANS ALL THE TIME...
HMPH... WELL, YOU'RE SO CLOSE TO BEING HUMAN, I SUPPOSE IT MAKES SENSE...
TOILET
ZHOOP——

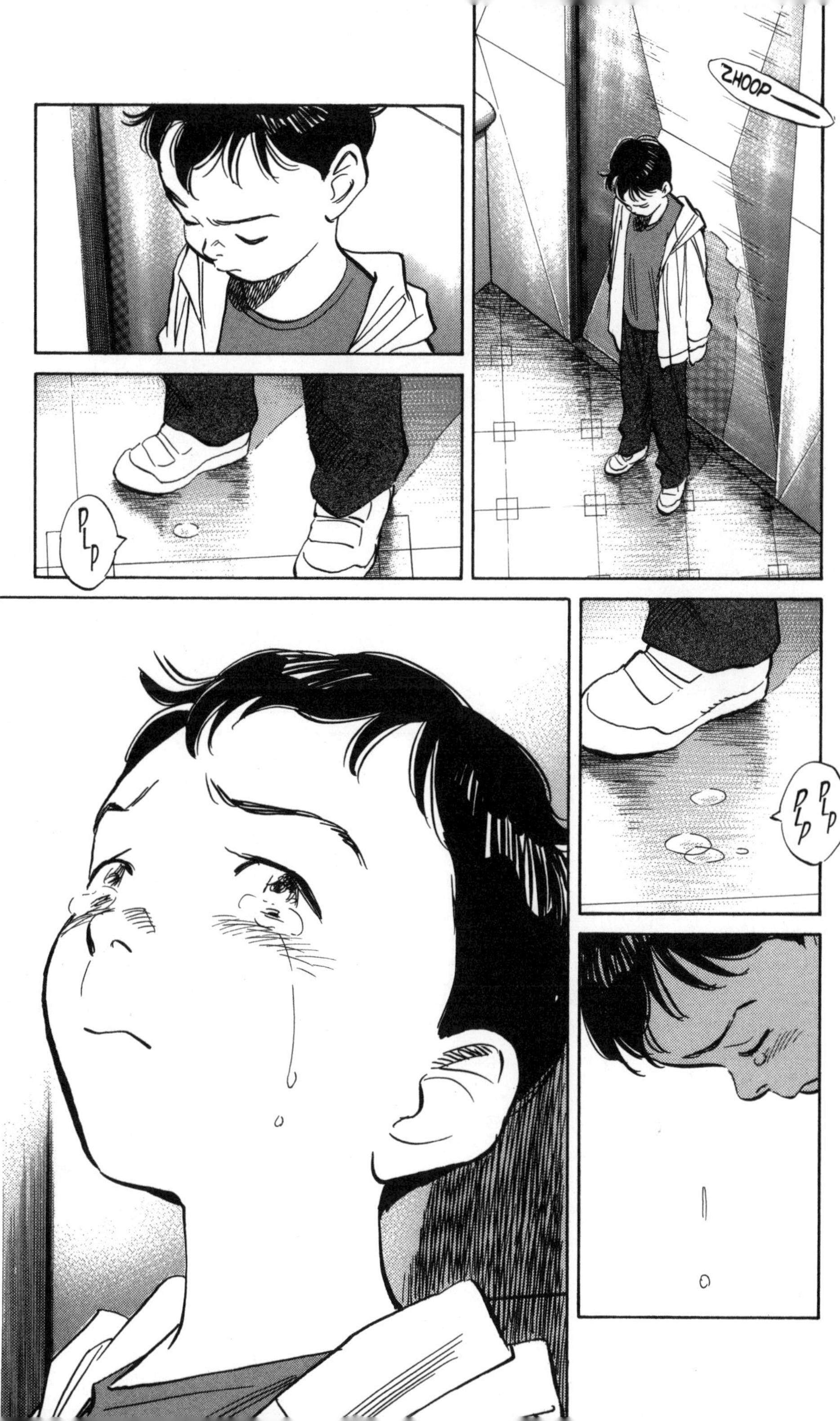
ZHOOP
PLP
PLP PLP

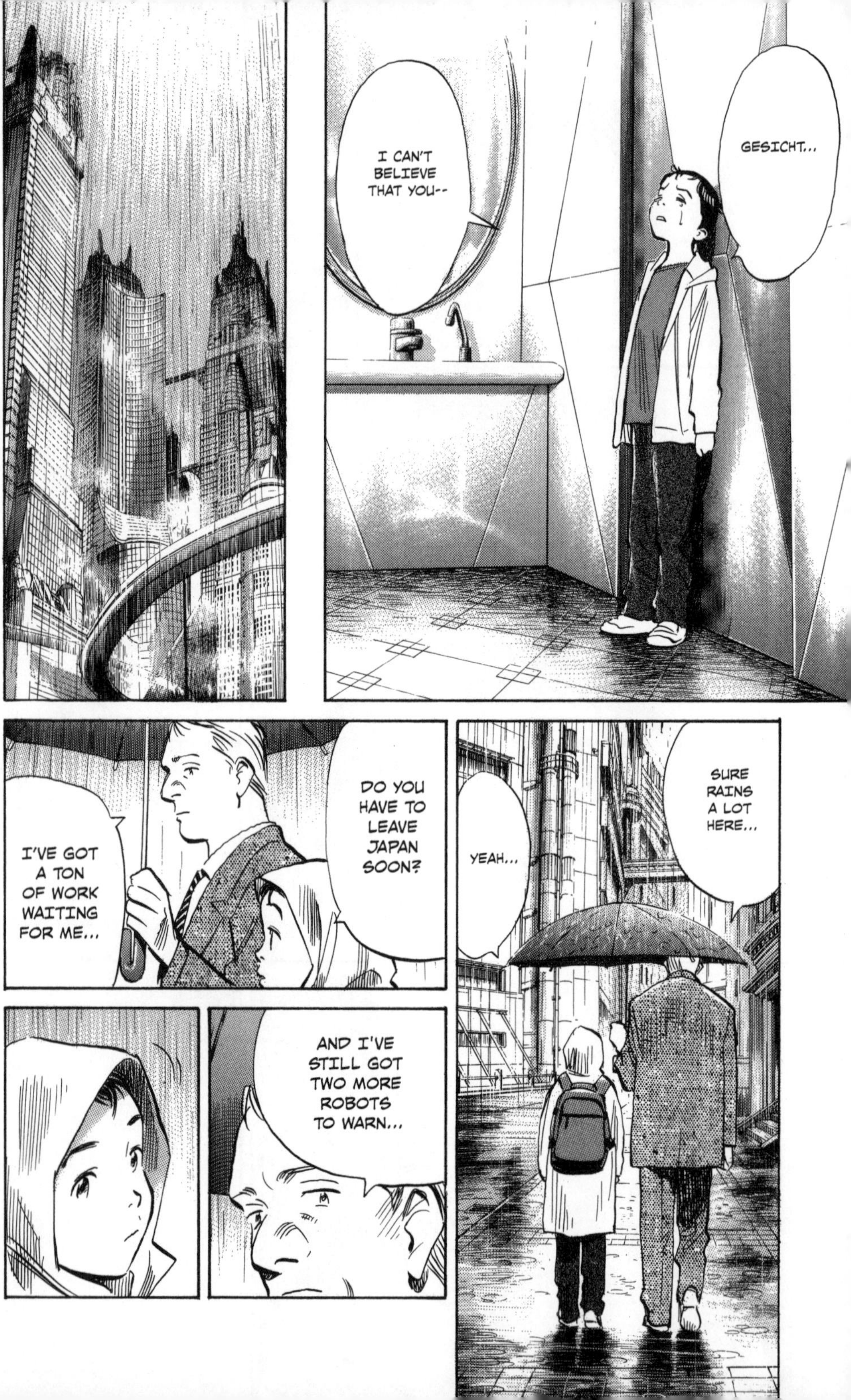
GESICHT...
I CAN'T BELIEVE THAT YOU--
SURE RAINS A LOT HERE...
YEAH...
DO YOU HAVE TO LEAVE JAPAN SOON?
I'VE GOT A TON OF WORK WAITING FOR ME...
AND I'VE STILL GOT TWO MORE ROBOTS TO WARN...

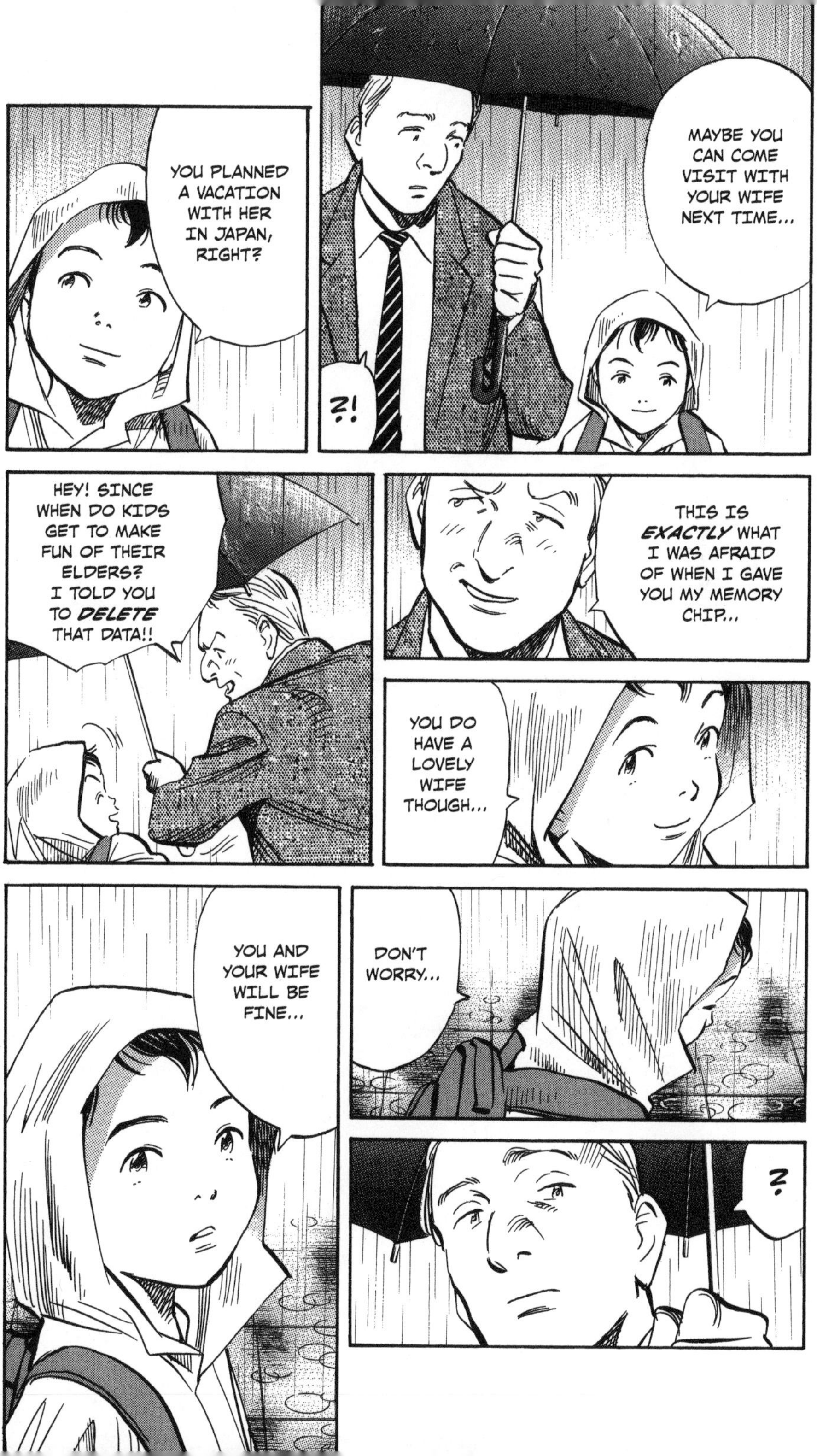
MAYBE YOU CAN COME VISIT WITH YOUR WIFE NEXT TIME...
?!
YOU PLANNED A VACATION WITH HER IN JAPAN, RIGHT?
THIS IS *EXACTLY* WHAT I WAS AFRAID OF WHEN I GAVE YOU MY MEMORY CHIP...
YOU DO HAVE A LOVELY WIFE THOUGH...
HEY! SINCE WHEN DO KIDS GET TO MAKE FUN OF THEIR ELDERS? I TOLD YOU TO *DELETE* THAT DATA!!
DON'T WORRY...
?
YOU AND YOUR WIFE WILL BE FINE...

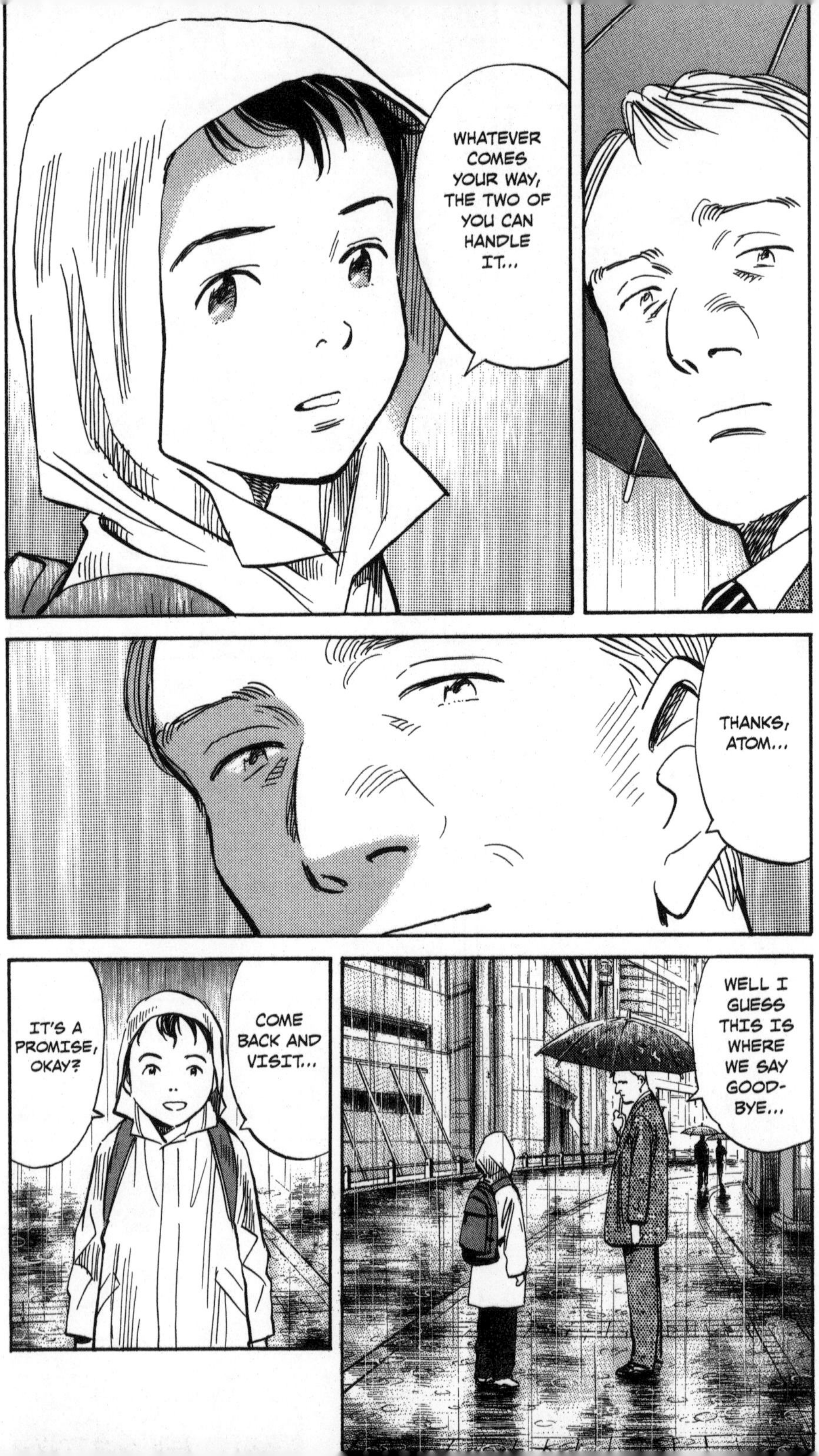
WHATEVER COMES YOUR WAY, THE TWO OF YOU CAN HANDLE IT...
THANKS, ATOM...
WELL I GUESS THIS IS WHERE WE SAY GOOD-BYE...
COME BACK AND VISIT...
IT'S A PROMISE, OKAY?

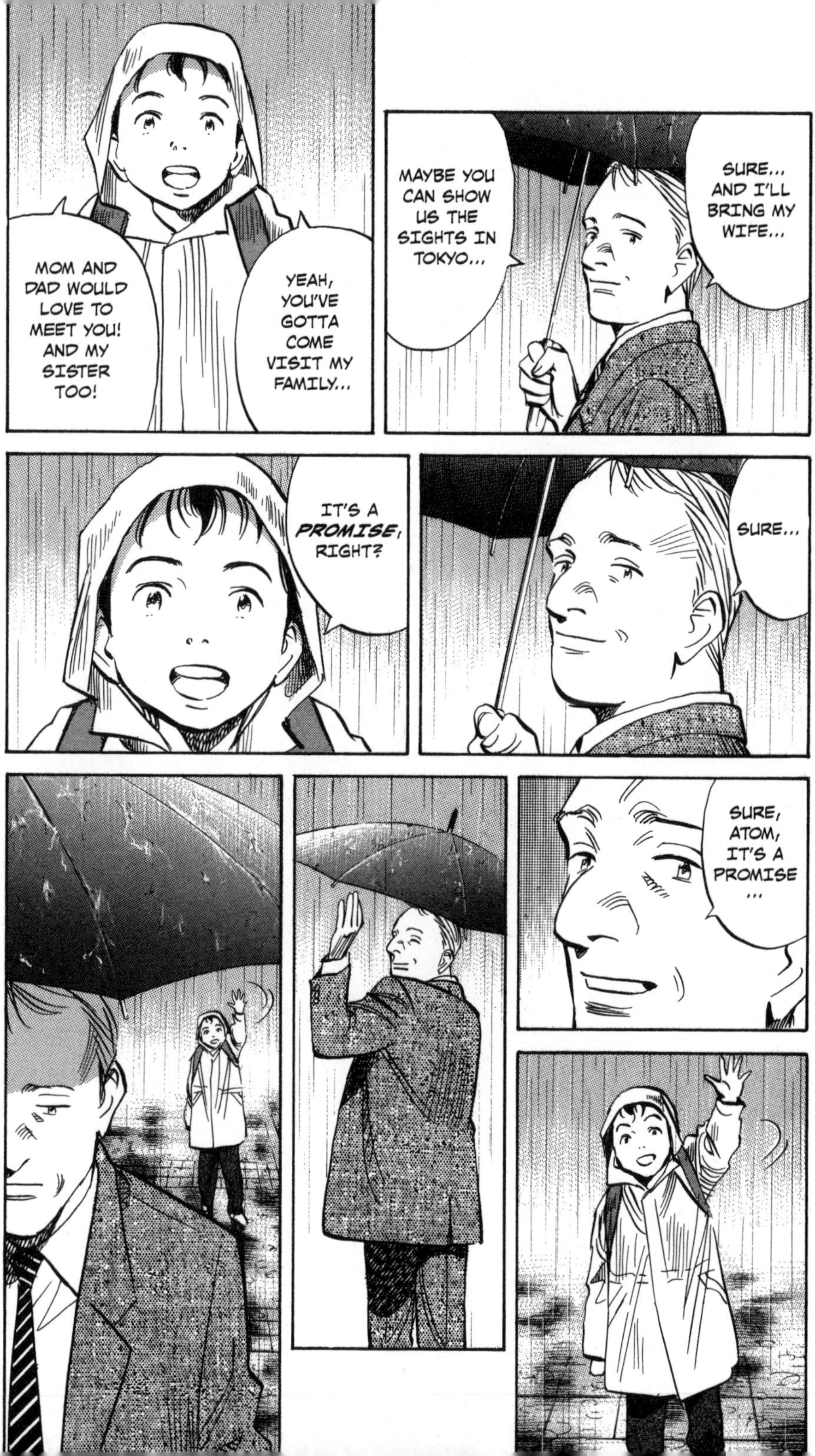
SURE... AND I'LL BRING MY WIFE...
MAYBE YOU CAN SHOW US THE SIGHTS IN TOKYO...
YEAH, YOU'VE GOTTA COME VISIT MY FAMILY...
MOM AND DAD WOULD LOVE TO MEET YOU! AND MY SISTER TOO!
SURE...
IT'S A *PROMISE*, RIGHT?
SURE, ATOM, IT'S A PROMISE...

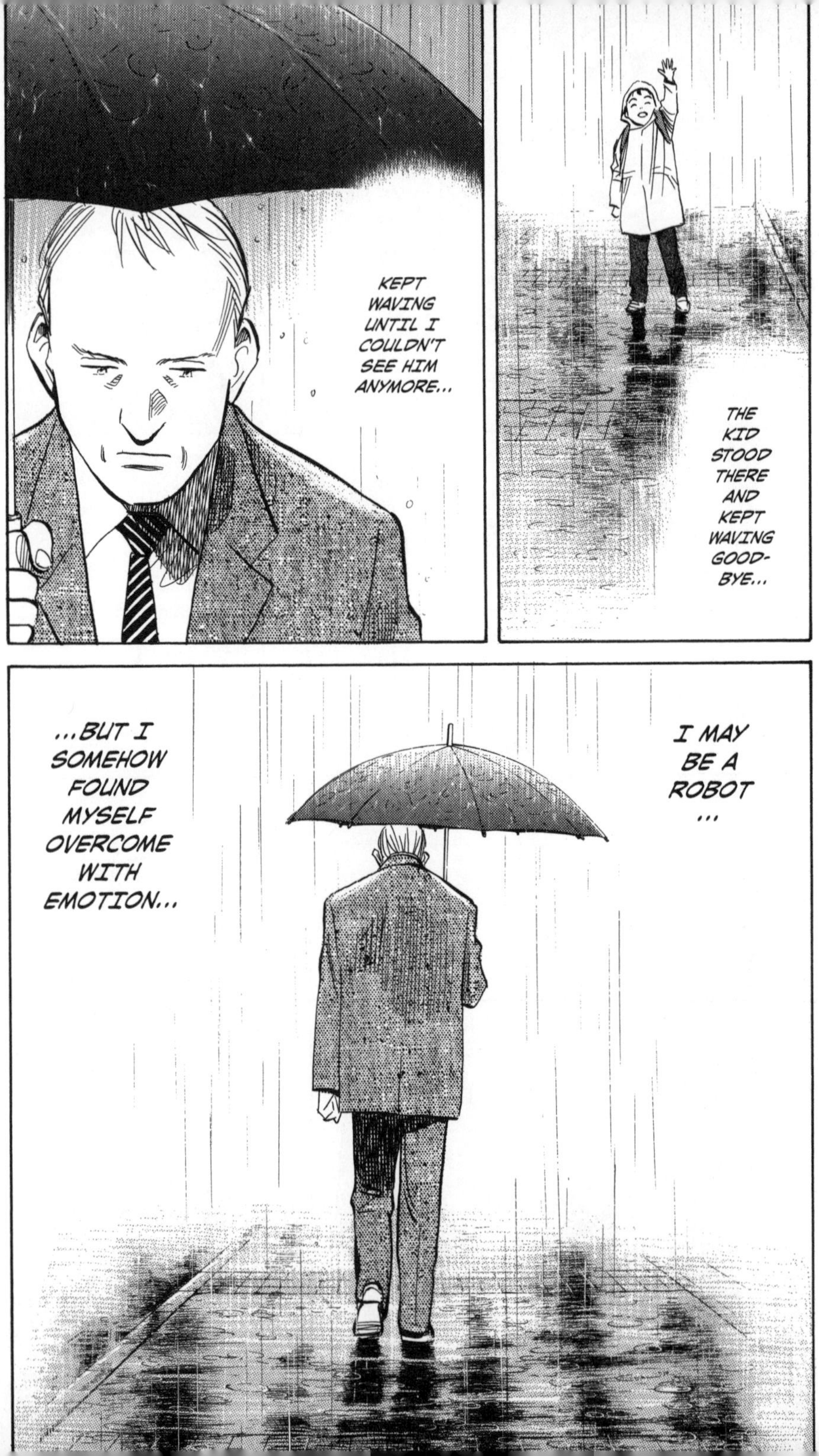
THE KID STOOD THERE AND KEPT WAVING GOOD-BYE...
KEPT WAVING UNTIL I COULDN'T SEE HIM ANYMORE...
I MAY BE A ROBOT ...
...BUT I SOMEHOW FOUND MYSELF OVERCOME WITH EMOTION...

Act 9 PROFESSOR OCHANOMIZU

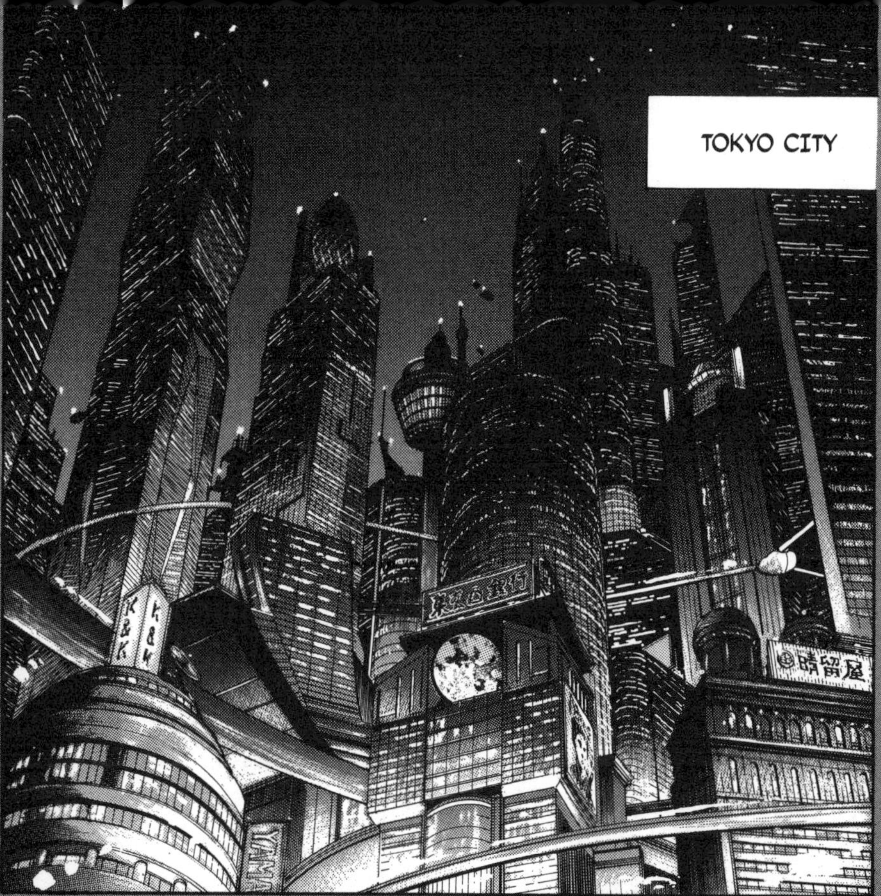
TOKYO CITY

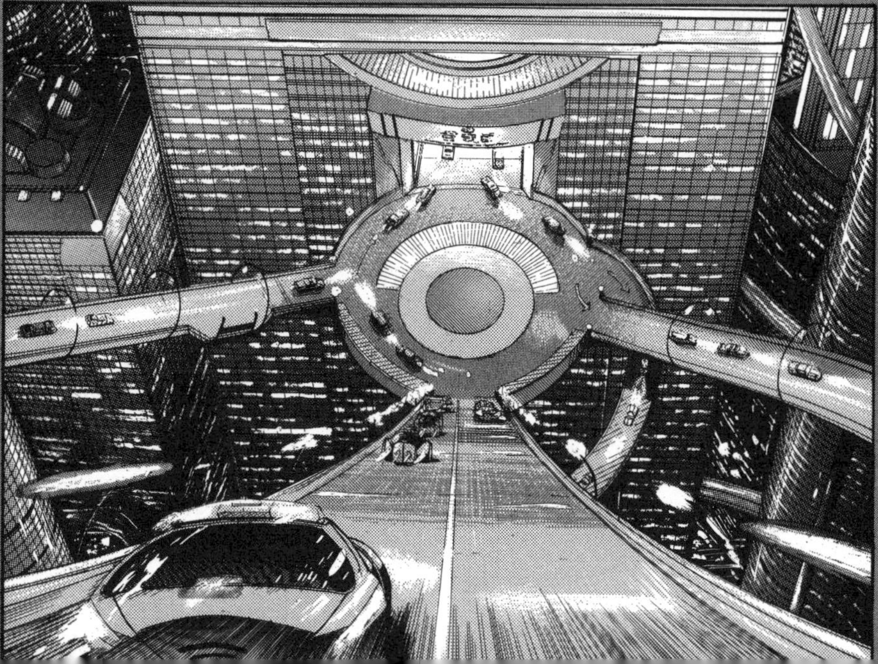

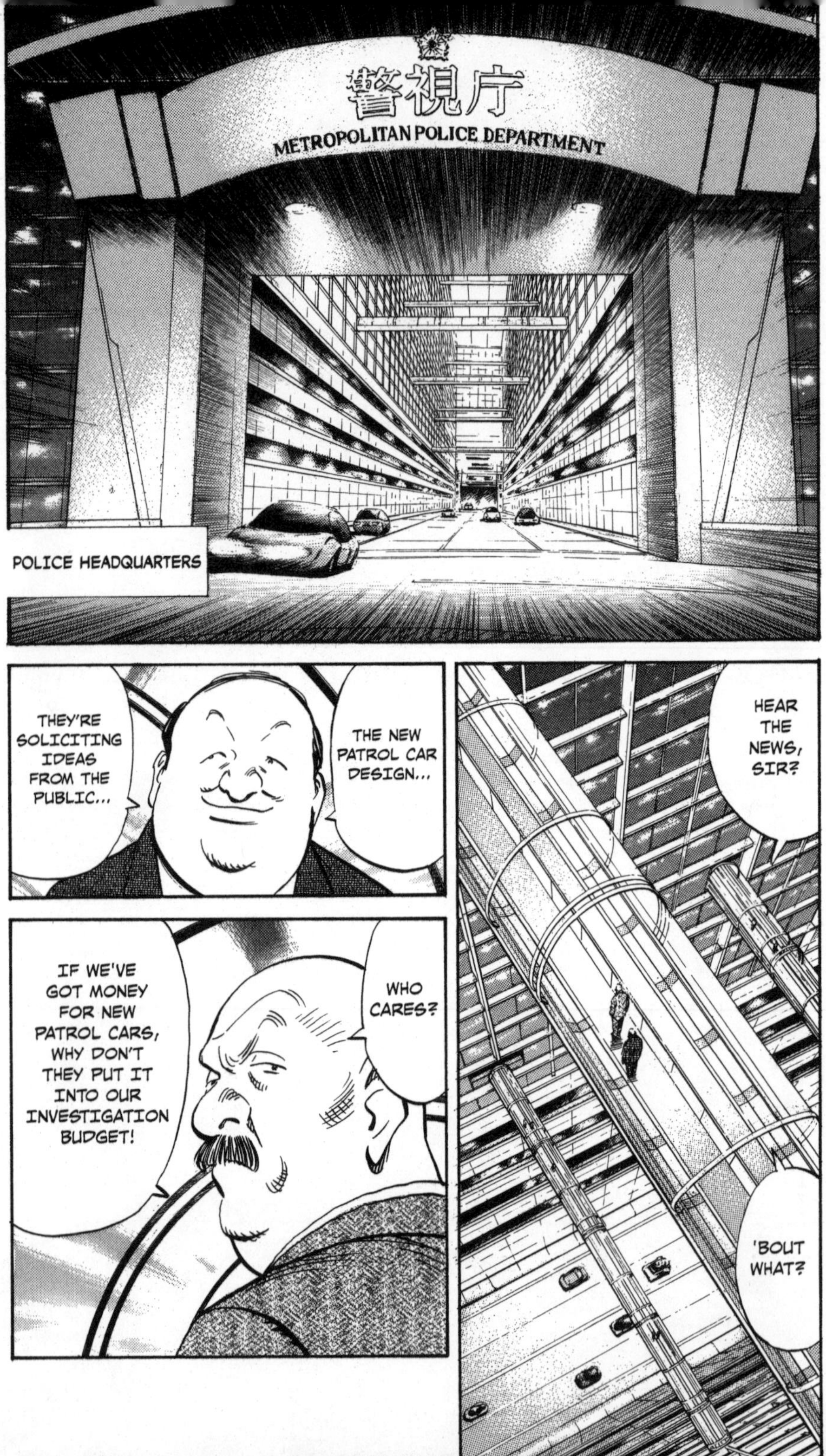
警視庁
METROPOLITAN POLICE DEPARTMENT
POLICE HEADQUARTERS
HEAR THE NEWS, SIR?
'BOUT WHAT?
THE NEW PATROL CAR DESIGN...
THEY'RE SOLICITING IDEAS FROM THE PUBLIC...
WHO CARES?
IF WE'VE GOT MONEY FOR NEW PATROL CARS, WHY DON'T THEY PUT IT INTO OUR INVESTIGATION BUDGET!

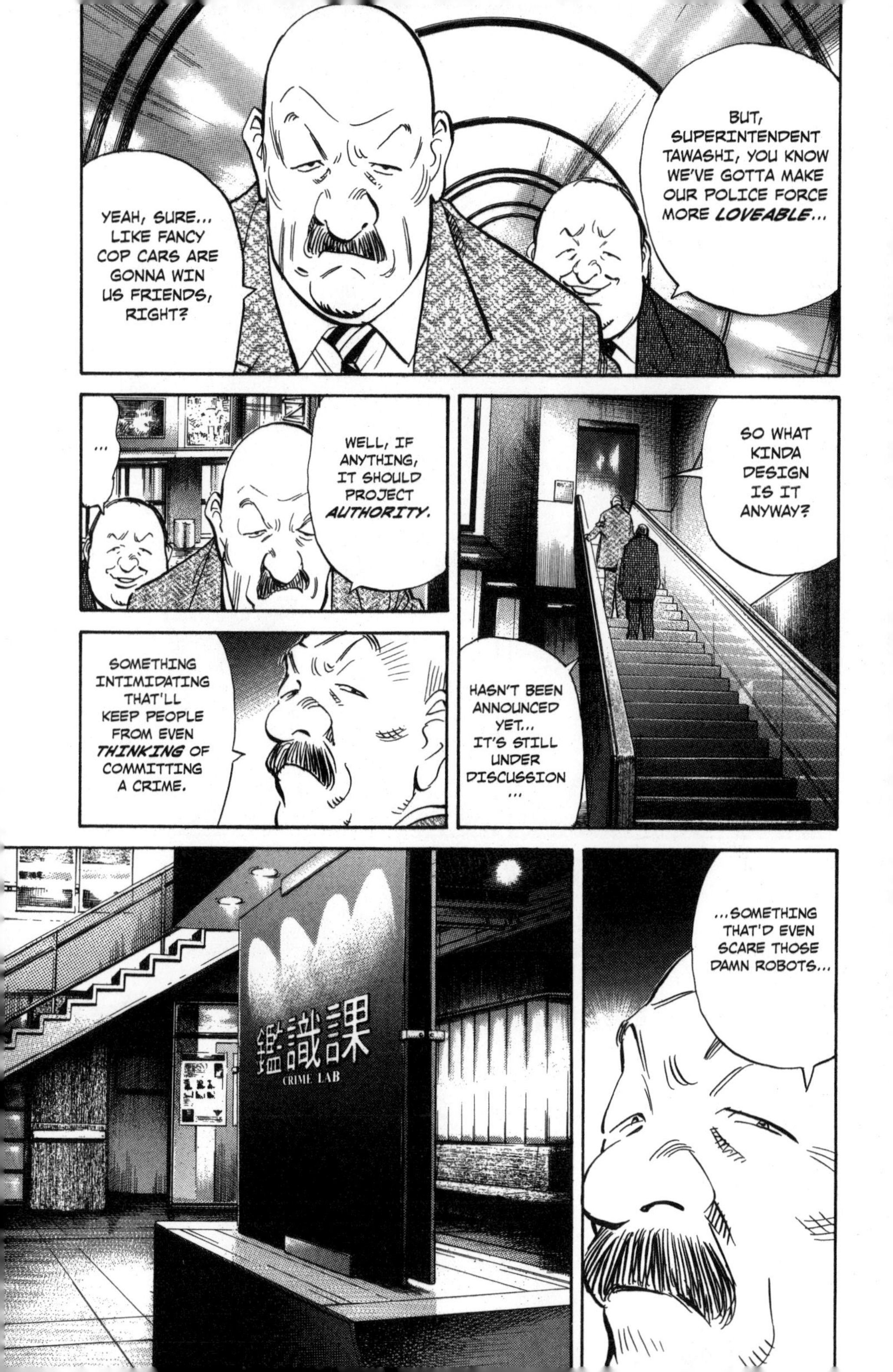
BUT, SUPERINTENDENT TAWASHI, YOU KNOW WE'VE GOTTA MAKE OUR POLICE FORCE MORE LOVEABLE...
YEAH, SURE... LIKE FANCY COP CARS ARE GONNA WIN US FRIENDS, RIGHT?
SO WHAT KINDA DESIGN IS IT ANYWAY?
HASN'T BEEN ANNOUNCED YET... IT'S STILL UNDER DISCUSSION...
WELL, IF ANYTHING, IT SHOULD PROJECT AUTHORITY.
...
SOMETHING INTIMIDATING THAT'LL KEEP PEOPLE FROM EVEN THINKING OF COMMITTING A CRIME.
...SOMETHING THAT'D EVEN SCARE THOSE DAMN ROBOTS...
鑑識課
CRIME LAB

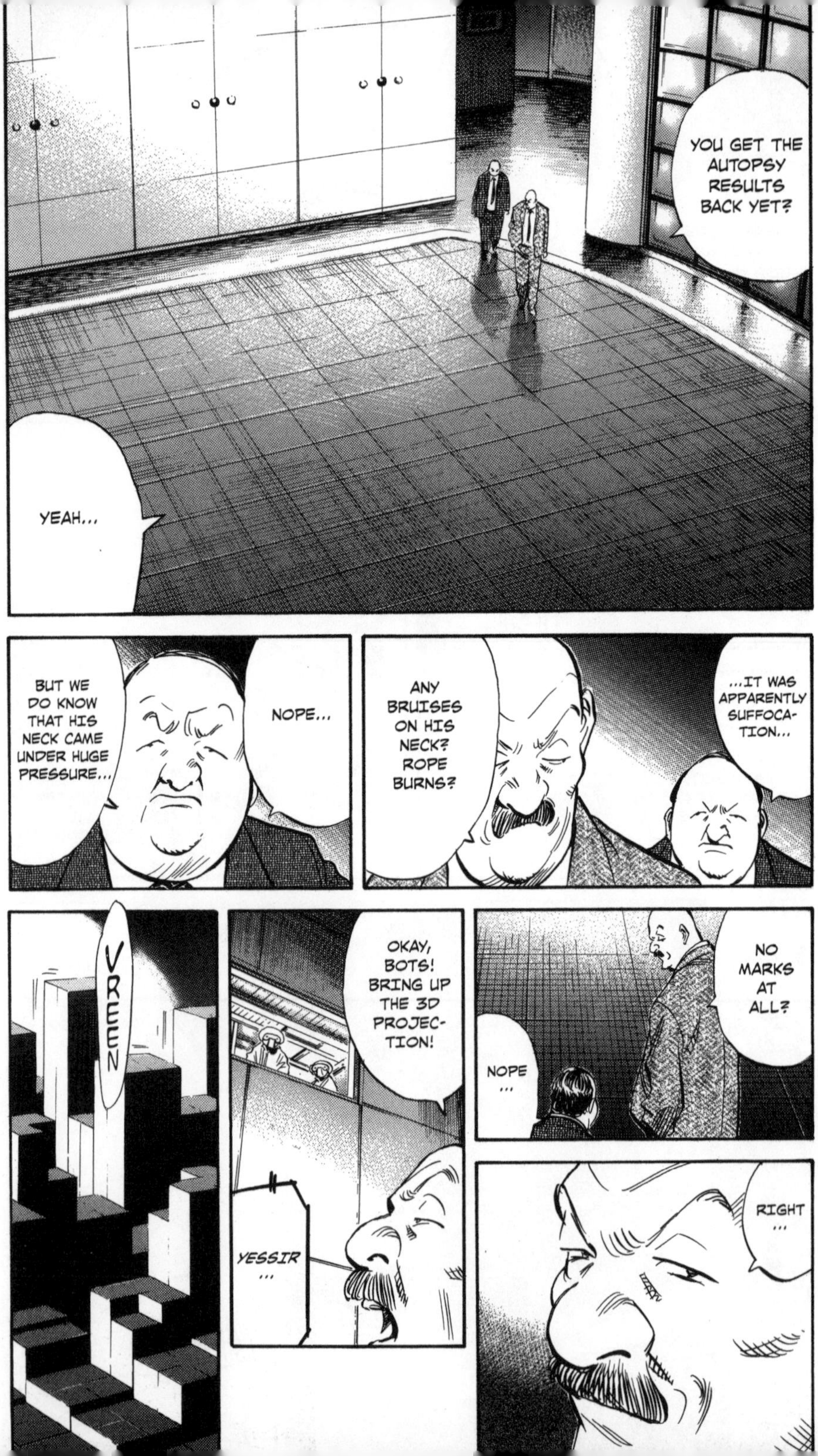
YOU GET THE AUTOPSY RESULTS BACK YET?
YEAH...
...IT WAS APPARENTLY SUFFOCATION...
ANY BRUISES ON HIS NECK? ROPE BURNS?
NOPE...
BUT WE DO KNOW THAT HIS NECK CAME UNDER HUGE PRESSURE...
NO MARKS AT ALL?
NOPE ...
RIGHT ...
OKAY, BOTS! BRING UP THE 3D PROJECTION!
YESSIR ...
VREEN

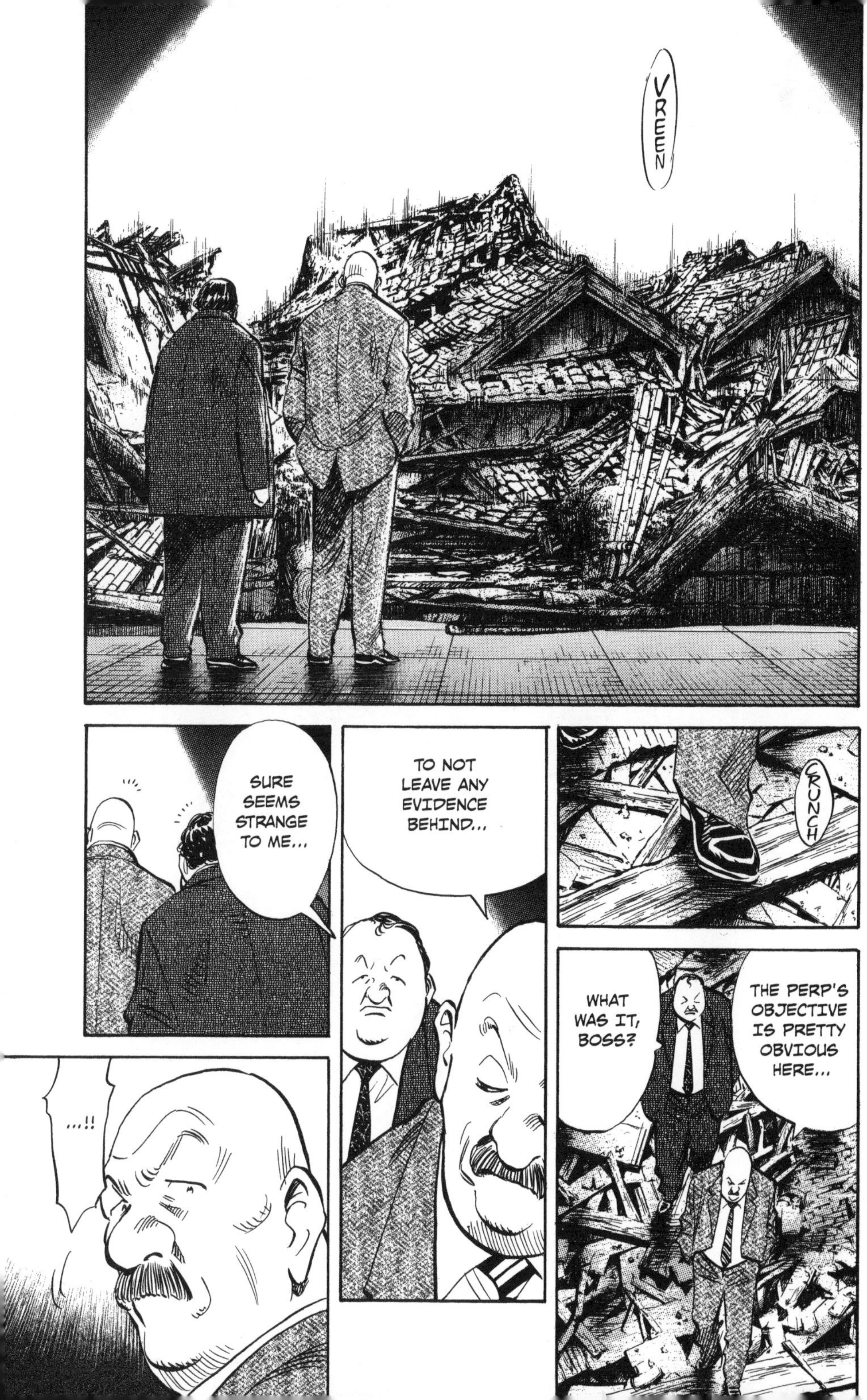
VREEN
CRUNCH
THE PERP'S OBJECTIVE IS PRETTY OBVIOUS HERE...
WHAT WAS IT, BOSS?
TO NOT LEAVE ANY EVIDENCE BEHIND...
SURE SEEMS STRANGE TO ME...
...!!

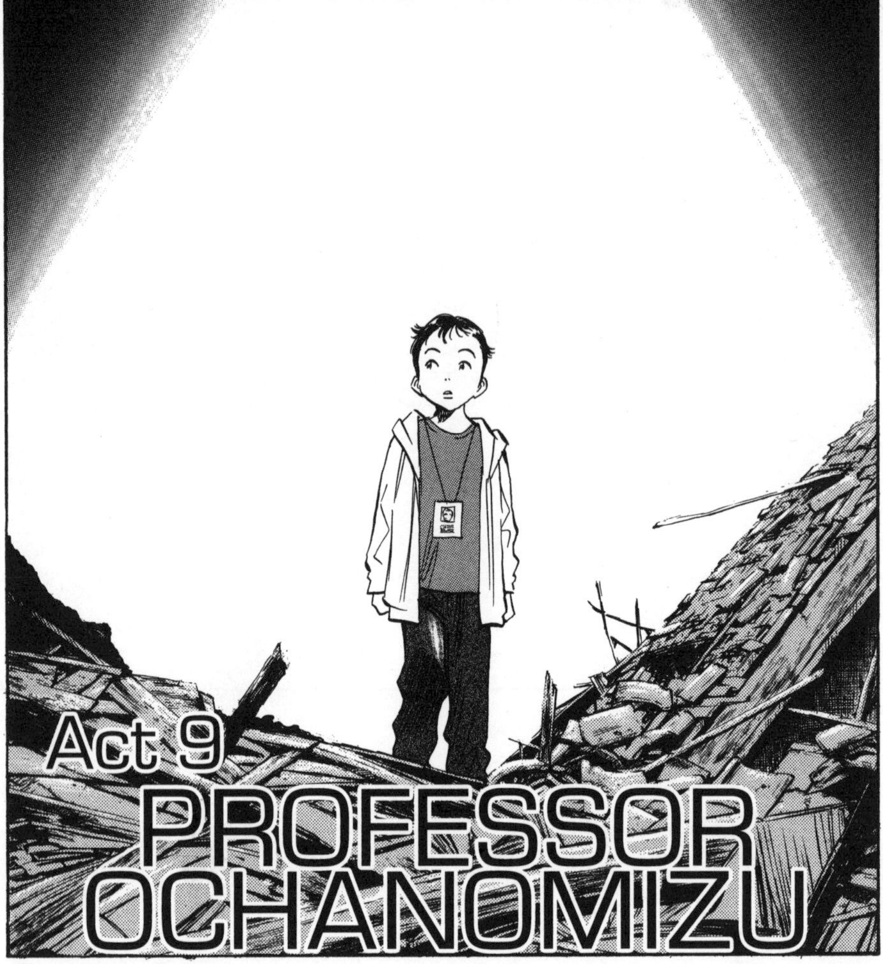
Act 9
PROFESSOR OCHANOMIZU

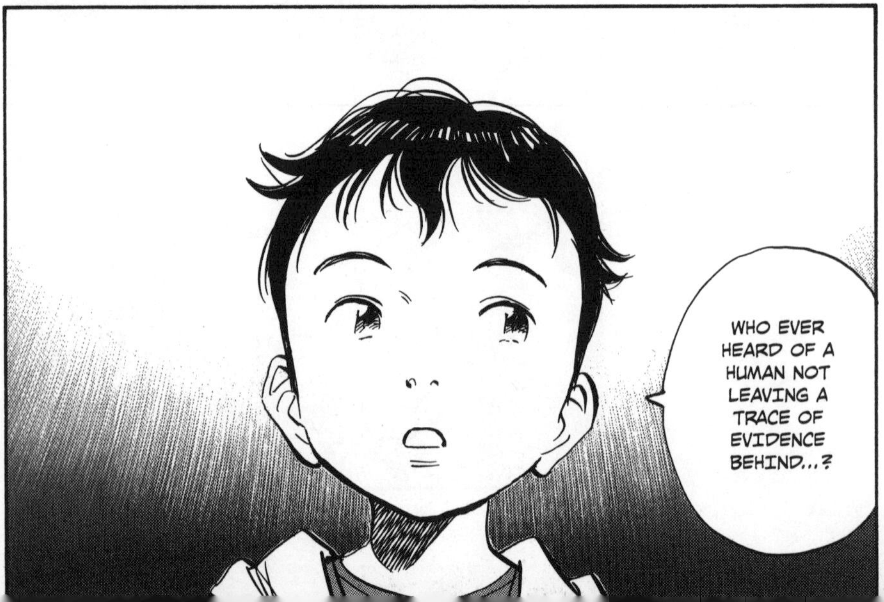
WHO EVER HEARD OF A HUMAN NOT LEAVING A TRACE OF EVIDENCE BEHIND...?

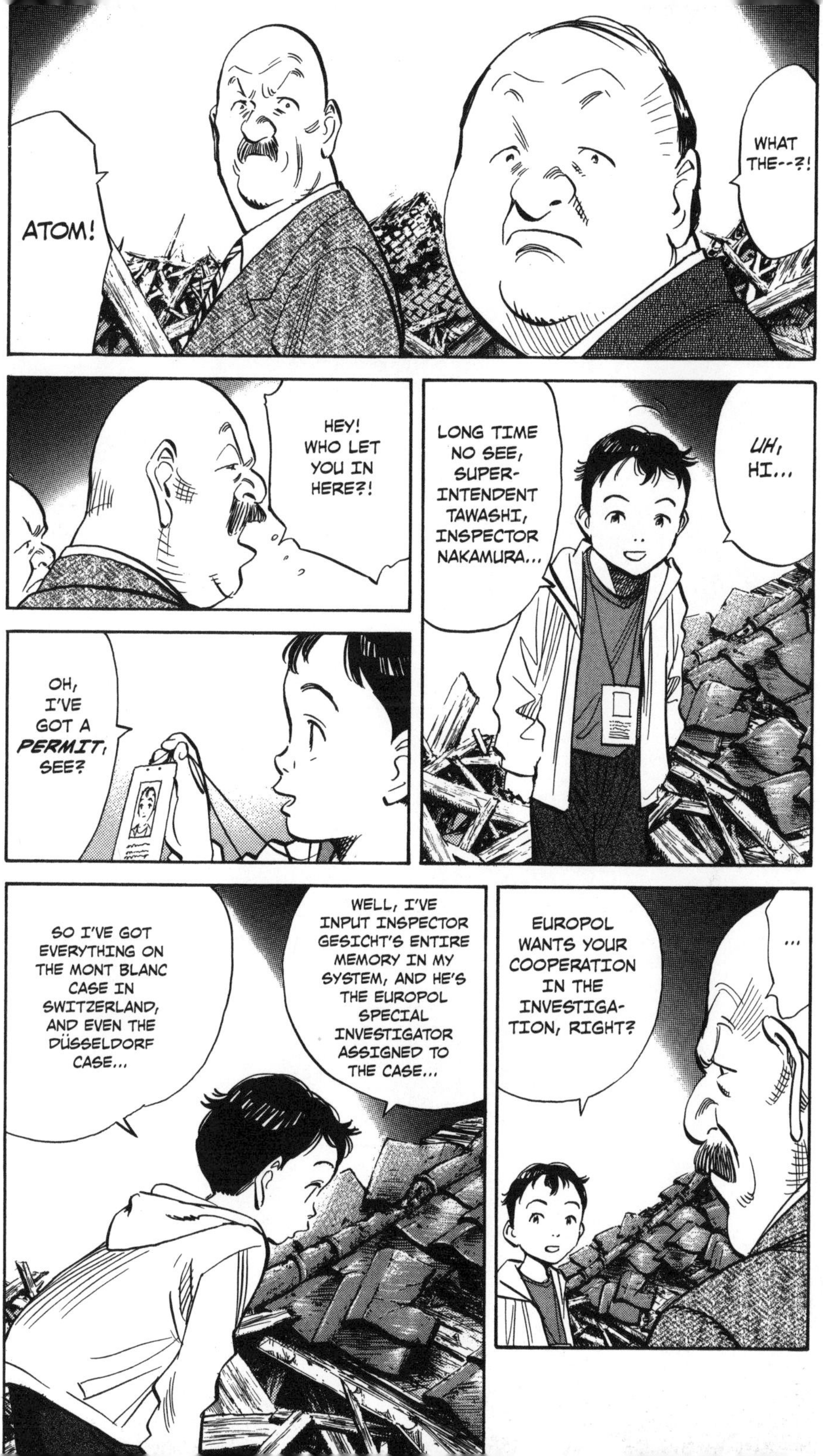
WHAT THE--?!
ATOM!
UH, HI...
LONG TIME NO SEE, SUPER-INTENDENT TAWASHI, INSPECTOR NAKAMURA...
HEY! WHO LET YOU IN HERE?!
OH, I'VE GOT A *PERMIT*, SEE?
...
EUROPOL WANTS YOUR COOPERATION IN THE INVESTIGA-TION, RIGHT?
WELL, I'VE INPUT INSPECTOR GESICHT'S ENTIRE MEMORY IN MY SYSTEM, AND HE'S THE EUROPOL SPECIAL INVESTIGATOR ASSIGNED TO THE CASE...
SO I'VE GOT EVERYTHING ON THE MONT BLANC CASE IN SWITZERLAND, AND EVEN THE DÜSSELDORF CASE...

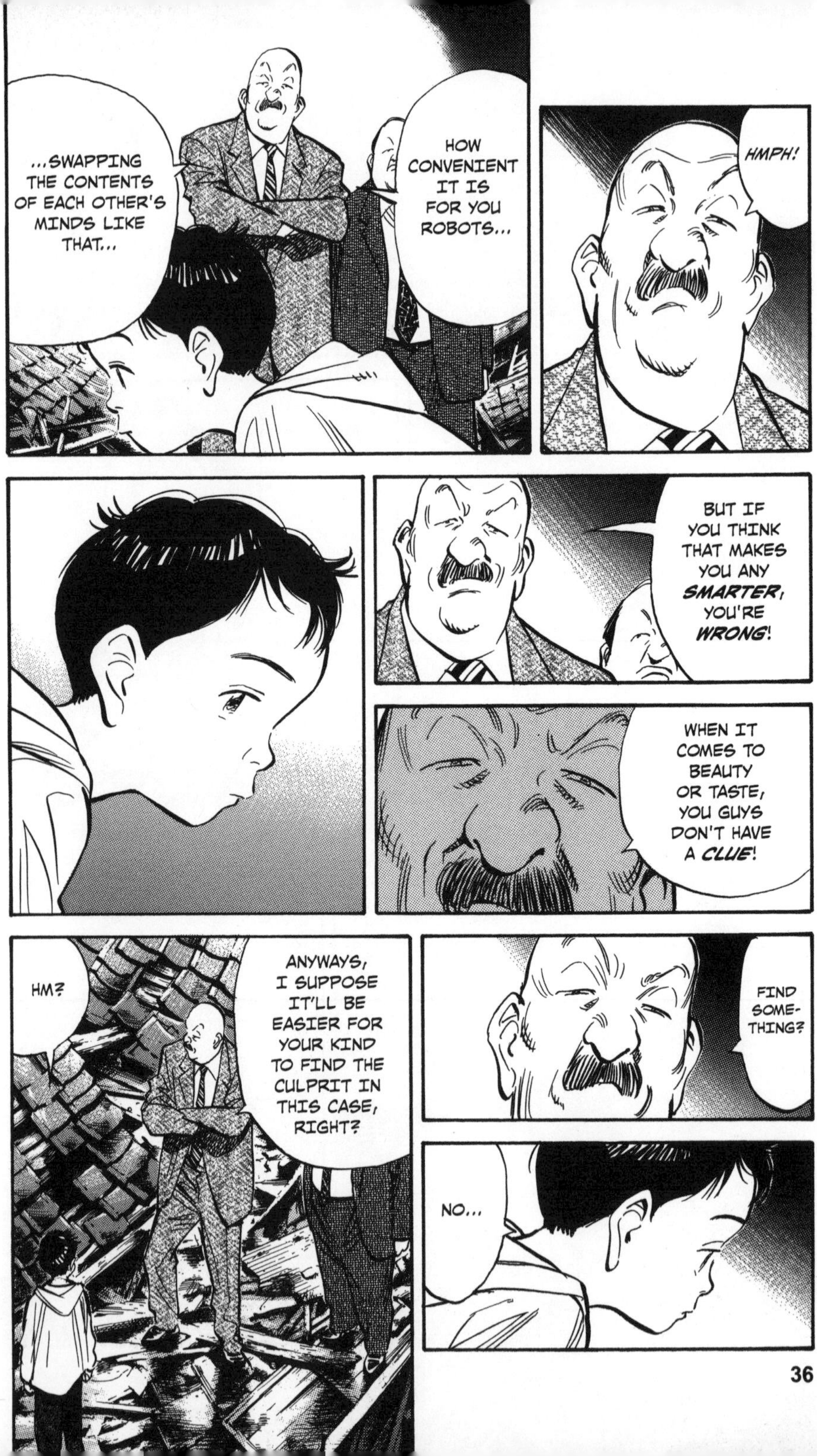

HMPH!
HOW CONVENIENT IT IS FOR YOU ROBOTS...
...SWAPPING THE CONTENTS OF EACH OTHER'S MINDS LIKE THAT...
BUT IF YOU THINK THAT MAKES YOU ANY *SMARTER*, YOU'RE *WRONG*!
WHEN IT COMES TO BEAUTY OR TASTE, YOU GUYS DON'T HAVE A *CLUE*!
FIND SOMETHING?
NO...
ANYWAYS, I SUPPOSE IT'LL BE EASIER FOR YOUR KIND TO FIND THE CULPRIT IN THIS CASE, RIGHT?
HM?

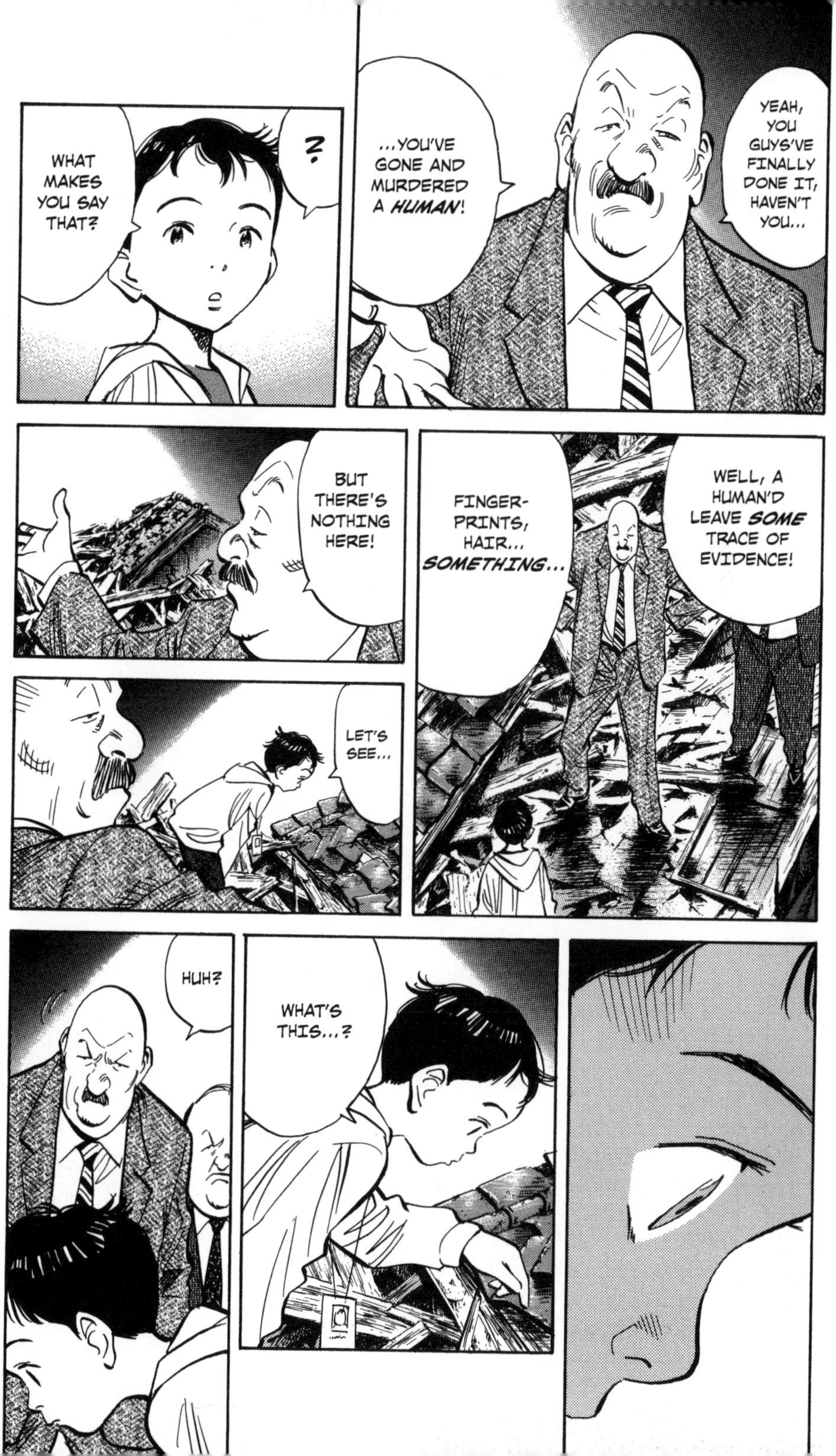
YEAH, YOU GUYS'VE FINALLY DONE IT, HAVEN'T YOU...
...YOU'VE GONE AND MURDERED A *HUMAN*!
?
WHAT MAKES YOU SAY THAT?
WELL, A HUMAN'D LEAVE *SOME* TRACE OF EVIDENCE!
FINGER-PRINTS, HAIR... *SOMETHING*...
BUT THERE'S NOTHING HERE!
LET'S SEE...
WHAT'S THIS...?
HUH?

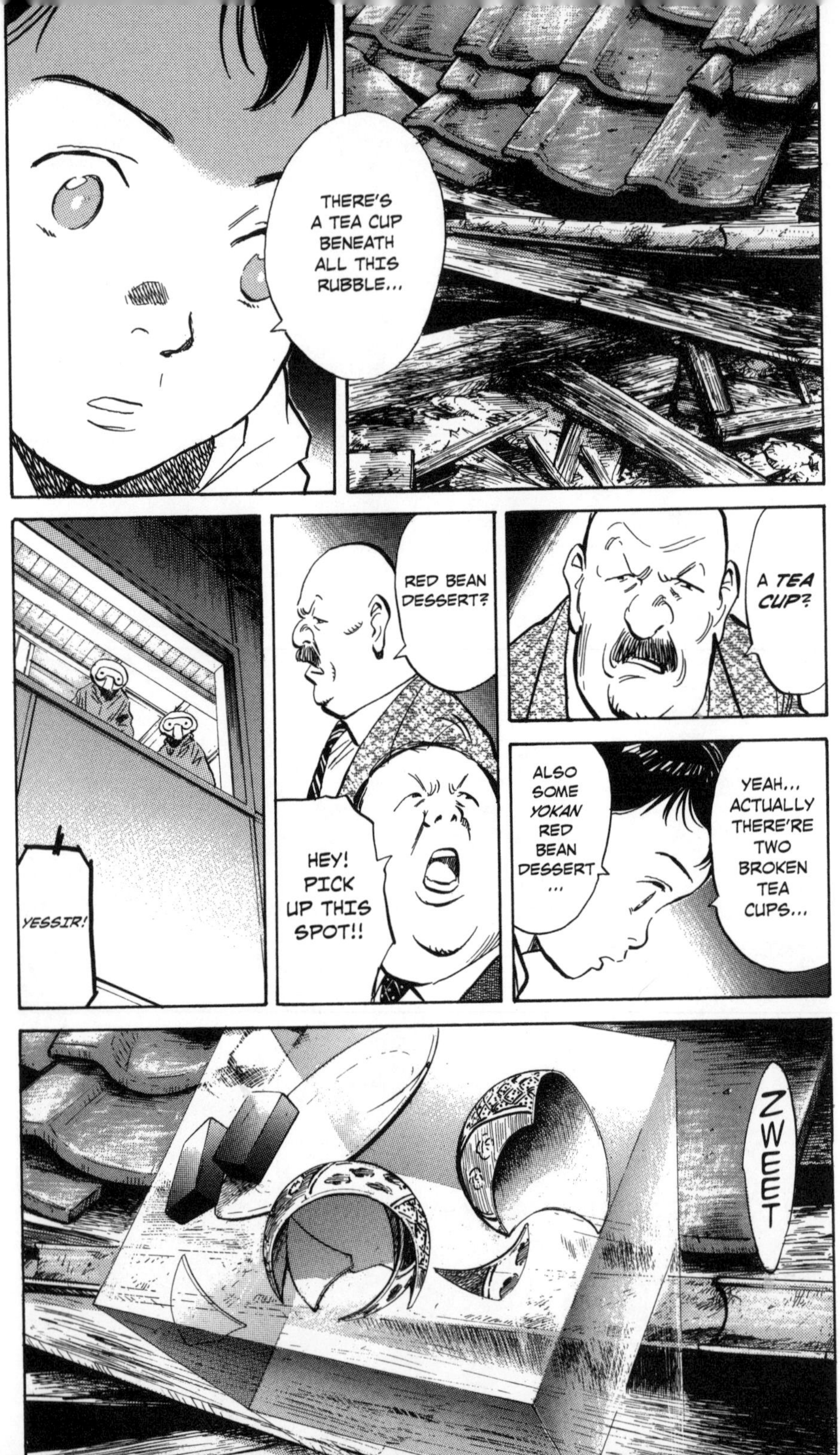
THERE'S A TEA CUP BENEATH ALL THIS RUBBLE...
A *TEA CUP*?
YEAH... ACTUALLY THERE'RE TWO BROKEN TEA CUPS...
ALSO SOME *YOKAN* RED BEAN DESSERT...
RED BEAN DESSERT?
HEY! PICK UP THIS SPOT!!
YESSIR!
ZWEET

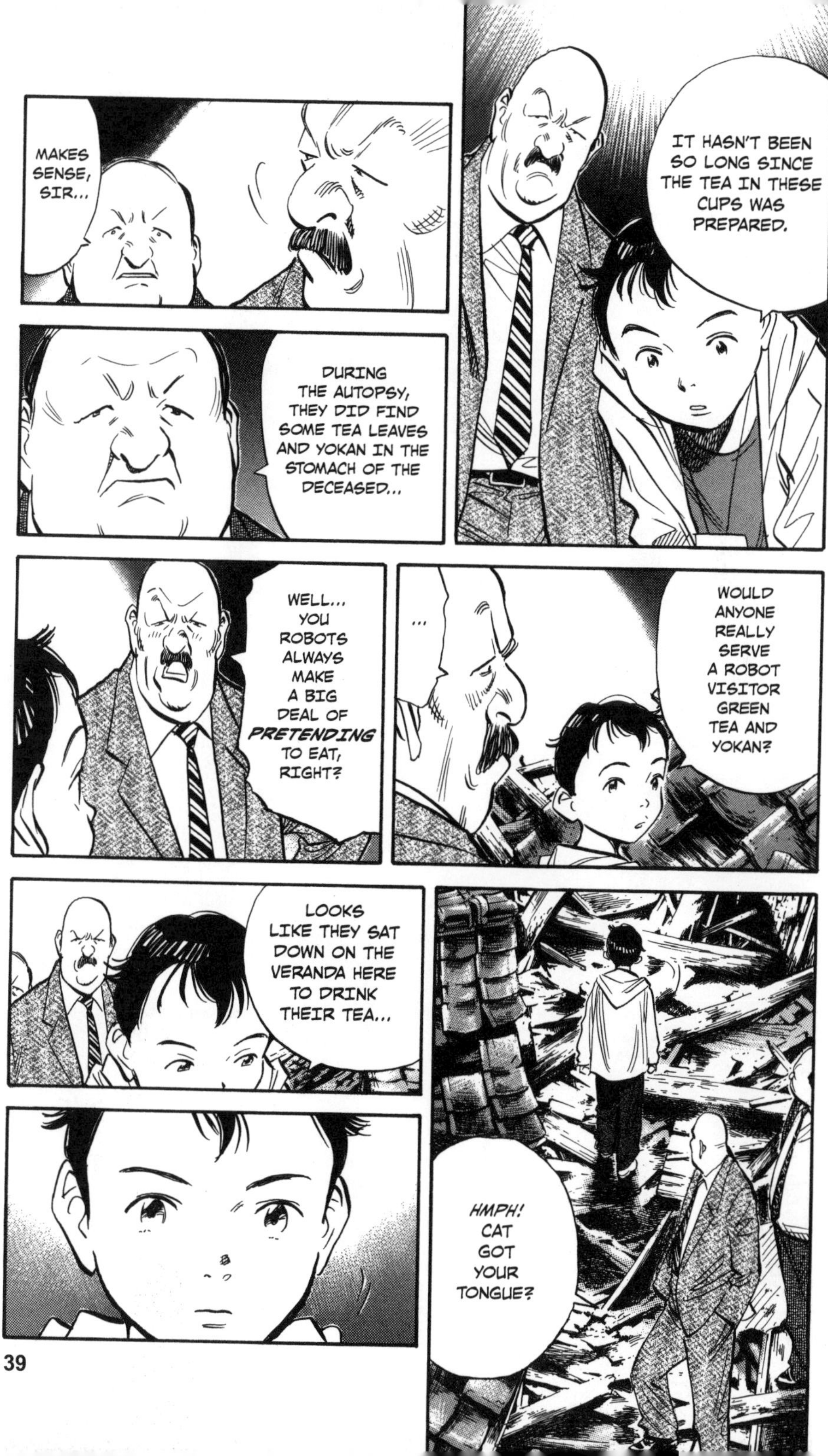
IT HASN'T BEEN SO LONG SINCE THE TEA IN THESE CUPS WAS PREPARED.
MAKES SENSE, SIR...
DURING THE AUTOPSY, THEY DID FIND SOME TEA LEAVES AND YOKAN IN THE STOMACH OF THE DECEASED...
WOULD ANYONE REALLY SERVE A ROBOT VISITOR GREEN TEA AND YOKAN?
...
WELL... YOU ROBOTS ALWAYS MAKE A BIG DEAL OF *PRETENDING* TO EAT, RIGHT?
HMPH! CAT GOT YOUR TONGUE?
LOOKS LIKE THEY SAT DOWN ON THE VERANDA HERE TO DRINK THEIR TEA...

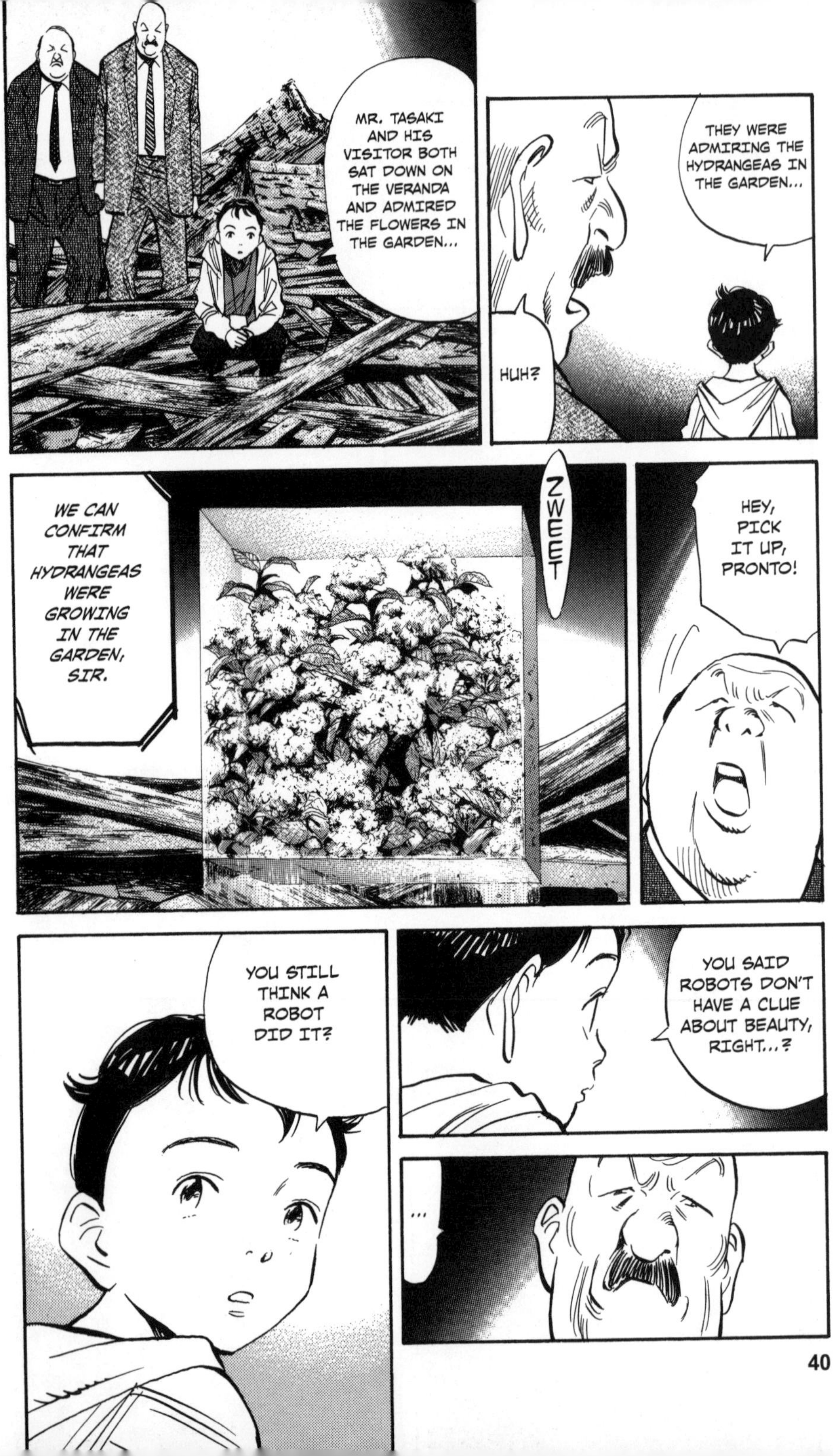

THEY WERE ADMIRING THE HYDRANGEAS IN THE GARDEN...
HUH?
MR. TASAKI AND HIS VISITOR BOTH SAT DOWN ON THE VERANDA AND ADMIRED THE FLOWERS IN THE GARDEN...
HEY, PICK IT UP, PRONTO!
ZWEET
WE CAN CONFIRM THAT HYDRANGEAS WERE GROWING IN THE GARDEN, SIR.
YOU SAID ROBOTS DON'T HAVE A CLUE ABOUT BEAUTY, RIGHT...?
...
YOU STILL THINK A ROBOT DID IT?

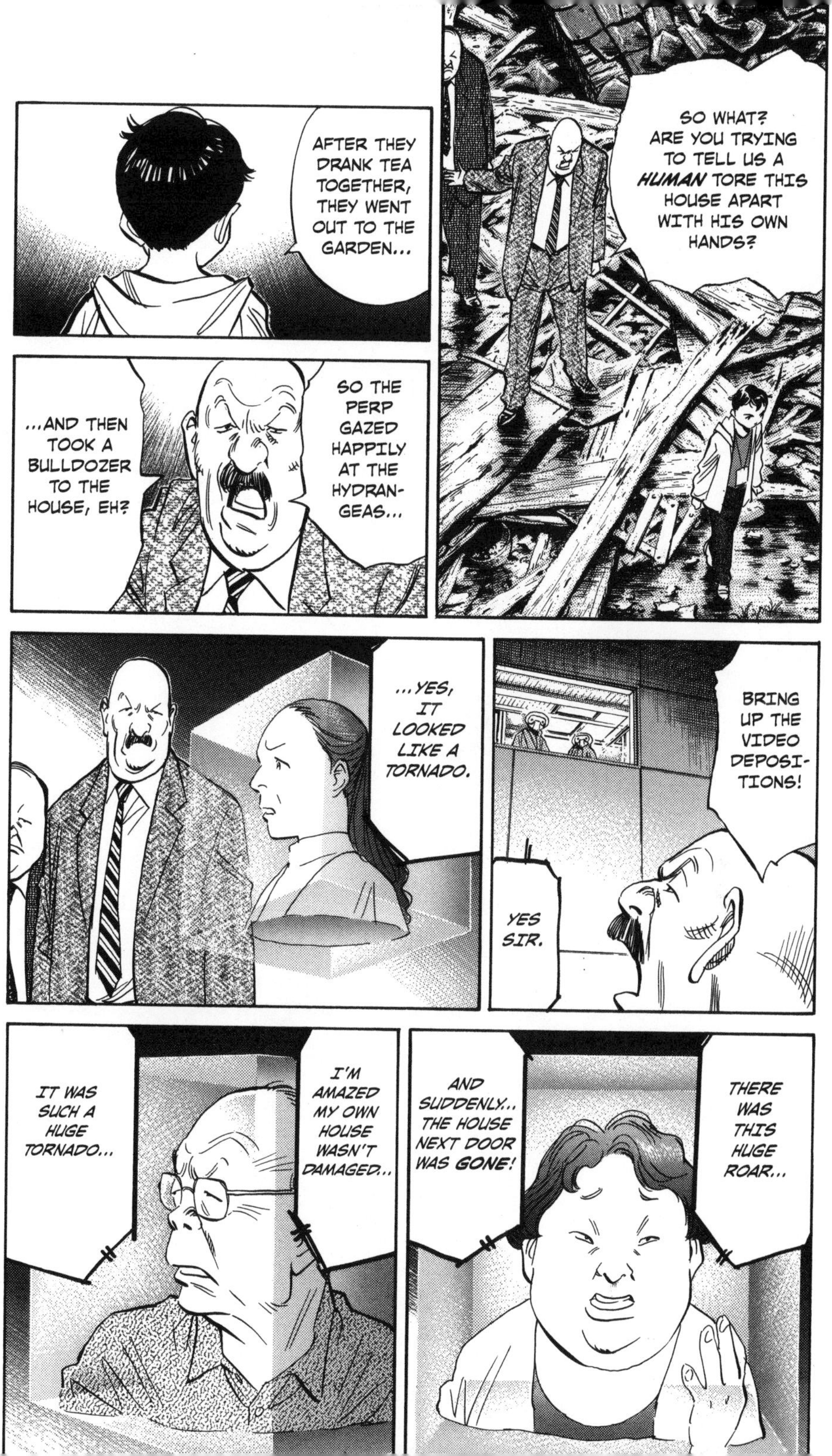
SO WHAT? ARE YOU TRYING TO TELL US A HUMAN TORE THIS HOUSE APART WITH HIS OWN HANDS?
AFTER THEY DRANK TEA TOGETHER, THEY WENT OUT TO THE GARDEN...
SO THE PERP GAZED HAPPILY AT THE HYDRANGEAS...
...AND THEN TOOK A BULLDOZER TO THE HOUSE, EH?
BRING UP THE VIDEO DEPOSITIONS!
YES SIR.
...YES, IT LOOKED LIKE A TORNADO.
THERE WAS THIS HUGE ROAR...
AND SUDDENLY... THE HOUSE NEXT DOOR WAS GONE!
I'M AMAZED MY OWN HOUSE WASN'T DAMAGED...
IT WAS SUCH A HUGE TORNADO...

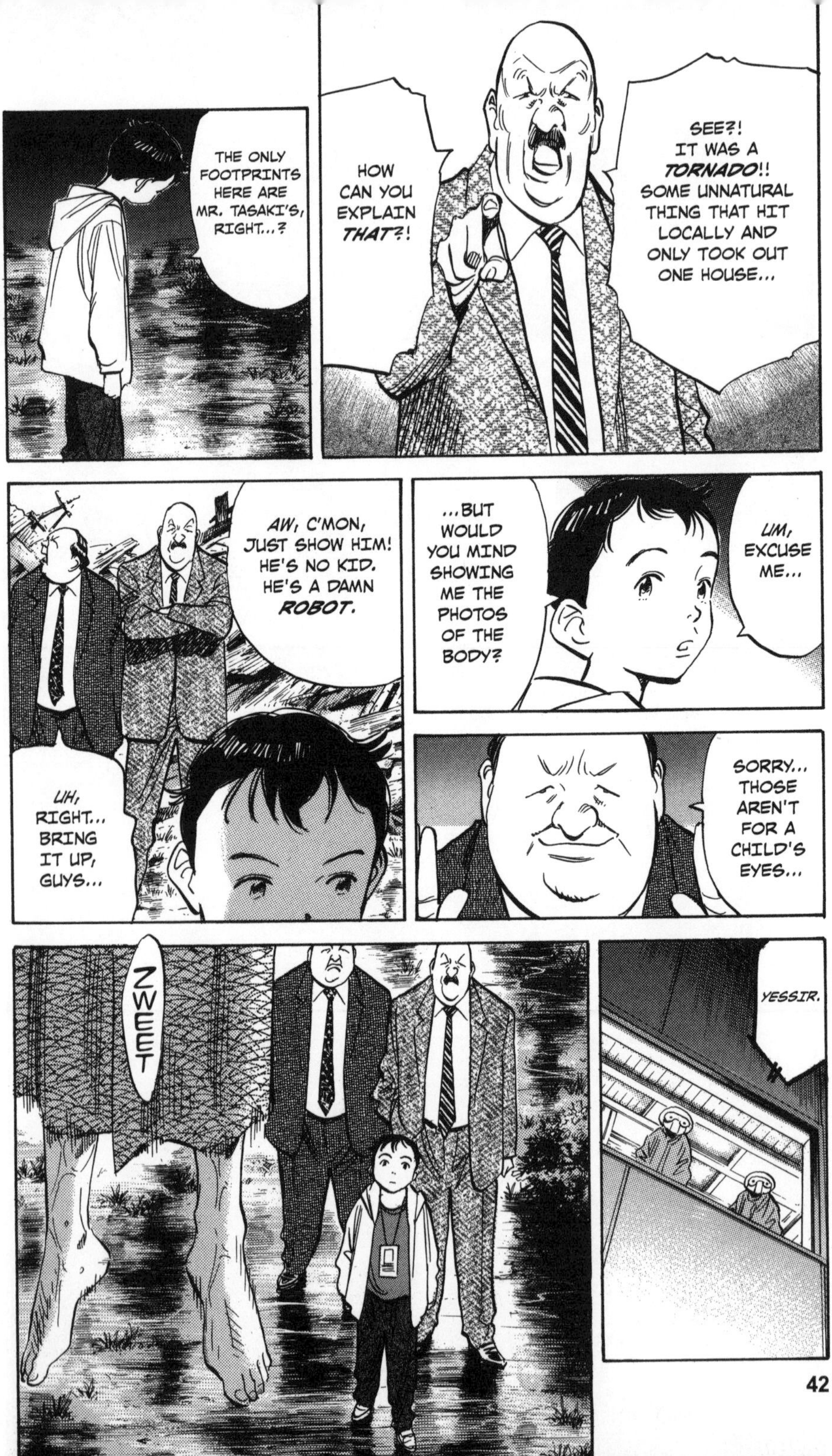
SEE?! IT WAS A *TORNADO*!! SOME UNNATURAL THING THAT HIT LOCALLY AND ONLY TOOK OUT ONE HOUSE...
HOW CAN YOU EXPLAIN *THAT*?!
THE ONLY FOOTPRINTS HERE ARE MR. TASAKI'S, RIGHT...?
UM, EXCUSE ME...
...BUT WOULD YOU MIND SHOWING ME THE PHOTOS OF THE BODY?
SORRY... THOSE AREN'T FOR A CHILD'S EYES...
AW, C'MON, JUST SHOW HIM! HE'S NO KID. HE'S A DAMN ***ROBOT***.
UH, RIGHT... BRING IT UP, GUYS...
YESSIR.
ZWEET

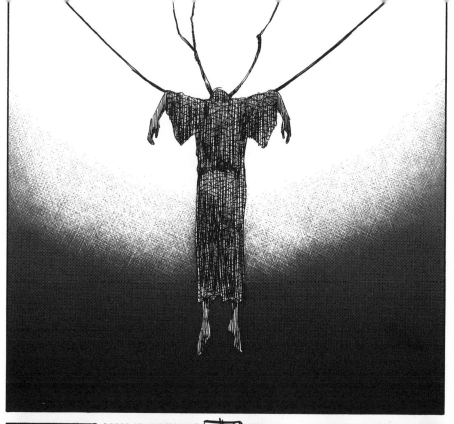

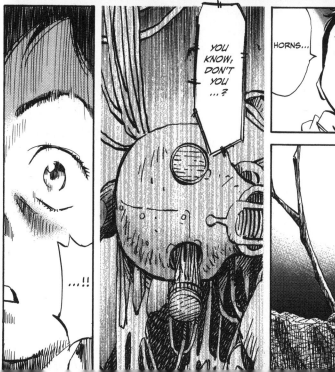

YOU KNOW, DON'T YOU...?

HORNS...

....!!

THE GOD OF DEATH WAS DEPICTED WITH HORNS...
...AND IN THE ROMAN MYTHOS...
ARGH...
GESICHT'S MEMORIES...
PLUTO ...

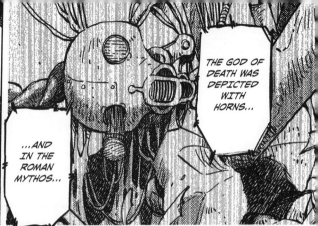

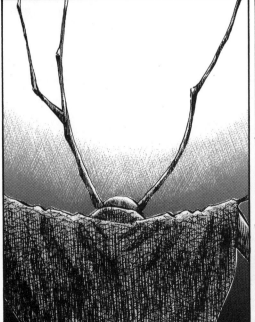

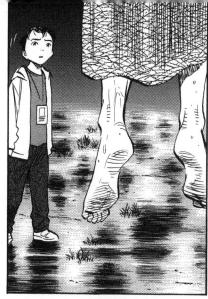

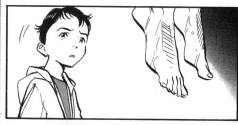

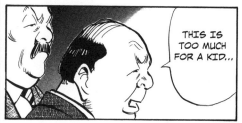

THIS IS TOO MUCH FOR A KID...
...
UM...
DO YOU KNOW IF JUNICHIRO TASAKI USED A PEN?
THERE *IS* A CALLOUS ON THE TOP JOINT OF HIS RIGHT MIDDLE FINGER... HE WAS APPARENTLY AN OLD-SCHOOL ANALOG TYPE...
NO, THERE'S SOMETHING ELSE. IT'S BEEN MOSTLY WASHED AWAY BY THE RAIN...
...BUT I CAN SEE FAINT TRACES OF *INK* ON HIS HAND...

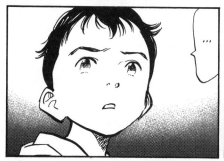

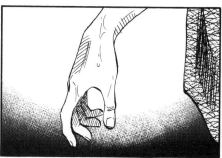

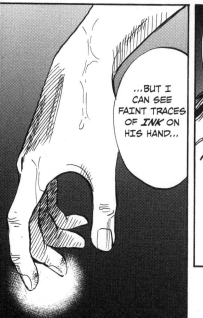

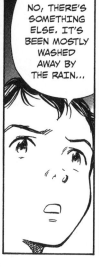

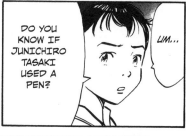

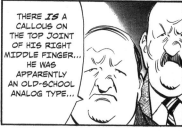

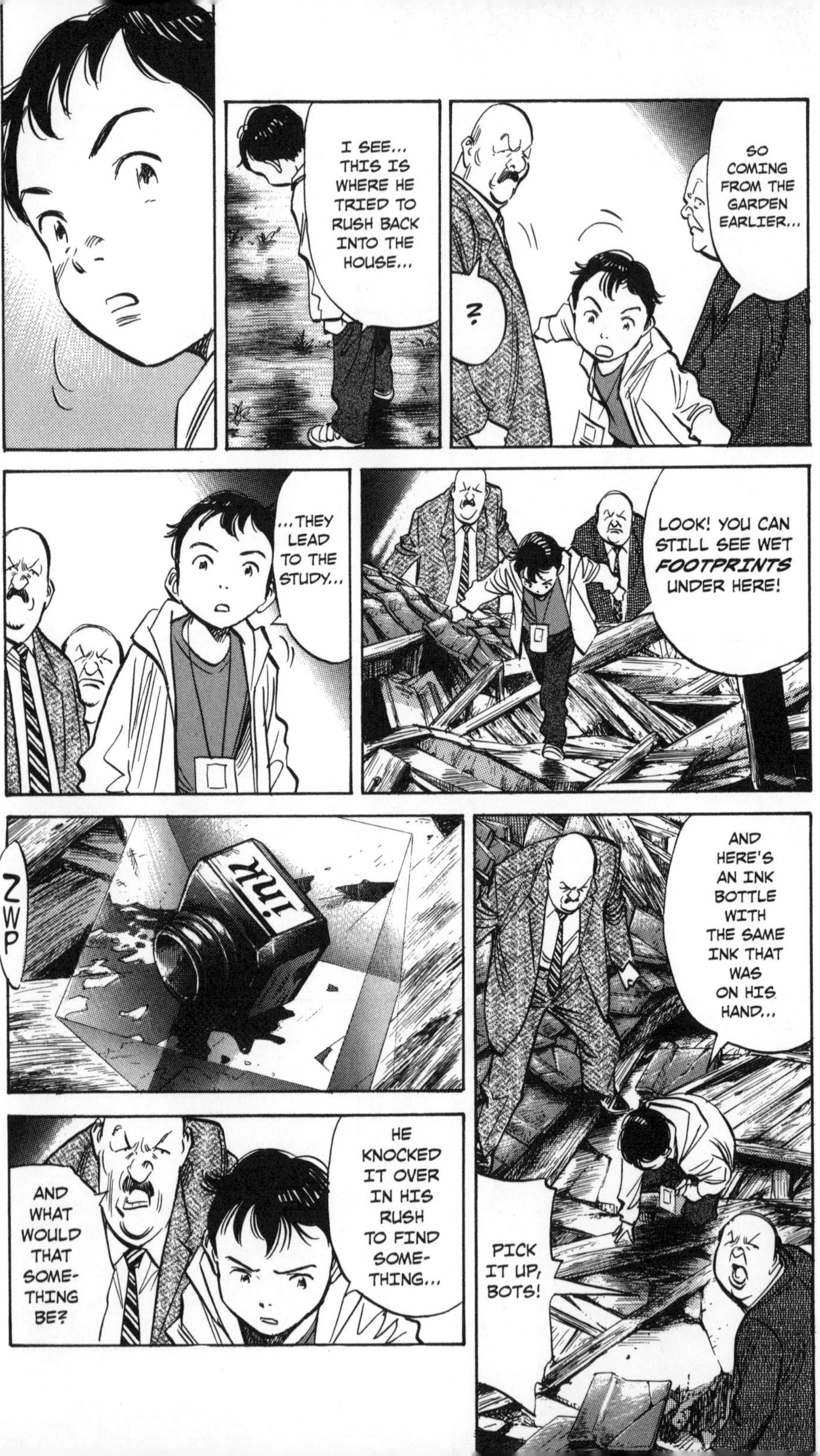
SO COMING FROM THE GARDEN EARLIER...
?
I SEE... THIS IS WHERE HE TRIED TO RUSH BACK INTO THE HOUSE...
LOOK! YOU CAN STILL SEE WET FOOTPRINTS UNDER HERE!
...THEY LEAD TO THE STUDY...
AND HERE'S AN INK BOTTLE WITH THE SAME INK THAT WAS ON HIS HAND...
PICK IT UP, BOTS!
ink
ZWP
HE KNOCKED IT OVER IN HIS RUSH TO FIND SOME-THING...
AND WHAT WOULD THAT SOME-THING BE?

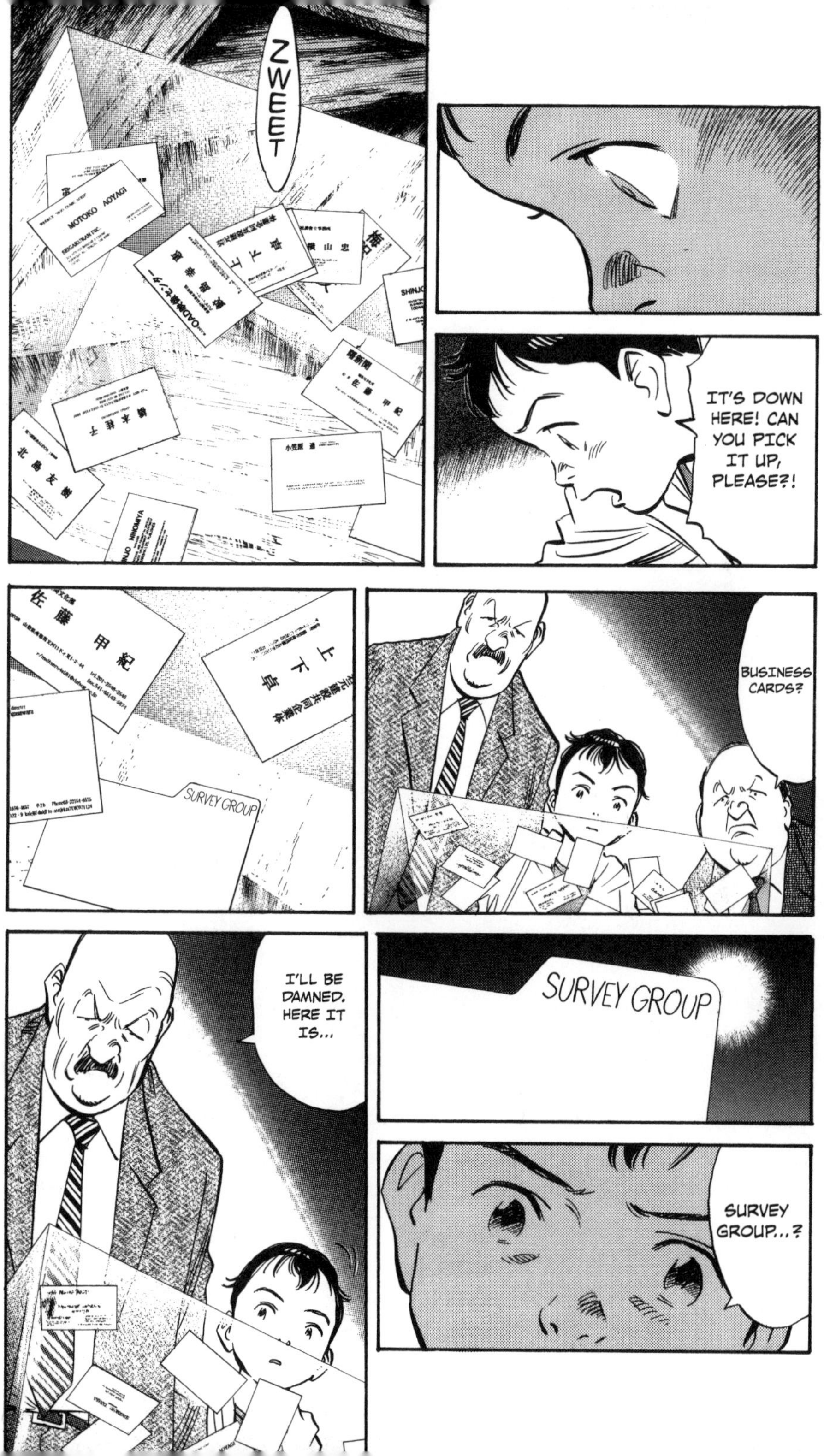
IT'S DOWN HERE! CAN YOU PICK IT UP, PLEASE?!
ZWEET
MOTOKO AOYAGI
BUSINESS CARDS?
佐藤 甲紀
上下卓
SURVEY GROUP
SURVEY GROUP
SURVEY GROUP...?
I'LL BE DAMNED. HERE IT IS...

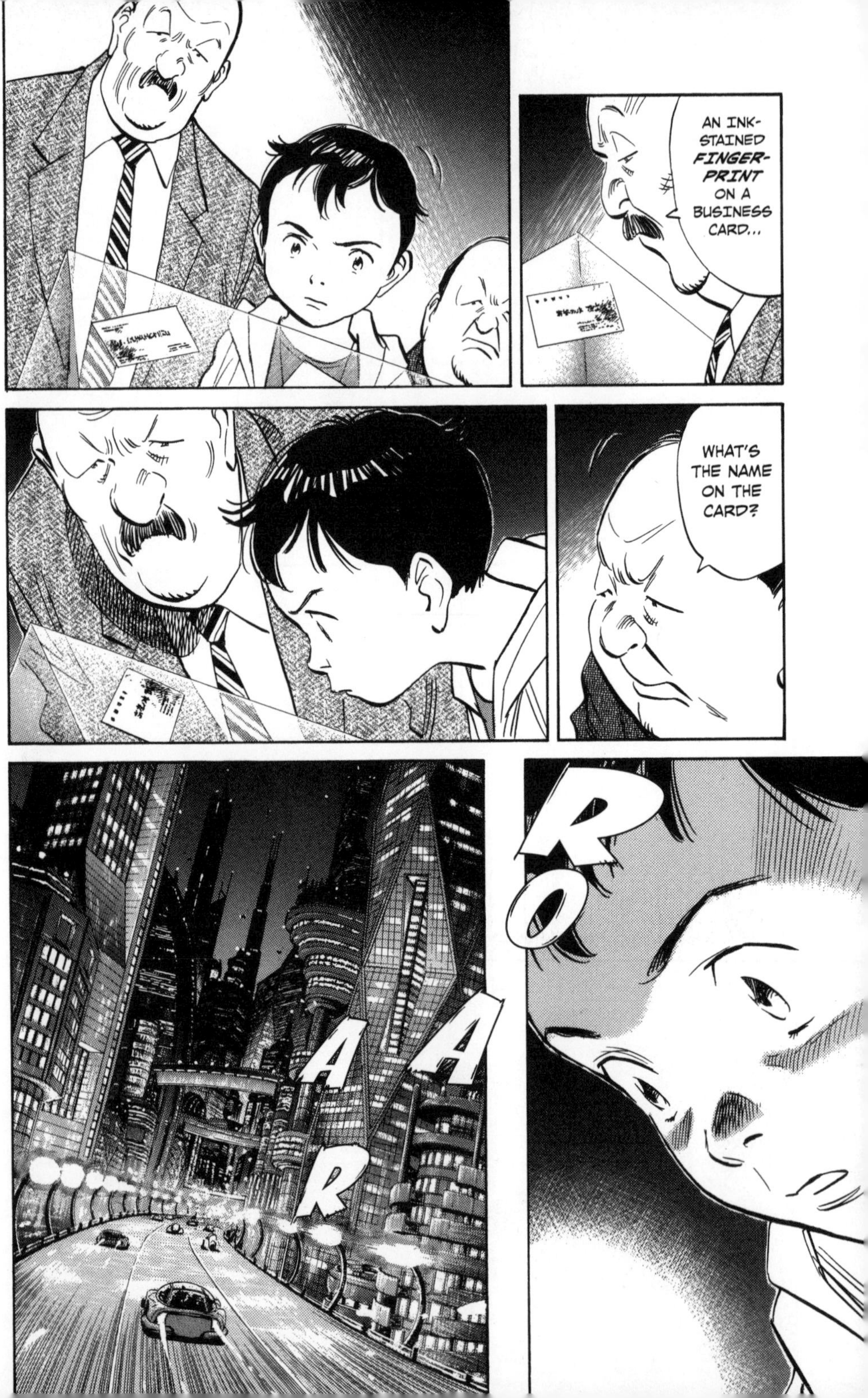
AN INK-STAINED FINGER-PRINT ON A BUSINESS CARD...
WHAT'S THE NAME ON THE CARD?
ROAAR

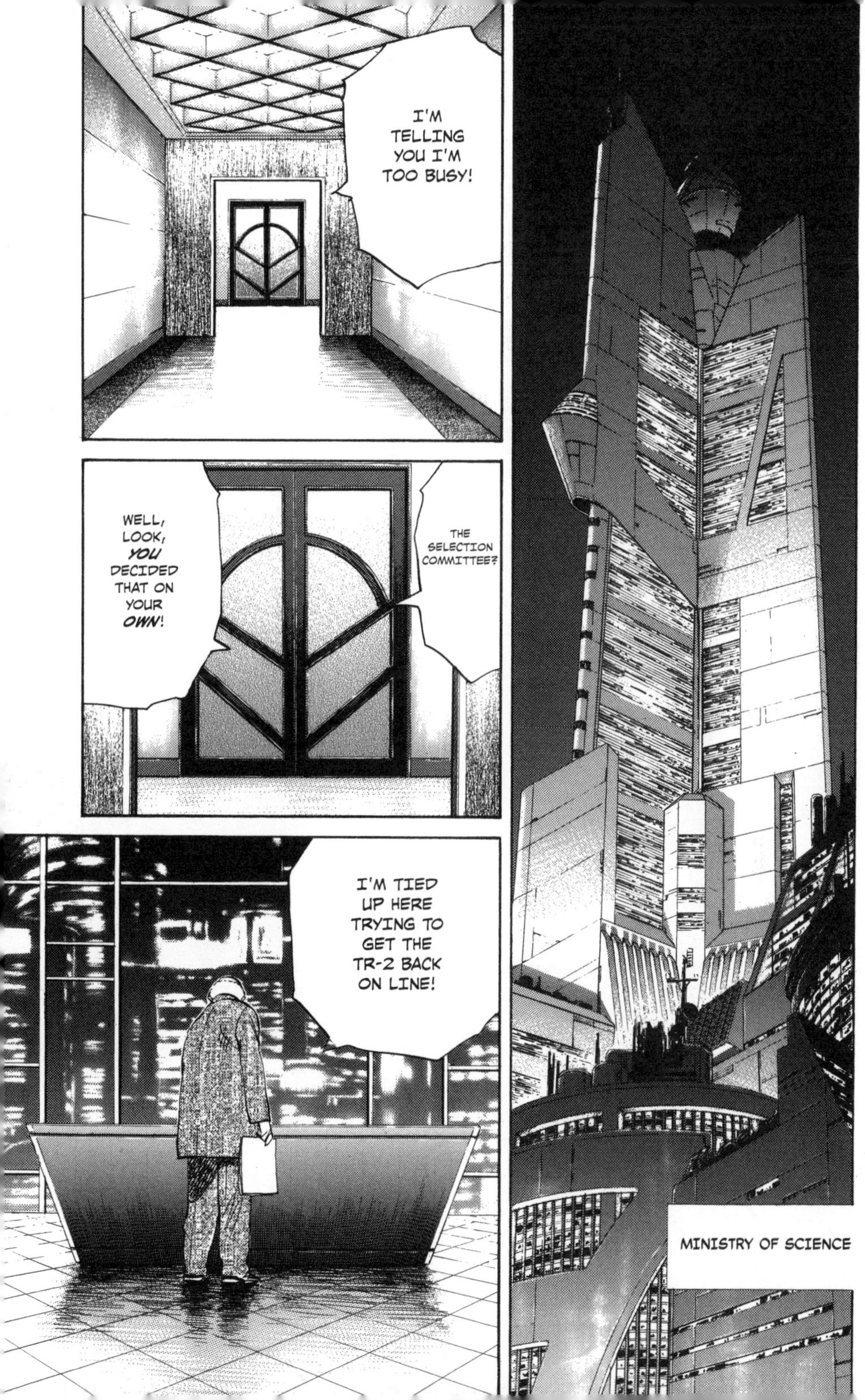
MINISTRY OF SCIENCE
I'M TELLING YOU I'M TOO BUSY!
THE SELECTION COMMITTEE?
WELL, LOOK, *YOU* DECIDED THAT ON YOUR *OWN*!
I'M TIED UP HERE TRYING TO GET THE TR-2 BACK ON LINE!

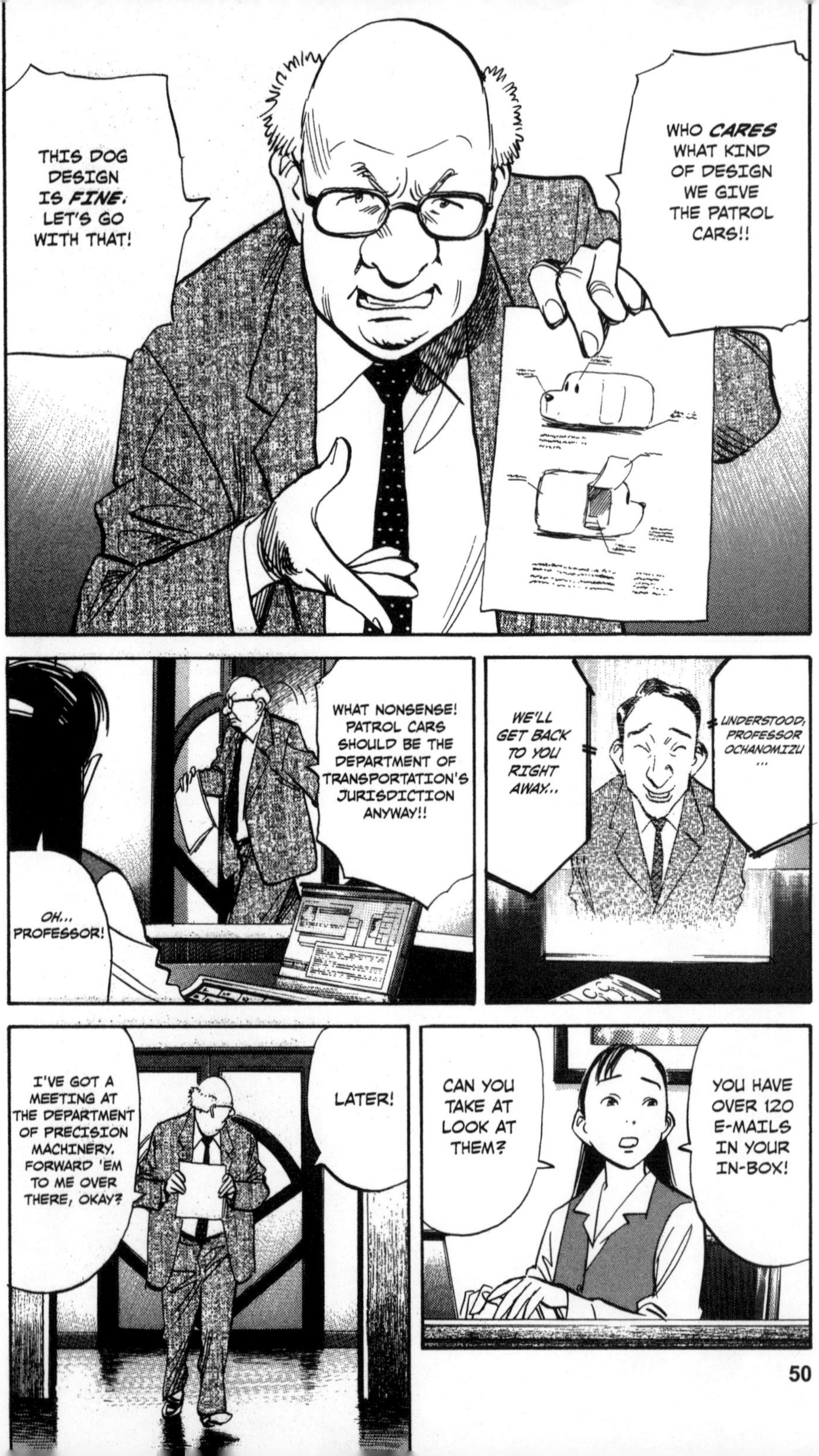
WHO CARES WHAT KIND OF DESIGN WE GIVE THE PATROL CARS!!
THIS DOG DESIGN IS FINE. LET'S GO WITH THAT!
UNDERSTOOD, PROFESSOR OCHANOMIZU...
WE'LL GET BACK TO YOU RIGHT AWAY...
WHAT NONSENSE! PATROL CARS SHOULD BE THE DEPARTMENT OF TRANSPORTATION'S JURISDICTION ANYWAY!!
OH... PROFESSOR!
YOU HAVE OVER 120 E-MAILS IN YOUR IN-BOX!
CAN YOU TAKE AT LOOK AT THEM?
LATER!
I'VE GOT A MEETING AT THE DEPARTMENT OF PRECISION MACHINERY. FORWARD 'EM TO ME OVER THERE, OKAY?

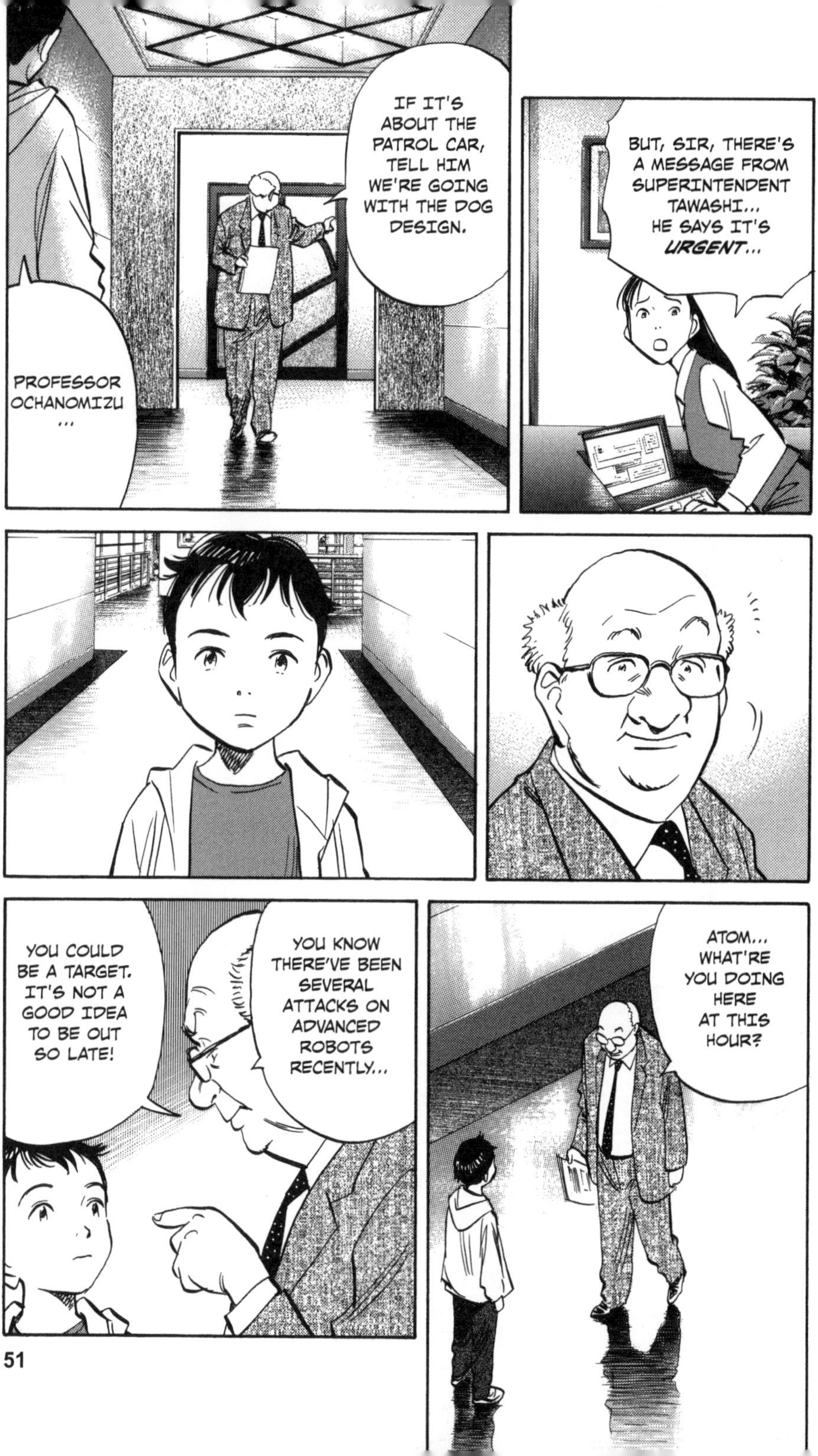
BUT, SIR, THERE'S A MESSAGE FROM SUPERINTENDENT TAWASHI... HE SAYS IT'S *URGENT*...
IF IT'S ABOUT THE PATROL CAR, TELL HIM WE'RE GOING WITH THE DOG DESIGN.
PROFESSOR OCHANOMIZU ...
ATOM... WHAT'RE YOU DOING HERE AT THIS HOUR?
YOU KNOW THERE'VE BEEN SEVERAL ATTACKS ON ADVANCED ROBOTS RECENTLY...
YOU COULD BE A TARGET. IT'S NOT A GOOD IDEA TO BE OUT SO LATE!

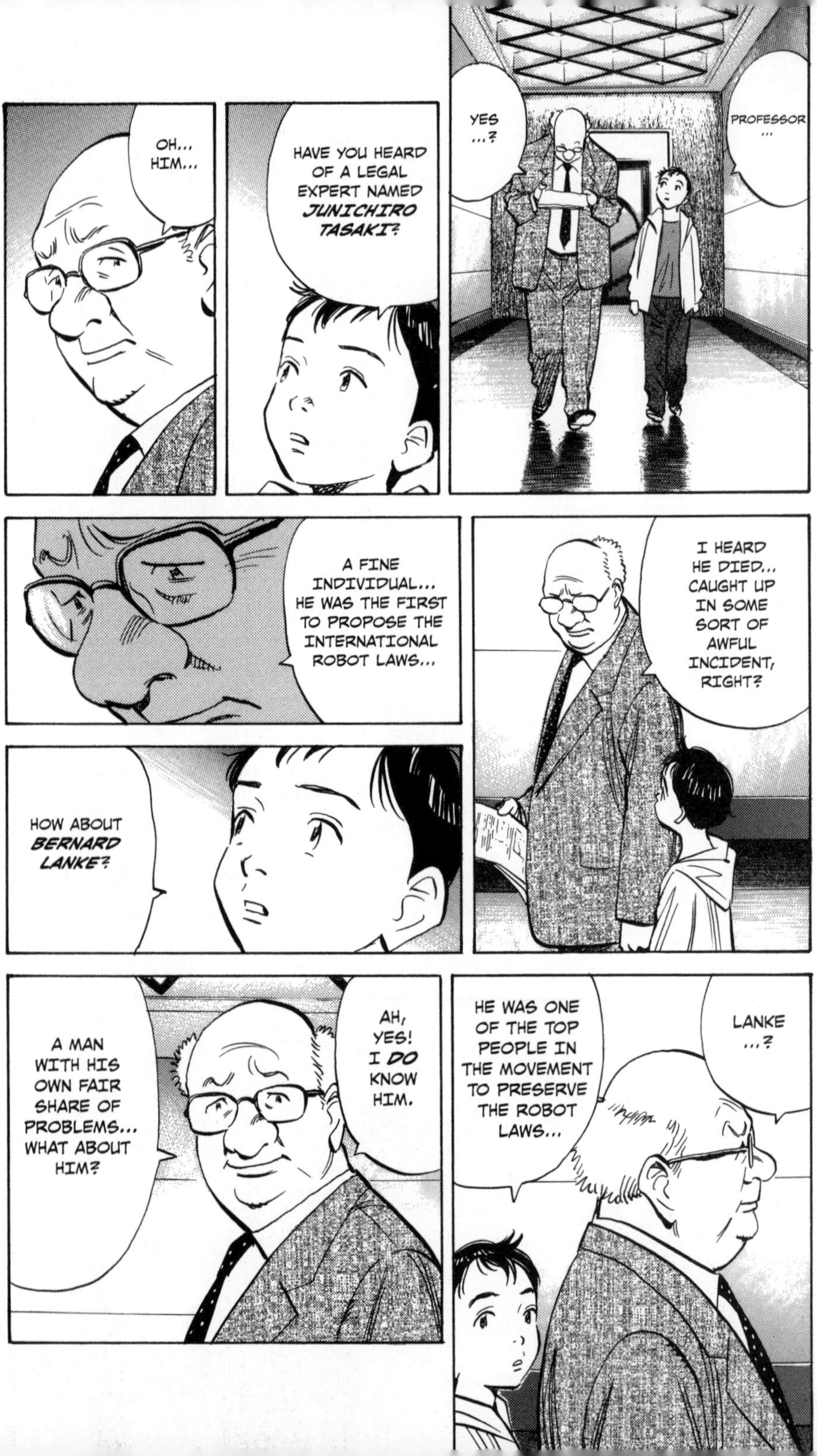
PROFESSOR ...
YES ...?
HAVE YOU HEARD OF A LEGAL EXPERT NAMED *JUNICHIRO TASAKI*?
OH... HIM...
I HEARD HE DIED... CAUGHT UP IN SOME SORT OF AWFUL INCIDENT, RIGHT?
A FINE INDIVIDUAL... HE WAS THE FIRST TO PROPOSE THE INTERNATIONAL ROBOT LAWS...
HOW ABOUT *BERNARD LANKE*?
LANKE ...?
HE WAS ONE OF THE TOP PEOPLE IN THE MOVEMENT TO PRESERVE THE ROBOT LAWS...
AH, YES! I *DO* KNOW HIM.
A MAN WITH HIS OWN FAIR SHARE OF PROBLEMS... WHAT ABOUT HIM?

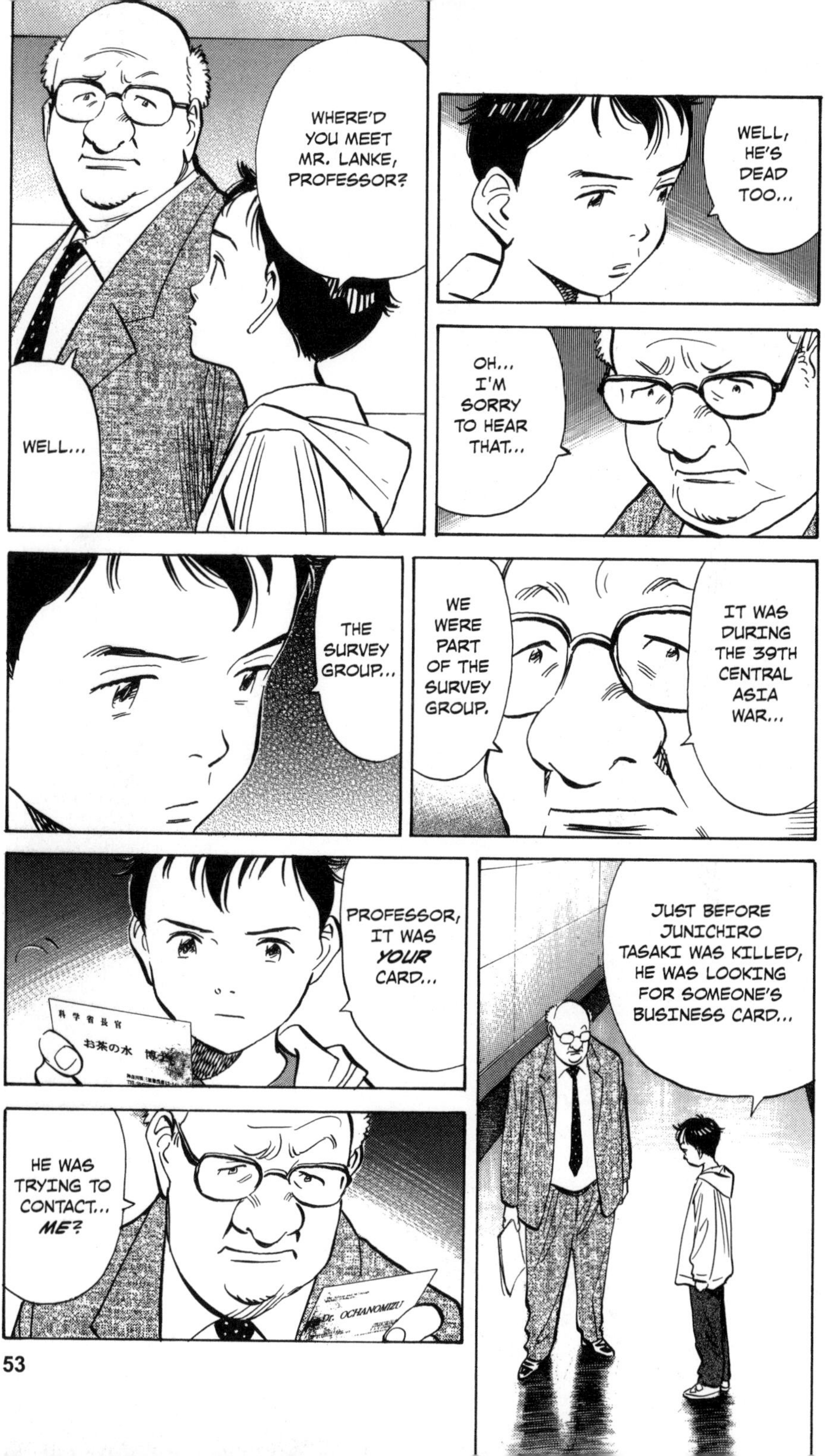
WELL, HE'S DEAD TOO...
OH... I'M SORRY TO HEAR THAT...
WHERE'D YOU MEET MR. LANKE, PROFESSOR?
WELL...
IT WAS DURING THE 39TH CENTRAL ASIA WAR...
WE WERE PART OF THE SURVEY GROUP.
THE SURVEY GROUP...
JUST BEFORE JUNICHIRO TASAKI WAS KILLED, HE WAS LOOKING FOR SOMEONE'S BUSINESS CARD...
PROFESSOR, IT WAS ***YOUR*** CARD...
科学省長官
お茶の水
HE WAS TRYING TO CONTACT... ***ME***?
Dr. OCHANOMIZU

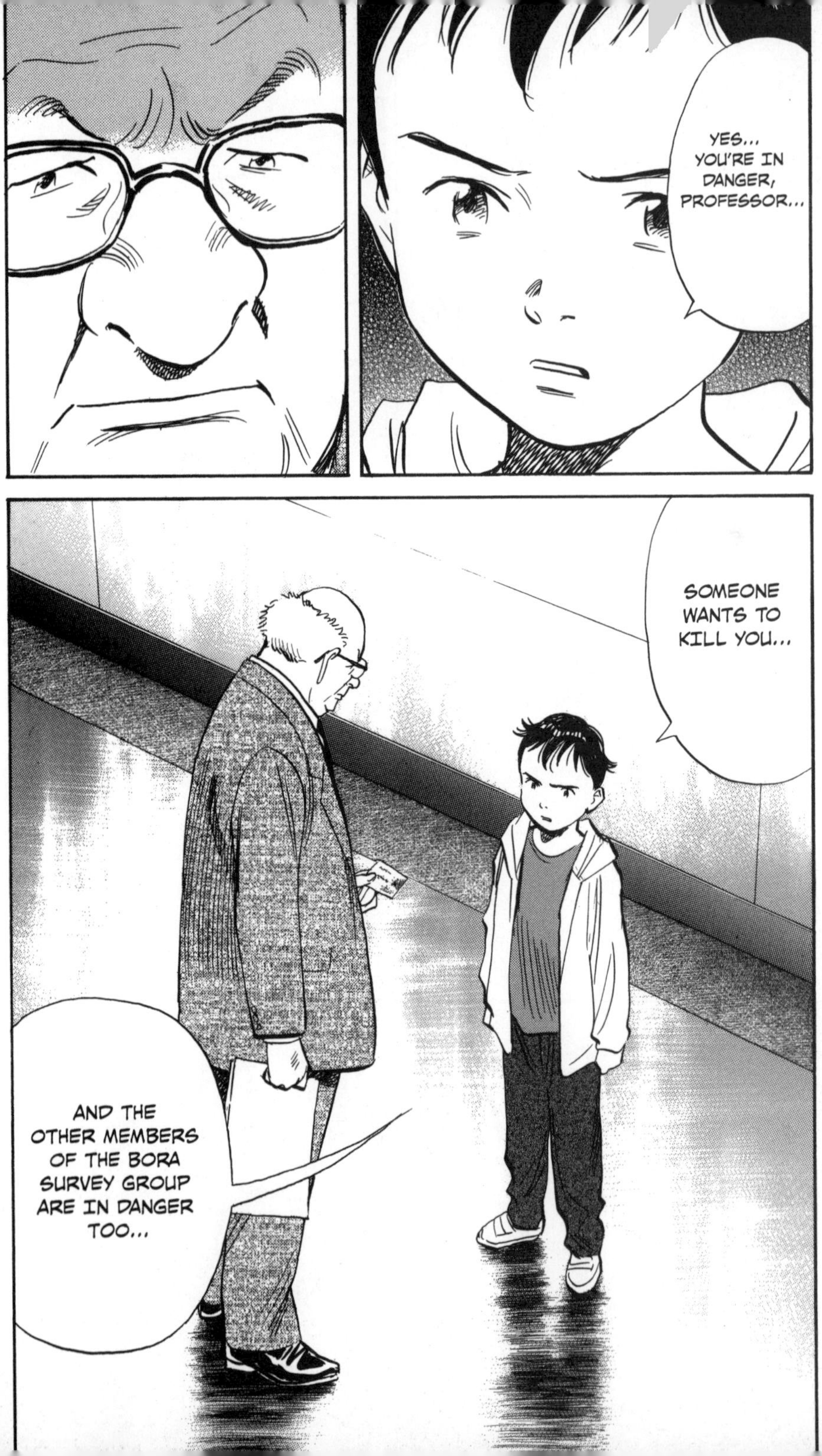
YES... YOU'RE IN DANGER, PROFESSOR...
SOMEONE WANTS TO KILL YOU...
AND THE OTHER MEMBERS OF THE BORA SURVEY GROUP ARE IN DANGER TOO...

Act 10 HERCULES

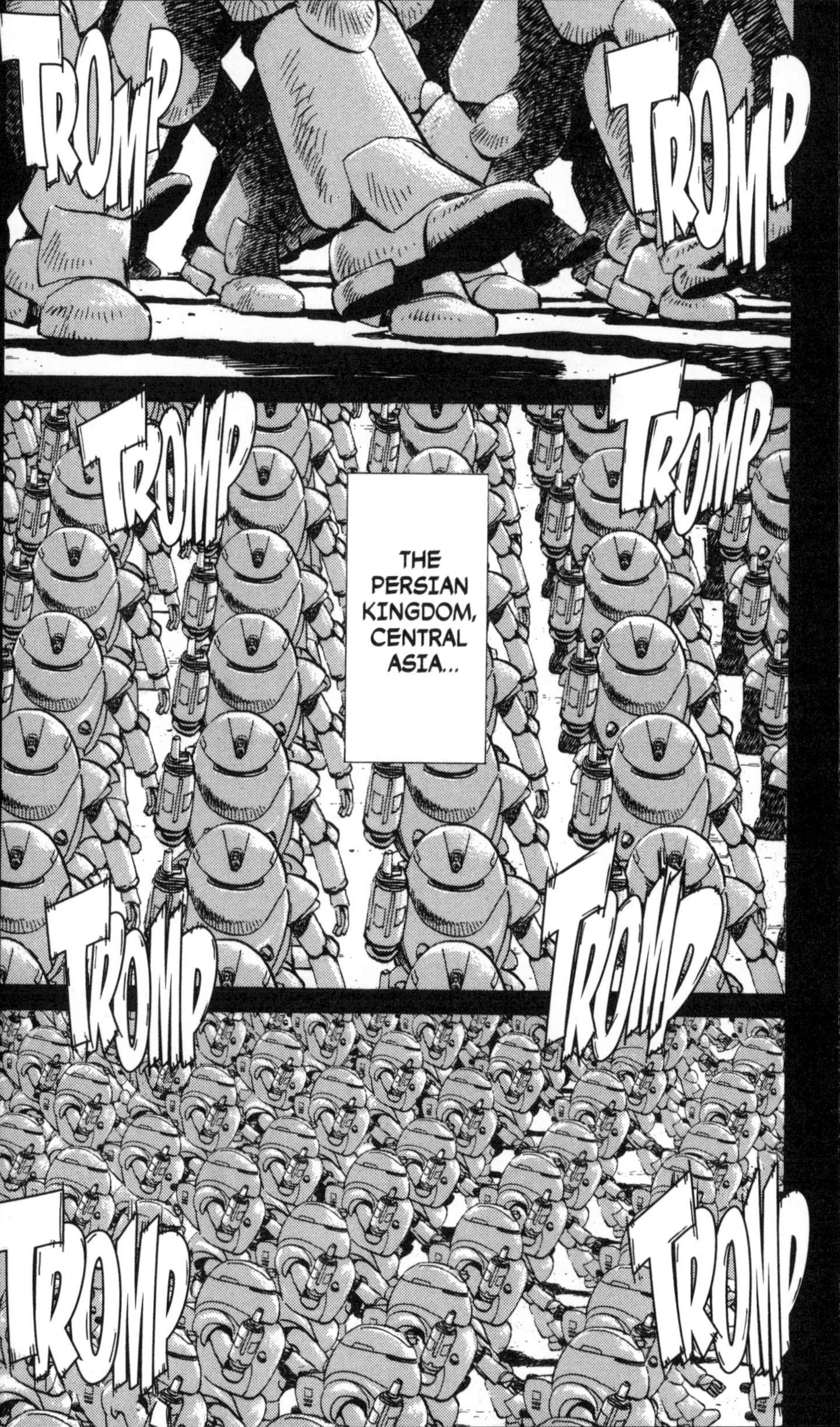
TROMP
TROMP
TROMP
TROMP
THE PERSIAN KINGDOM, CENTRAL ASIA...
TROMP
TROMP
TROMP
TROMP

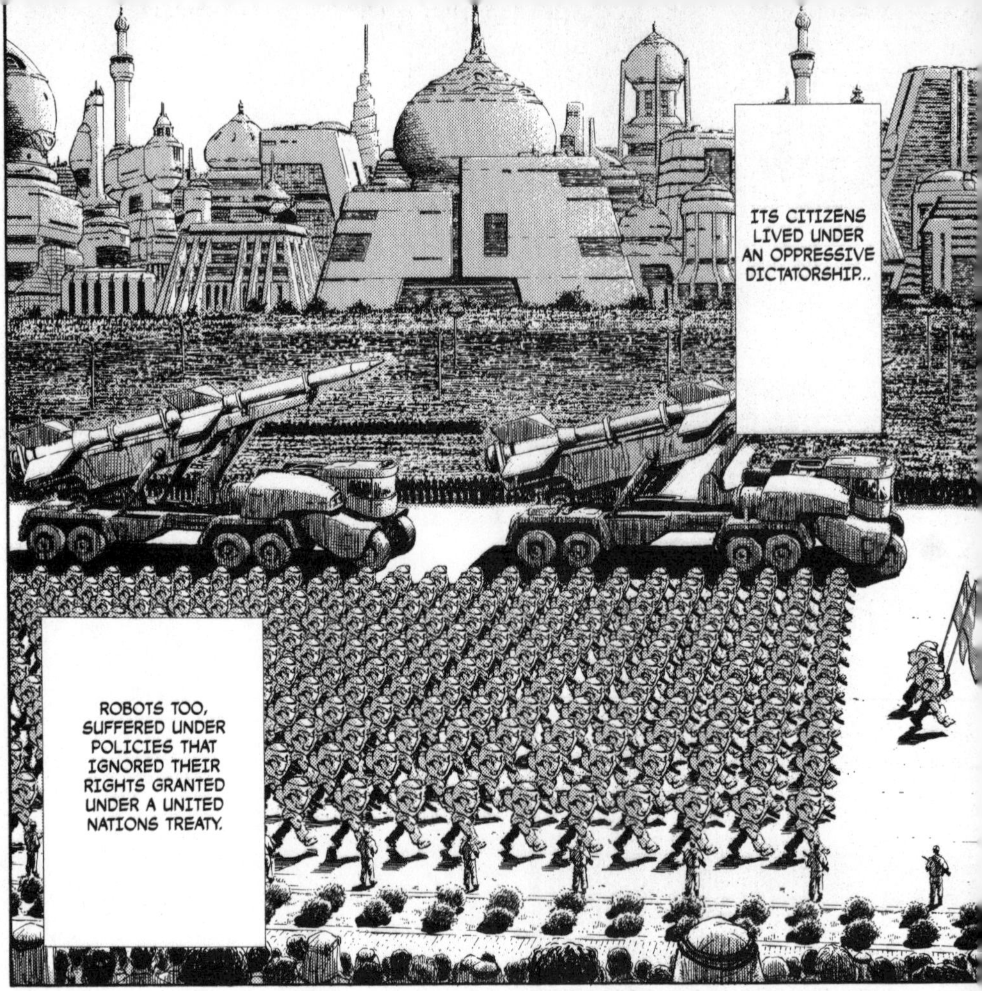
ITS CITIZENS LIVED UNDER AN OPPRESSIVE DICTATORSHIP...
ROBOTS TOO, SUFFERED UNDER POLICIES THAT IGNORED THEIR RIGHTS GRANTED UNDER A UNITED NATIONS TREATY.
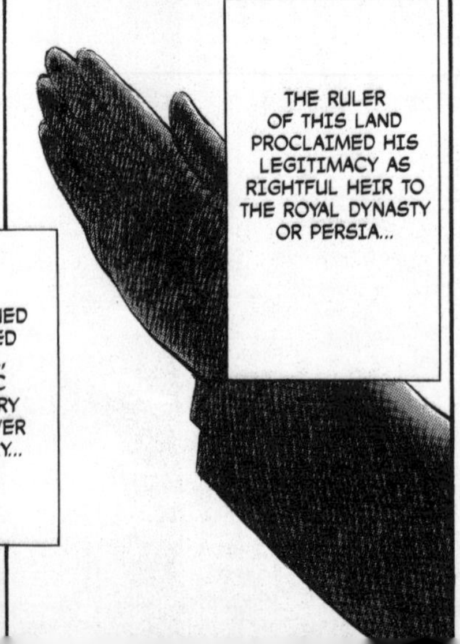
THE RULER OF THIS LAND PROCLAIMED HIS LEGITIMACY AS RIGHTFUL HEIR TO THE ROYAL DYNASTY OR PERSIA...
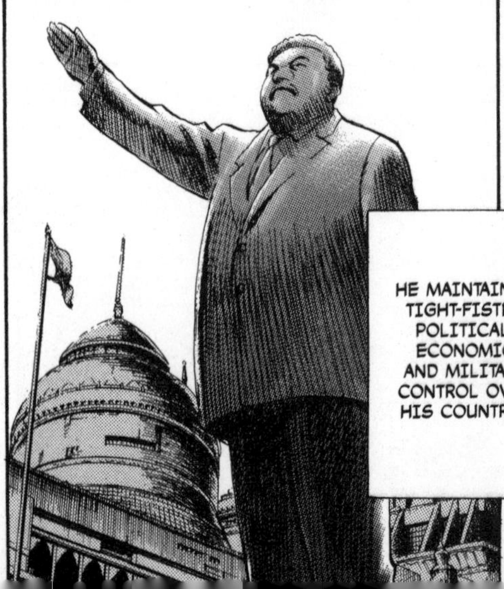
HE MAINTAINED TIGHT-FISTED POLITICAL, ECONOMIC AND MILITARY CONTROL OVER HIS COUNTRY...

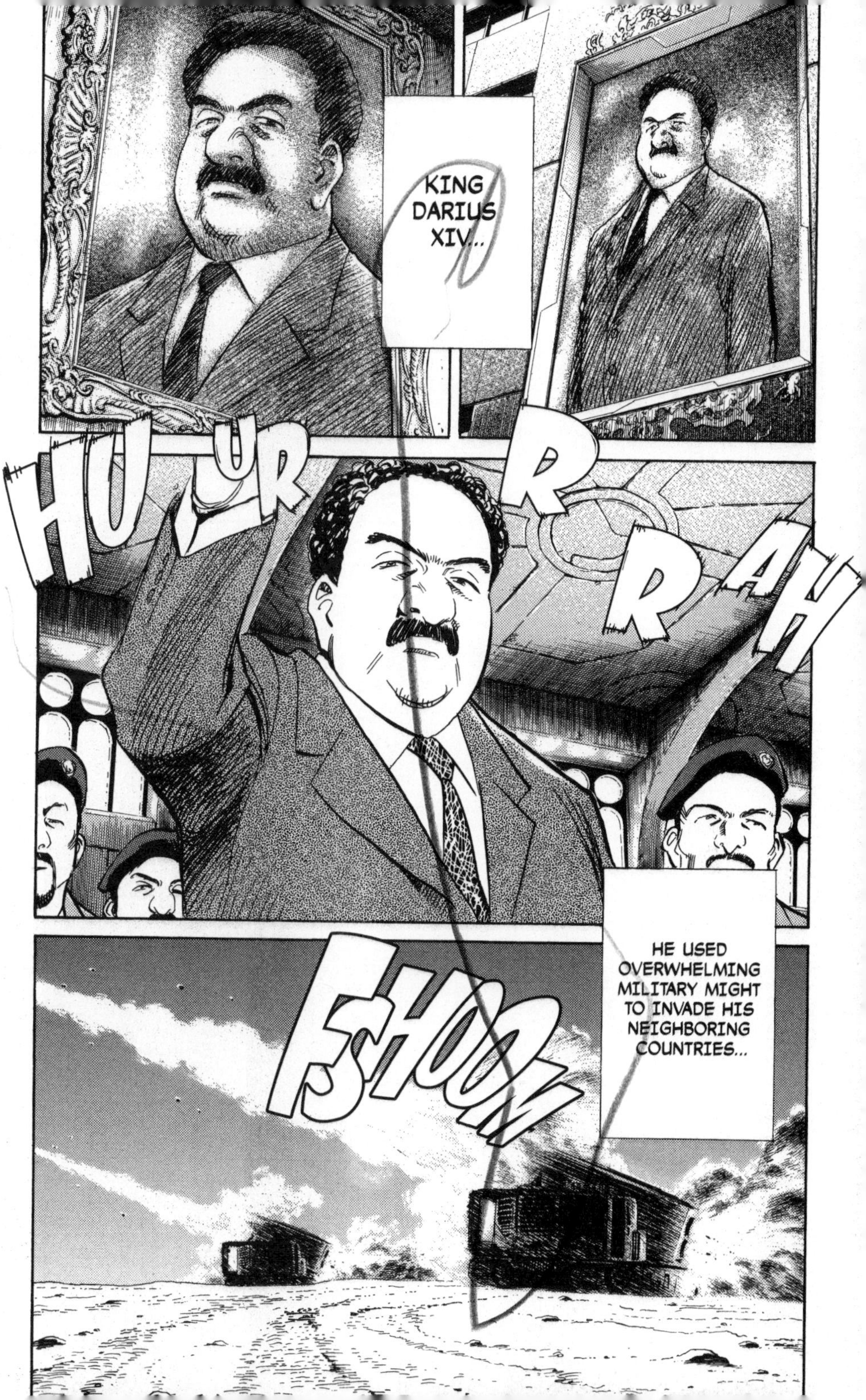
KING DARIUS XIV...
HUURRRAH
HE USED OVERWHELMING MILITARY MIGHT TO INVADE HIS NEIGHBORING COUNTRIES...
FSHOOM

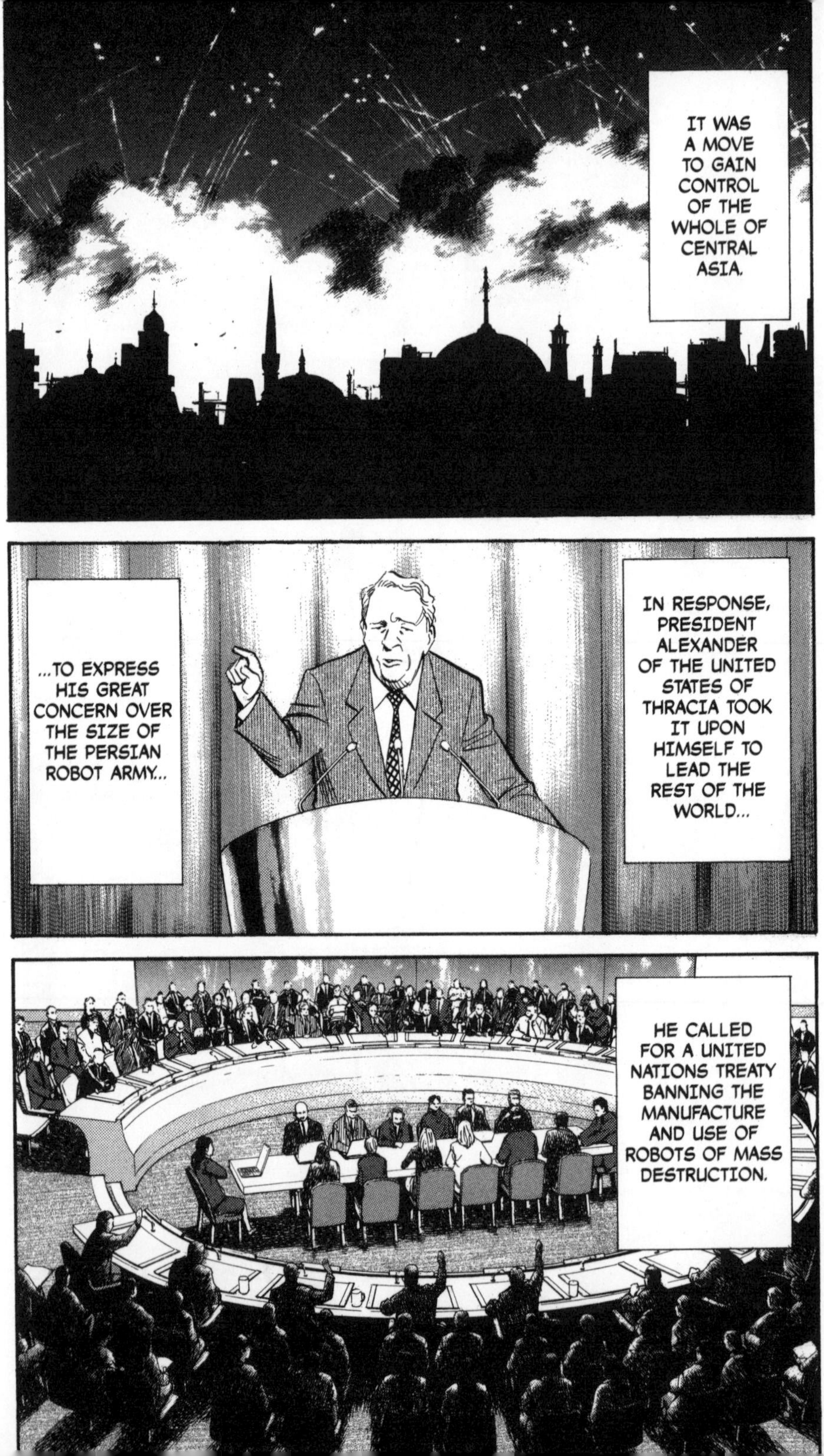
IT WAS A MOVE TO GAIN CONTROL OF THE WHOLE OF CENTRAL ASIA.
IN RESPONSE, PRESIDENT ALEXANDER OF THE UNITED STATES OF THRACIA TOOK IT UPON HIMSELF TO LEAD THE REST OF THE WORLD...
...TO EXPRESS HIS GREAT CONCERN OVER THE SIZE OF THE PERSIAN ROBOT ARMY...
HE CALLED FOR A UNITED NATIONS TREATY BANNING THE MANUFACTURE AND USE OF ROBOTS OF MASS DESTRUCTION.

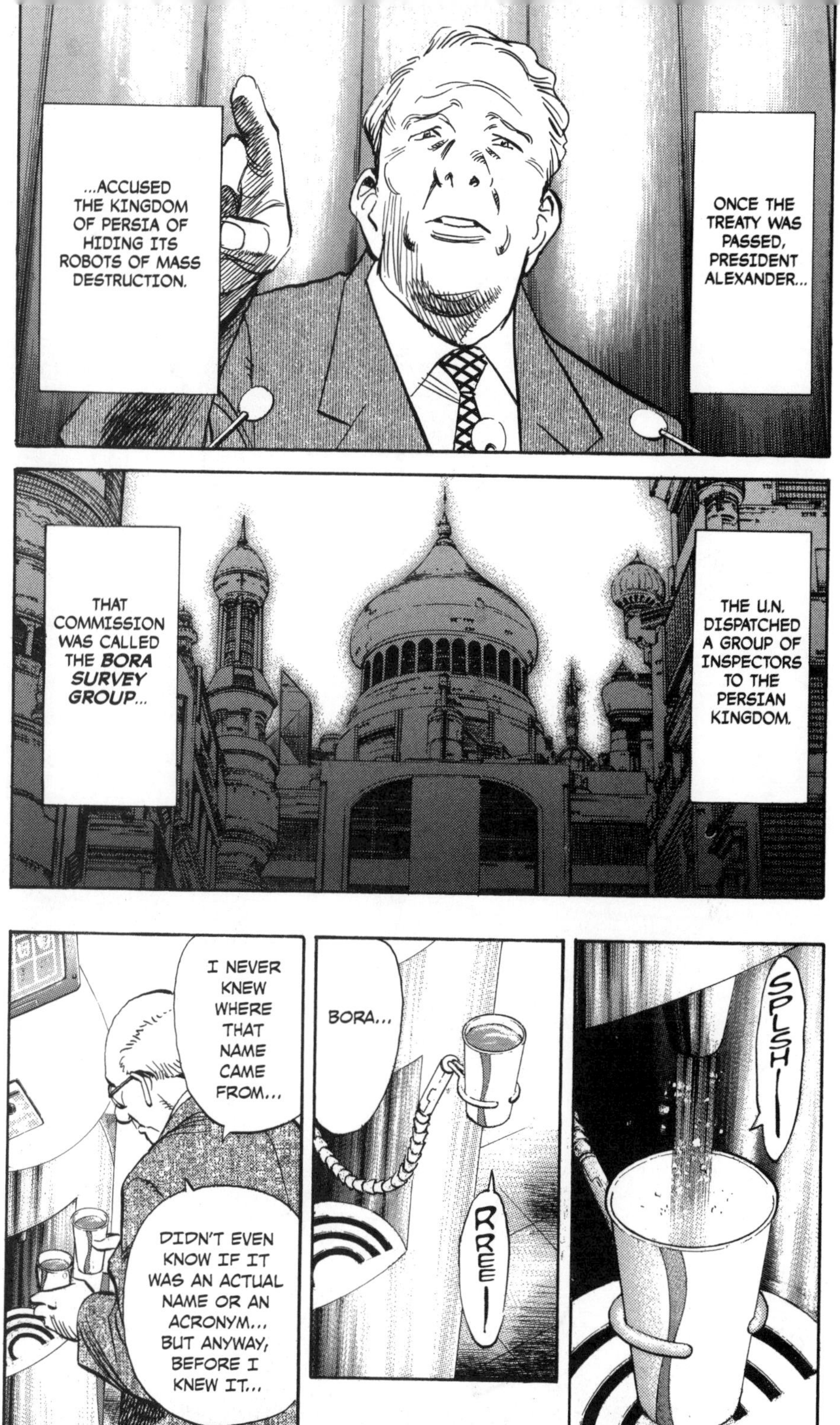
ONCE THE TREATY WAS PASSED, PRESIDENT ALEXANDER...
...ACCUSED THE KINGDOM OF PERSIA OF HIDING ITS ROBOTS OF MASS DESTRUCTION.
THE U.N. DISPATCHED A GROUP OF INSPECTORS TO THE PERSIAN KINGDOM.
THAT COMMISSION WAS CALLED THE ***BORA SURVEY GROUP***...
SPLSHI
BORA...
RREI
I NEVER KNEW WHERE THAT NAME CAME FROM...
DIDN'T EVEN KNOW IF IT WAS AN ACTUAL NAME OR AN ACRONYM... BUT ANYWAY, BEFORE I KNEW IT...

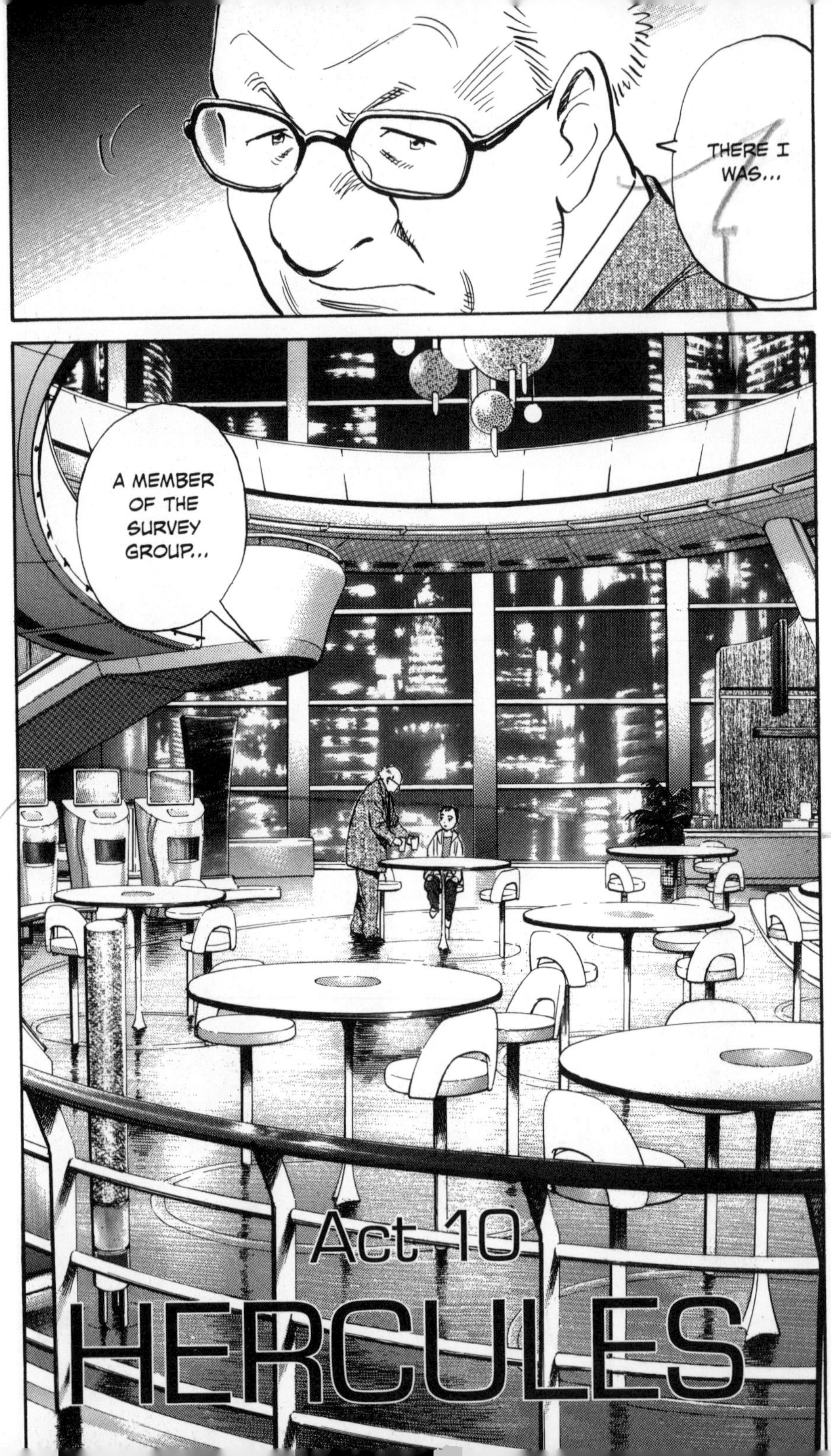
THERE I WAS...
A MEMBER OF THE SURVEY GROUP...
Act 10
HERCULES

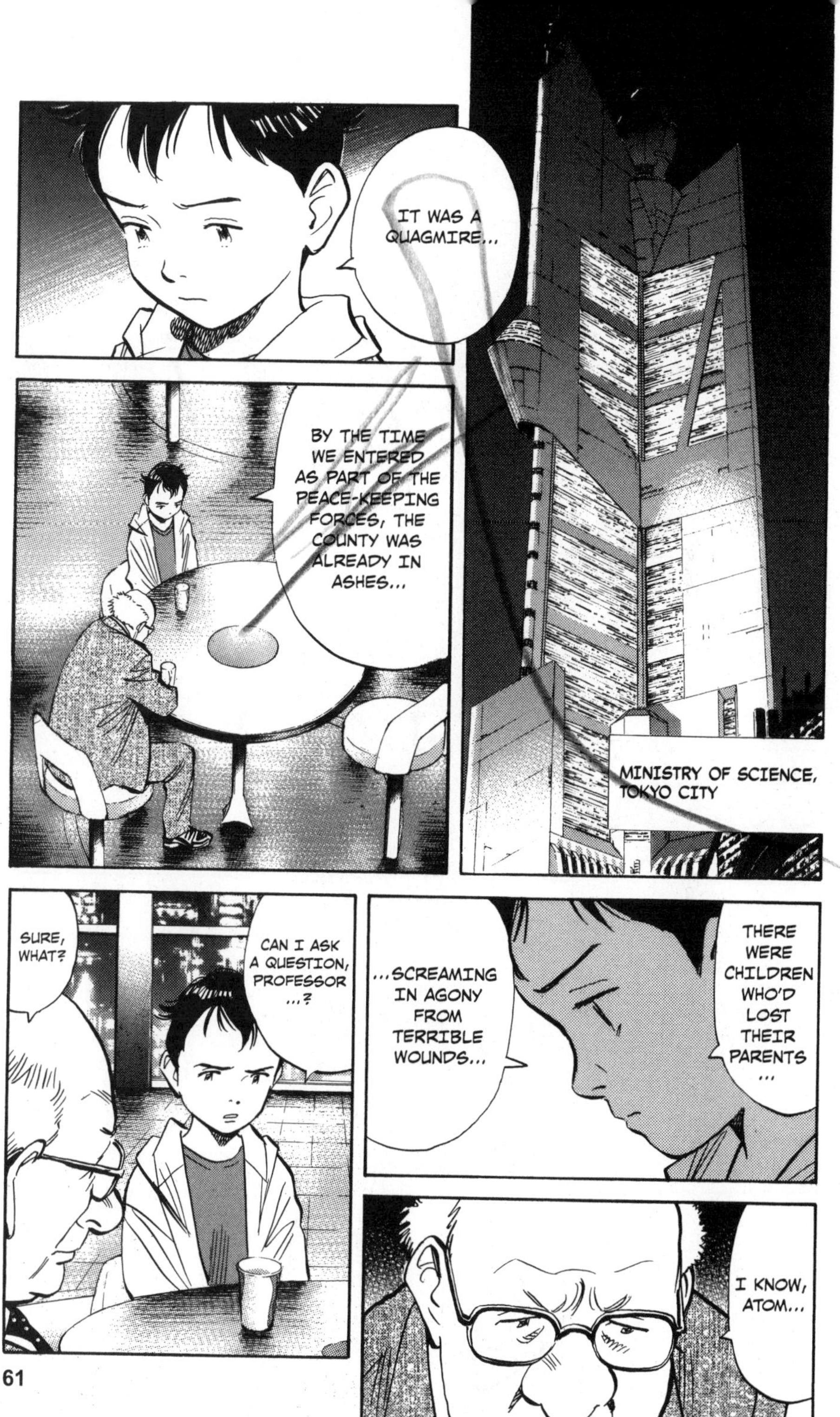

MINISTRY OF SCIENCE, TOKYO CITY
IT WAS A QUAGMIRE...
BY THE TIME WE ENTERED AS PART OF THE PEACE-KEEPING FORCES, THE COUNTY WAS ALREADY IN ASHES...
THERE WERE CHILDREN WHO'D LOST THEIR PARENTS ...
...SCREAMING IN AGONY FROM TERRIBLE WOUNDS...
I KNOW, ATOM...
CAN I ASK A QUESTION, PROFESSOR ...?
SURE, WHAT?

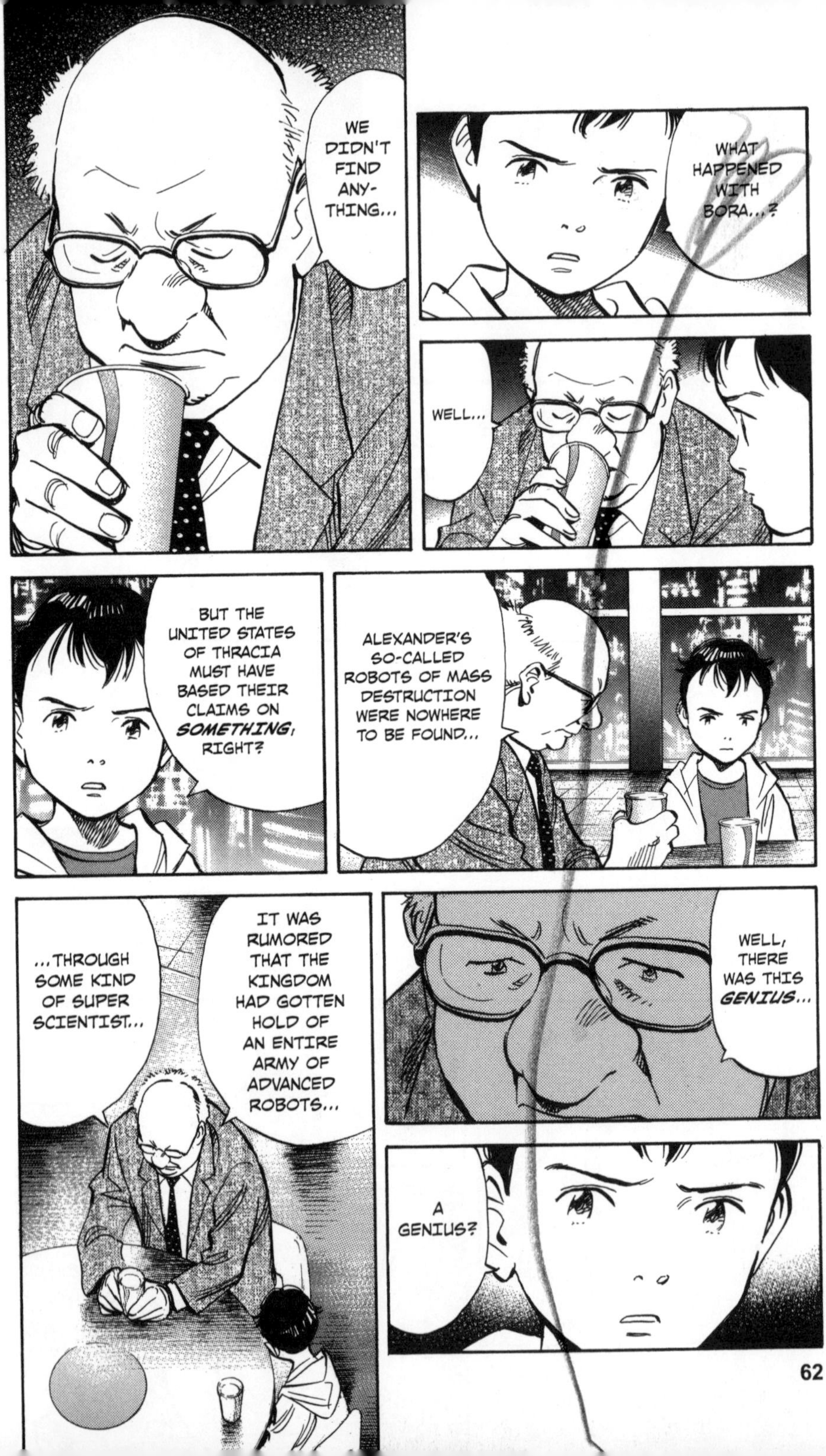
WHAT HAPPENED WITH BORA...?
WELL...
WE DIDN'T FIND ANYTHING...
ALEXANDER'S SO-CALLED ROBOTS OF MASS DESTRUCTION WERE NOWHERE TO BE FOUND...
BUT THE UNITED STATES OF THRACIA MUST HAVE BASED THEIR CLAIMS ON *SOMETHING*, RIGHT?
WELL, THERE WAS THIS *GENIUS*...
A GENIUS?
IT WAS RUMORED THAT THE KINGDOM HAD GOTTEN HOLD OF AN ENTIRE ARMY OF ADVANCED ROBOTS...
...THROUGH SOME KIND OF SUPER SCIENTIST...

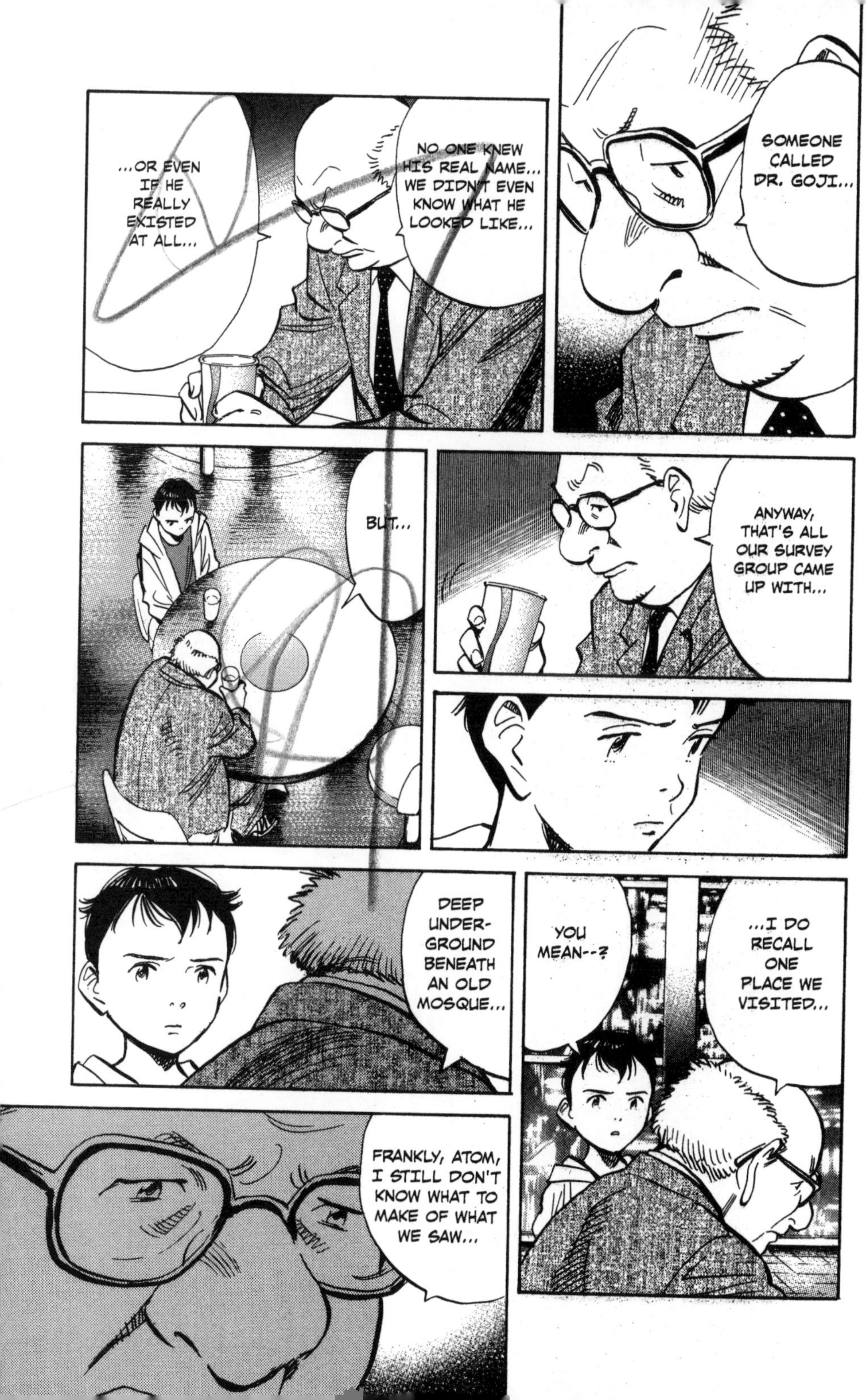
SOMEONE CALLED DR. GOJI...
NO ONE KNEW HIS REAL NAME... WE DIDN'T EVEN KNOW WHAT HE LOOKED LIKE...
...OR EVEN IF HE REALLY EXISTED AT ALL...
ANYWAY, THAT'S ALL OUR SURVEY GROUP CAME UP WITH...
BUT...
...I DO RECALL ONE PLACE WE VISITED...
YOU MEAN--?
DEEP UNDER-GROUND BENEATH AN OLD MOSQUE...
FRANKLY, ATOM, I STILL DON'T KNOW WHAT TO MAKE OF WHAT WE SAW...

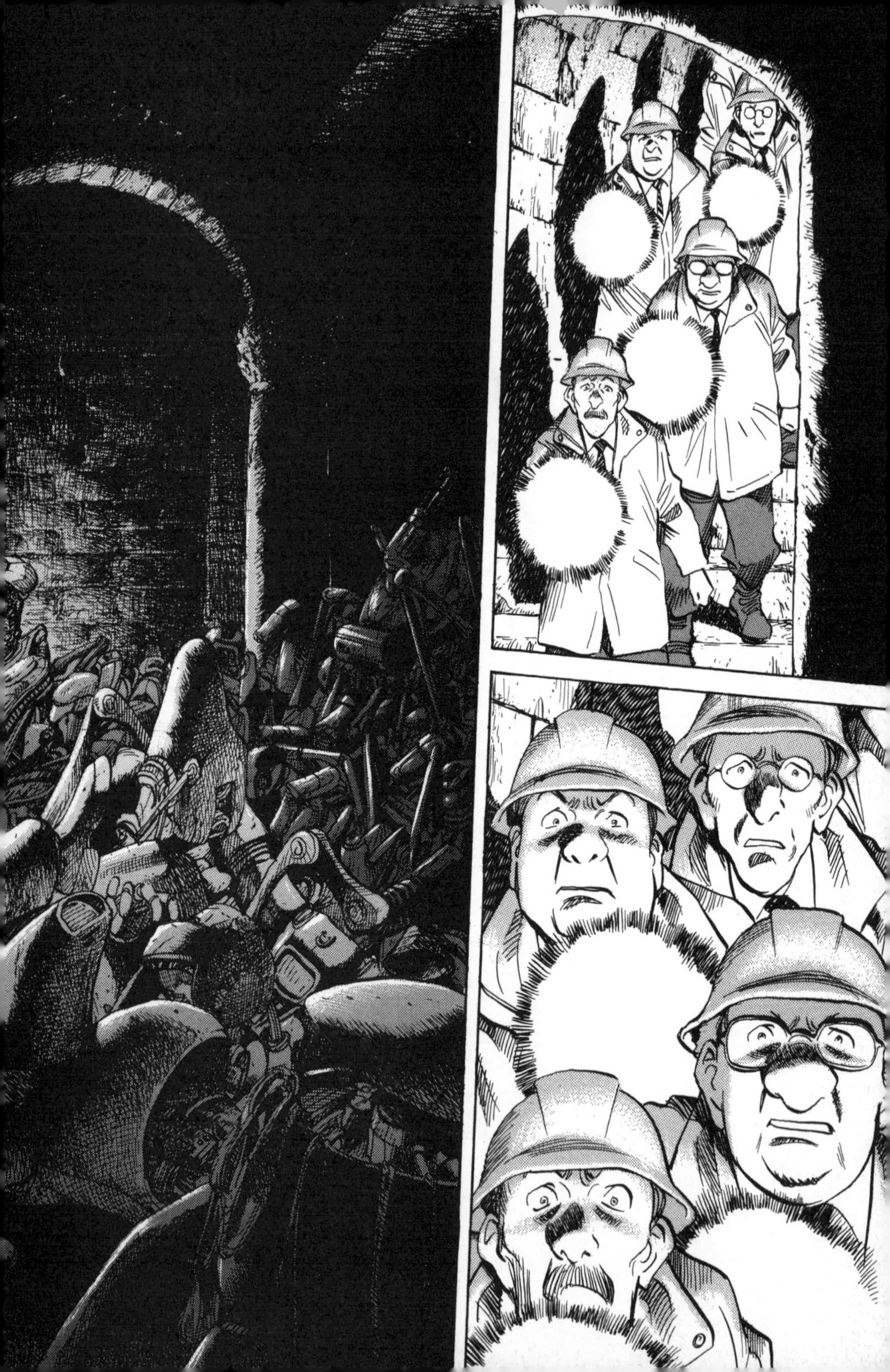

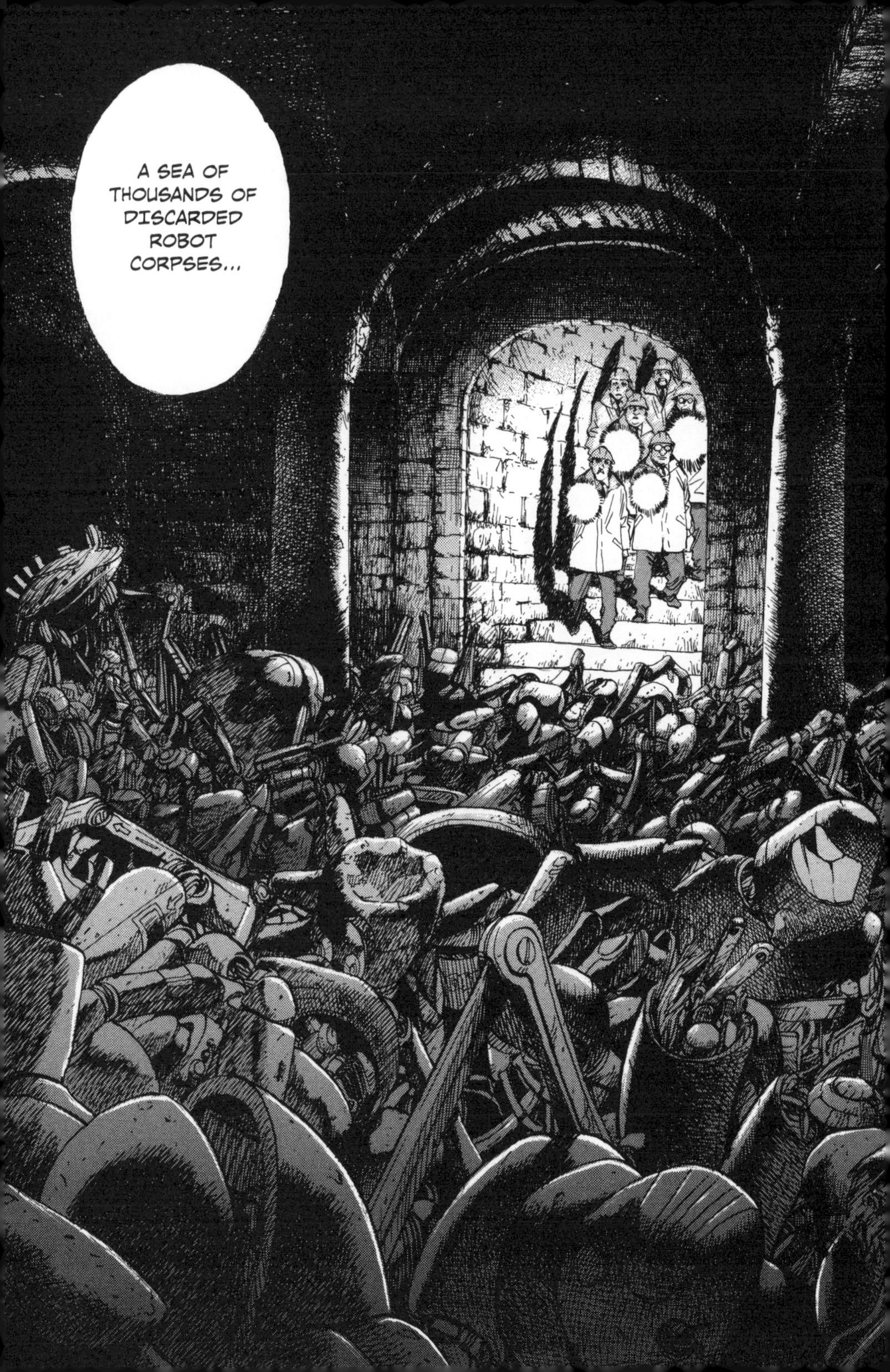
A SEA OF THOUSANDS OF DISCARDED ROBOT CORPSES...

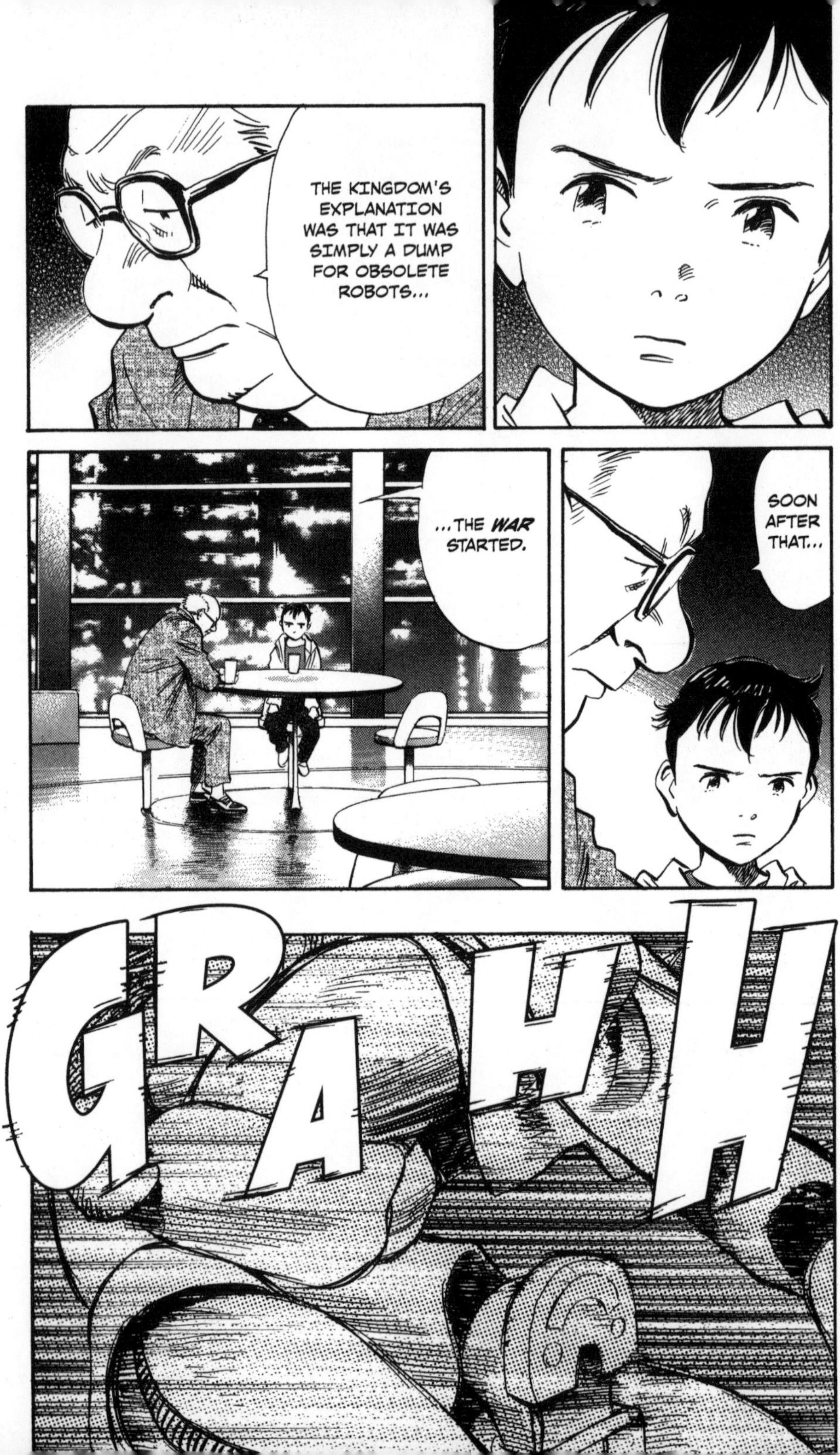
THE KINGDOM'S EXPLANATION WAS THAT IT WAS SIMPLY A DUMP FOR OBSOLETE ROBOTS...
SOON AFTER THAT...
...THE WAR STARTED.
GRAHH

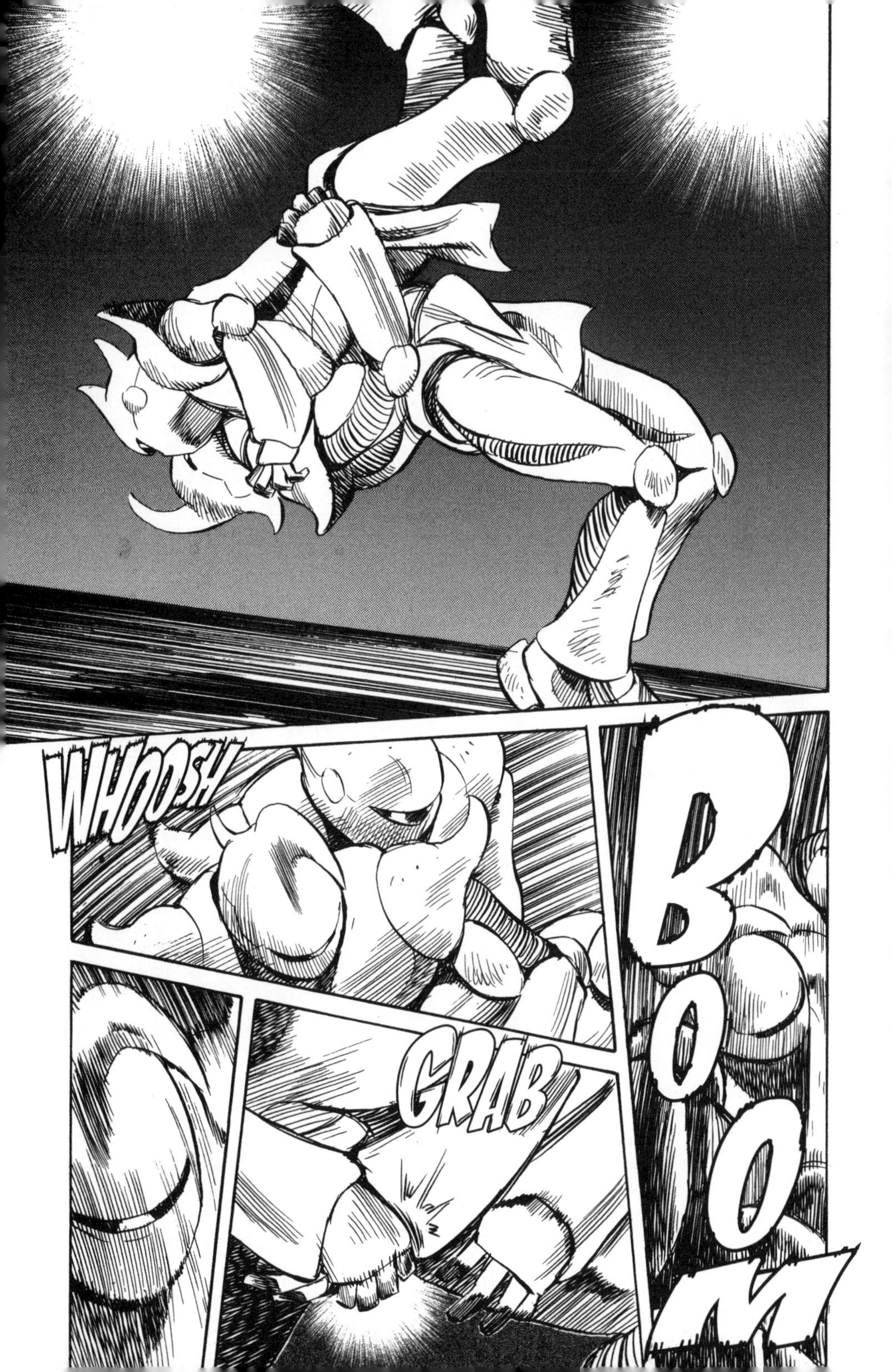
BOOM
WHOOSH
GRAB

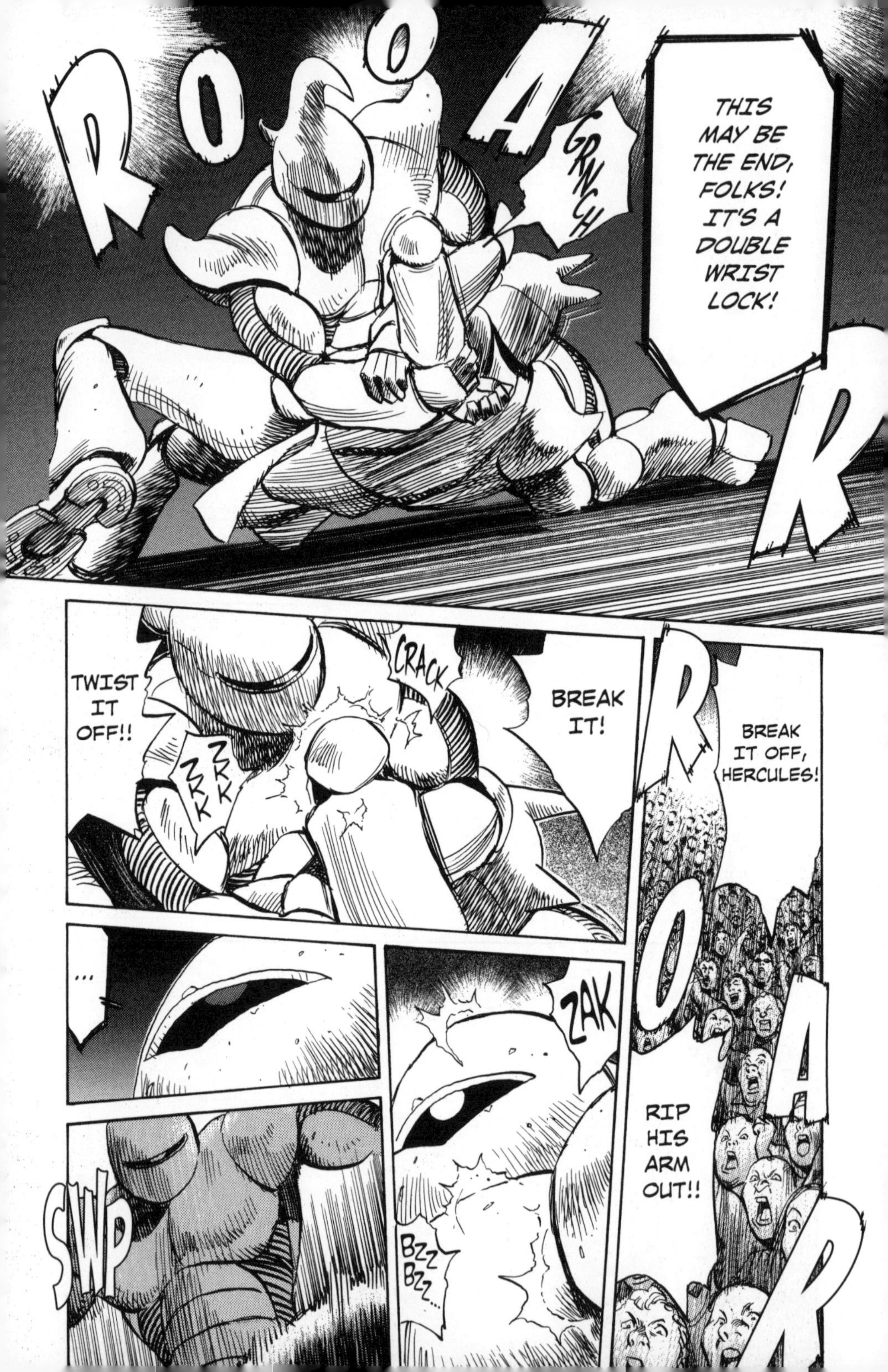
THIS MAY BE THE END, FOLKS! IT'S A DOUBLE WRIST LOCK!
GRNCH
ROOOAR
ROAR
BREAK IT OFF, HERCULES!
RIP HIS ARM OUT!!
BREAK IT!
CRACK
TWIST IT OFF!!
ZRK ZRK
ZAK
BZZ BZZ...
...
SWP

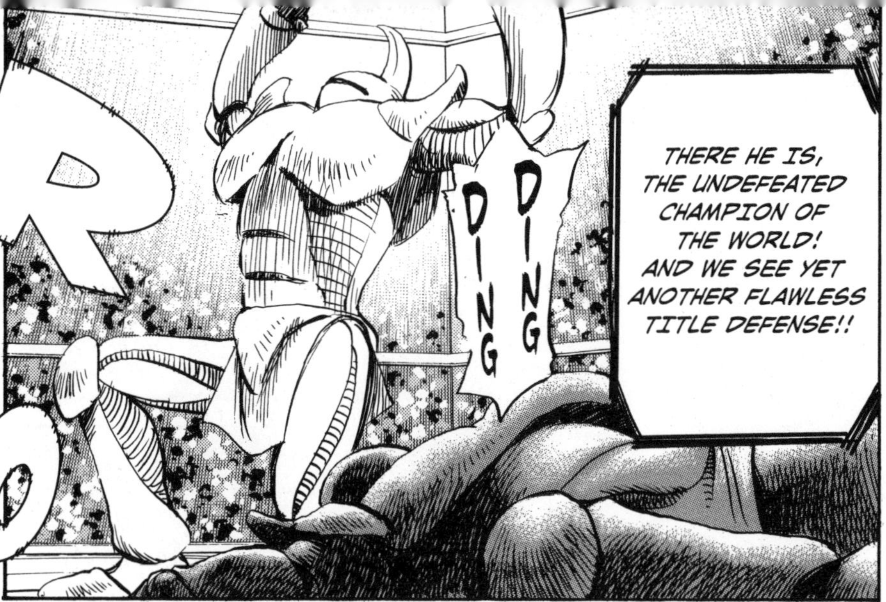
THERE HE IS, THE UNDEFEATED CHAMPION OF THE WORLD! AND WE SEE YET ANOTHER FLAWLESS TITLE DEFENSE!!
DING DING
R
O
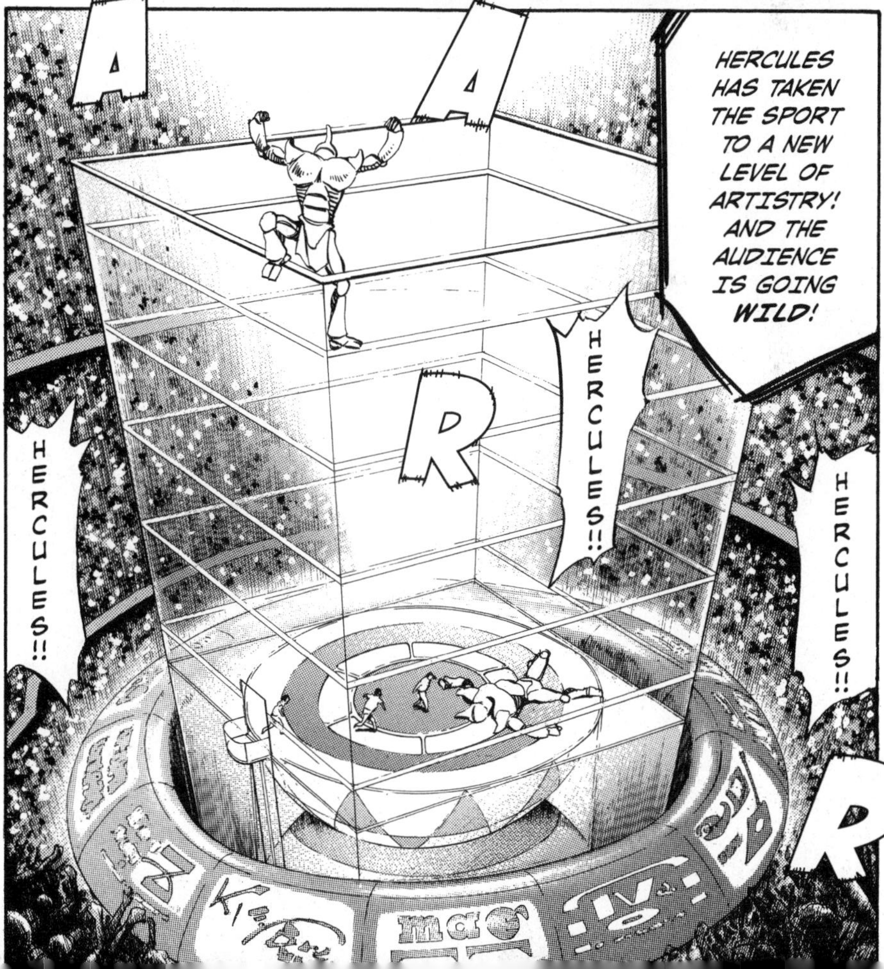
HERCULES HAS TAKEN THE SPORT TO A NEW LEVEL OF ARTISTRY! AND THE AUDIENCE IS GOING **WILD**!
A
A
HERCULES!!
R
HERCULES!!
HERCULES!!
R

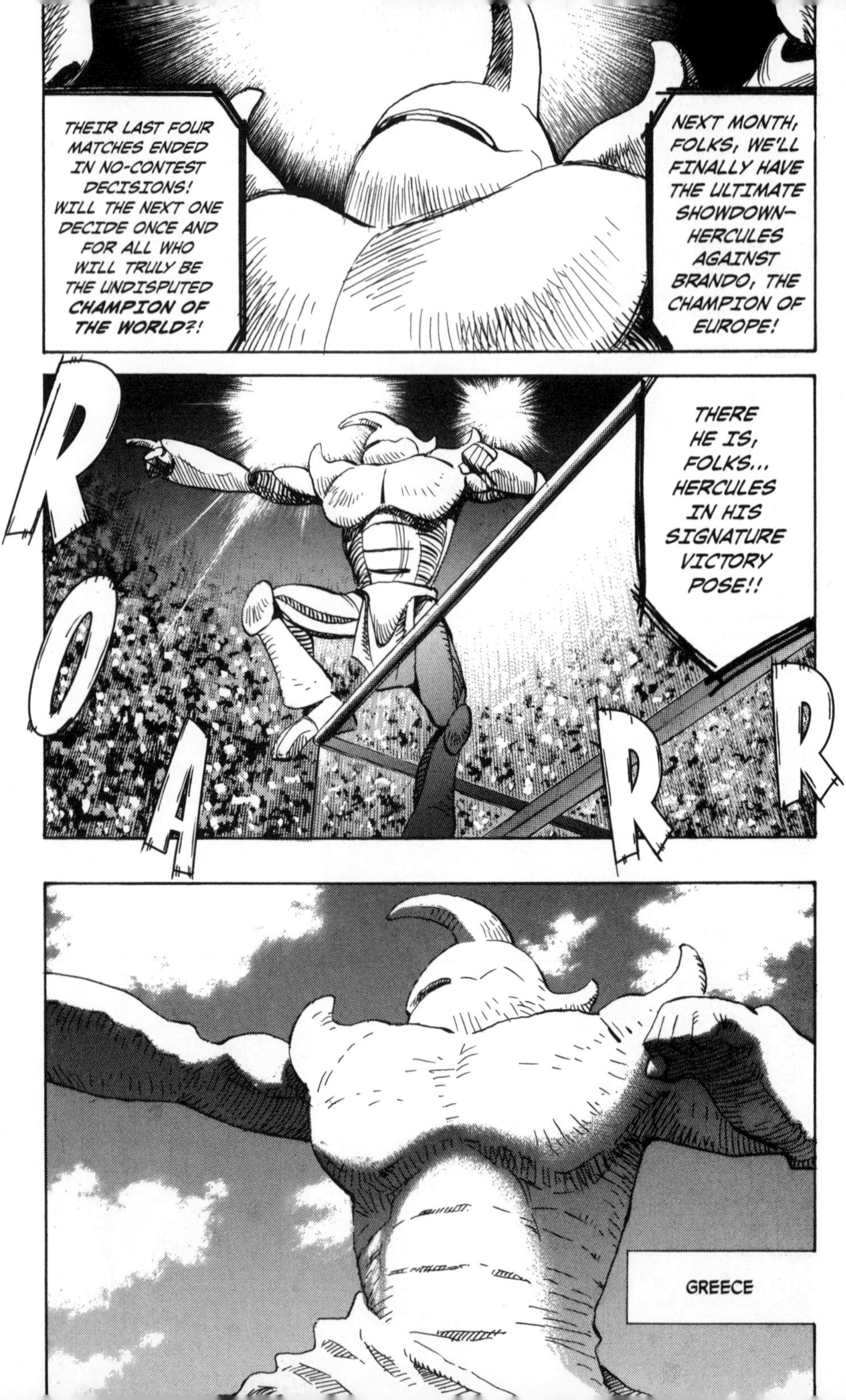
NEXT MONTH, FOLKS, WE'LL FINALLY HAVE THE ULTIMATE SHOWDOWN– HERCULES AGAINST BRANDO, THE CHAMPION OF EUROPE!
THEIR LAST FOUR MATCHES ENDED IN NO-CONTEST DECISIONS! WILL THE NEXT ONE DECIDE ONCE AND FOR ALL WHO WILL TRULY BE THE UNDISPUTED CHAMPION OF THE WORLD?!
THERE HE IS, FOLKS... HERCULES IN HIS SIGNATURE VICTORY POSE!!
ROARR
GREECE

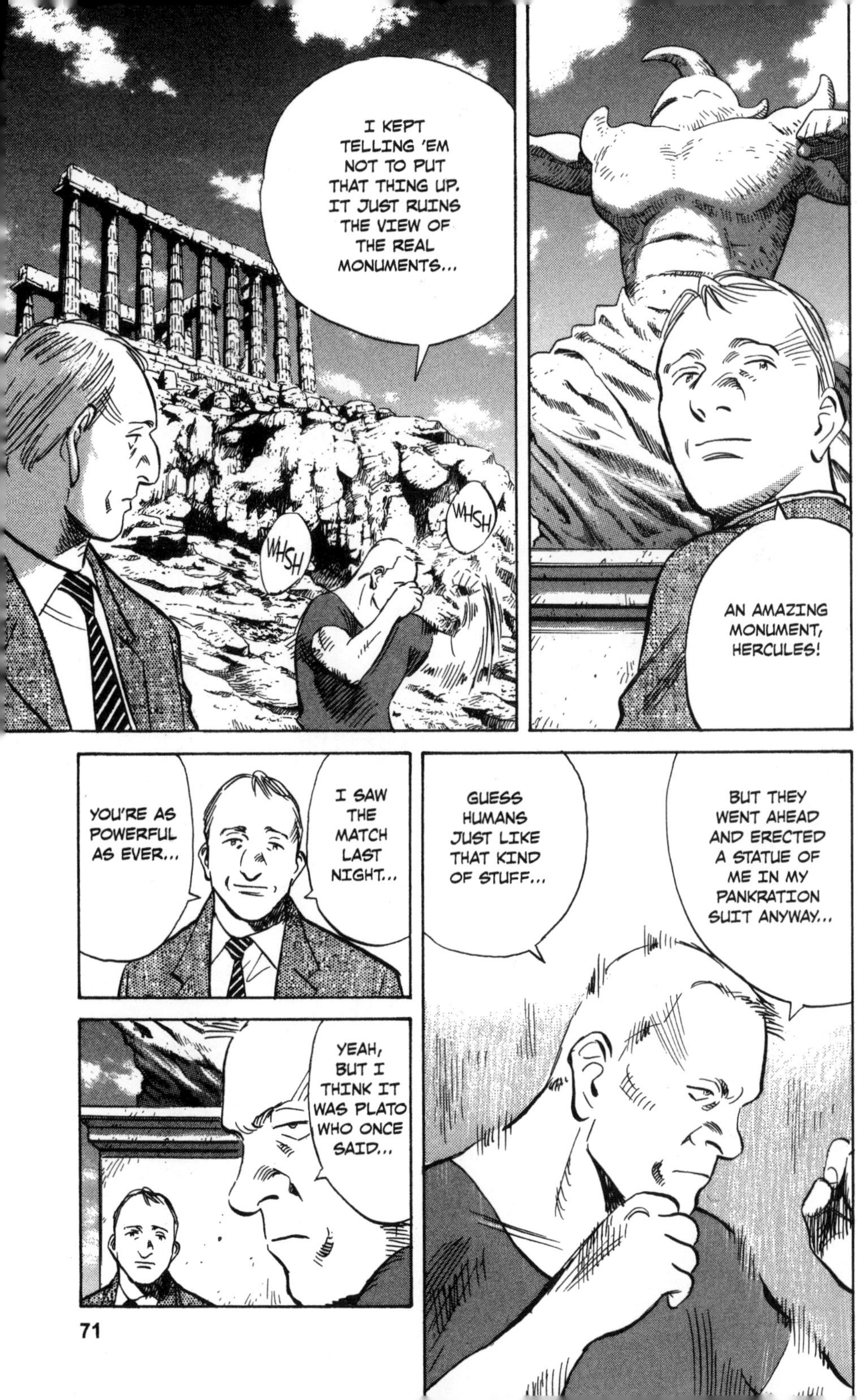
AN AMAZING MONUMENT, HERCULES!
I KEPT TELLING 'EM NOT TO PUT THAT THING UP. IT JUST RUINS THE VIEW OF THE REAL MONUMENTS...
WHSH
WHSH
BUT THEY WENT AHEAD AND ERECTED A STATUE OF ME IN MY PANKRATION SUIT ANYWAY...
GUESS HUMANS JUST LIKE THAT KIND OF STUFF...
I SAW THE MATCH LAST NIGHT...
YOU'RE AS POWERFUL AS EVER...
YEAH, BUT I THINK IT WAS PLATO WHO ONCE SAID...

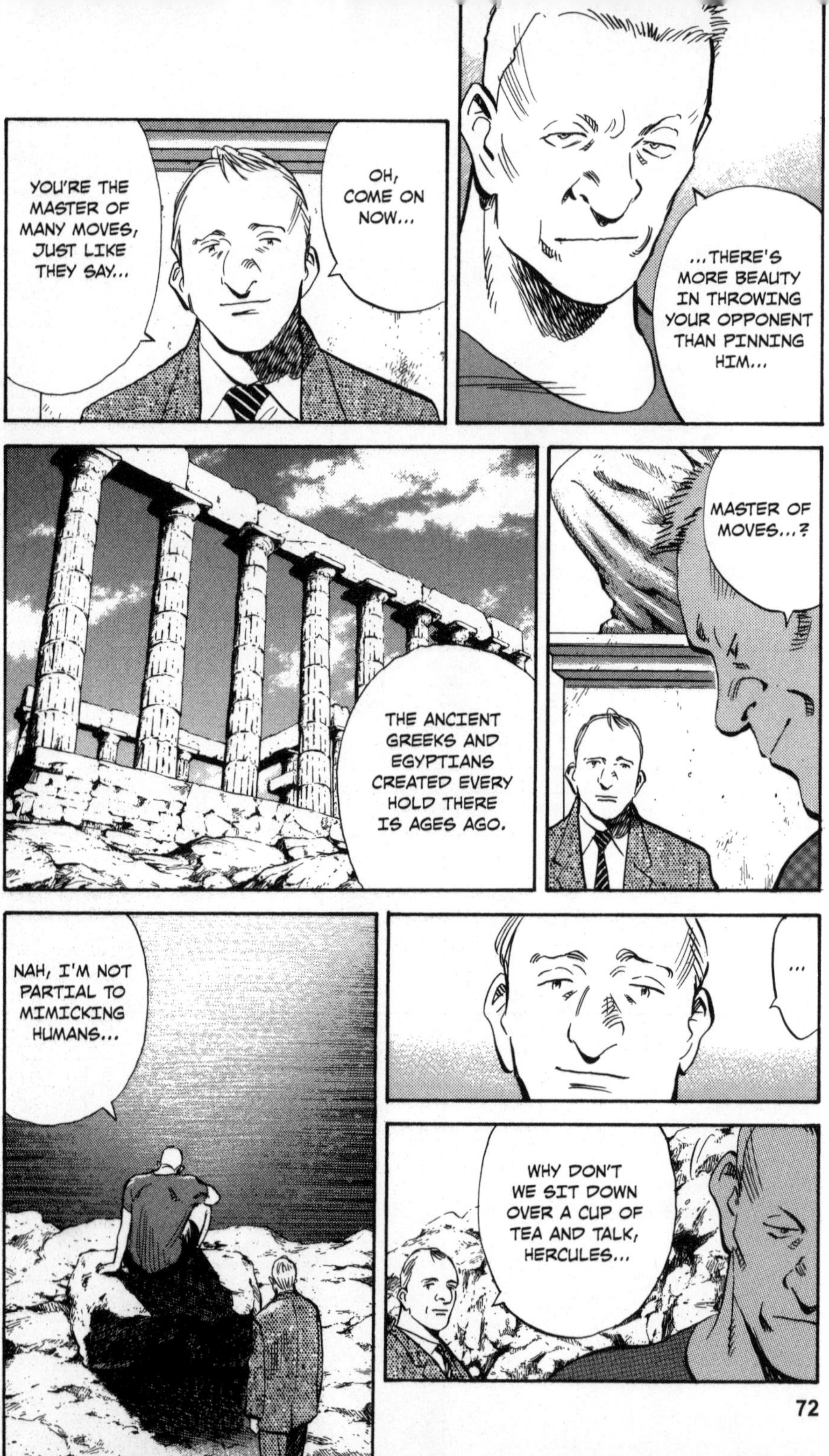
...THERE'S MORE BEAUTY IN THROWING YOUR OPPONENT THAN PINNING HIM...
OH, COME ON NOW...
YOU'RE THE MASTER OF MANY MOVES, JUST LIKE THEY SAY...
MASTER OF MOVES...?
THE ANCIENT GREEKS AND EGYPTIANS CREATED EVERY HOLD THERE IS AGES AGO.
...
WHY DON'T WE SIT DOWN OVER A CUP OF TEA AND TALK, HERCULES...
NAH, I'M NOT PARTIAL TO MIMICKING HUMANS...

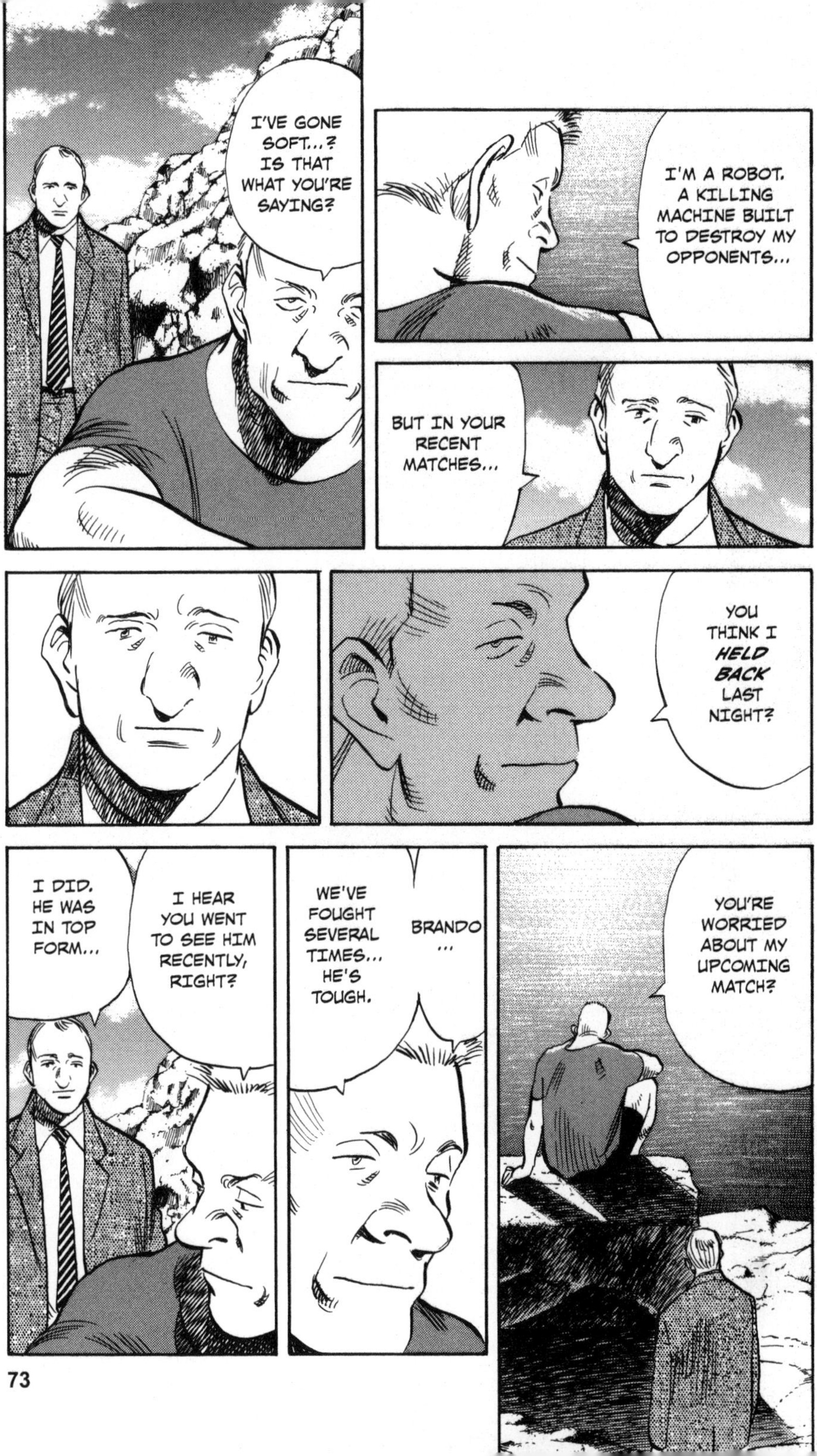
I'M A ROBOT. A KILLING MACHINE BUILT TO DESTROY MY OPPONENTS...
BUT IN YOUR RECENT MATCHES...
I'VE GONE SOFT...? IS THAT WHAT YOU'RE SAYING?
YOU THINK I *HELD BACK* LAST NIGHT?
YOU'RE WORRIED ABOUT MY UPCOMING MATCH?
BRANDO...
WE'VE FOUGHT SEVERAL TIMES... HE'S TOUGH.
I HEAR YOU WENT TO SEE HIM RECENTLY, RIGHT?
I DID. HE WAS IN TOP FORM...

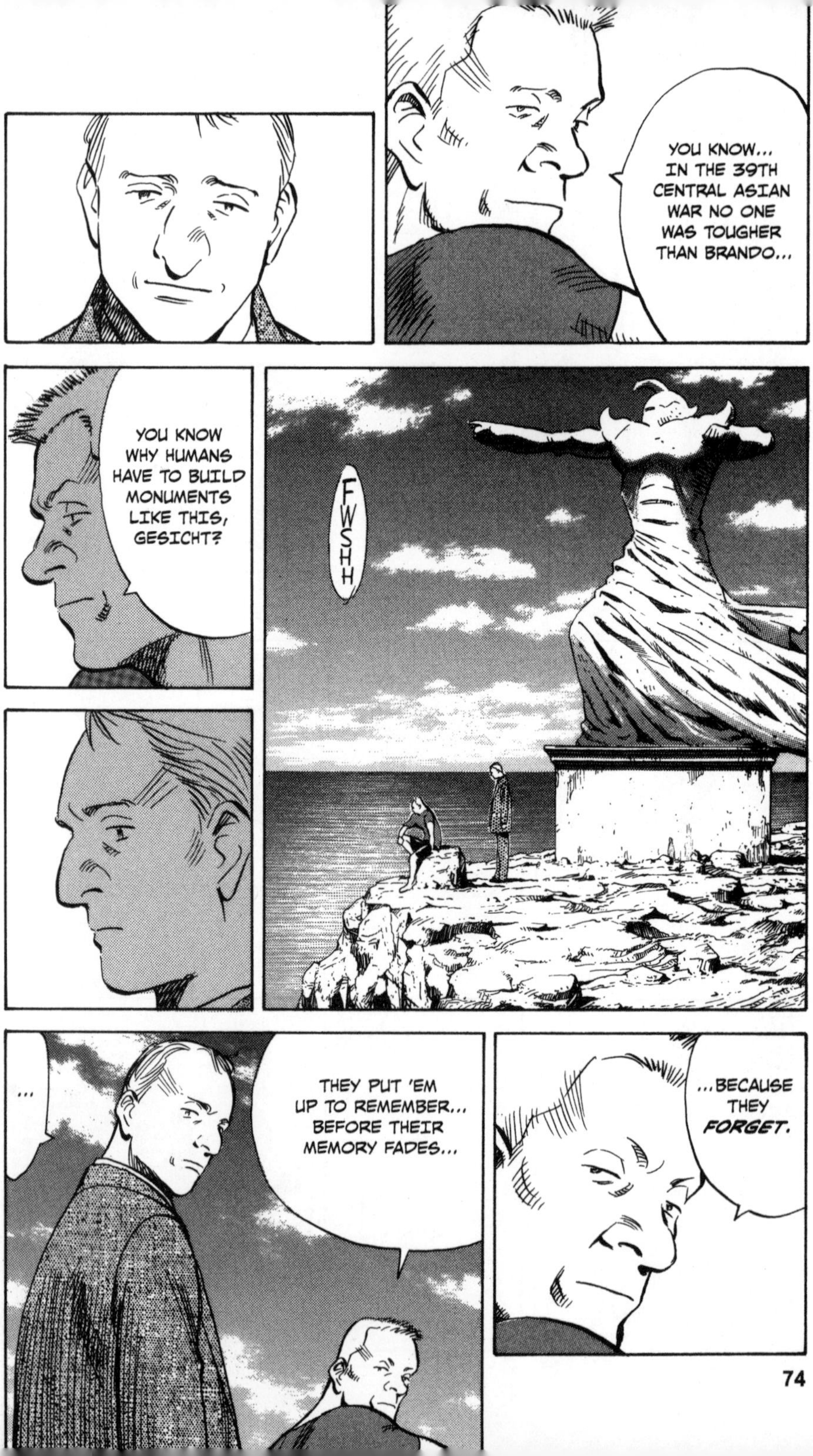
YOU KNOW... IN THE 39TH CENTRAL ASIAN WAR NO ONE WAS TOUGHER THAN BRANDO...
FWSHH
YOU KNOW WHY HUMANS HAVE TO BUILD MONUMENTS LIKE THIS, GESICHT?
...BECAUSE THEY *FORGET*.
THEY PUT 'EM UP TO REMEMBER... BEFORE THEIR MEMORY FADES...
...

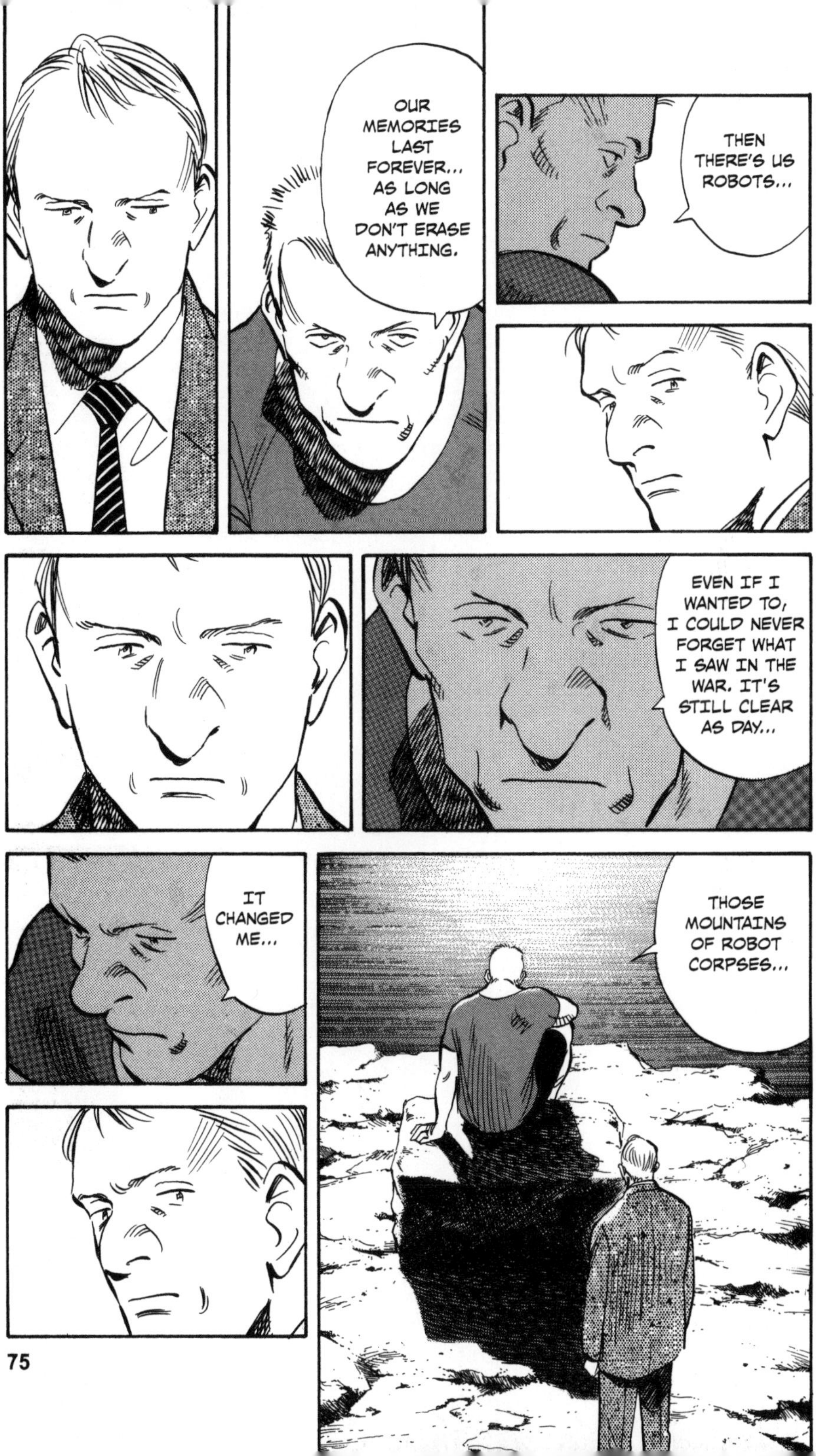
THEN THERE'S US ROBOTS...
OUR MEMORIES LAST FOREVER... AS LONG AS WE DON'T ERASE ANYTHING.
EVEN IF I WANTED TO, I COULD NEVER FORGET WHAT I SAW IN THE WAR. IT'S STILL CLEAR AS DAY...
THOSE MOUNTAINS OF ROBOT CORPSES...
IT CHANGED ME...

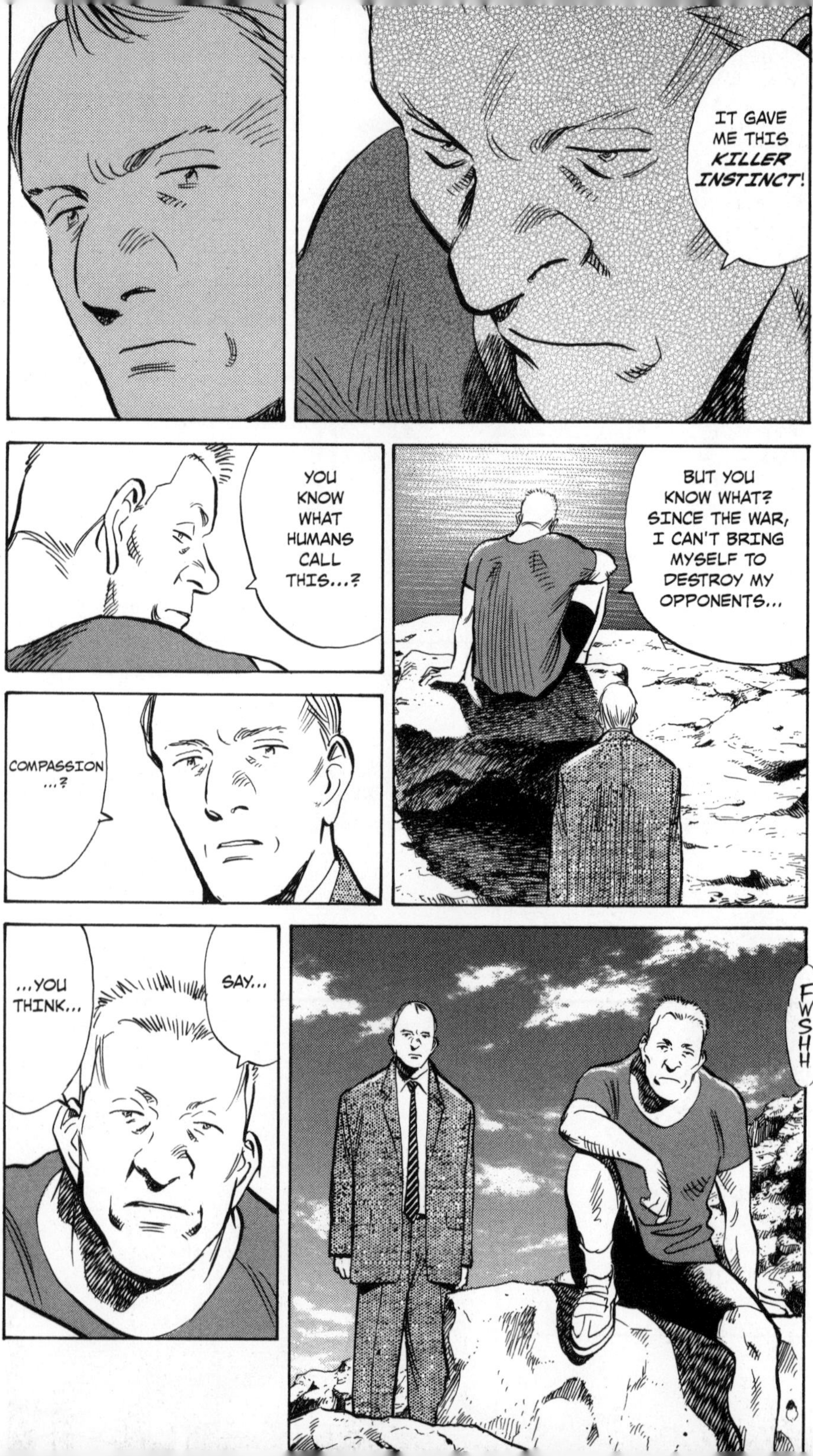
IT GAVE ME THIS *KILLER INSTINCT*!
BUT YOU KNOW WHAT? SINCE THE WAR, I CAN'T BRING MYSELF TO DESTROY MY OPPONENTS...
YOU KNOW WHAT HUMANS CALL THIS...?
COMPASSION...?
FWSHH
SAY...
...YOU THINK...

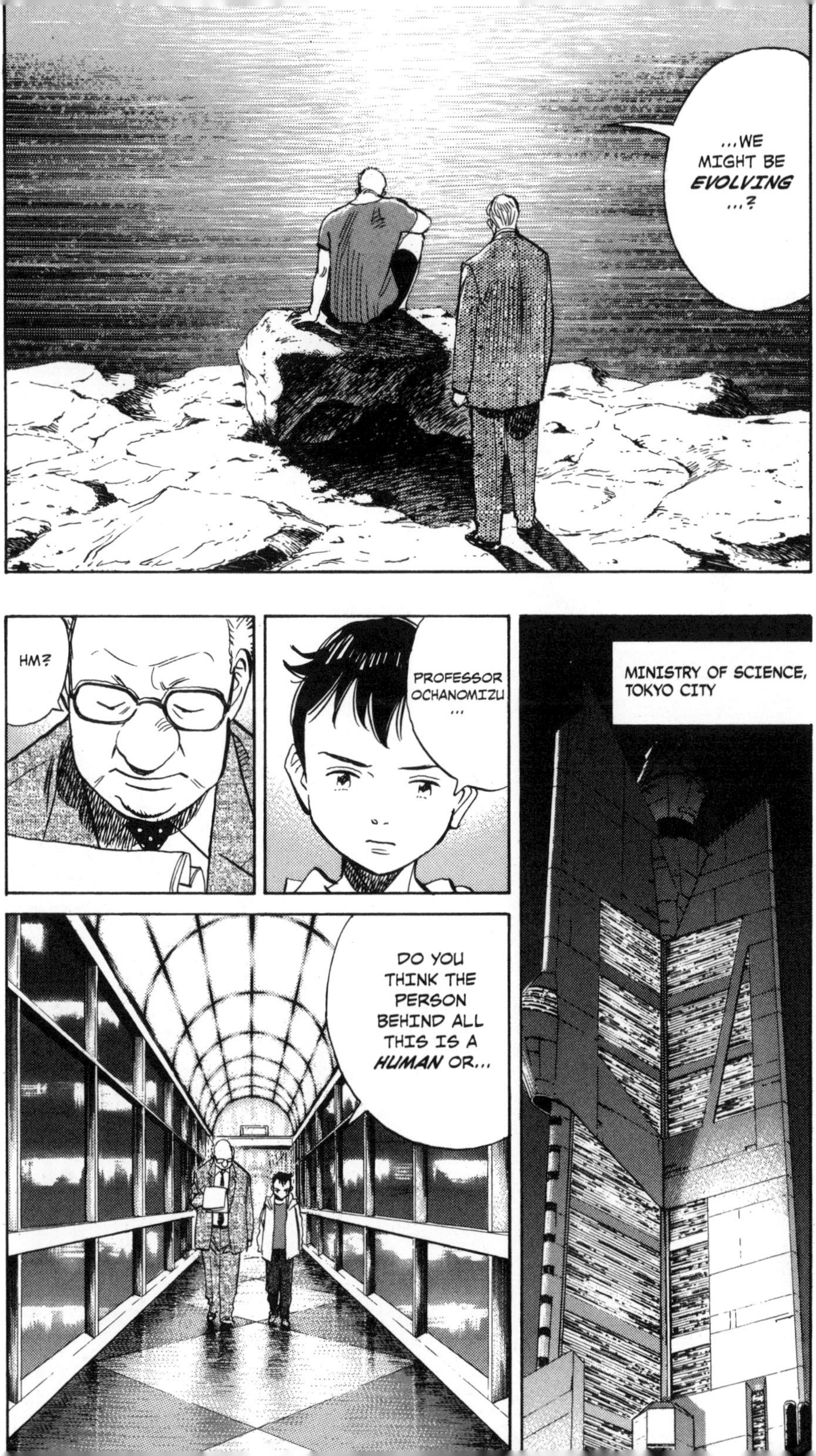
...WE MIGHT BE *EVOLVING* ...?
MINISTRY OF SCIENCE, TOKYO CITY
PROFESSOR OCHANOMIZU ...
HM?
DO YOU THINK THE PERSON BEHIND ALL THIS IS A *HUMAN* OR...

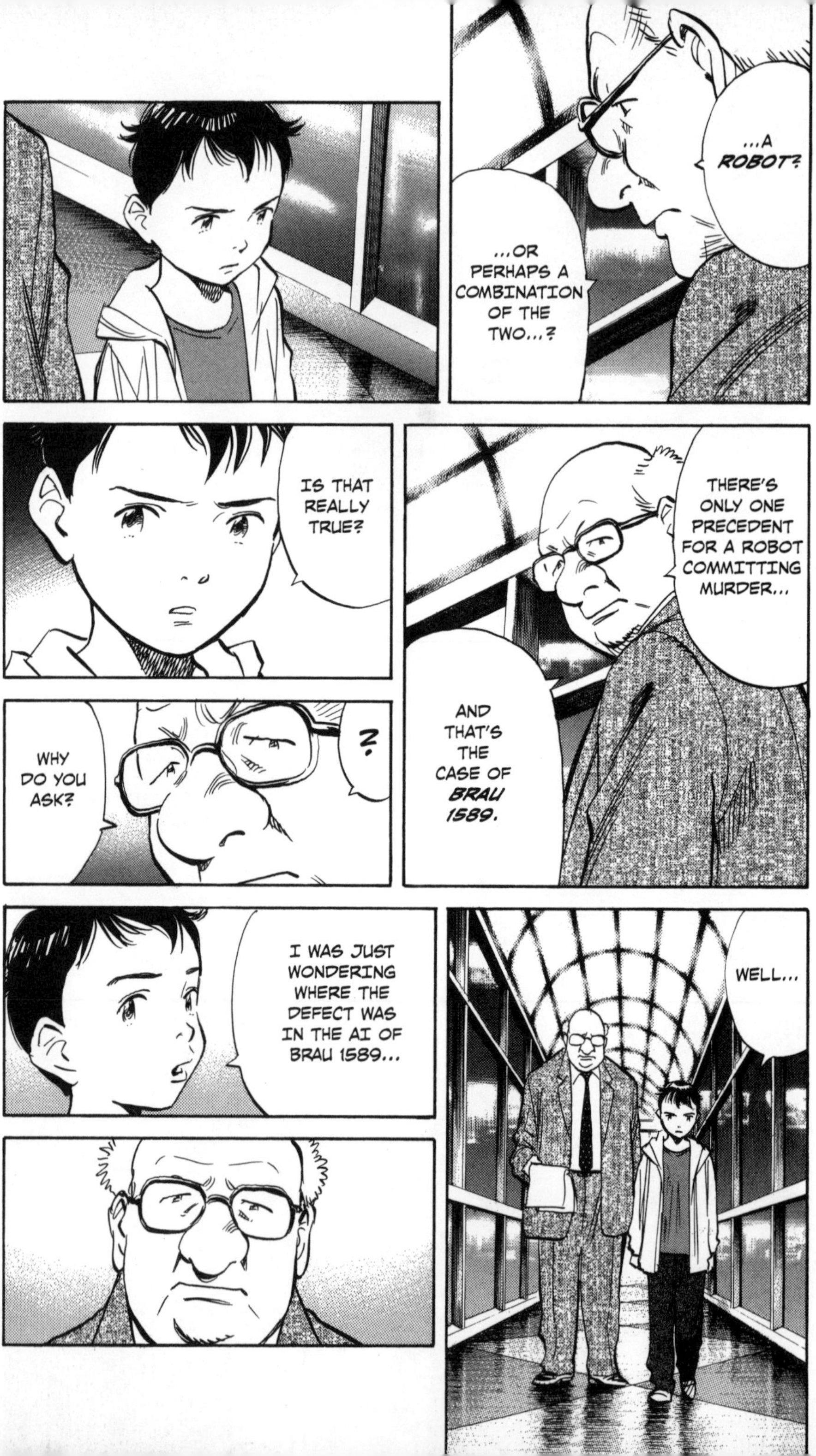
...A ROBOT?
...OR PERHAPS A COMBINATION OF THE TWO...?
THERE'S ONLY ONE PRECEDENT FOR A ROBOT COMMITTING MURDER...
AND THAT'S THE CASE OF BRAU 1589.
IS THAT REALLY TRUE?
?
WHY DO YOU ASK?
WELL...
I WAS JUST WONDERING WHERE THE DEFECT WAS IN THE AI OF BRAU 1589...

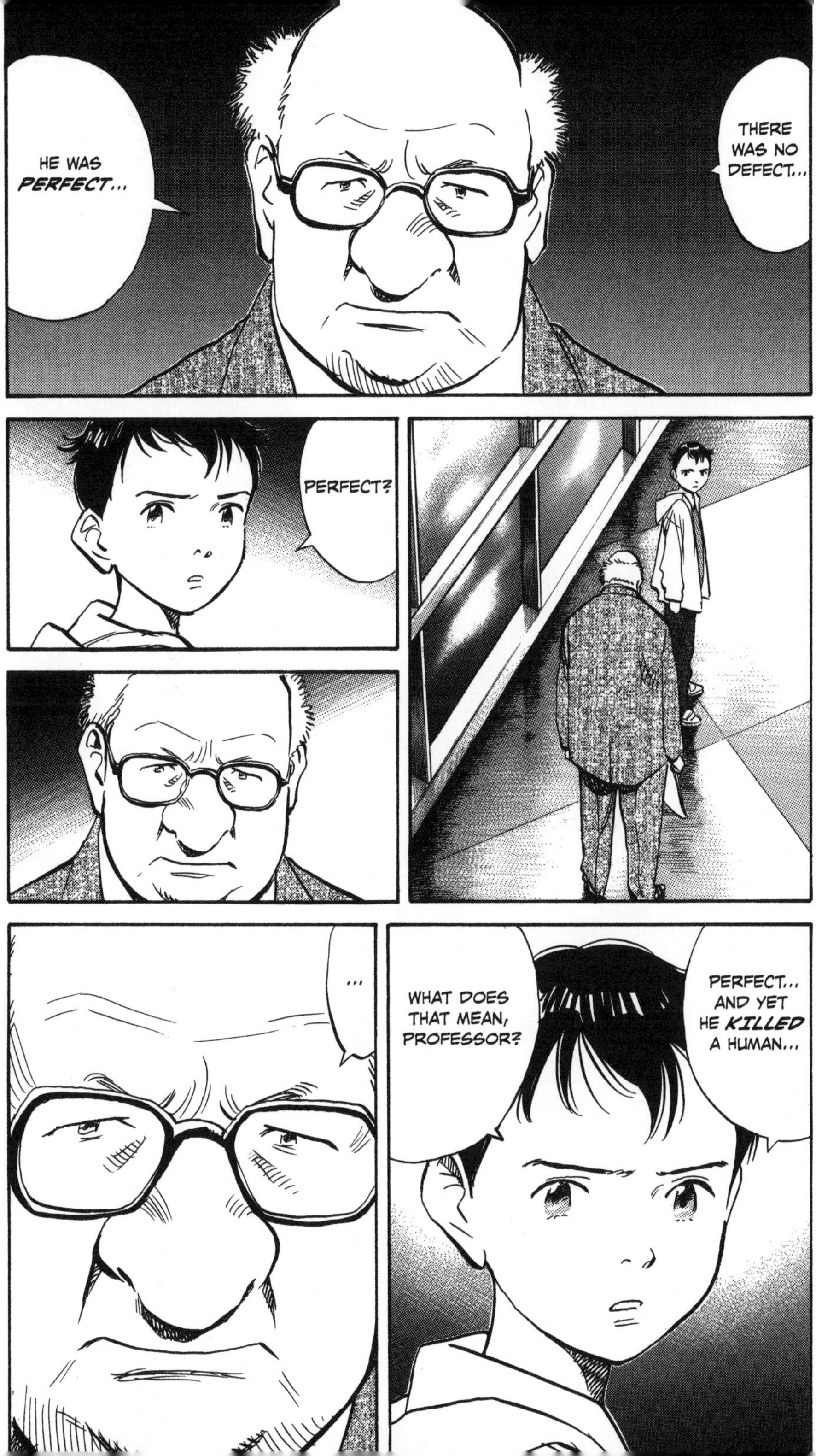
THERE WAS NO DEFECT...
HE WAS *PERFECT*...
PERFECT?
PERFECT... AND YET HE *KILLED* A HUMAN...
WHAT DOES THAT MEAN, PROFESSOR?
...

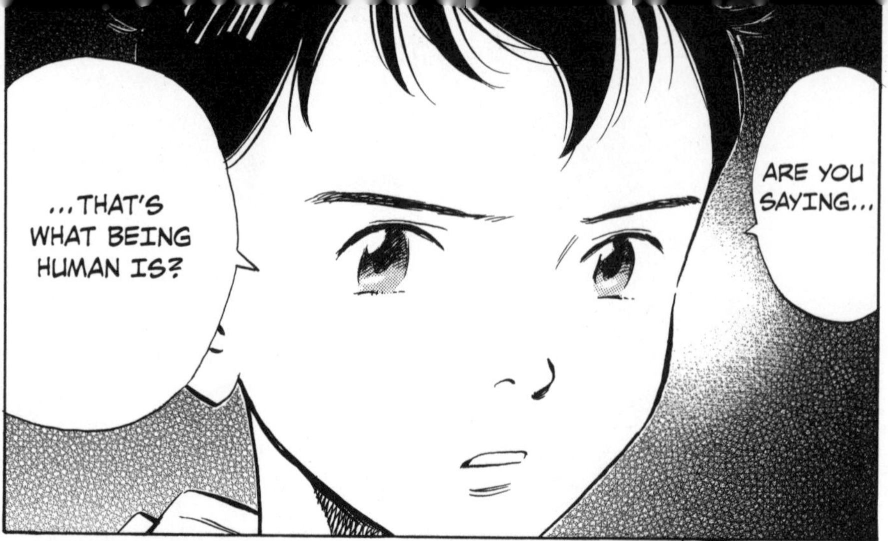
ARE YOU SAYING...
...THAT'S WHAT BEING HUMAN IS?

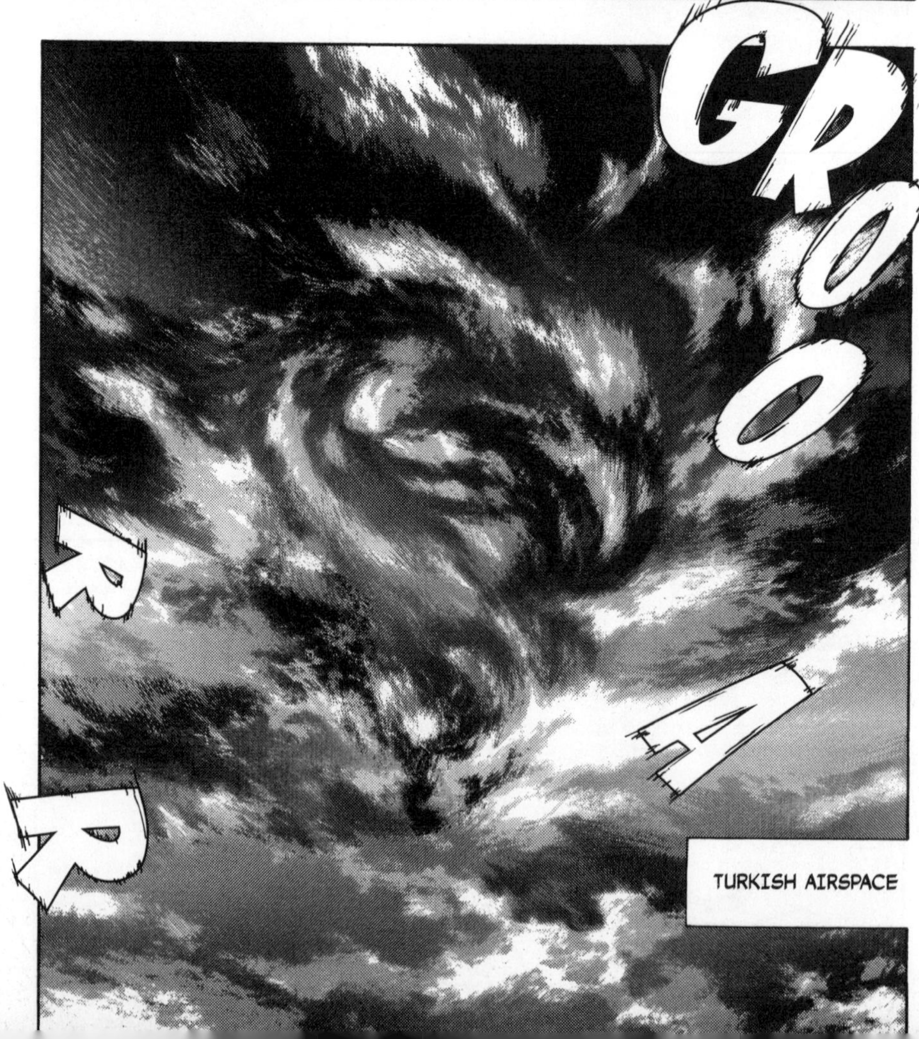
GROOOARR
TURKISH AIRSPACE

Act 11 PATCHING IN

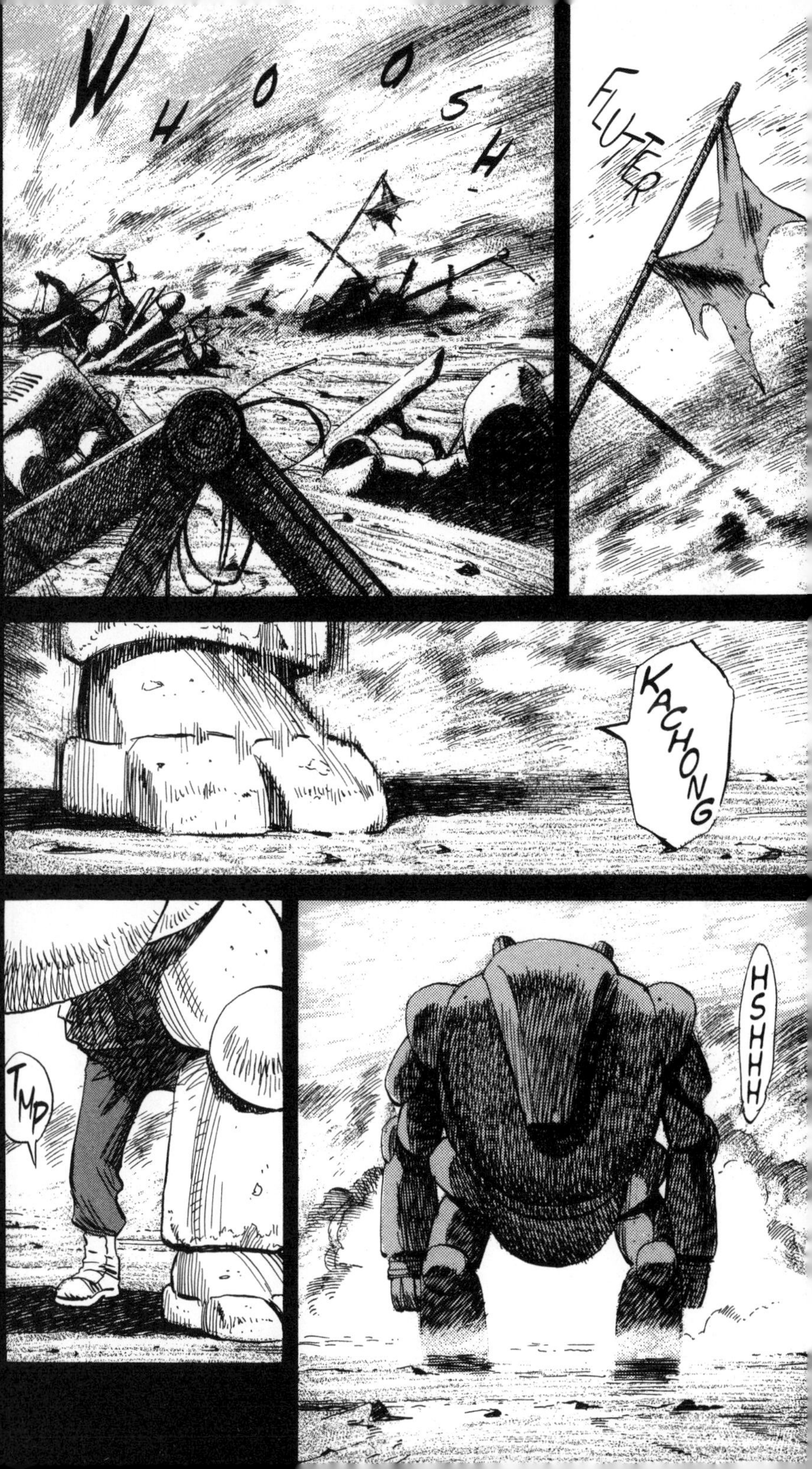
FLUTTER
WHOOSH
KACHONG
HSHHH
TMP

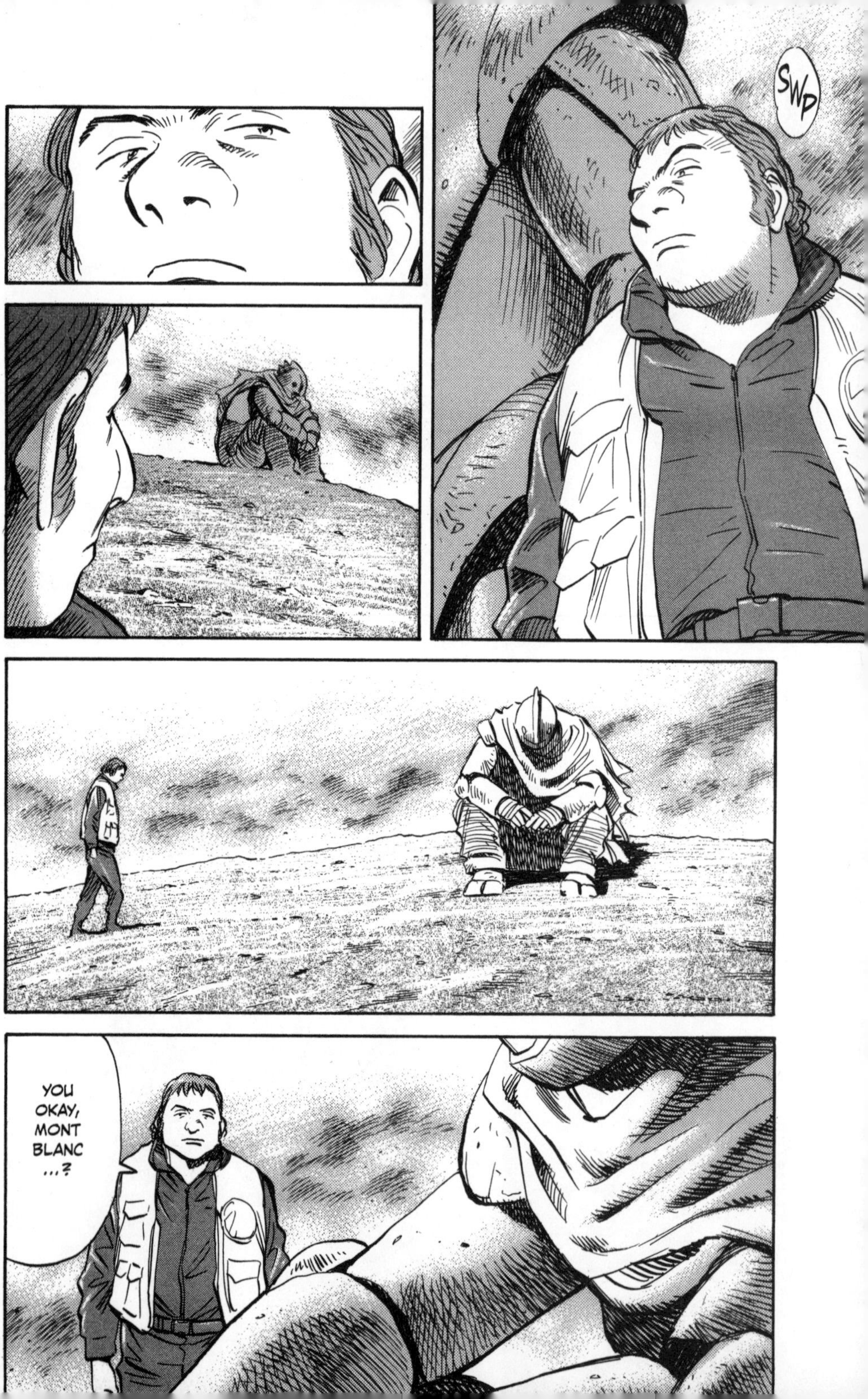
SWP
YOU OKAY, MONT BLANC ...?

...

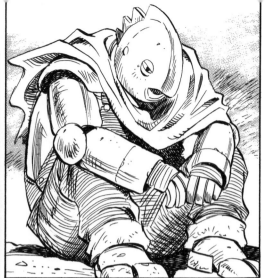

HOW MANY'D YOU DESTROY?

A LOT...

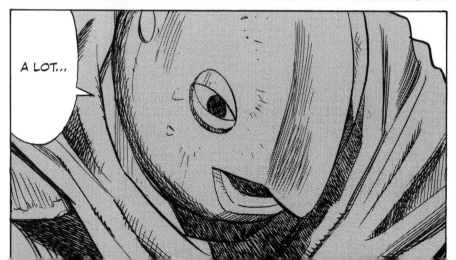

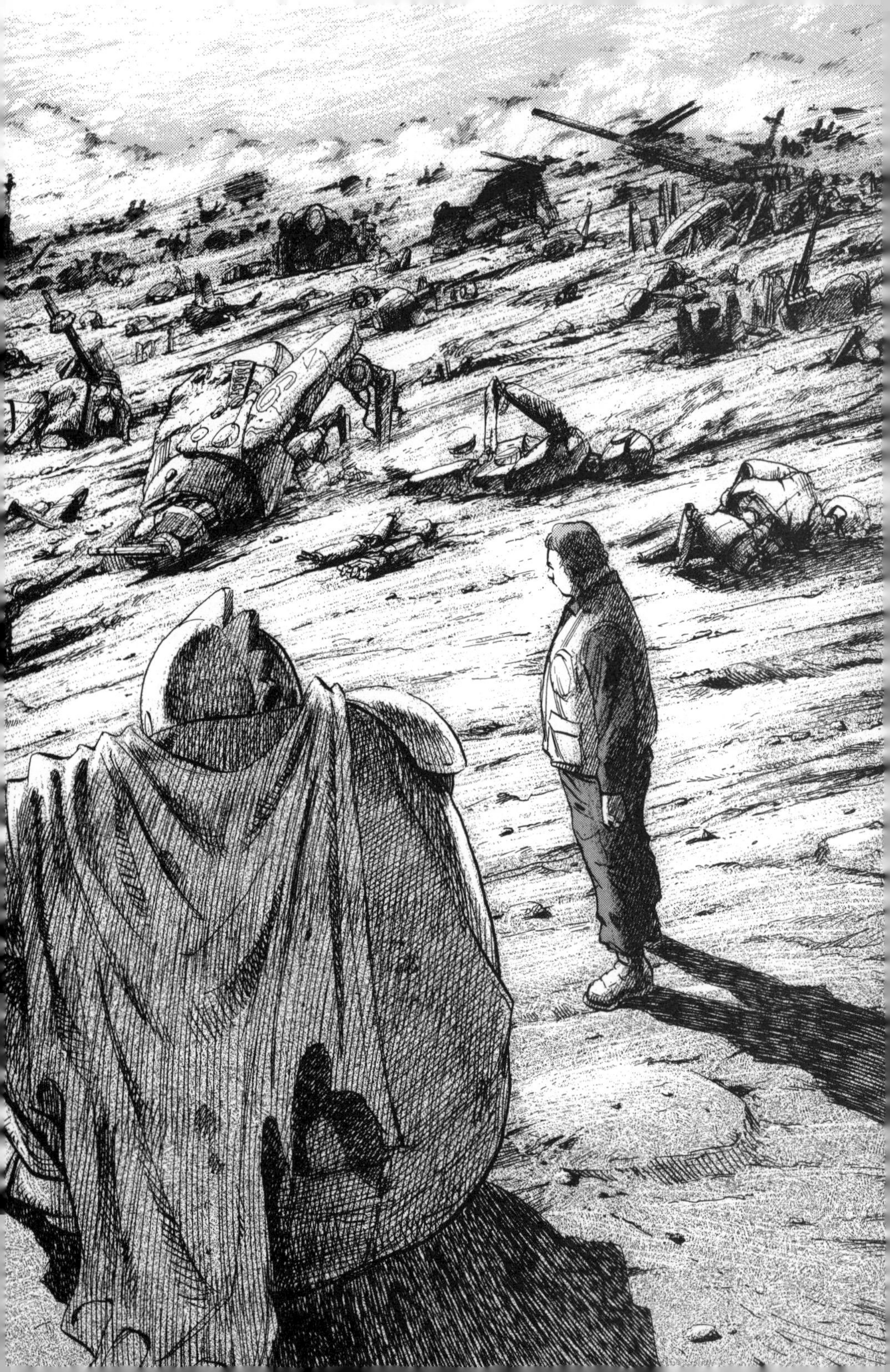

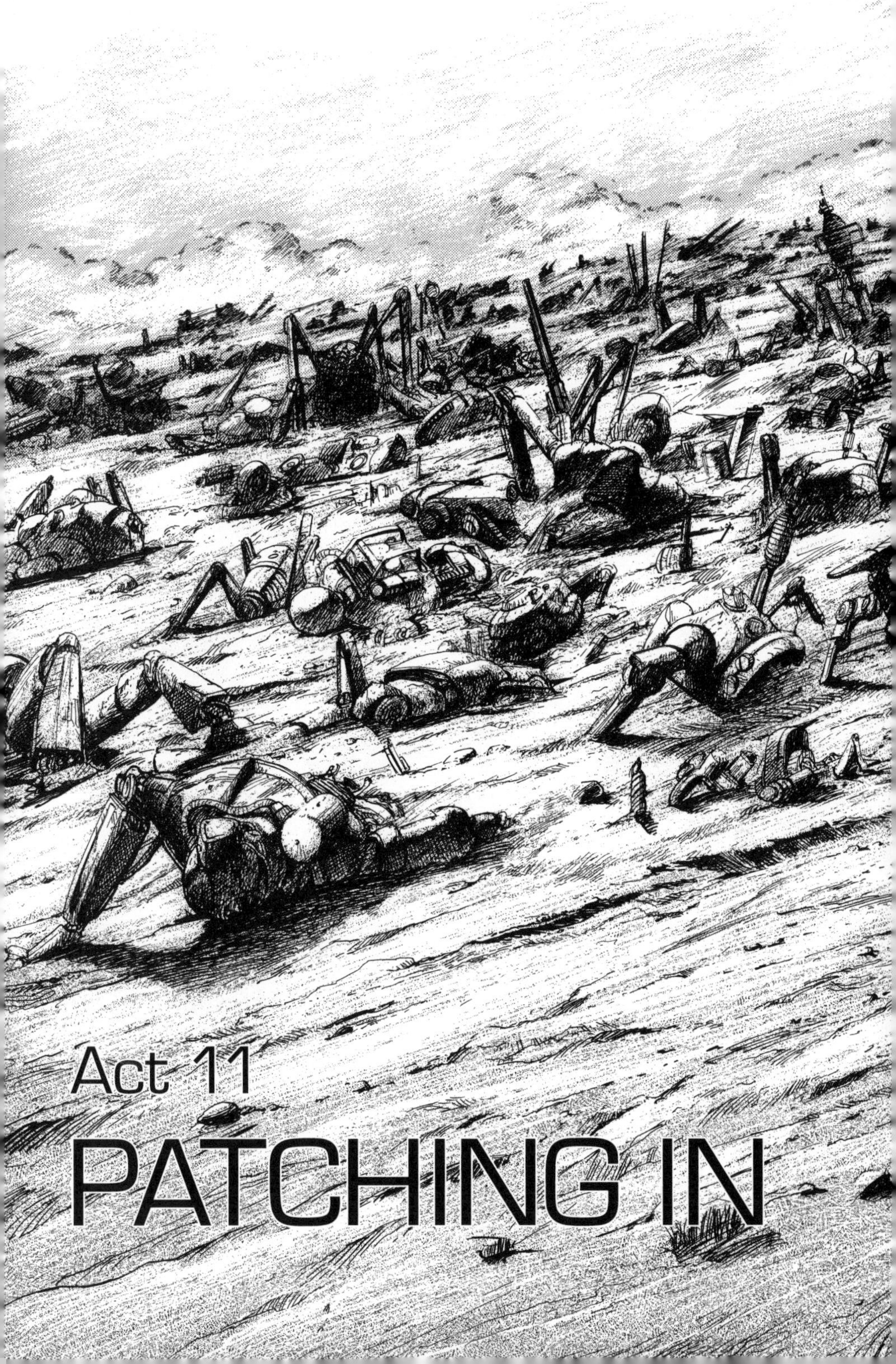

Act 11

PATCHING IN

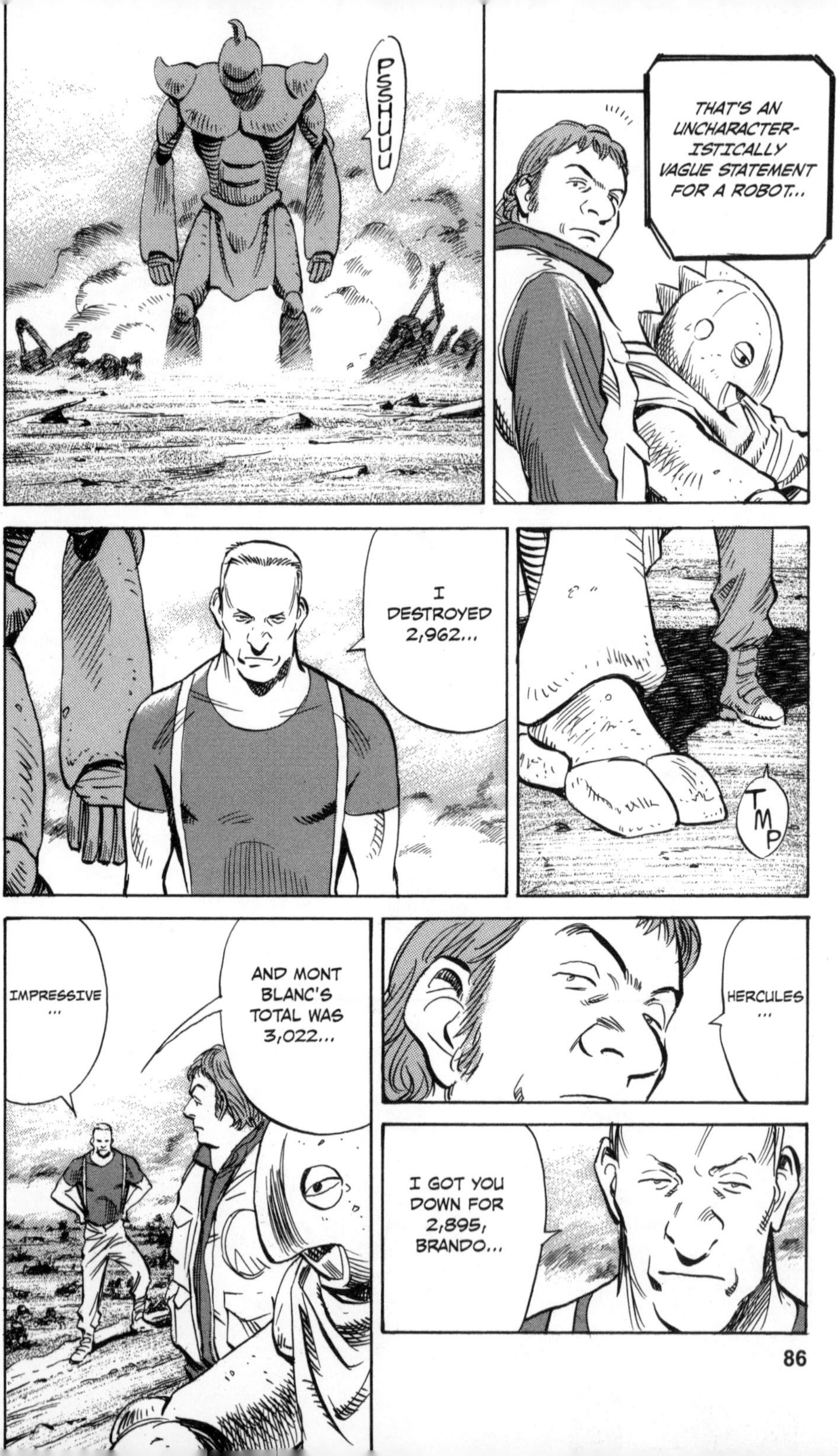
THAT'S AN UNCHARACTER-ISTICALLY VAGUE STATEMENT FOR A ROBOT...
PSSHUUU
TMP
I DESTROYED 2,962...
HERCULES...
I GOT YOU DOWN FOR 2,895, BRANDO...
AND MONT BLANC'S TOTAL WAS 3,022...
IMPRESSIVE...

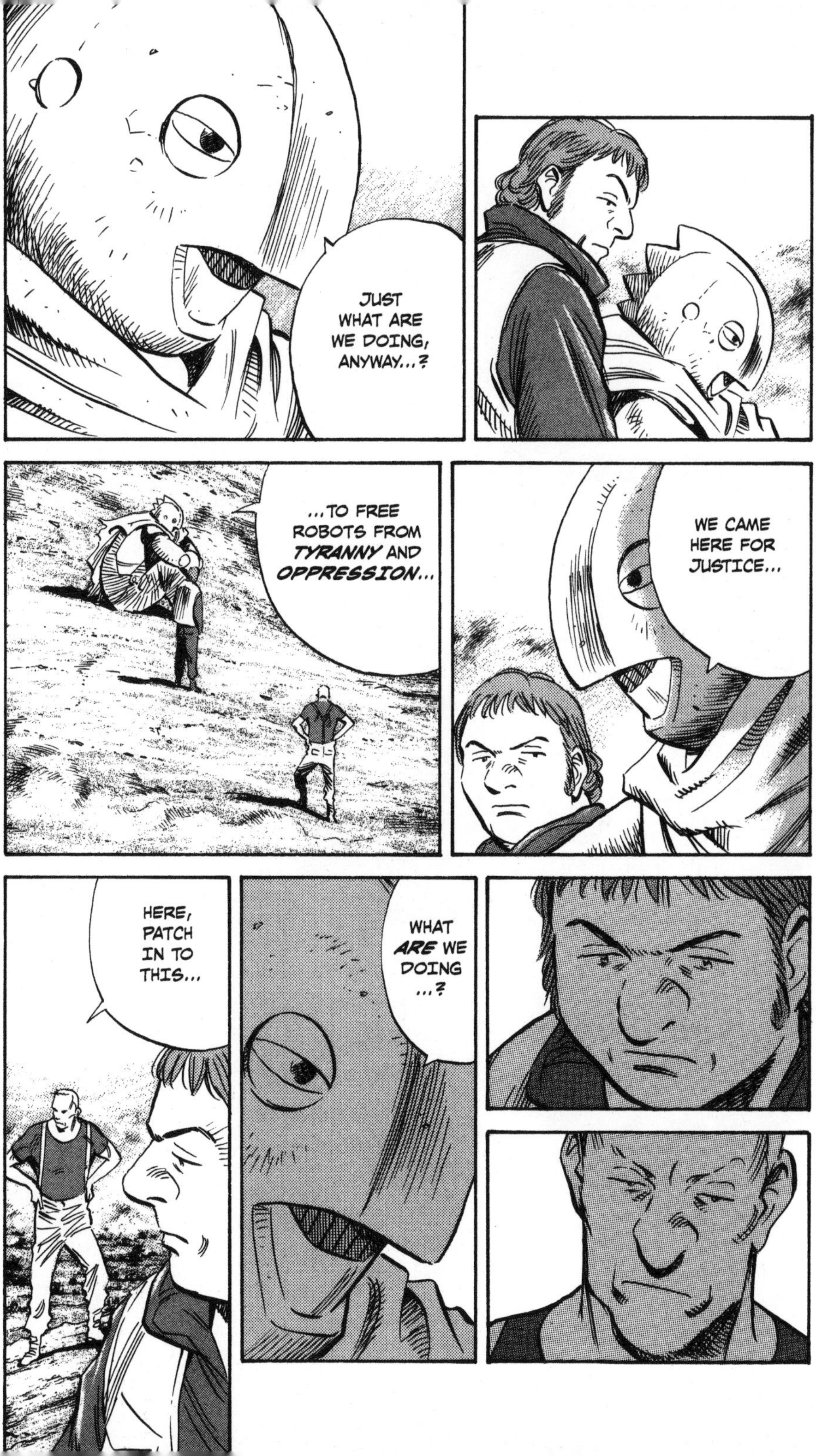
JUST WHAT ARE WE DOING, ANYWAY...?
WE CAME HERE FOR JUSTICE...
...TO FREE ROBOTS FROM *TYRANNY* AND *OPPRESSION*...
WHAT *ARE* WE DOING ...?
HERE, PATCH IN TO THIS...

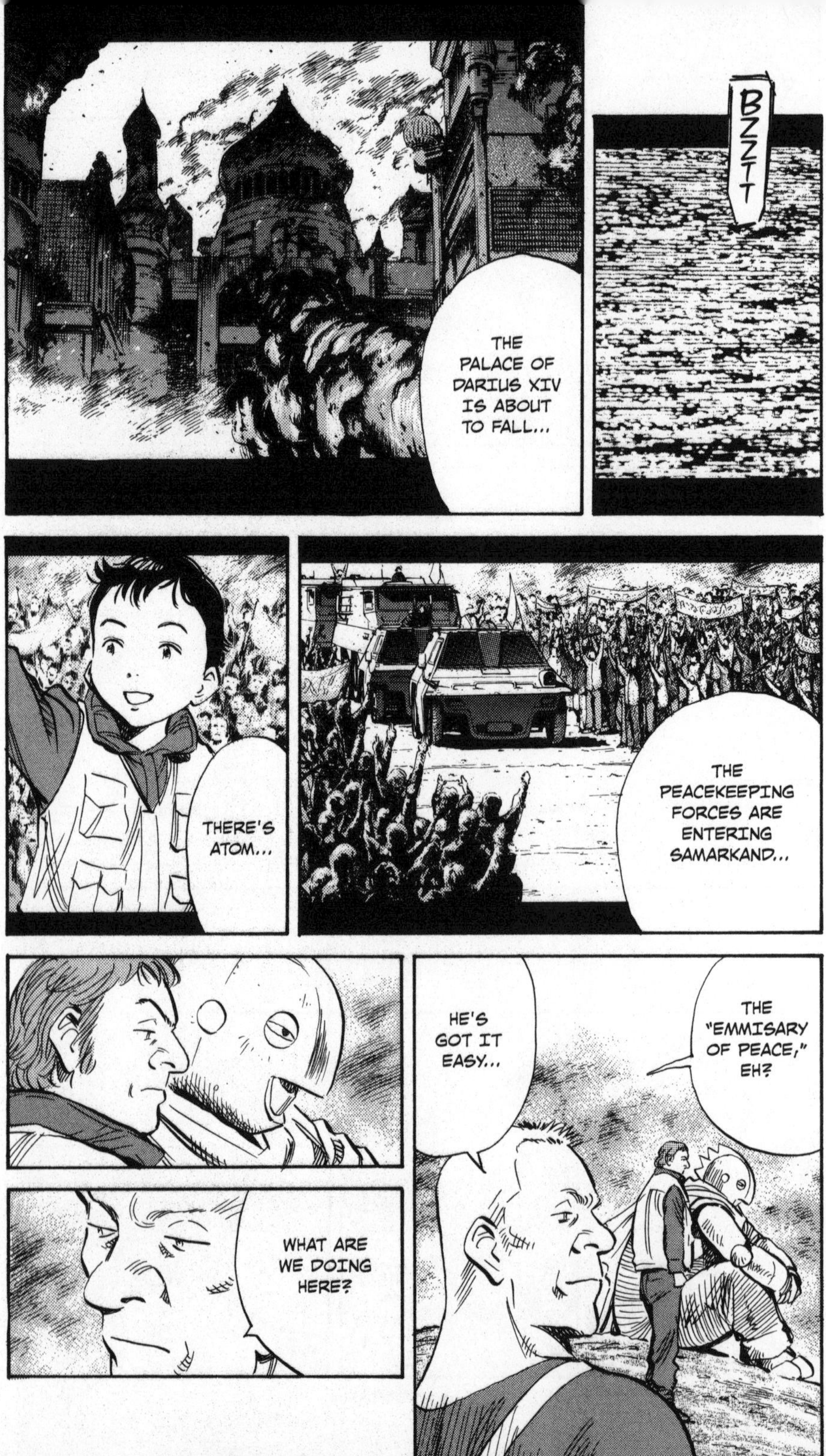
BZZTT
THE PALACE OF DARIUS XIV IS ABOUT TO FALL...
THE PEACEKEEPING FORCES ARE ENTERING SAMARKAND...
THERE'S ATOM...
THE "EMMISARY OF PEACE," EH?
HE'S GOT IT EASY...
WHAT ARE WE DOING HERE?

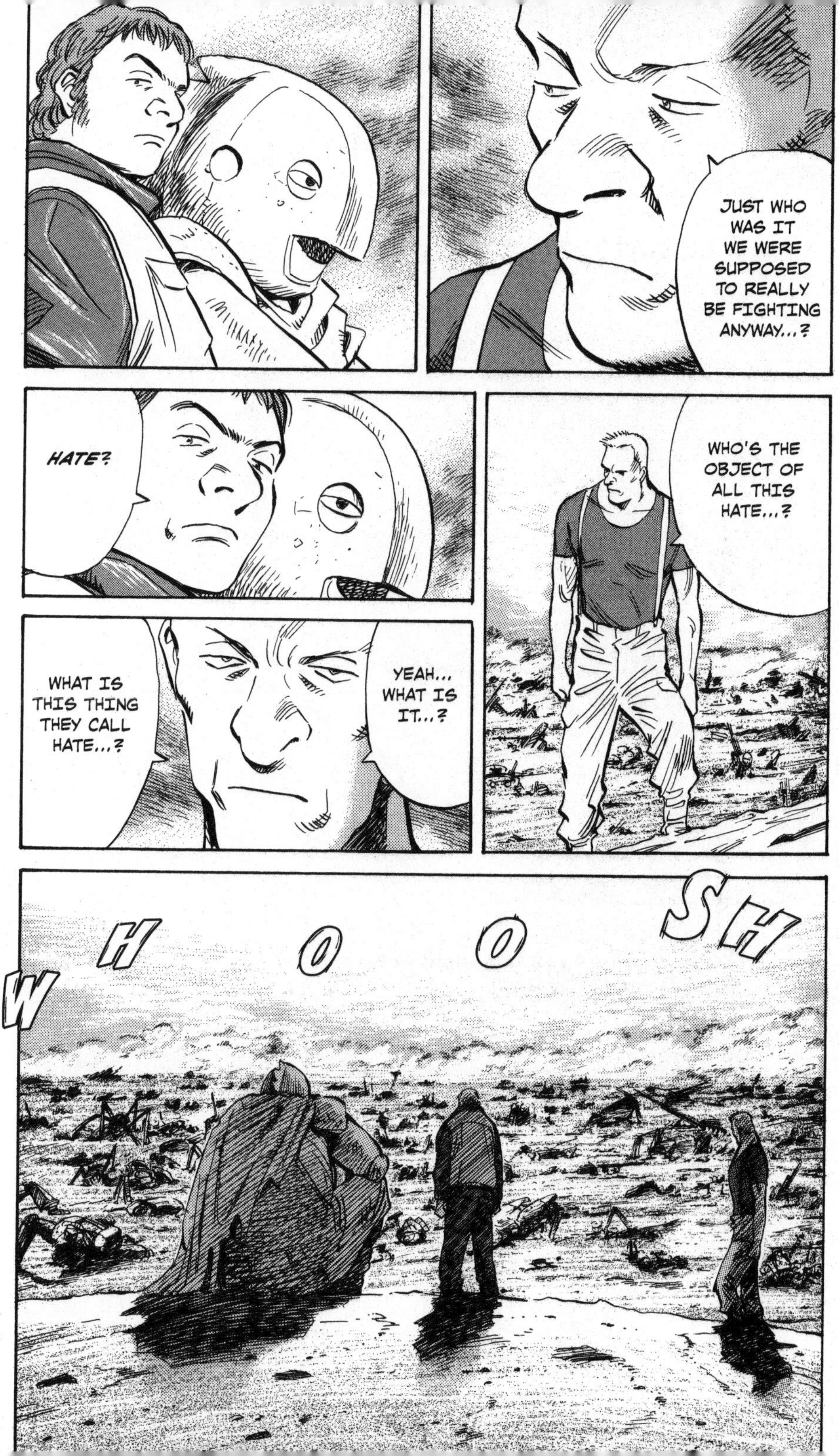
JUST WHO WAS IT WE WERE SUPPOSED TO REALLY BE FIGHTING ANYWAY...?
WHO'S THE OBJECT OF ALL THIS HATE...?
HATE?
YEAH... WHAT IS IT...?
WHAT IS THIS THING THEY CALL HATE...?
WHOOSH

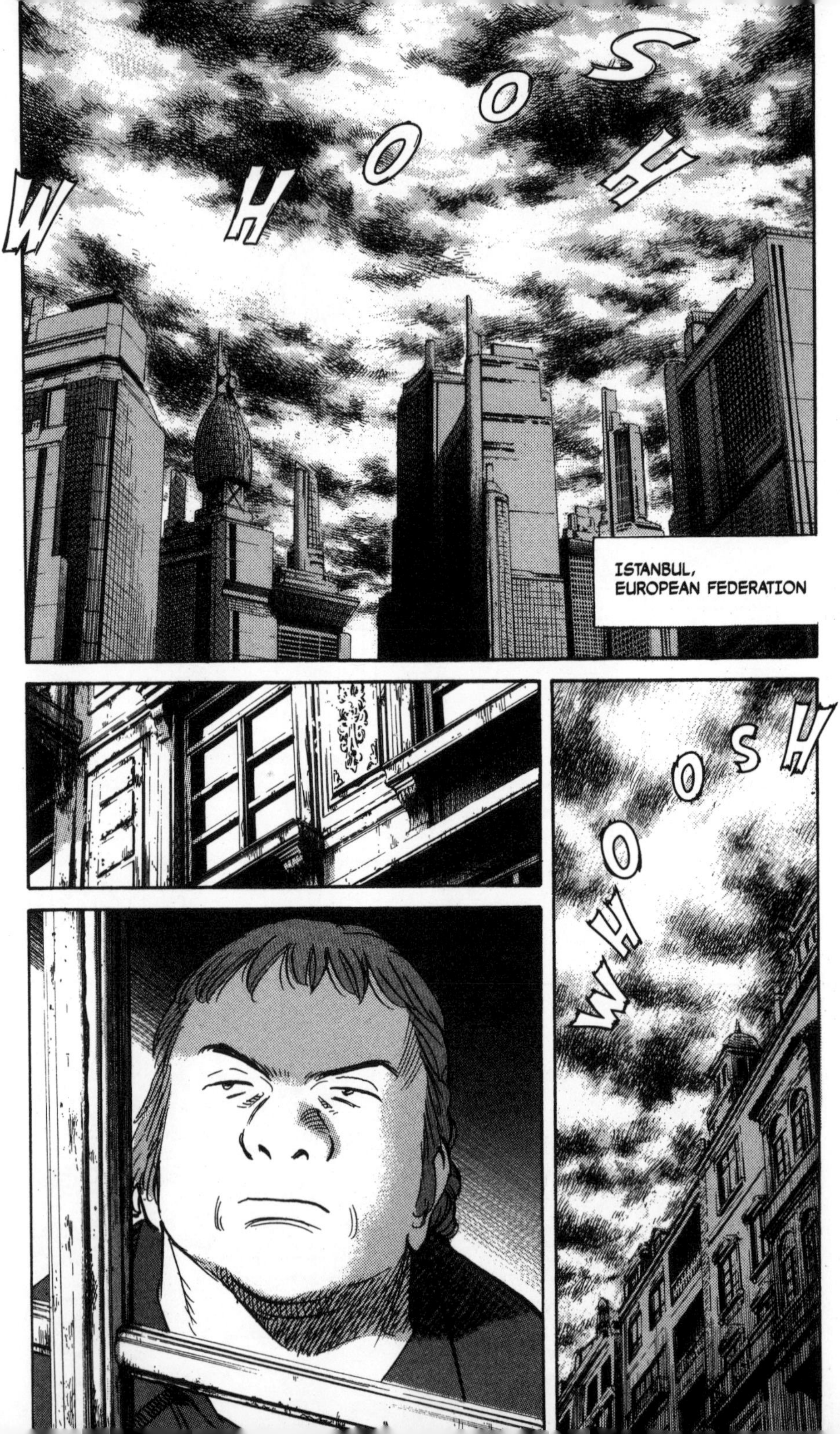
WHOOSH
ISTANBUL,
EUROPEAN FEDERATION
WHOOSH

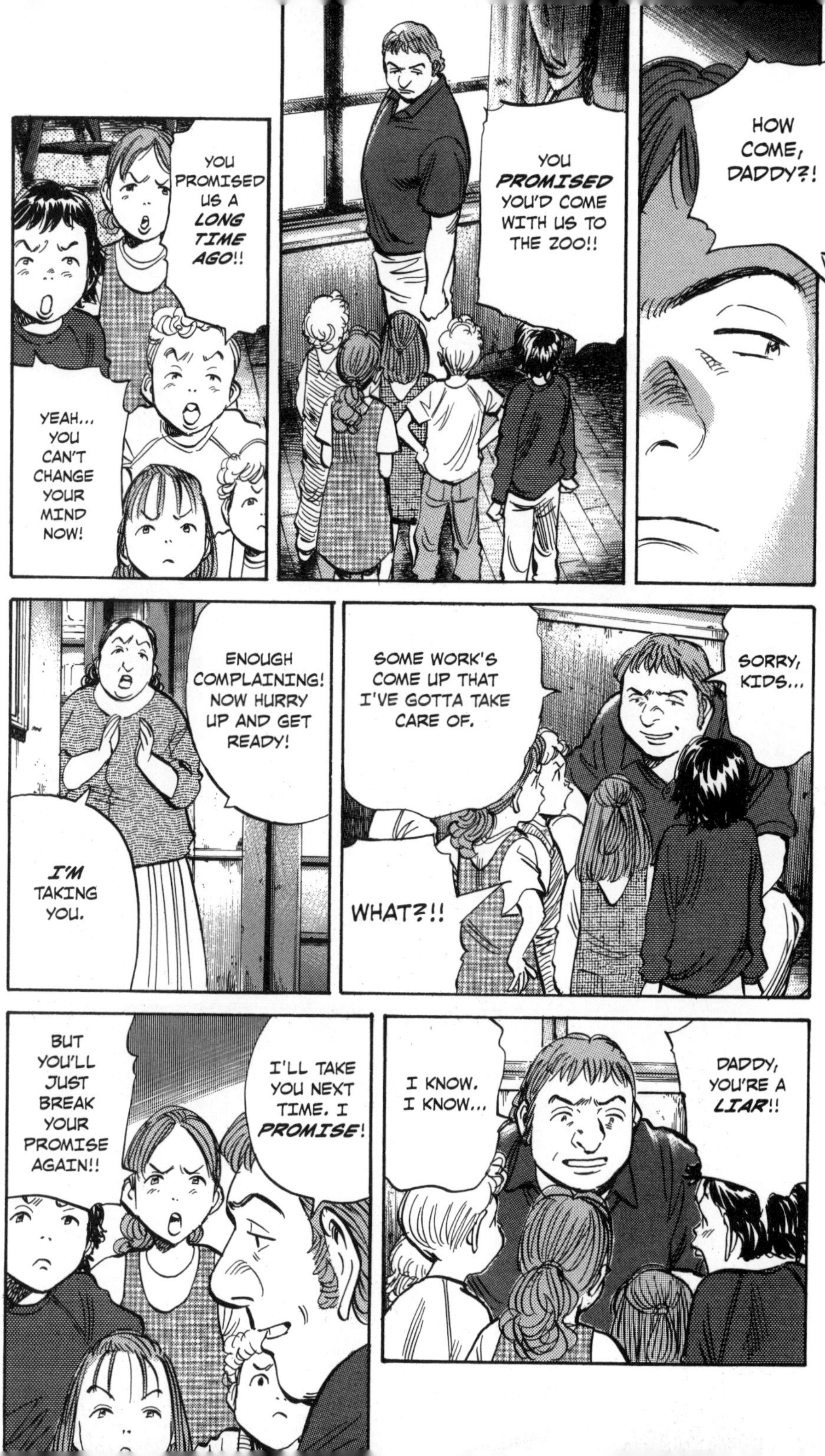
HOW COME, DADDY?!
YOU PROMISED YOU'D COME WITH US TO THE ZOO!!
YOU PROMISED US A LONG TIME AGO!!
YEAH... YOU CAN'T CHANGE YOUR MIND NOW!
SORRY, KIDS...
SOME WORK'S COME UP THAT I'VE GOTTA TAKE CARE OF.
WHAT?!!
ENOUGH COMPLAINING! NOW HURRY UP AND GET READY!
I'M TAKING YOU.
DADDY, YOU'RE A LIAR!!
I KNOW. I KNOW...
I'LL TAKE YOU NEXT TIME. I PROMISE!
BUT YOU'LL JUST BREAK YOUR PROMISE AGAIN!!

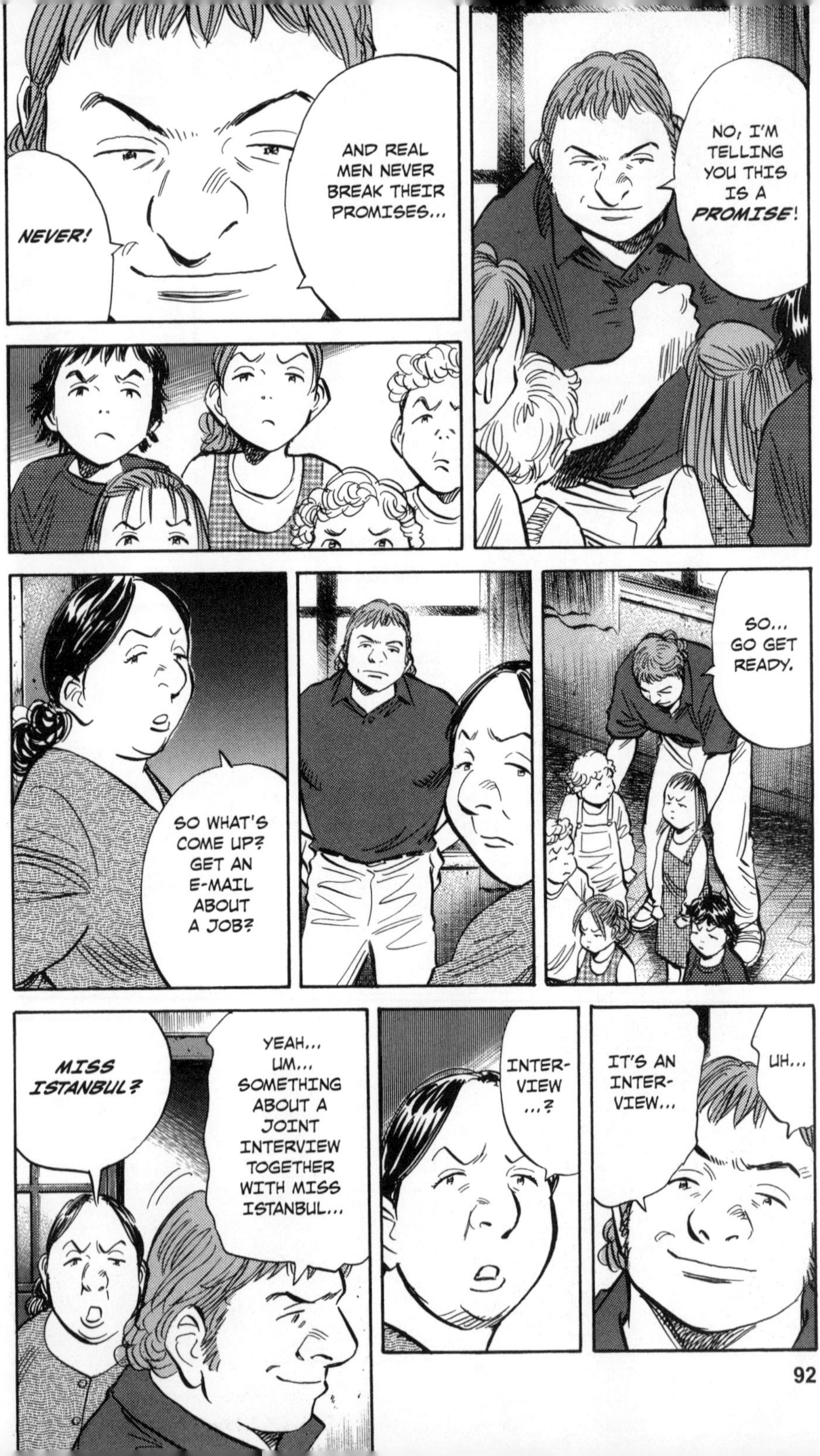
NO, I'M TELLING YOU THIS IS A PROMISE!
AND REAL MEN NEVER BREAK THEIR PROMISES...
NEVER!
SO... GO GET READY.
SO WHAT'S COME UP? GET AN E-MAIL ABOUT A JOB?
UH...
IT'S AN INTER-VIEW...
INTER-VIEW ...?
YEAH... UM... SOMETHING ABOUT A JOINT INTERVIEW TOGETHER WITH MISS ISTANBUL...
MISS ISTANBUL?

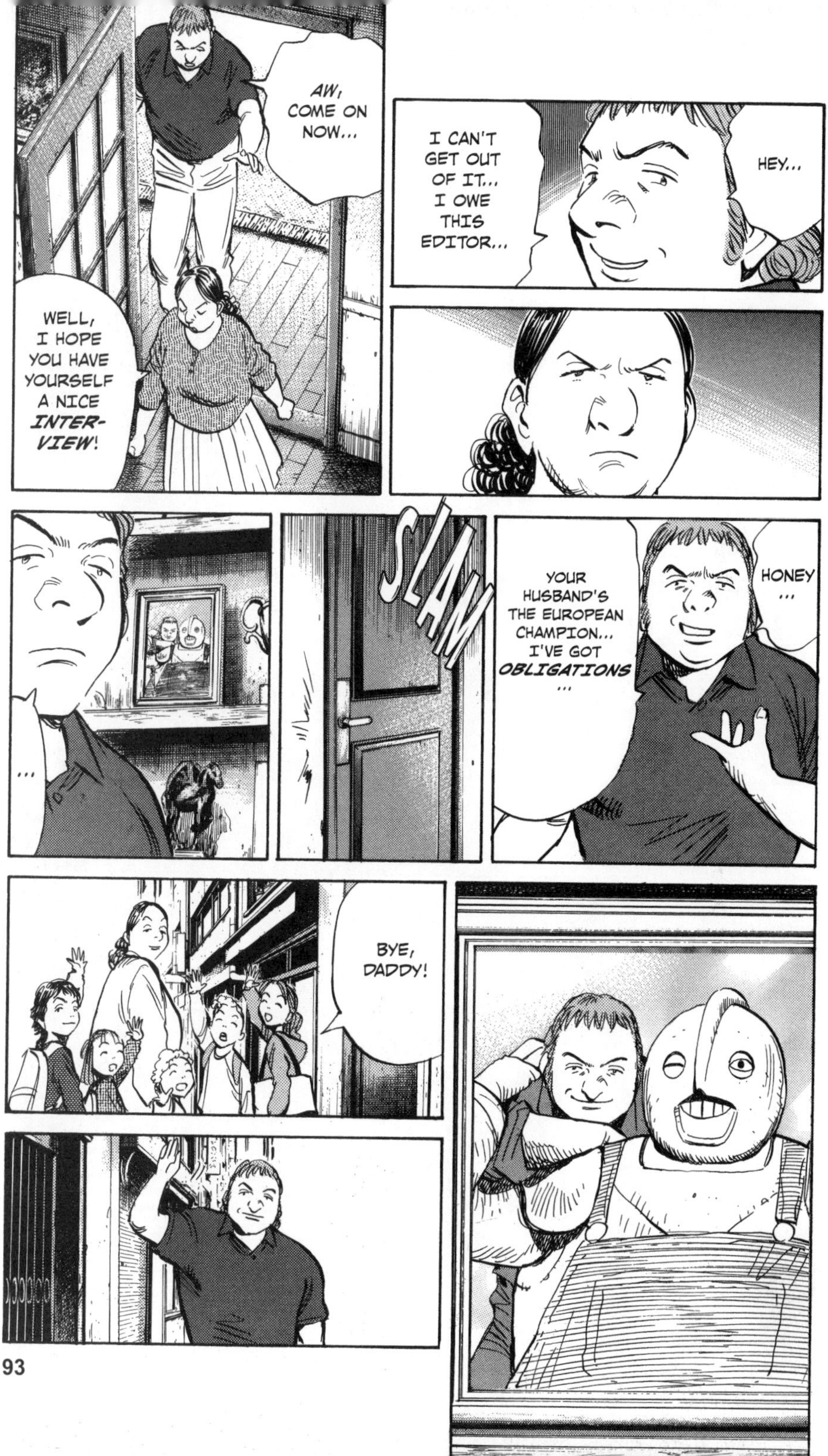
HEY...
I CAN'T GET OUT OF IT... I OWE THIS EDITOR...
AW, COME ON NOW...
WELL, I HOPE YOU HAVE YOURSELF A NICE *INTERVIEW*!
HONEY ...
YOUR HUSBAND'S THE EUROPEAN CHAMPION... I'VE GOT *OBLIGATIONS* ...
SLAM
...
BYE, DADDY!

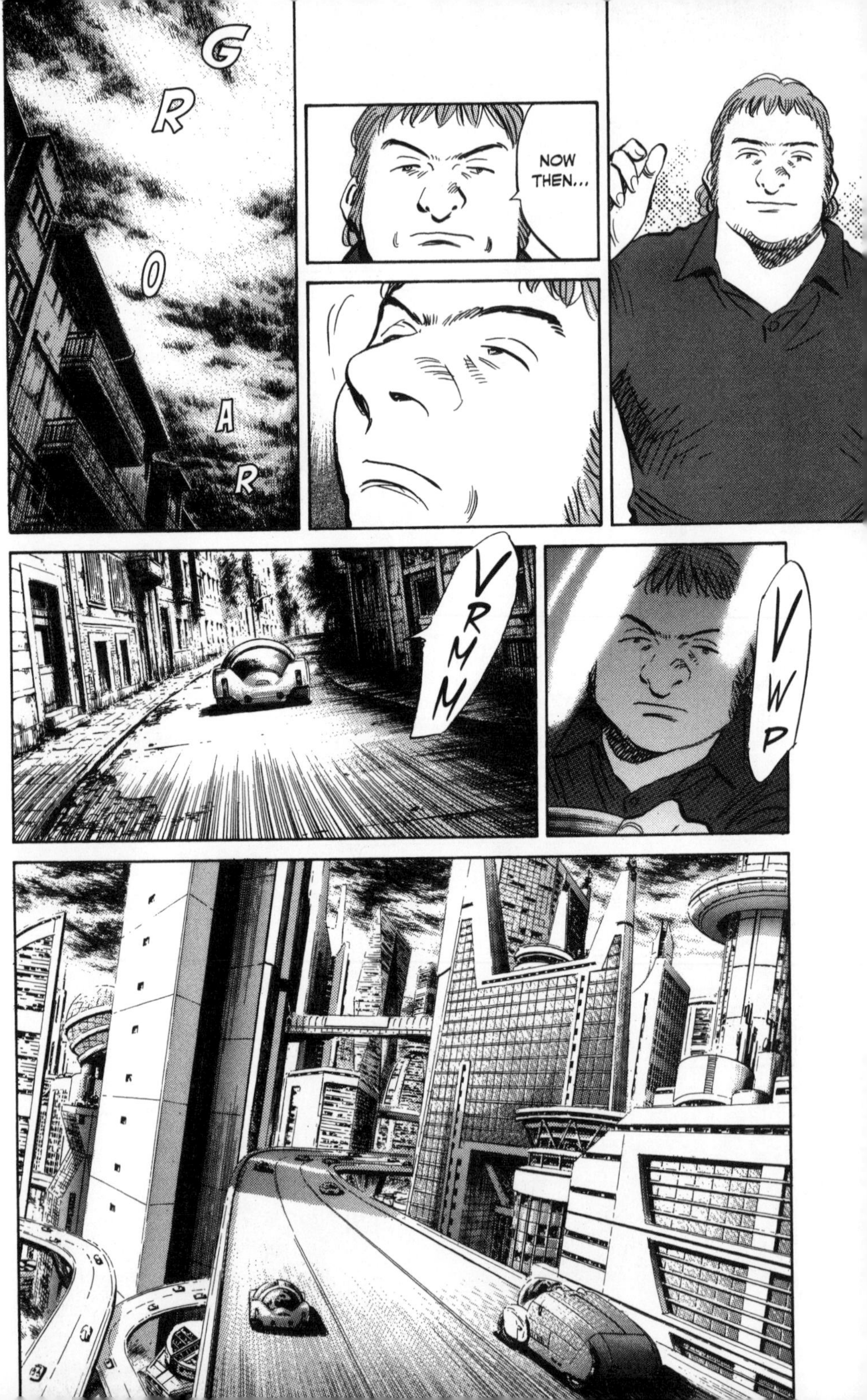
NOW THEN...
GROAR
VWP
VRMM

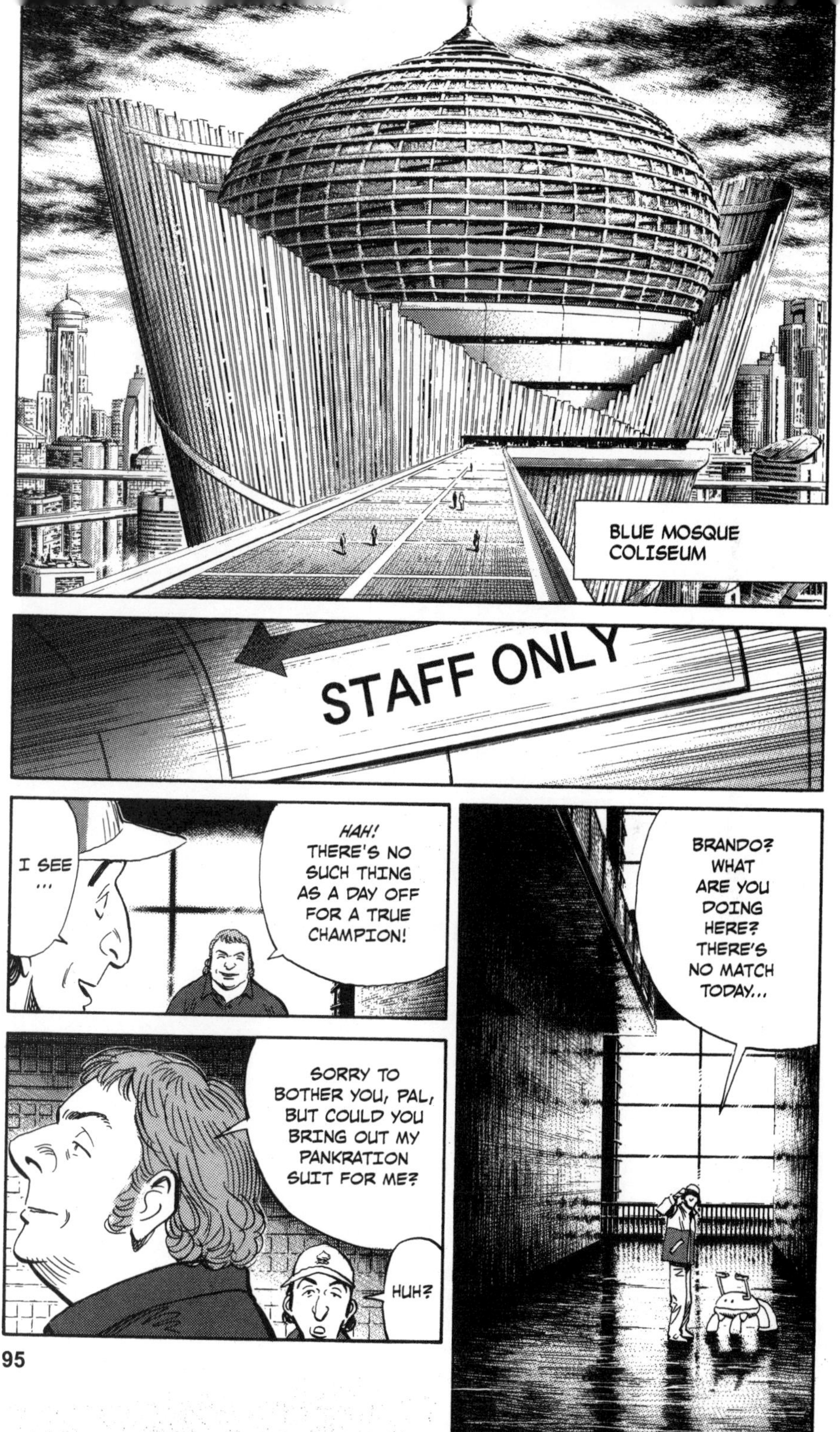
BLUE MOSQUE COLISEUM
STAFF ONLY
BRANDO? WHAT ARE YOU DOING HERE? THERE'S NO MATCH TODAY...
HAH! THERE'S NO SUCH THING AS A DAY OFF FOR A TRUE CHAMPION!
I SEE ...
SORRY TO BOTHER YOU, PAL, BUT COULD YOU BRING OUT MY PANKRATION SUIT FOR ME?
HUH?

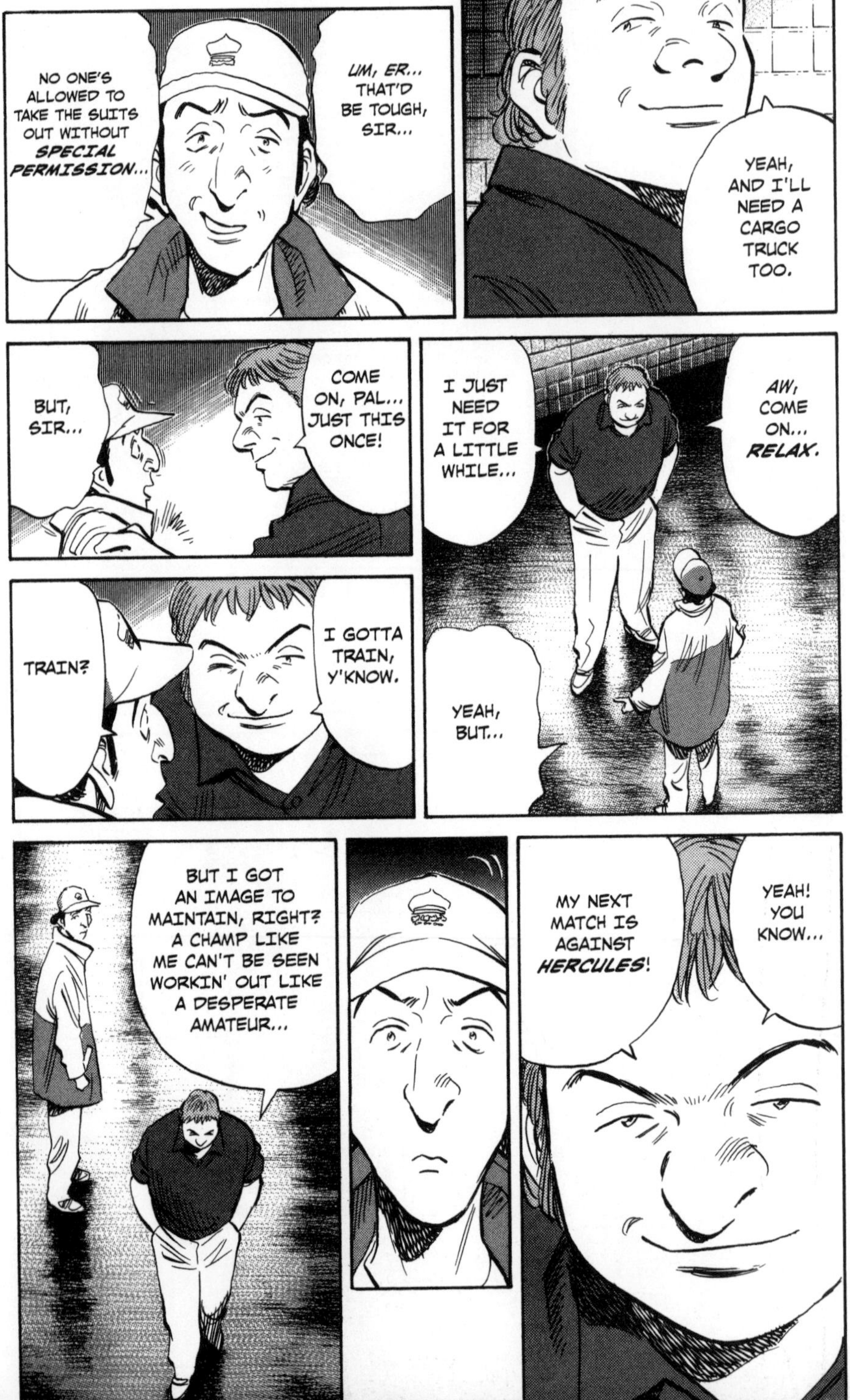
YEAH, AND I'LL NEED A CARGO TRUCK TOO.
UM, ER... THAT'D BE TOUGH, SIR...
NO ONE'S ALLOWED TO TAKE THE SUITS OUT WITHOUT SPECIAL PERMISSION...
AW, COME ON... RELAX.
I JUST NEED IT FOR A LITTLE WHILE...
YEAH, BUT...
COME ON, PAL... JUST THIS ONCE!
BUT, SIR...
I GOTTA TRAIN, Y'KNOW.
TRAIN?
YEAH! YOU KNOW...
MY NEXT MATCH IS AGAINST HERCULES!
BUT I GOT AN IMAGE TO MAINTAIN, RIGHT? A CHAMP LIKE ME CAN'T BE SEEN WORKIN' OUT LIKE A DESPERATE AMATEUR...

I GOTTA DO MY TRAINING ON THE *SLY*... GET IT?
...
VREEN
VREEN
VREEN
VREEN
I REALLY WISH I HAD MY OLD COMBAT SUIT, BUT THE ARMY'S GOT IT UNDER LOCK AND KEY...
WHAT'S THAT?
NOTHING... JUST TALKIN' TO MYSELF...
VREEN
VREEN

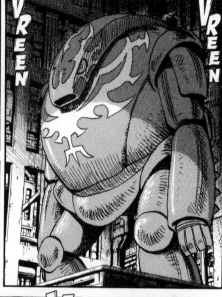

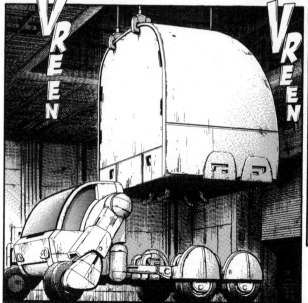

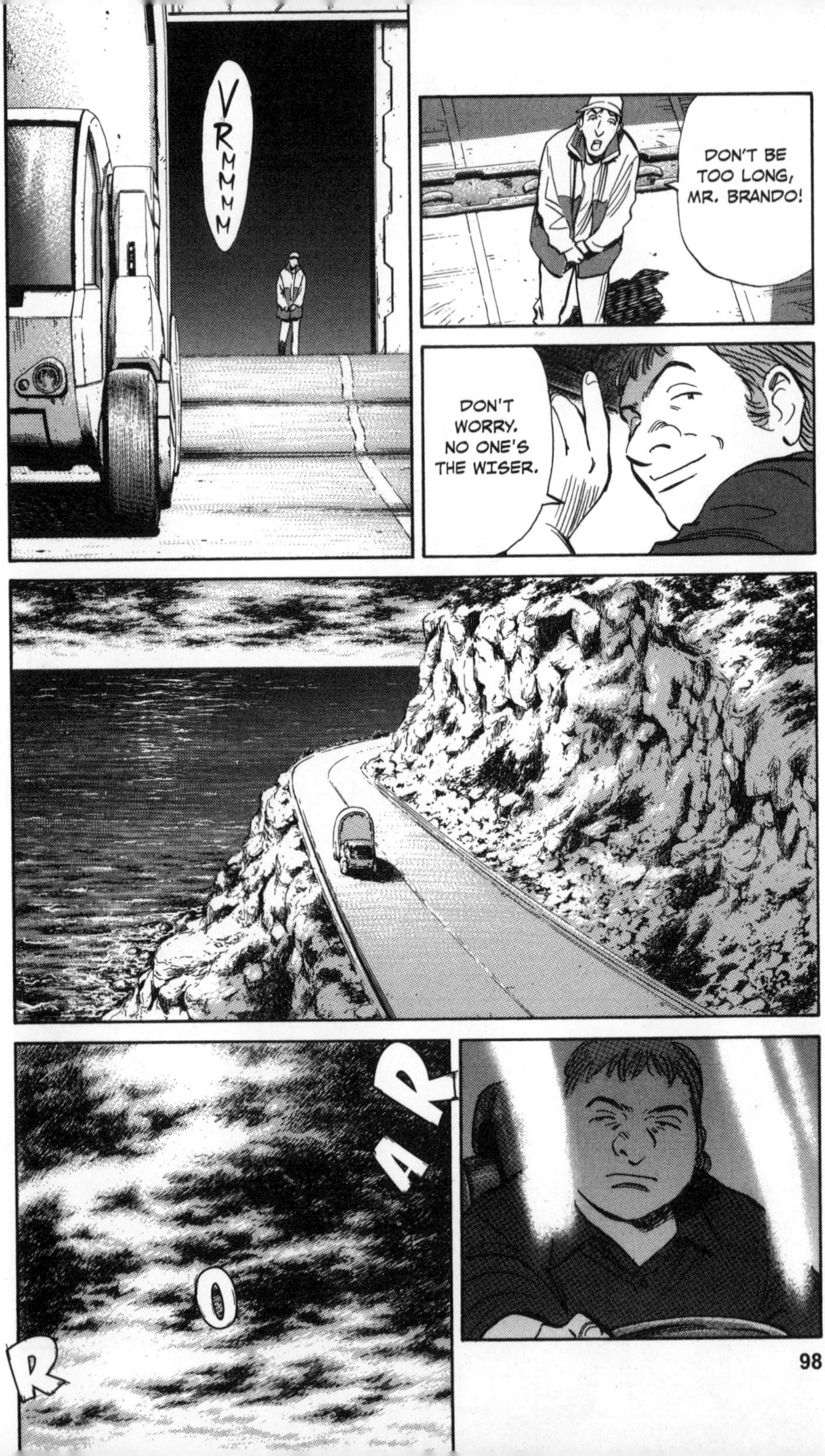
DON'T BE TOO LONG, MR. BRANDO!
DON'T WORRY. NO ONE'S THE WISER.
VRMMMM
ROAR

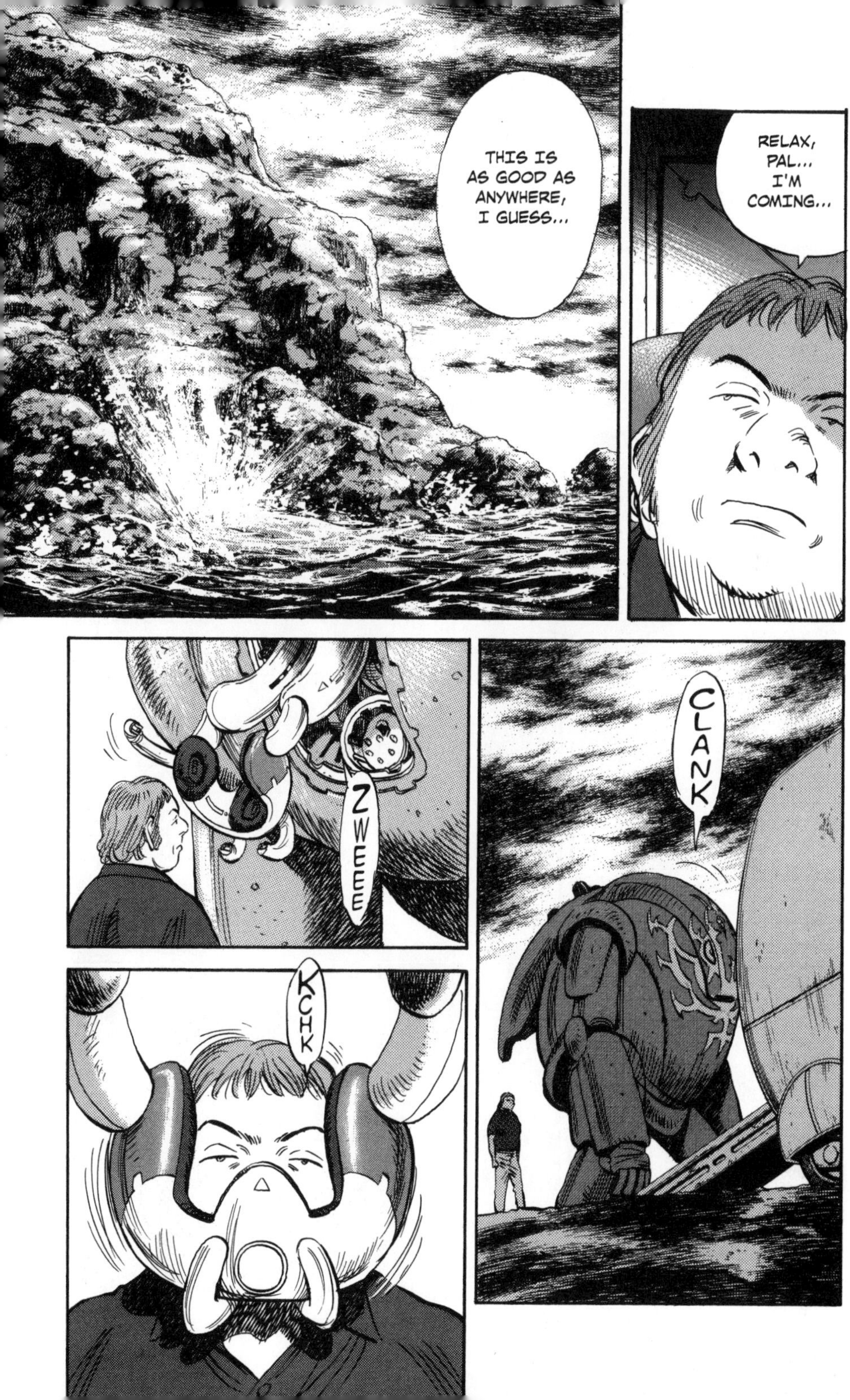
RELAX, PAL... I'M COMING...
THIS IS AS GOOD AS ANYWHERE, I GUESS...
CLANK
ZWEEE
KCHK

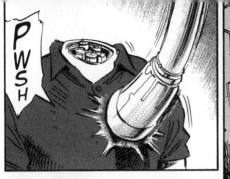
PWSH

GASCHUNK

SHMPP

CREE

VWOOSH

ZWEEE!

DOOM

KASHONK

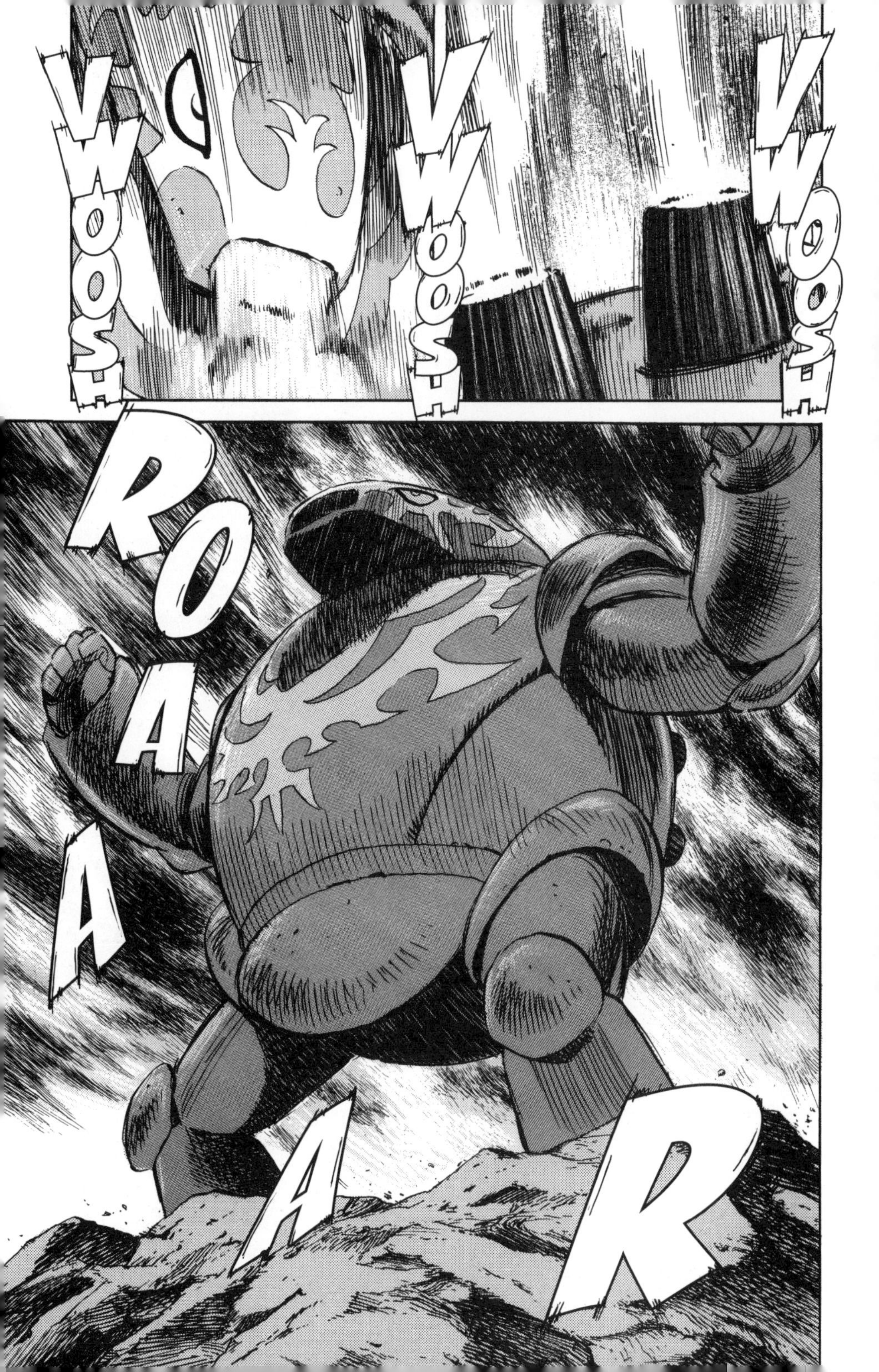
VWOOSH
VWOOSH
VWOOSH
ROAAAAR

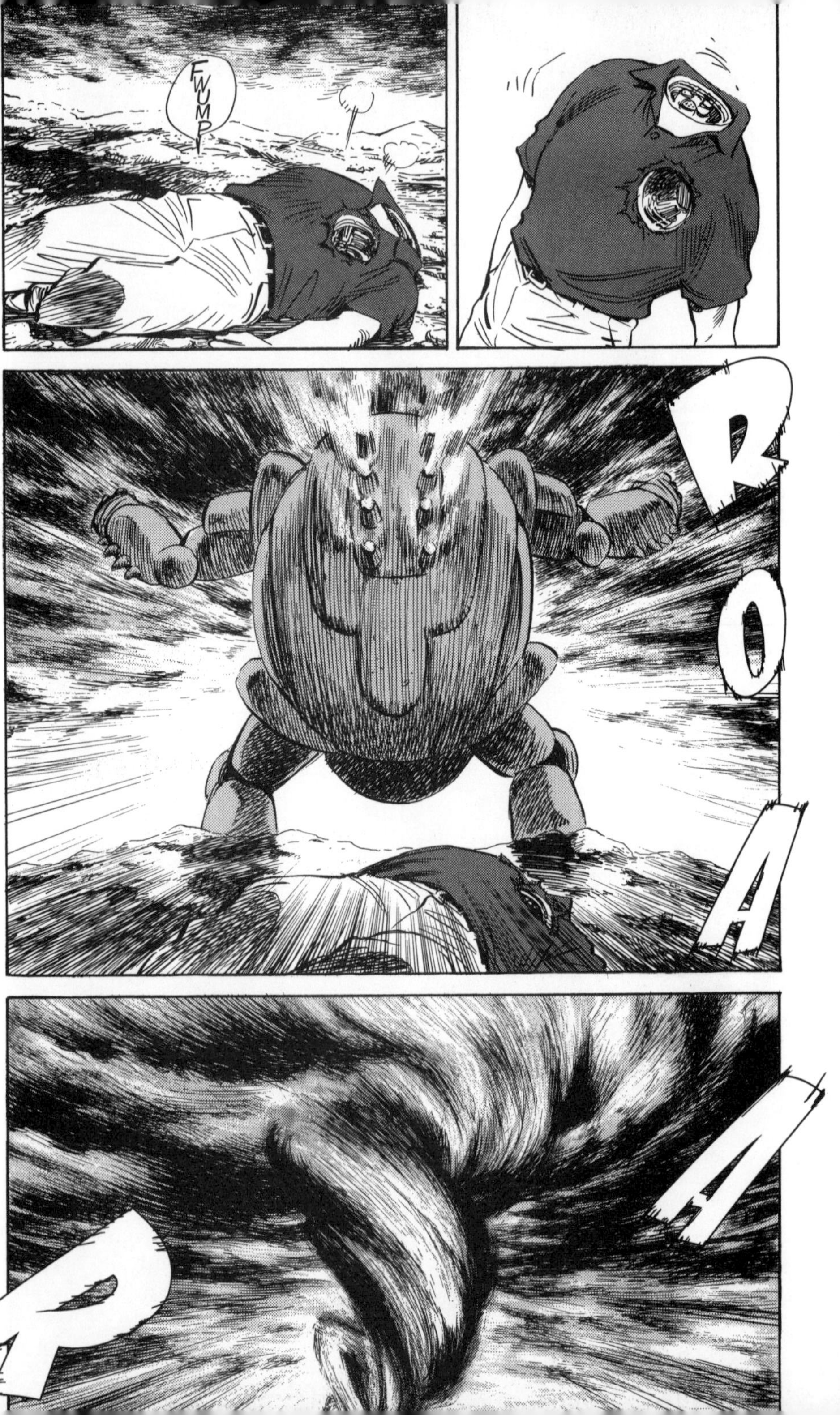
FWUMP
ROA
A
R

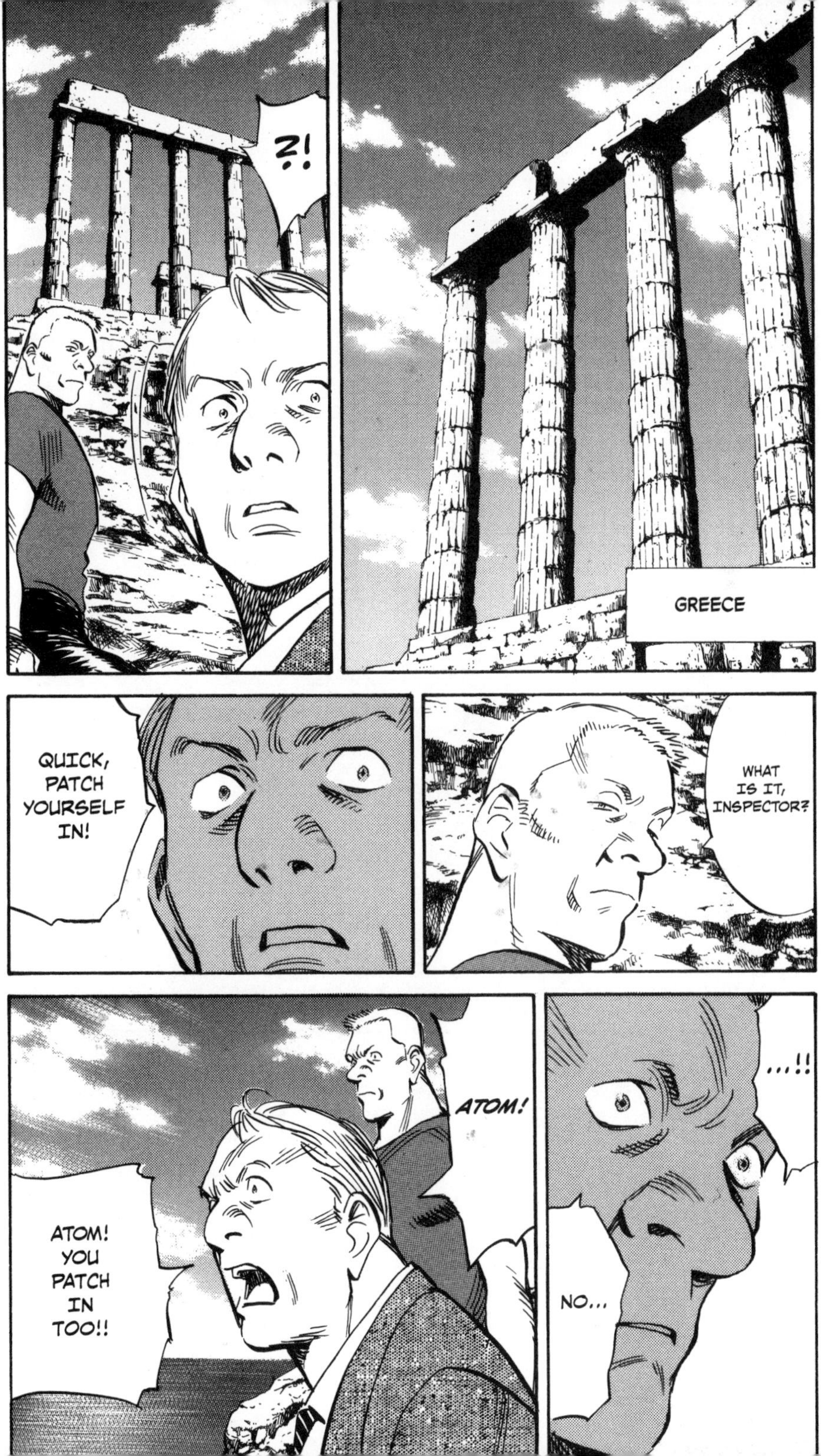
GREECE
?!
WHAT IS IT, INSPECTOR?
QUICK, PATCH YOURSELF IN!
...!!
NO...
ATOM!
ATOM! YOU PATCH IN TOO!!

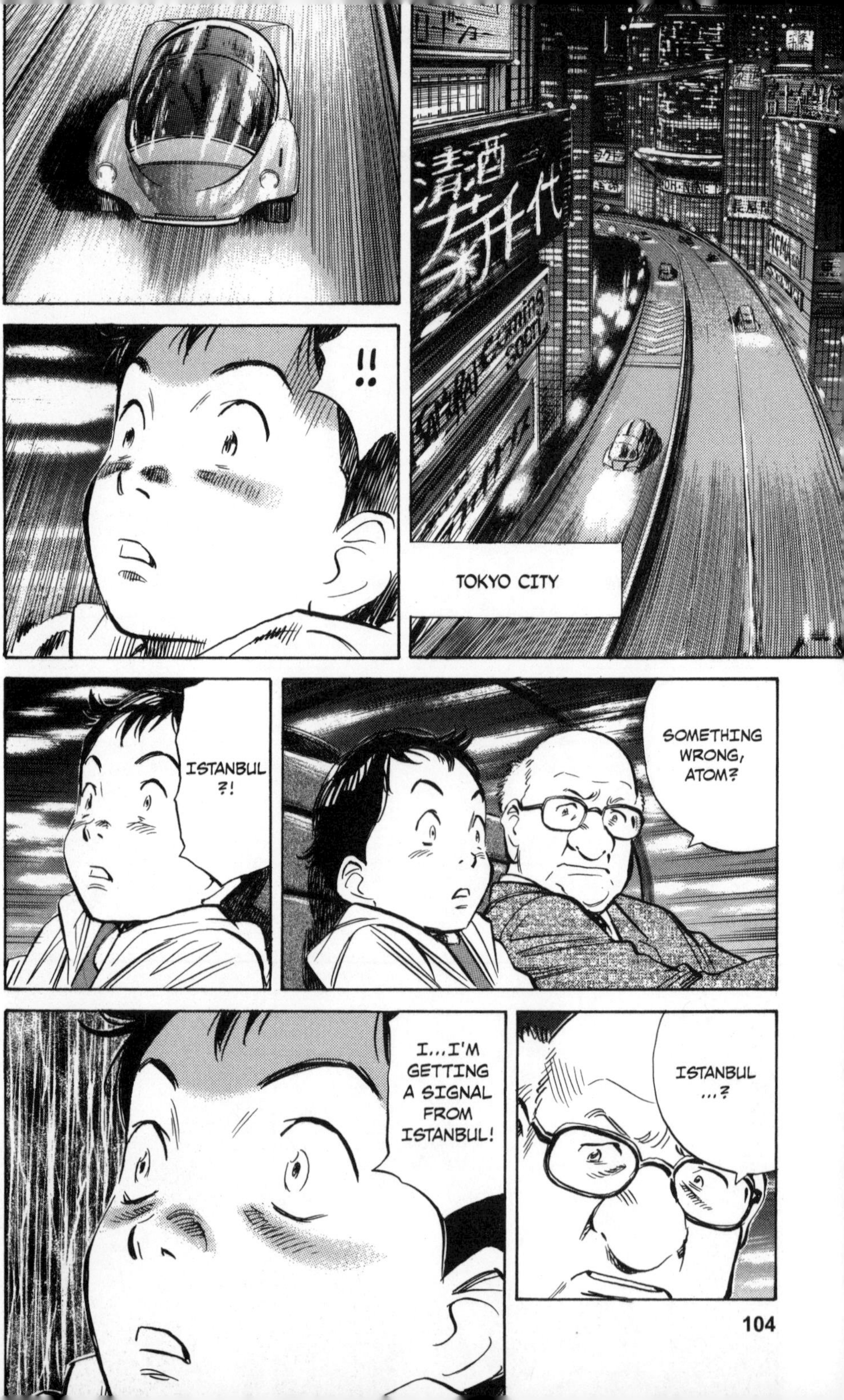
清酒
TOKYO CITY
!!
SOMETHING WRONG, ATOM?
ISTANBUL?!
ISTANBUL...?
I...I'M GETTING A SIGNAL FROM ISTANBUL!

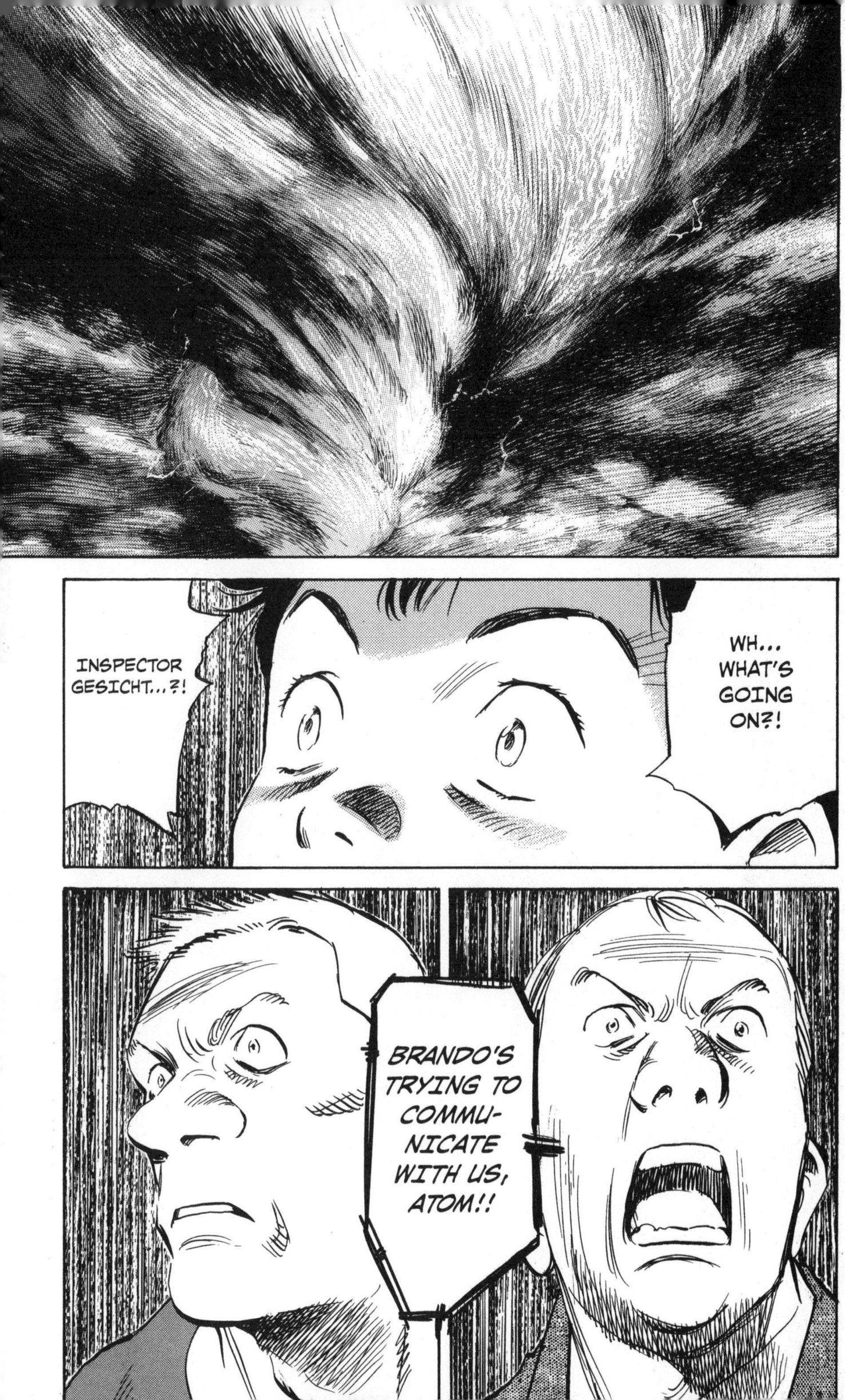
WH... WHAT'S GOING ON?!
INSPECTOR GESICHT...?!
BRANDO'S TRYING TO COMMUNICATE WITH US, ATOM!!

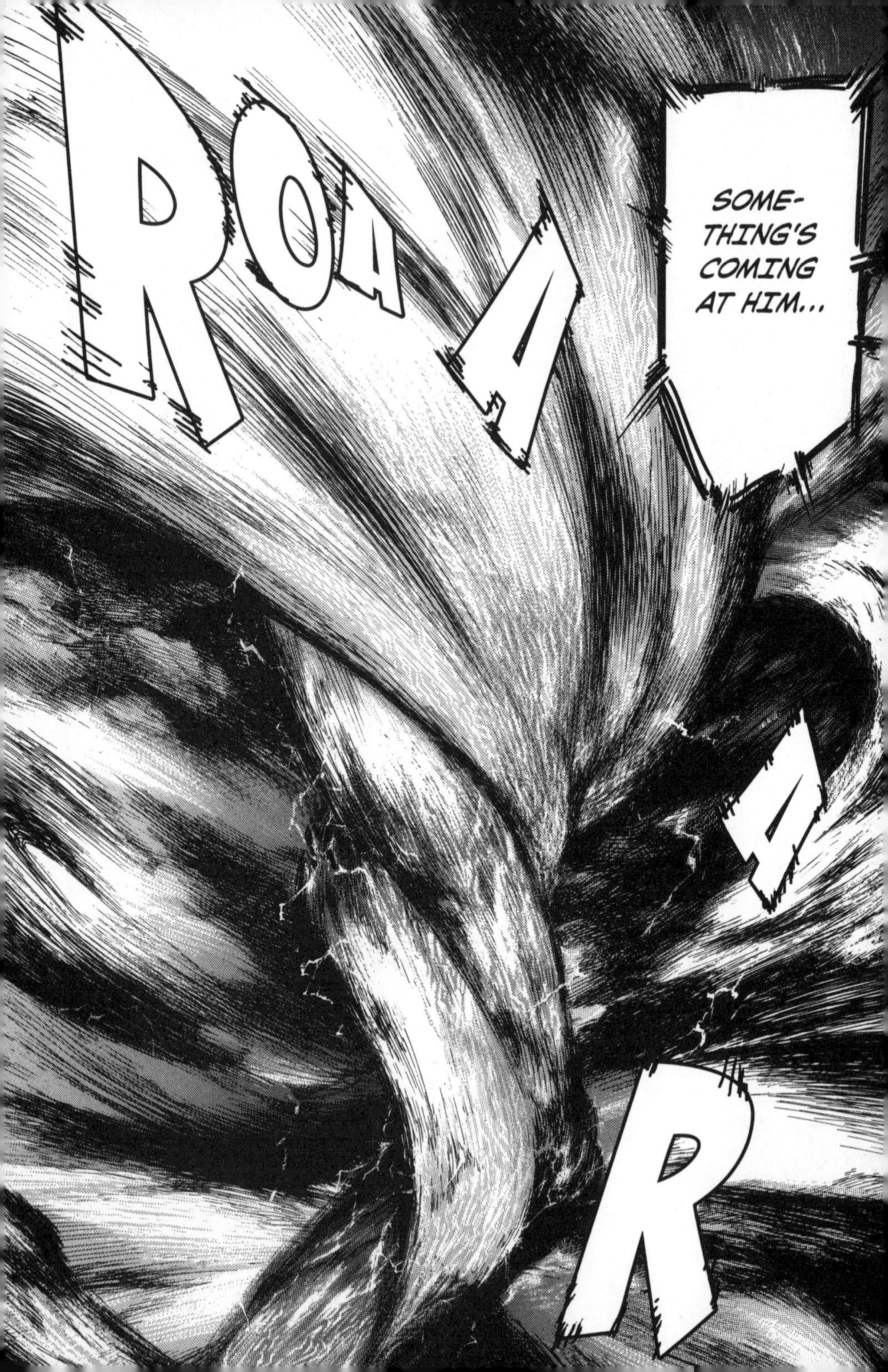
SOME-
THING'S
COMING
AT HIM...
ROAAAR

Act 12 Family Portrait

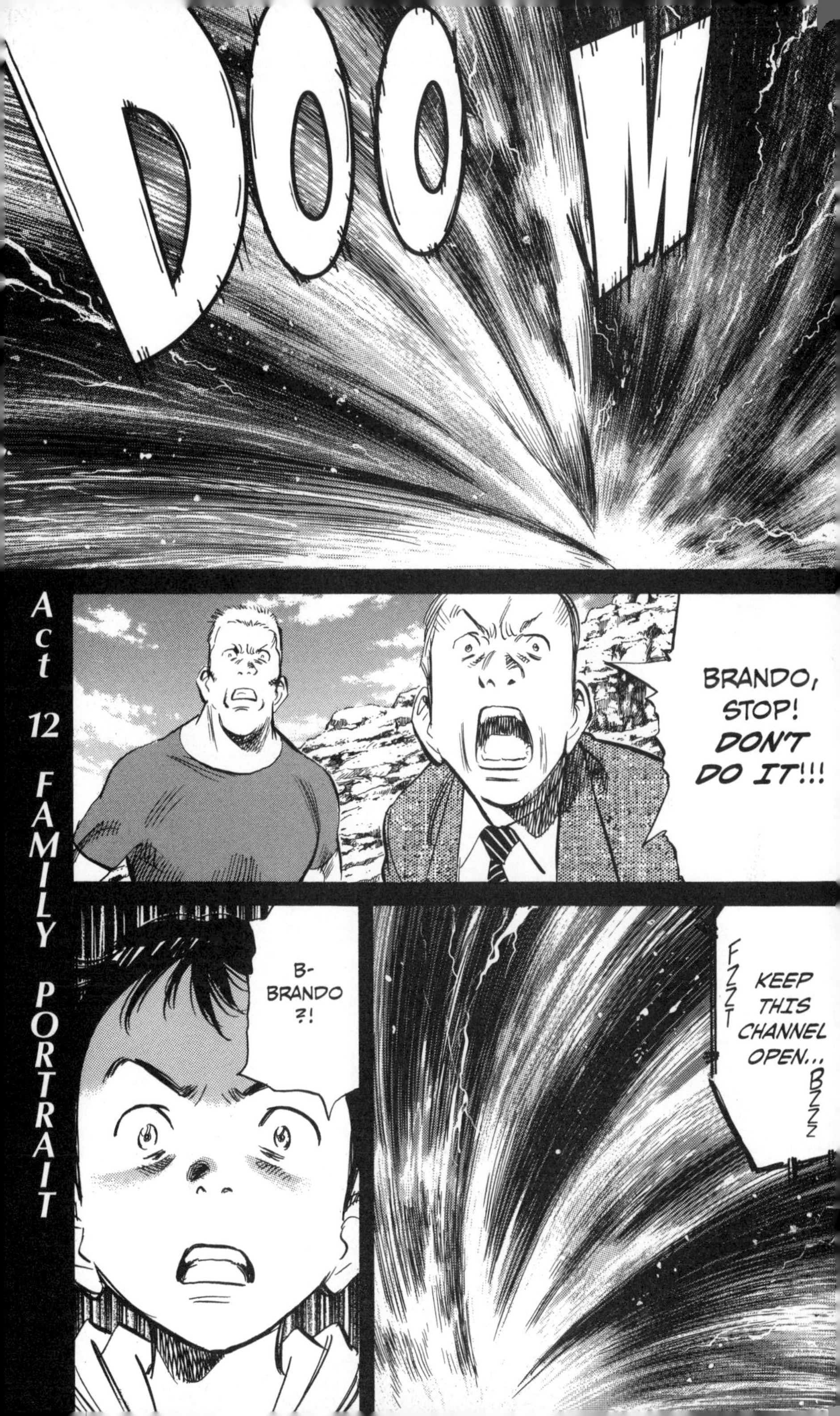
DOOOM
BRANDO, STOP! DON'T DO IT!!!
FZZT
KEEP THIS CHANNEL OPEN...
BZZZ
B-BRANDO?!

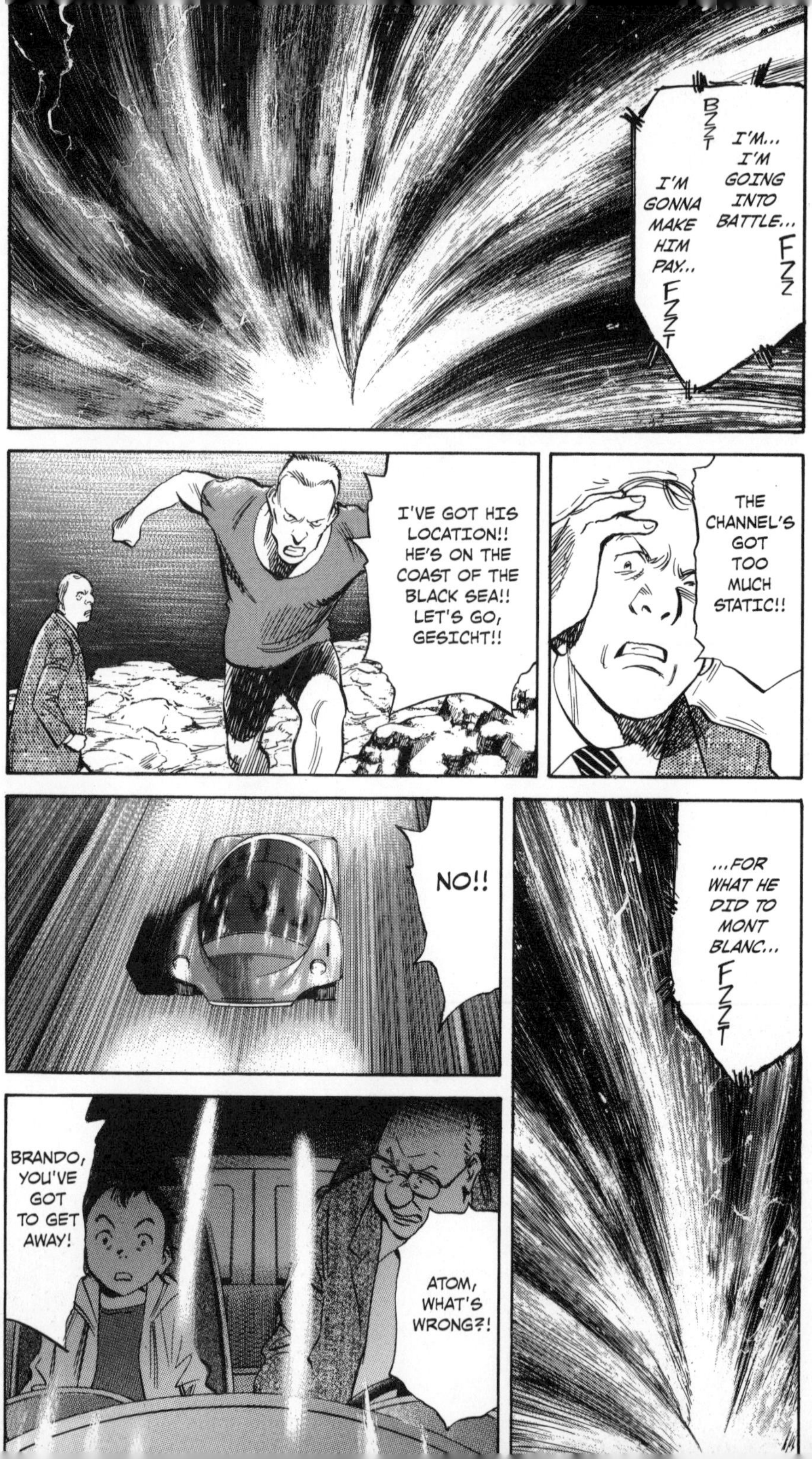
BZZT
I'M... I'M GOING INTO BATTLE...
FZZ
I'M GONNA MAKE HIM PAY...
FZZT
THE CHANNEL'S GOT TOO MUCH STATIC!!
I'VE GOT HIS LOCATION!! HE'S ON THE COAST OF THE BLACK SEA!! LET'S GO, GESICHT!!
...FOR WHAT HE DID TO MONT BLANC...
FZZT
NO!!
BRANDO, YOU'VE GOT TO GET AWAY!
ATOM, WHAT'S WRONG?!

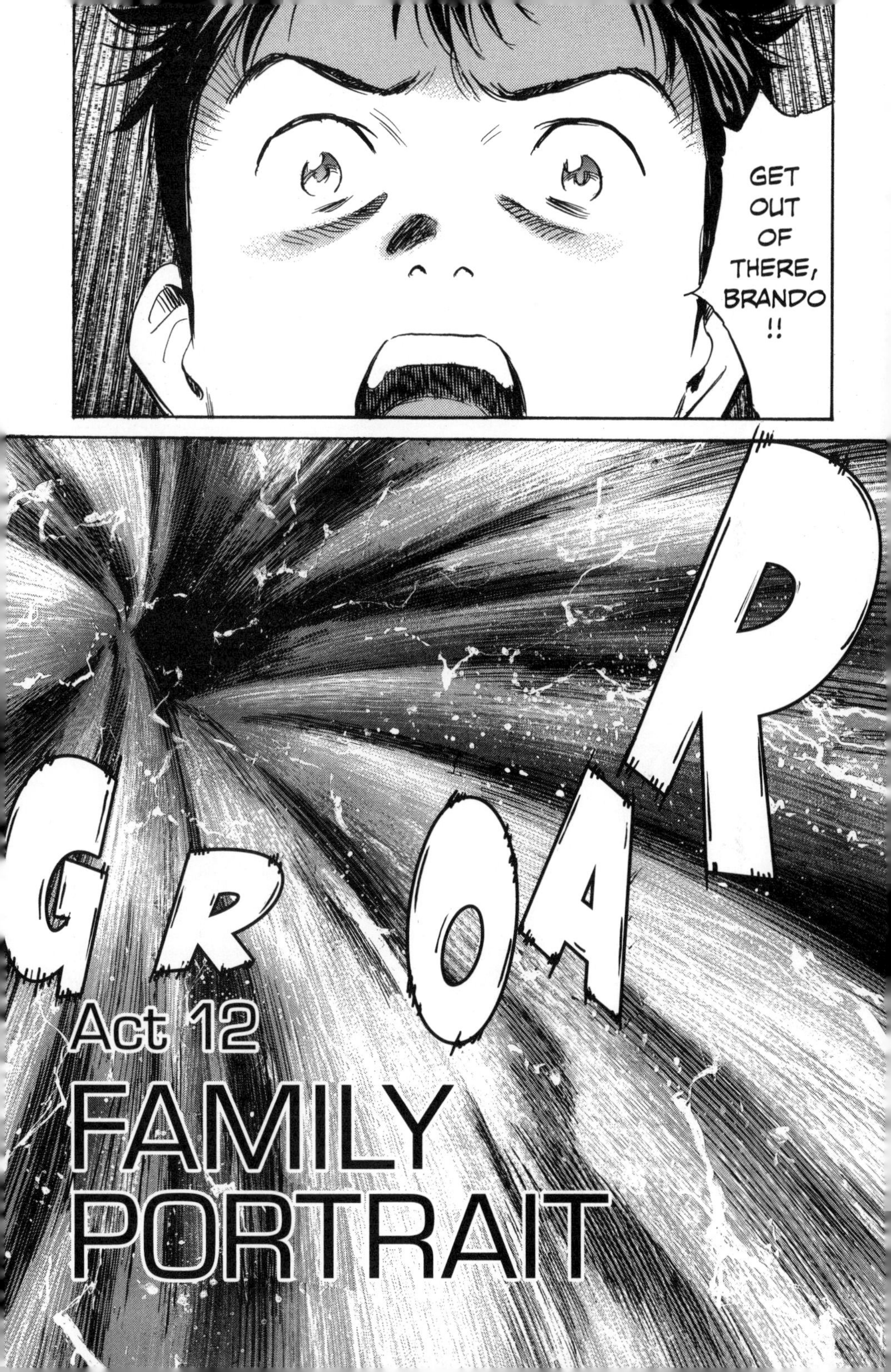
GET OUT OF THERE, BRANDO!!
GROAR

Act 12
FAMILY PORTRAIT

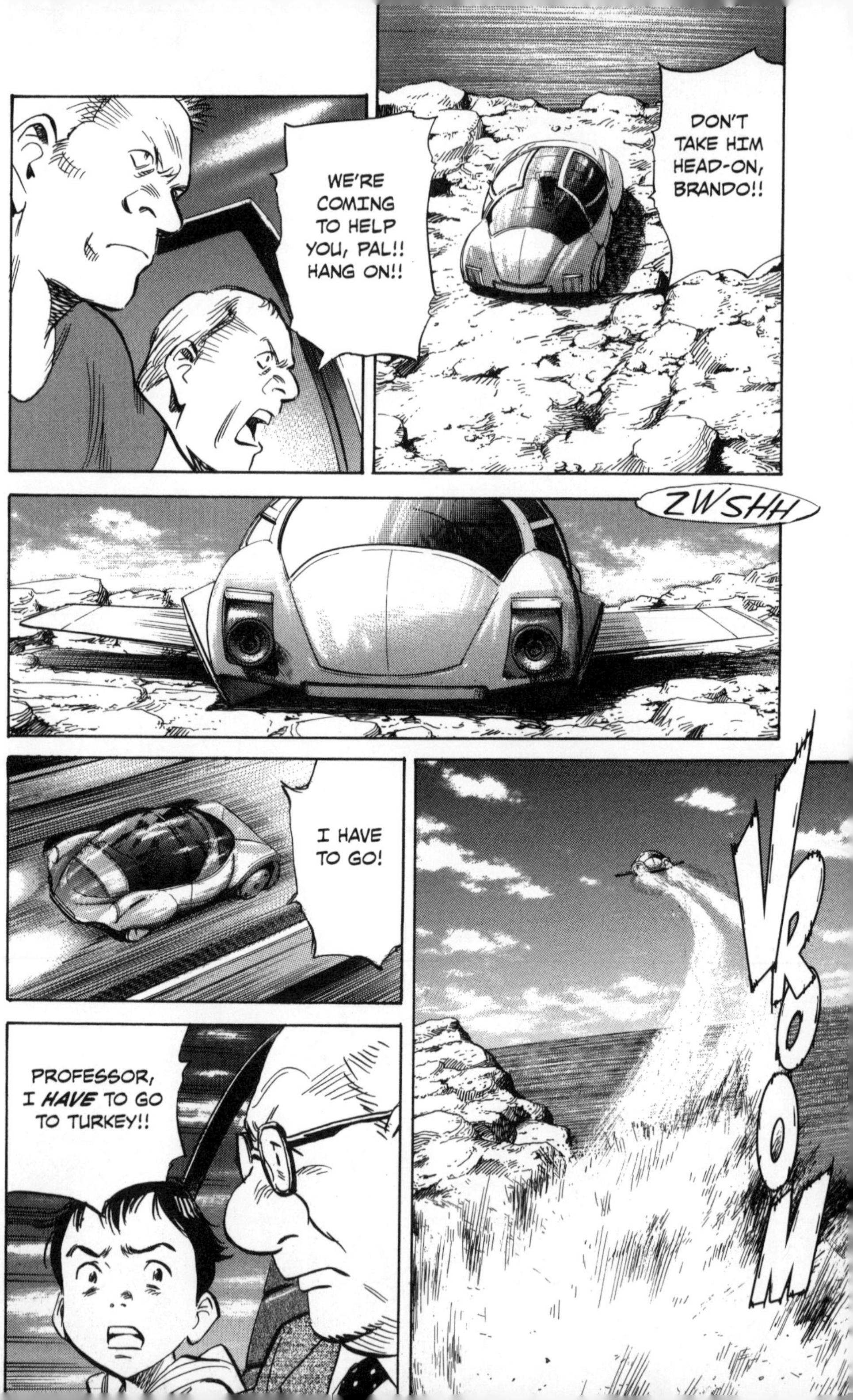
DON'T TAKE HIM HEAD-ON, BRANDO!!
WE'RE COMING TO HELP YOU, PAL!! HANG ON!!
ZWSHH
VROOM
I HAVE TO GO!
PROFESSOR, I *HAVE* TO GO TO TURKEY!!

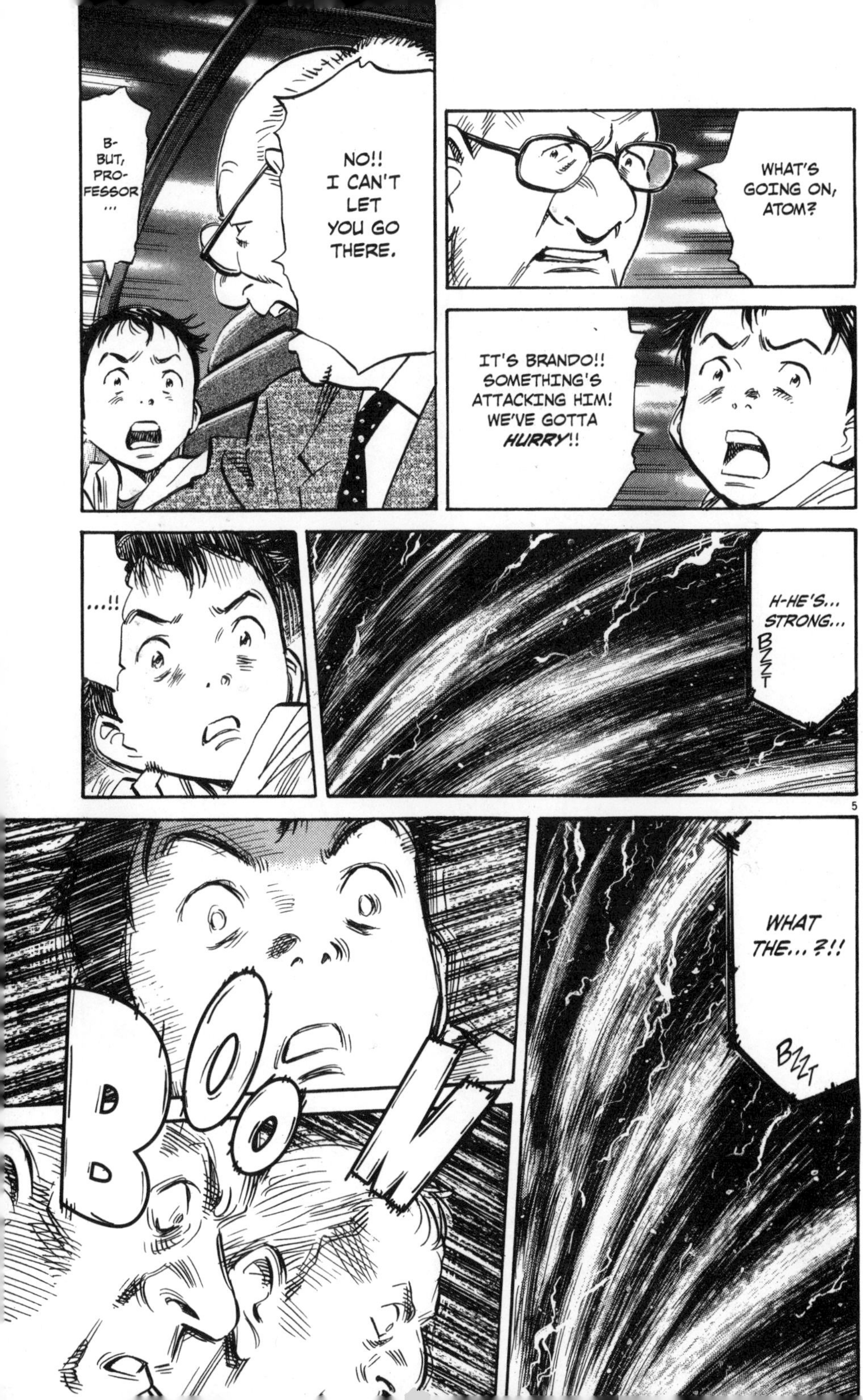
WHAT'S GOING ON, ATOM?
IT'S BRANDO!! SOMETHING'S ATTACKING HIM! WE'VE GOTTA *HURRY*!!
NO!! I CAN'T LET YOU GO THERE.
B-BUT, PRO-FESSOR...
H-HE'S... STRONG...
BZZT
...!!
WHAT THE...?!!
BZZT
BOOOM

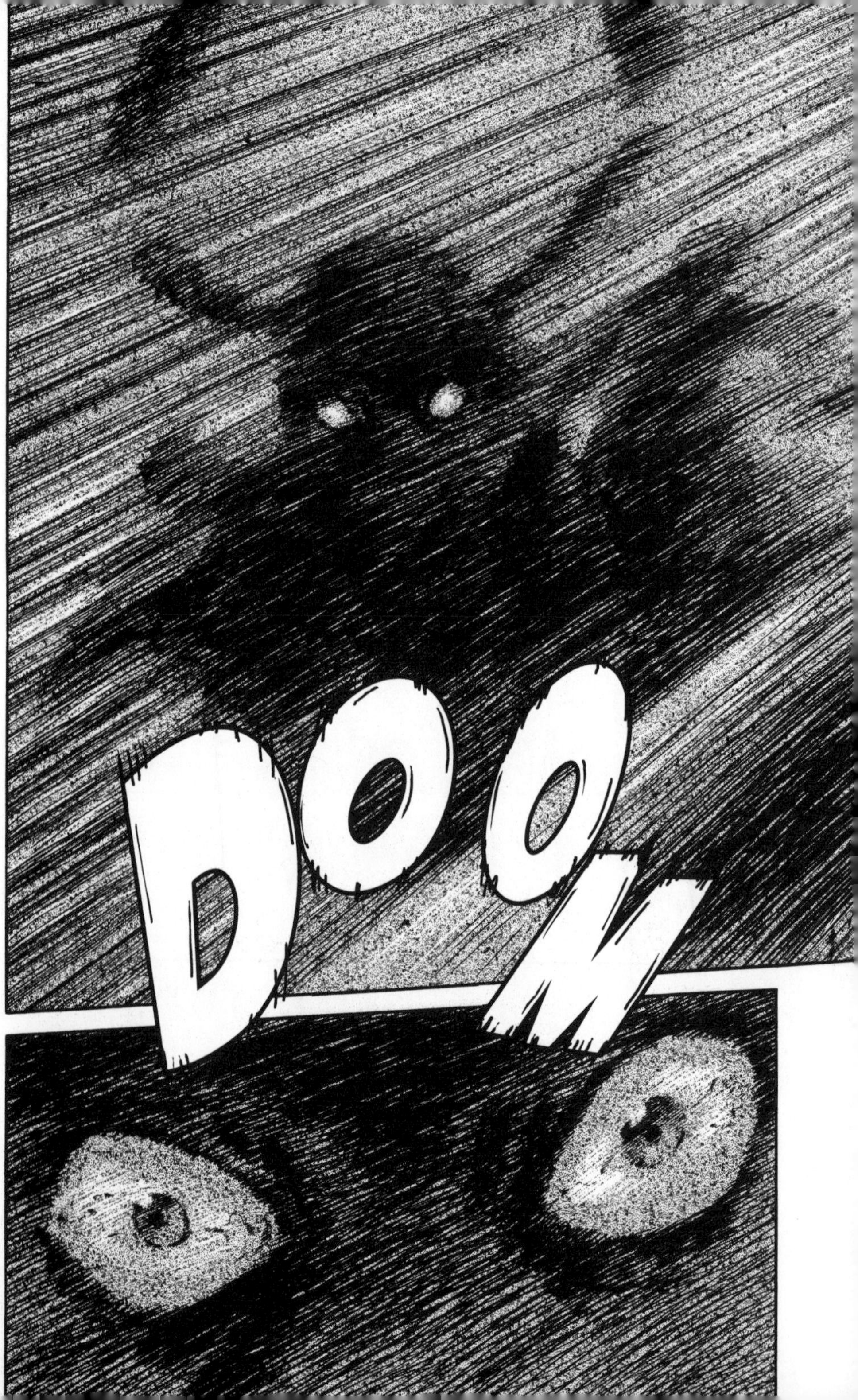
DOOM

WHAT *WAS* THAT?!

ATOM! WHAT'S HAPPENING?!!

WH- WHAT WAS THAT?!

BRANDO...

BRANDO! COME IN!!

BRANDO?!

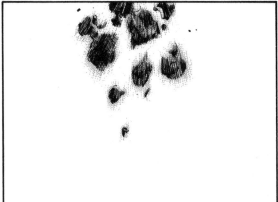

BRANDO!! ARE YOU THERE?!!

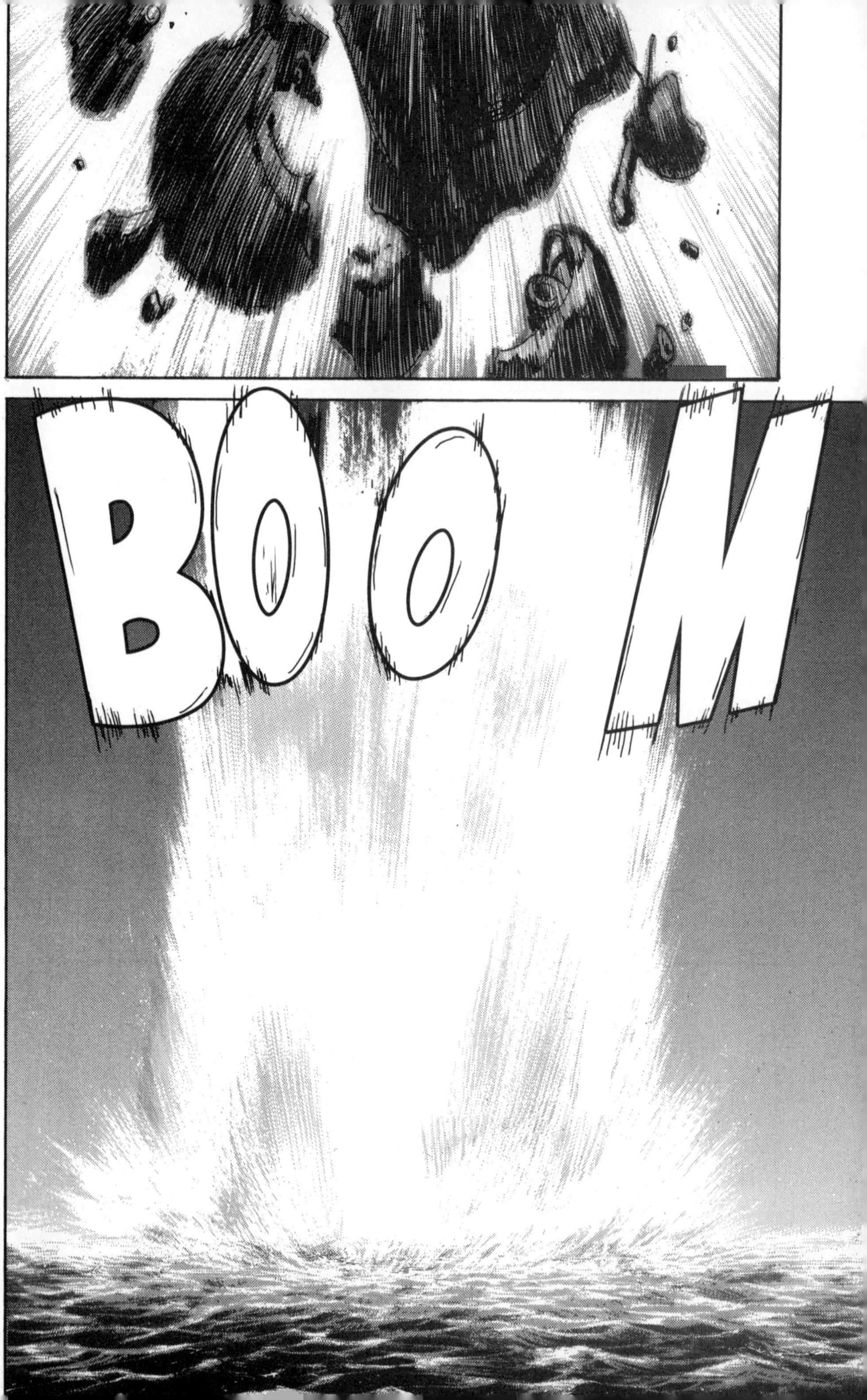
BOOOM

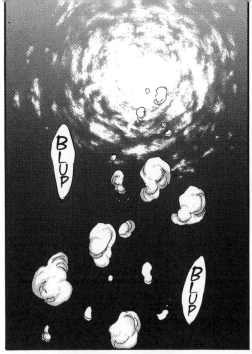

BLUP

BLUP

?!

THE SEA ...?

BRANDO!!

!!

I DID IT, GUYS... I BEAT HIM...

BRANDO!!

I DID IT...

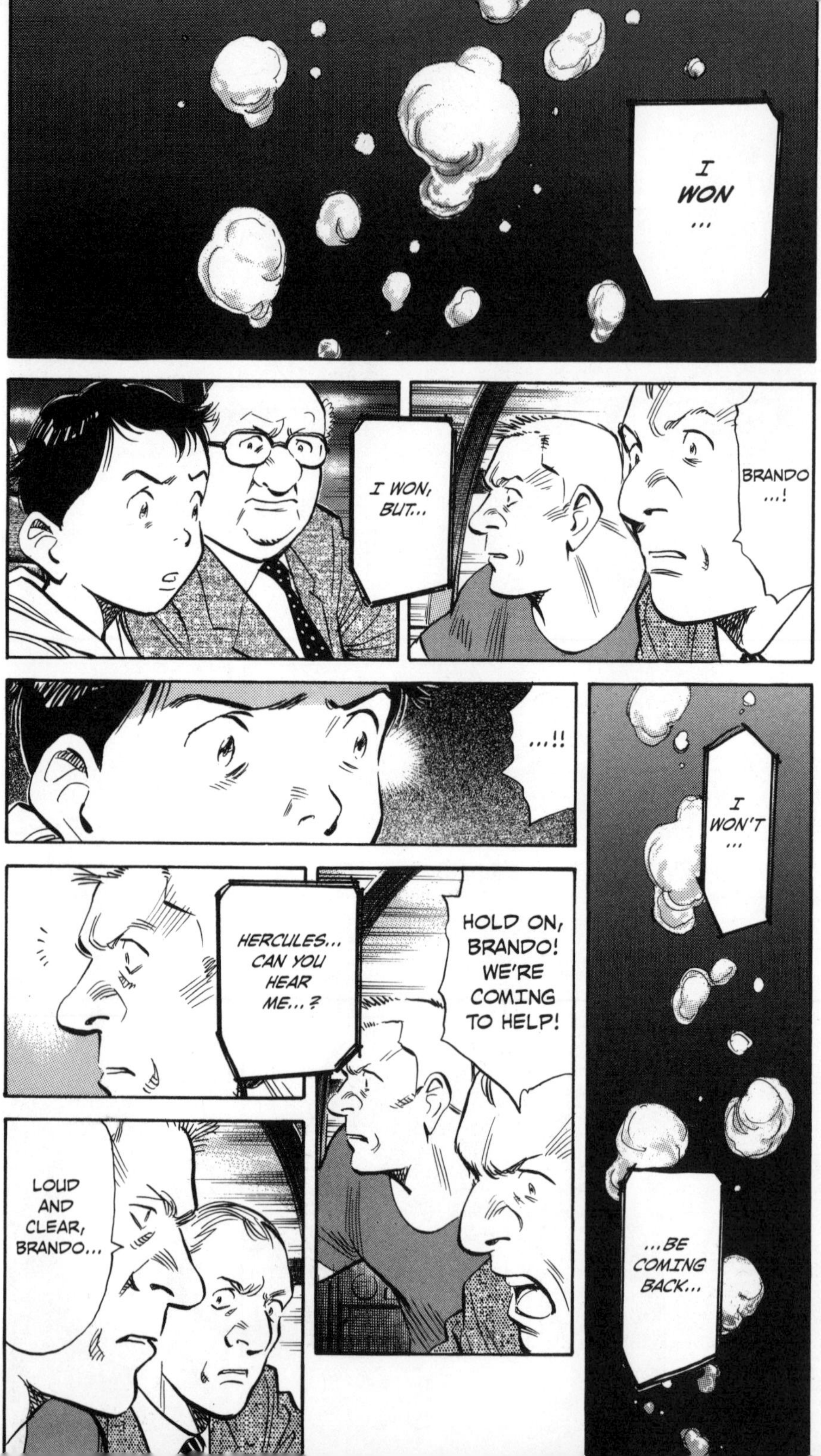
I WON...
BRANDO...!
I WON, BUT...
I WON'T...
...BE COMING BACK...
...!!
HOLD ON, BRANDO! WE'RE COMING TO HELP!
HERCULES... CAN YOU HEAR ME...?
LOUD AND CLEAR, BRANDO...

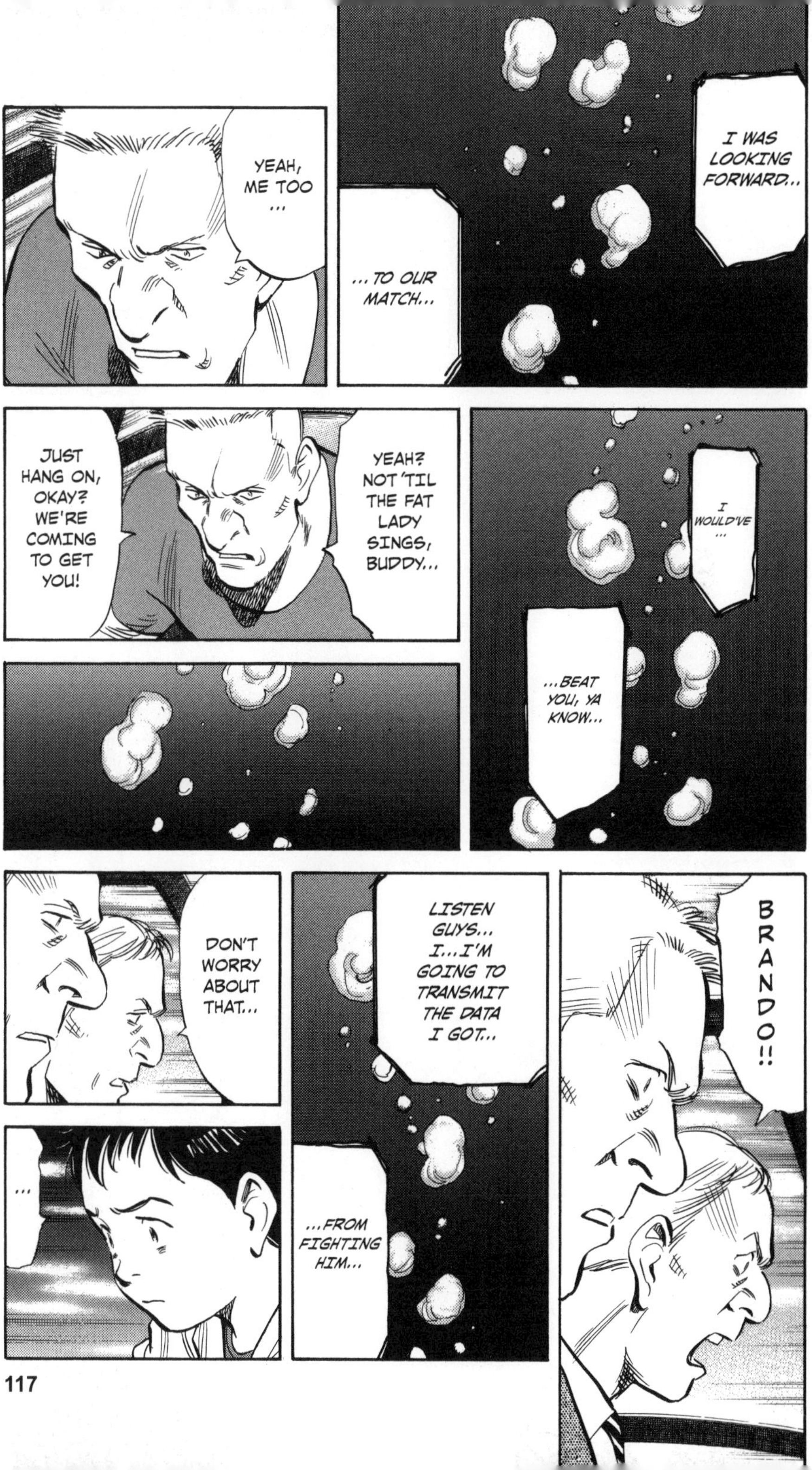
I WAS LOOKING FORWARD...
...TO OUR MATCH...
YEAH, ME TOO ...
I WOULD'VE ...
...BEAT YOU, YA KNOW...
YEAH? NOT 'TIL THE FAT LADY SINGS, BUDDY...
JUST HANG ON, OKAY? WE'RE COMING TO GET YOU!
BRANDO!!
LISTEN GUYS... I...I'M GOING TO TRANSMIT THE DATA I GOT...
...FROM FIGHTING HIM...
DON'T WORRY ABOUT THAT...
...

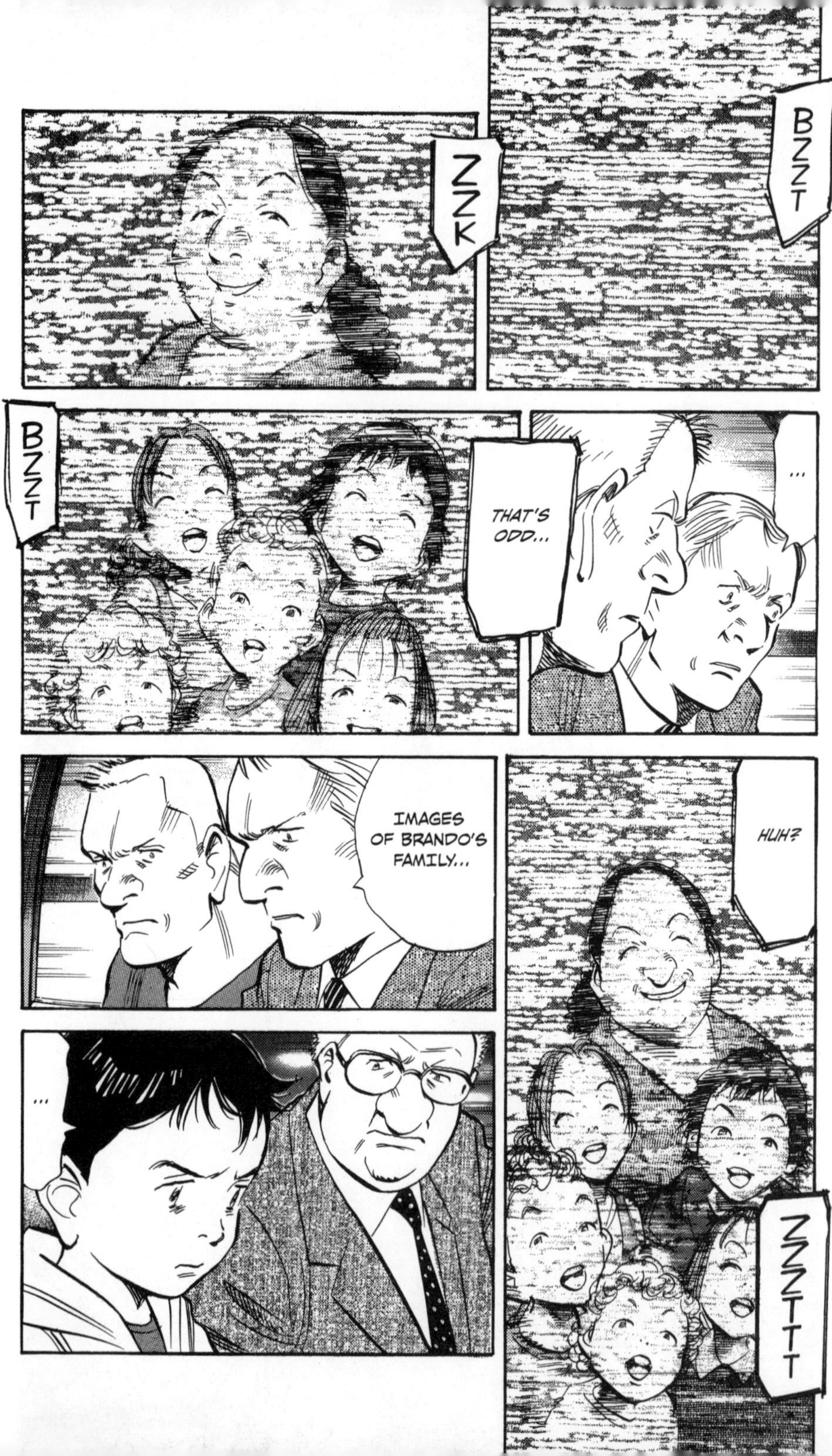
BZZT
ZZK
...
THAT'S ODD...
BZZT
HUH?
ZZZTTT
IMAGES OF BRANDO'S FAMILY...
...

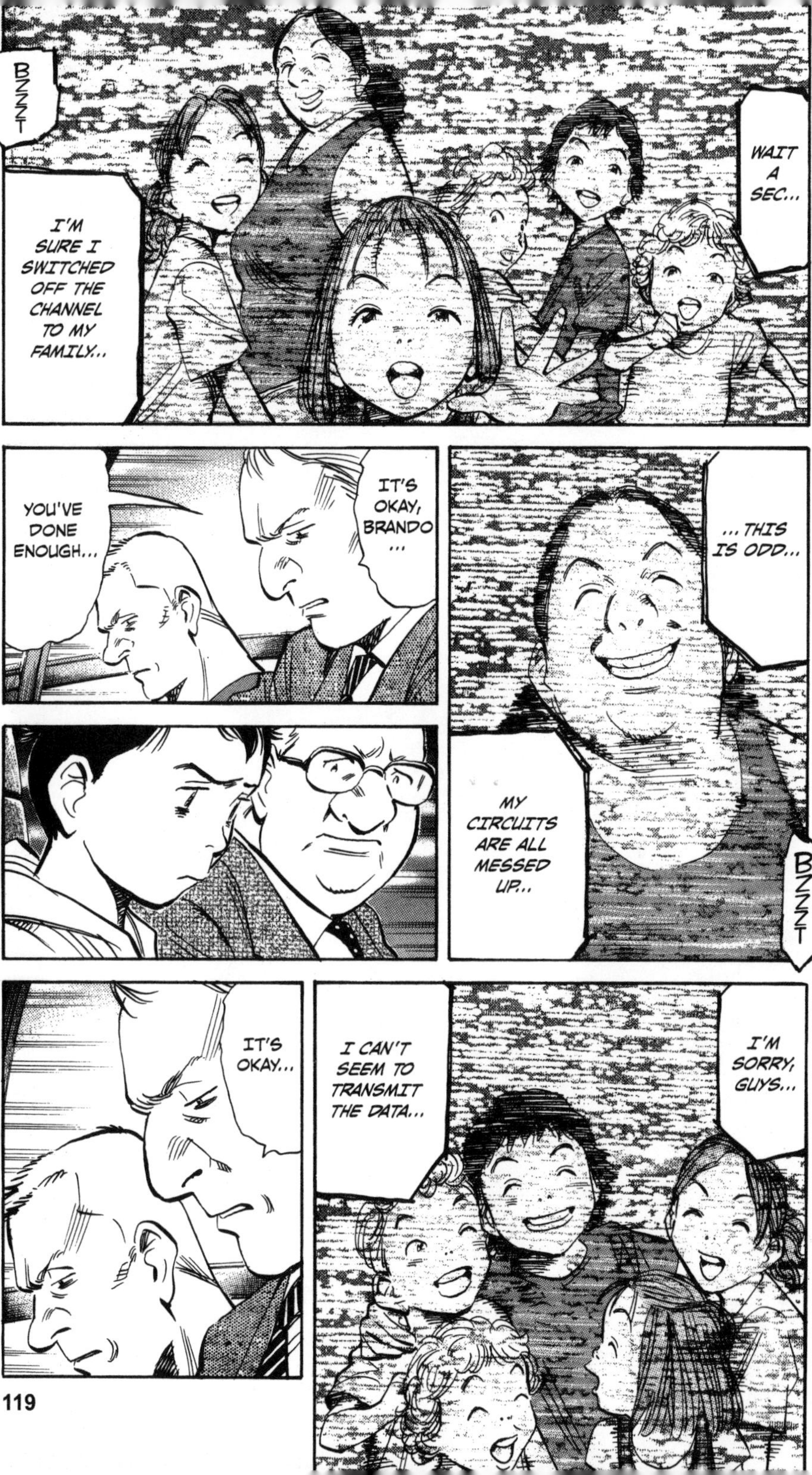
WAIT A SEC...
BZZZT
I'M SURE I SWITCHED OFF THE CHANNEL TO MY FAMILY...
...THIS IS ODD...
MY CIRCUITS ARE ALL MESSED UP...
BZZZT
IT'S OKAY, BRANDO...
YOU'VE DONE ENOUGH...
I'M SORRY, GUYS...
I CAN'T SEEM TO TRANSMIT THE DATA...
IT'S OKAY...

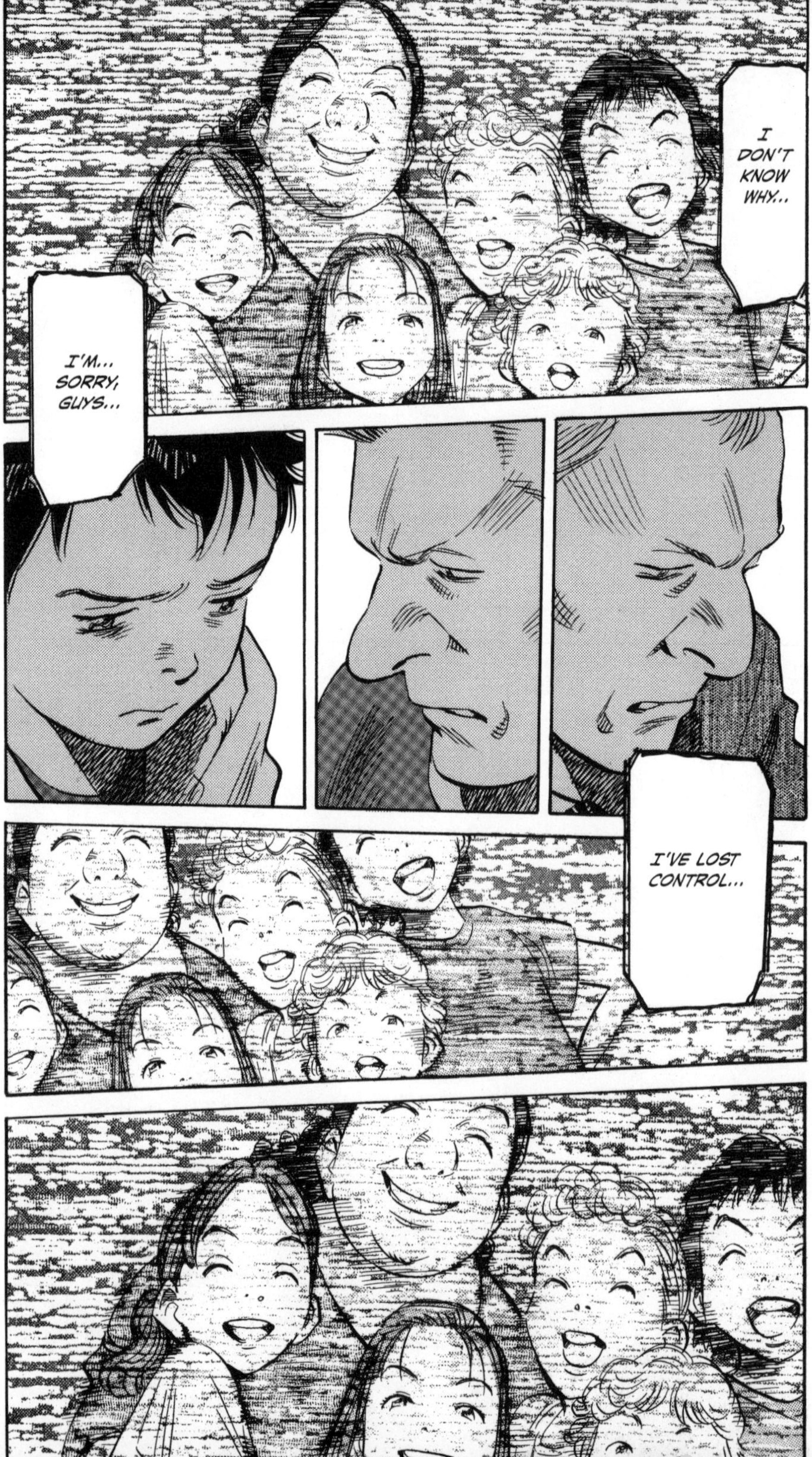
I DON'T KNOW WHY...
I'M... SORRY, GUYS...
I'VE LOST CONTROL...

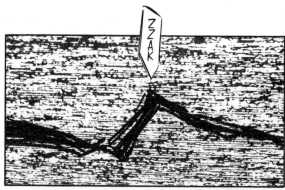

BRANDO...

...

?

YES...

INSPECTOR GESICHT...

BRANDO!!

I TOLD YOU I'M A LUCKY MAN...

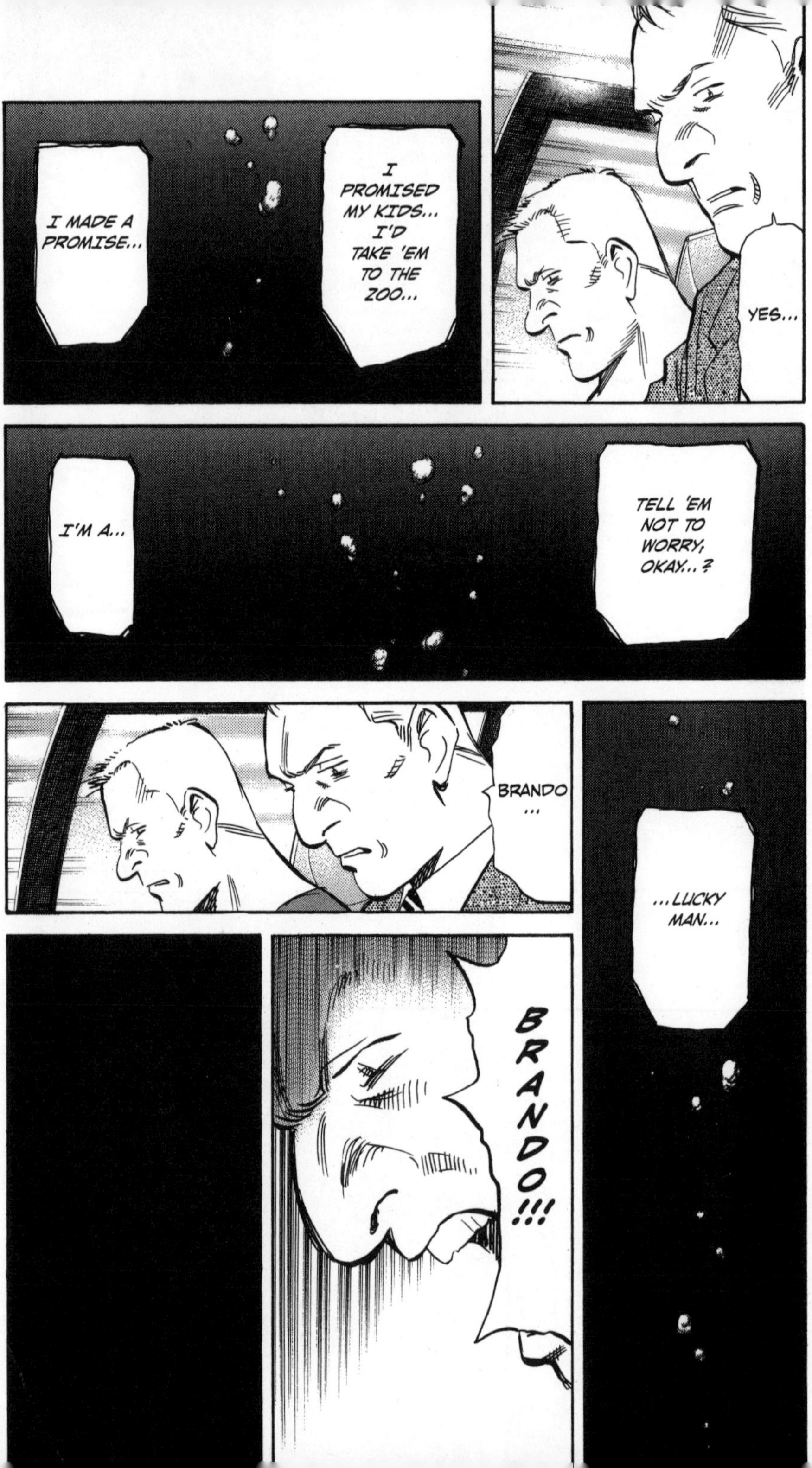
YES...
I PROMISED MY KIDS... I'D TAKE 'EM TO THE ZOO...
I MADE A PROMISE...
TELL 'EM NOT TO WORRY, OKAY...?
I'M A...
...LUCKY MAN...
BRANDO ...
BRANDOO!!!

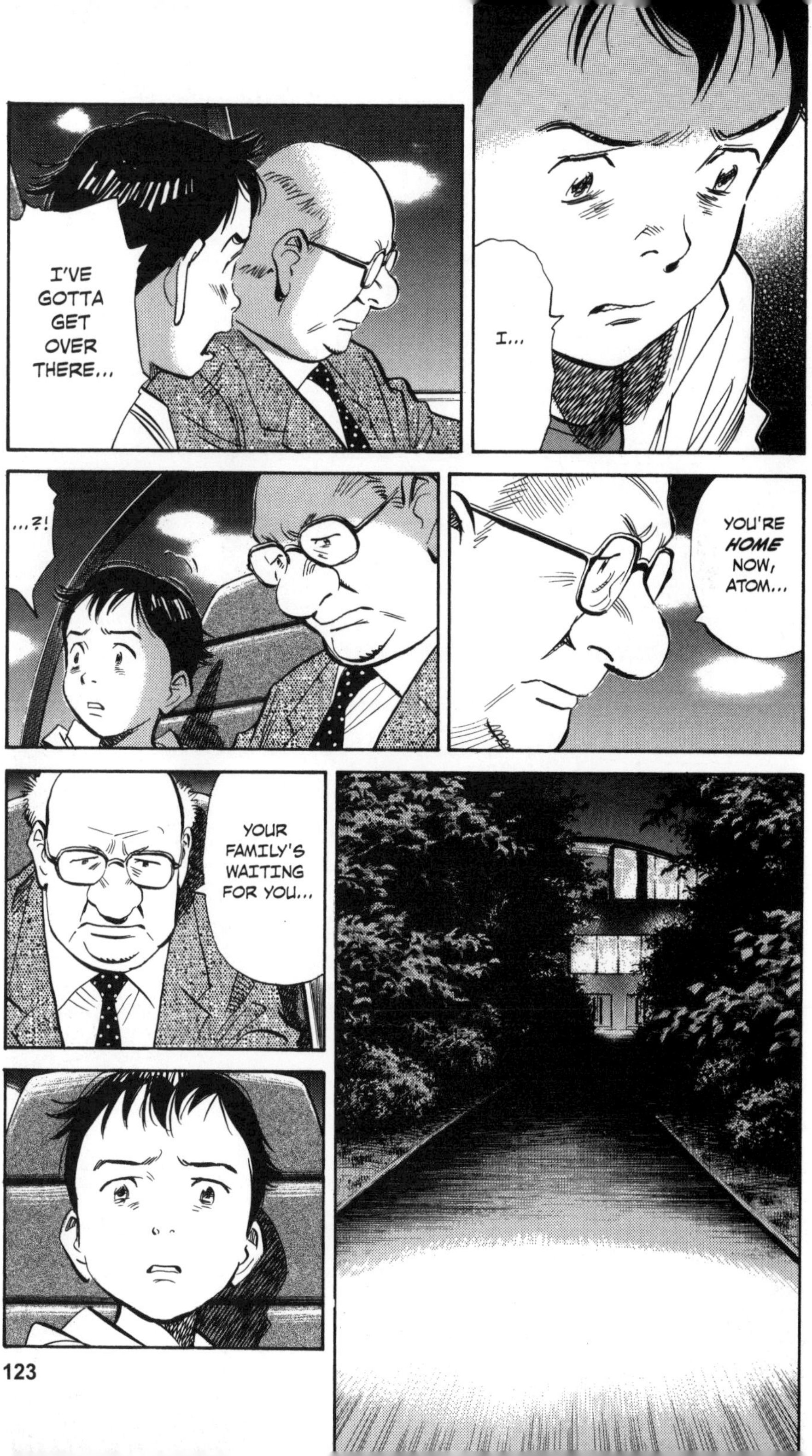
I...
I'VE GOTTA GET OVER THERE...
YOU'RE *HOME* NOW, ATOM...
...?!
YOUR FAMILY'S WAITING FOR YOU...

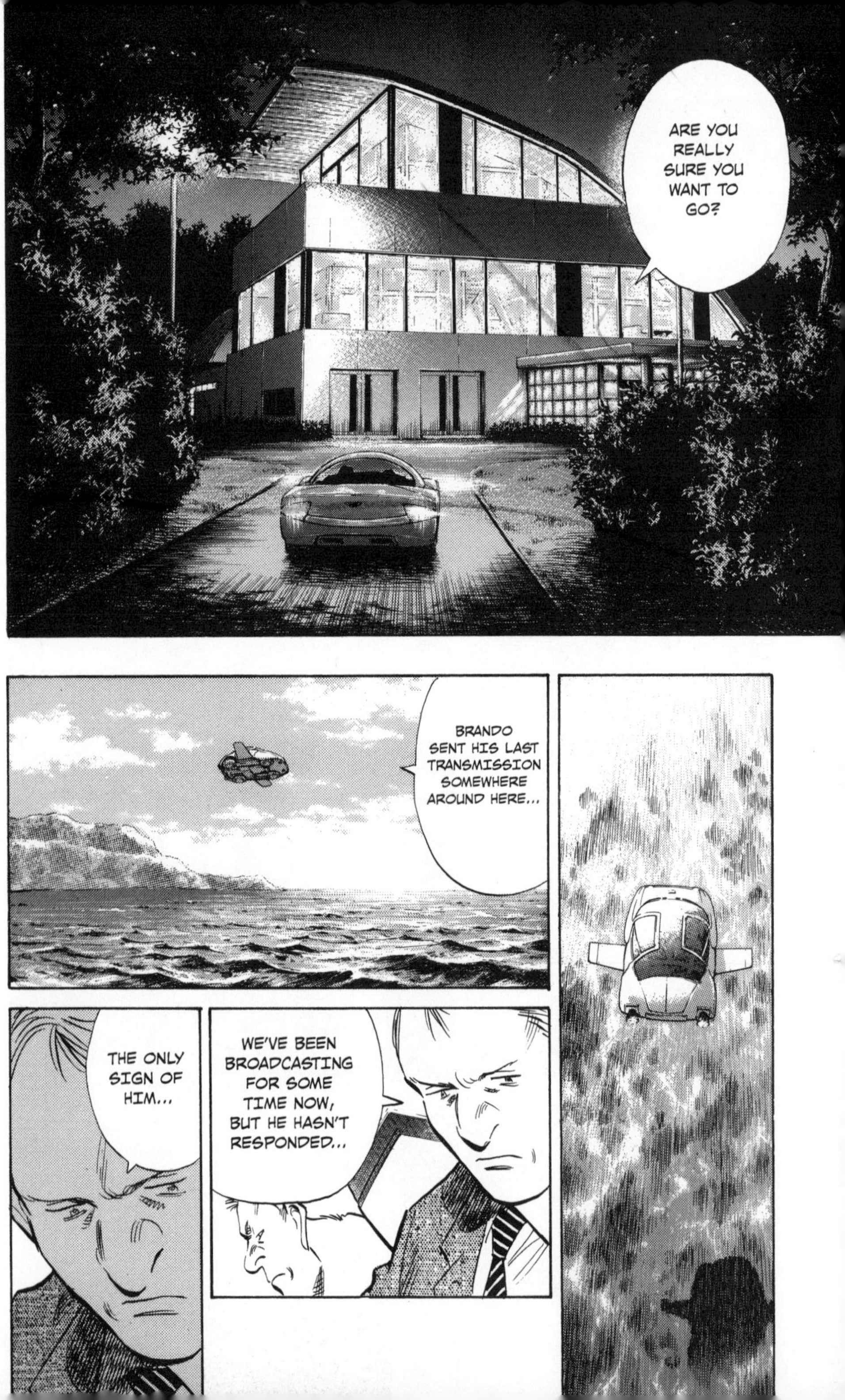
ARE YOU REALLY SURE YOU WANT TO GO?
BRANDO SENT HIS LAST TRANSMISSION SOMEWHERE AROUND HERE...
WE'VE BEEN BROADCASTING FOR SOME TIME NOW, BUT HE HASN'T RESPONDED...
THE ONLY SIGN OF HIM...

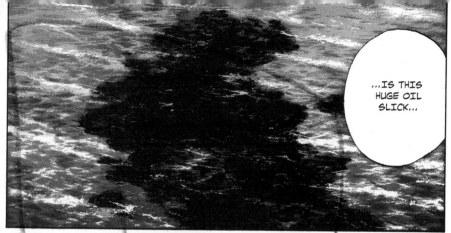

...IS THIS HUGE OIL SLICK...

...SHOW ONLY SHARDS OF WRECKAGE ON THE SEA FLOOR... I WONDER IF...

BOTTOM SCANS...

...PARTS OF HIS OPPONENT ARE DOWN THERE TOO...

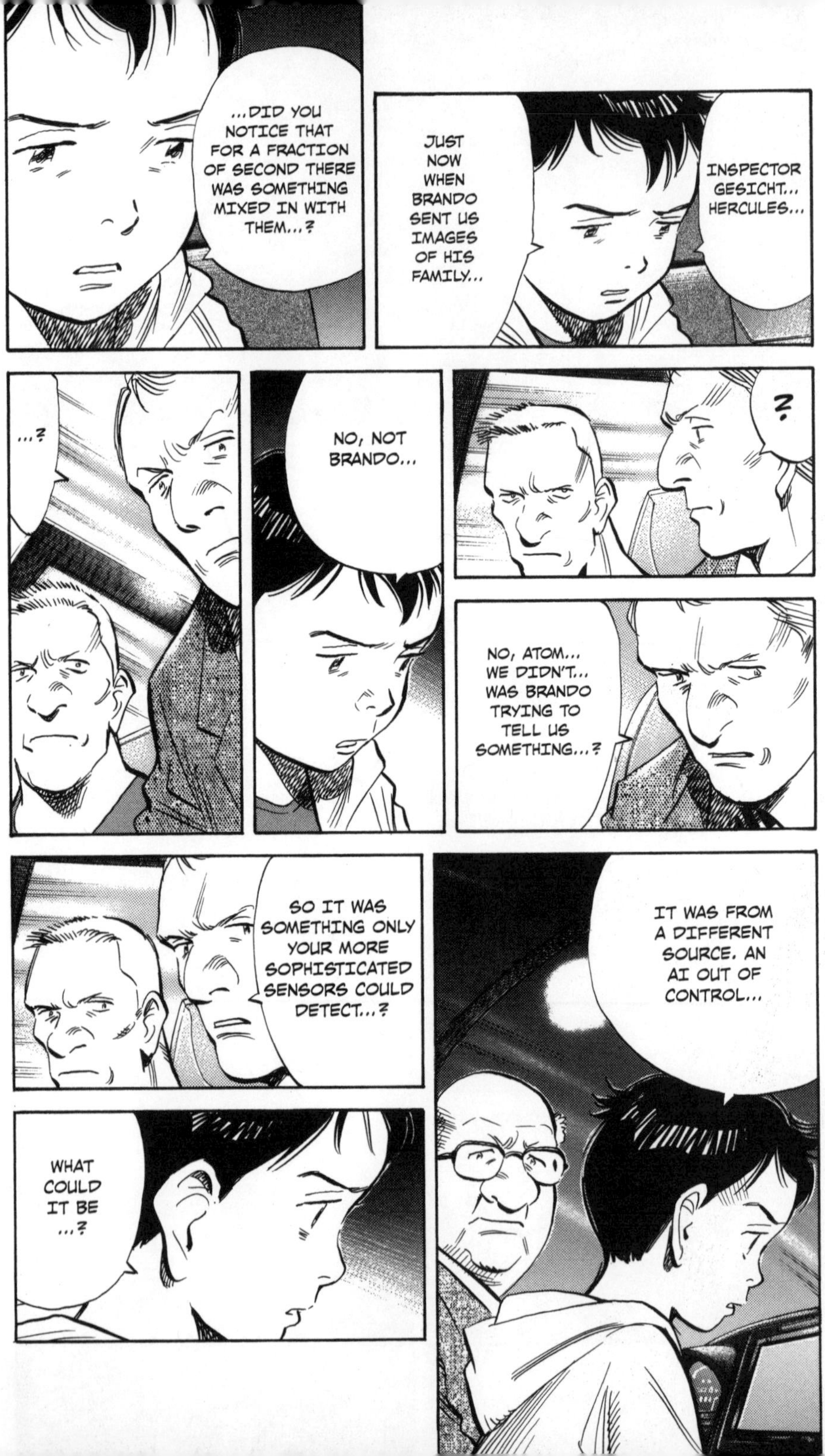
INSPECTOR GESICHT... HERCULES...
JUST NOW WHEN BRANDO SENT US IMAGES OF HIS FAMILY...
...DID YOU NOTICE THAT FOR A FRACTION OF SECOND THERE WAS SOMETHING MIXED IN WITH THEM...?
?
NO, ATOM... WE DIDN'T... WAS BRANDO TRYING TO TELL US SOMETHING...?
NO, NOT BRANDO...
...?
IT WAS FROM A DIFFERENT SOURCE. AN AI OUT OF CONTROL...
SO IT WAS SOMETHING ONLY YOUR MORE SOPHISTICATED SENSORS COULD DETECT...?
WHAT COULD IT BE ...?

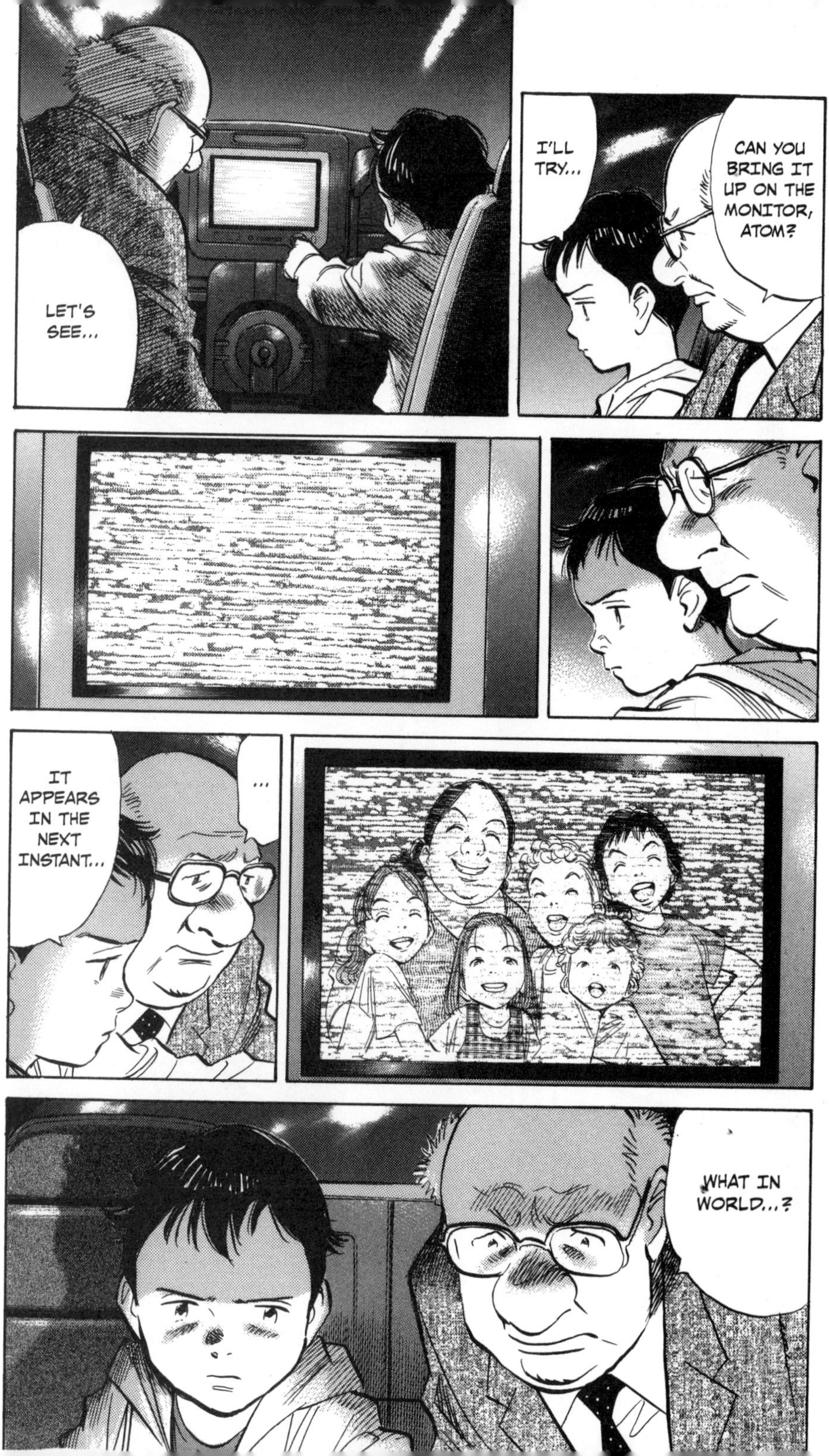
CAN YOU BRING IT UP ON THE MONITOR, ATOM?
I'LL TRY...
LET'S SEE...
...
IT APPEARS IN THE NEXT INSTANT...
WHAT IN WORLD...?

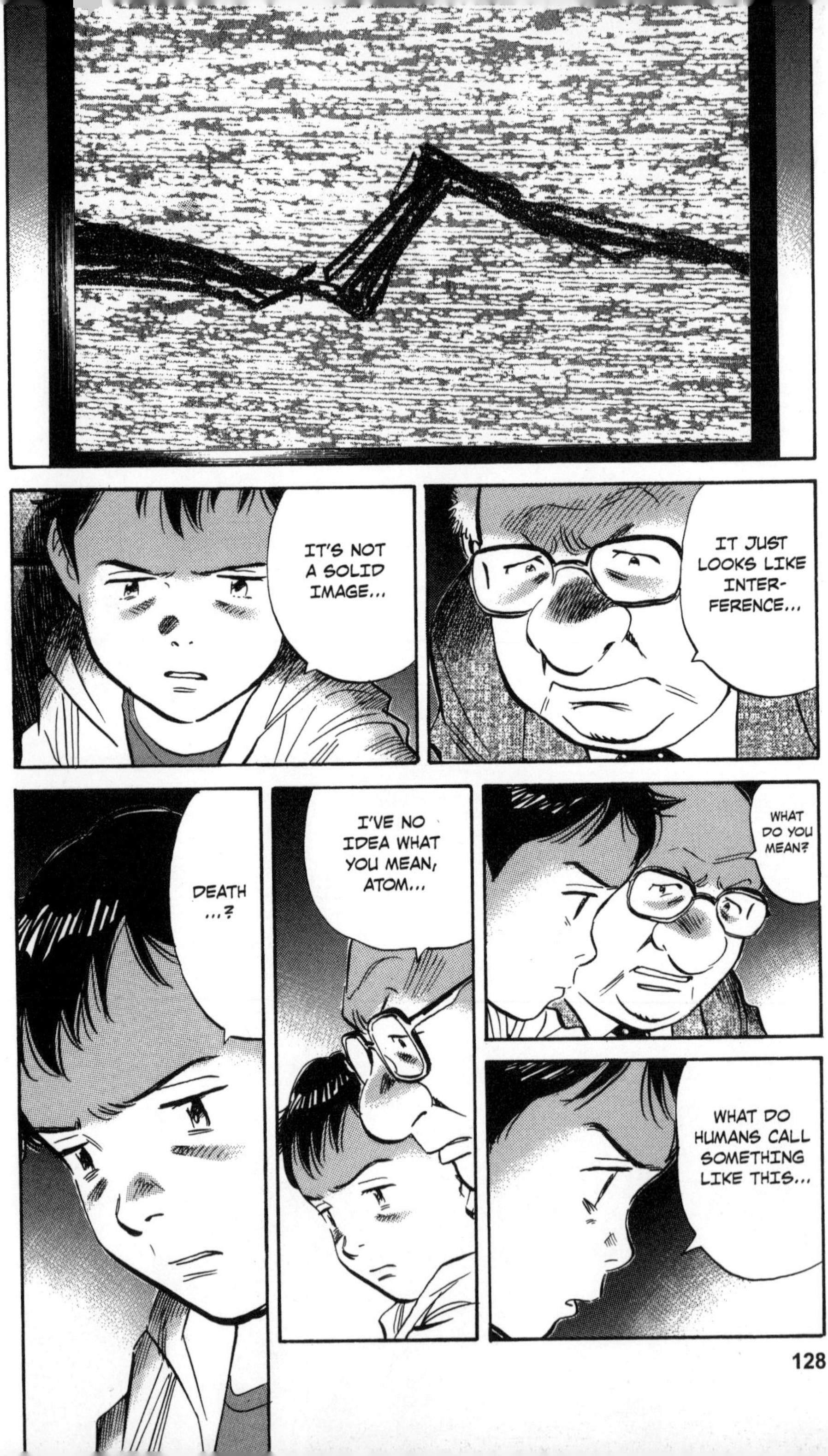
IT JUST LOOKS LIKE INTER-FERENCE...
IT'S NOT A SOLID IMAGE...
WHAT DO YOU MEAN?
WHAT DO HUMANS CALL SOMETHING LIKE THIS...
I'VE NO IDEA WHAT YOU MEAN, ATOM...
DEATH...?

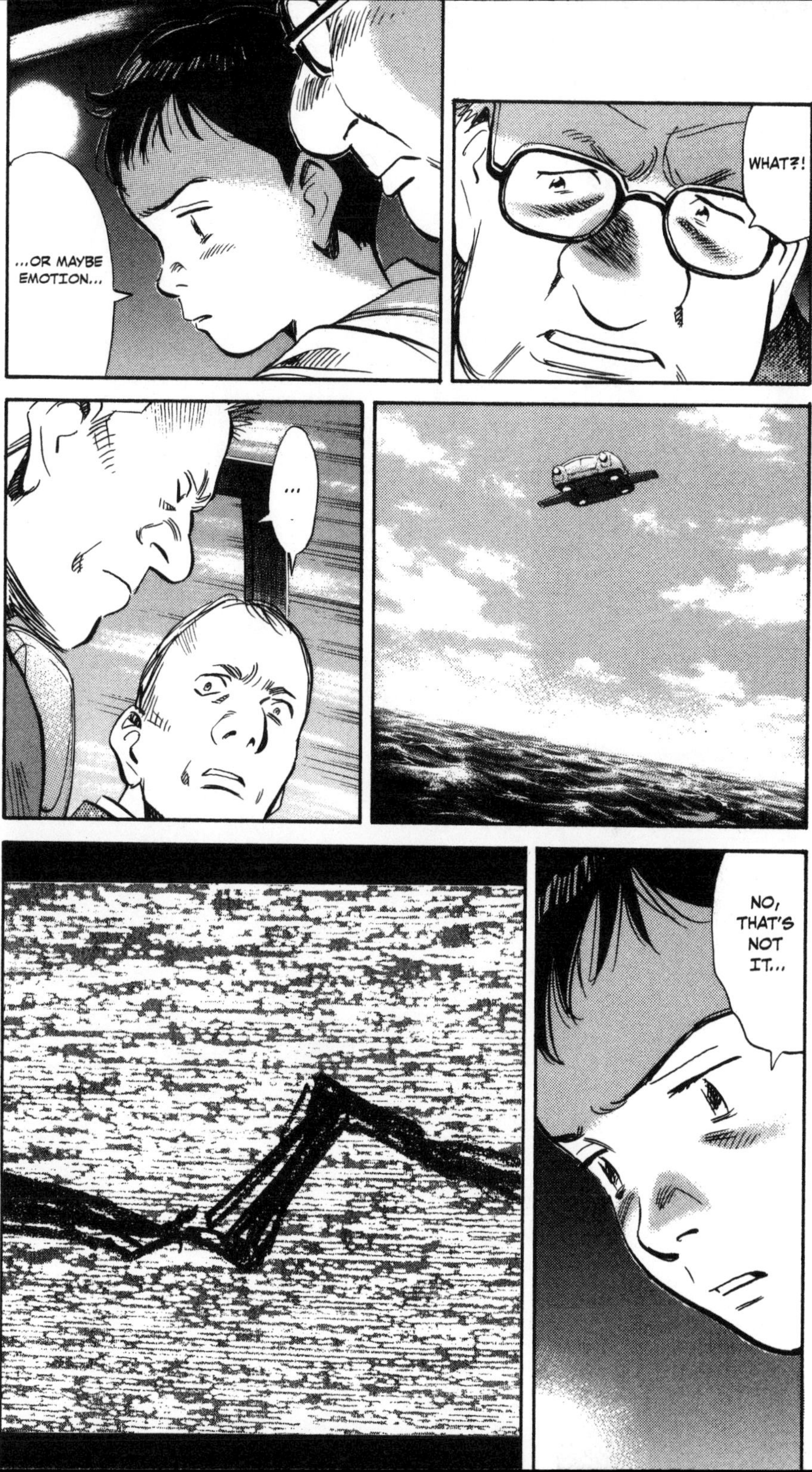
...OR MAYBE EMOTION...
WHAT?!
...
NO, THAT'S NOT IT...

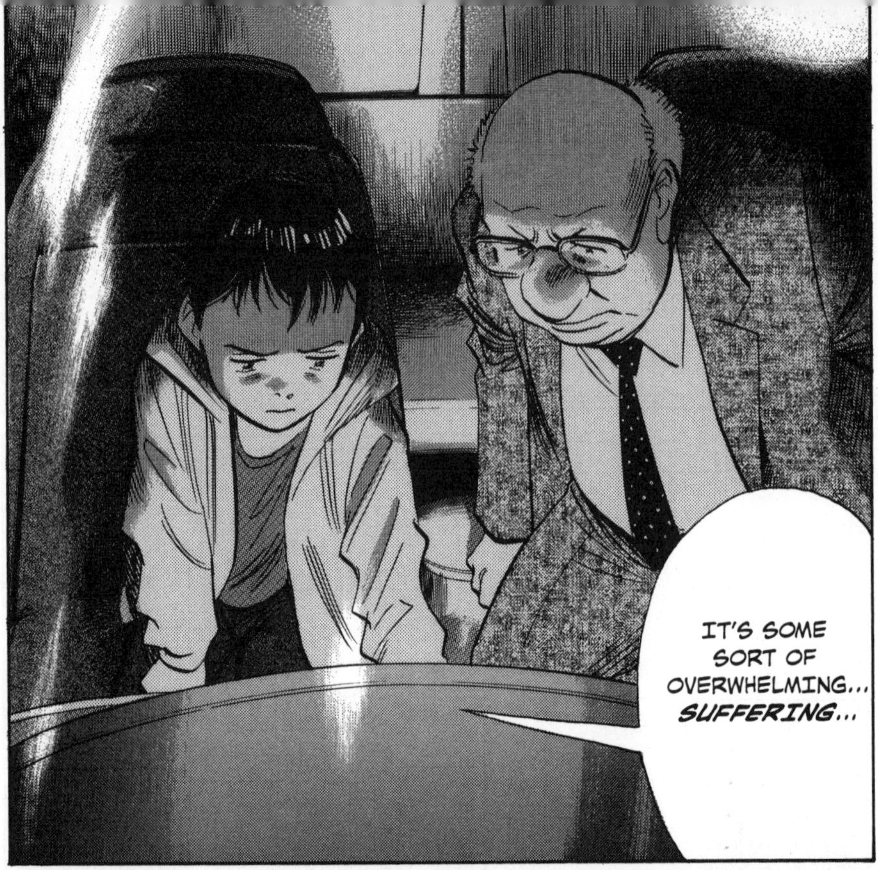
IT'S SOME SORT OF OVERWHELMING... *SUFFERING*...
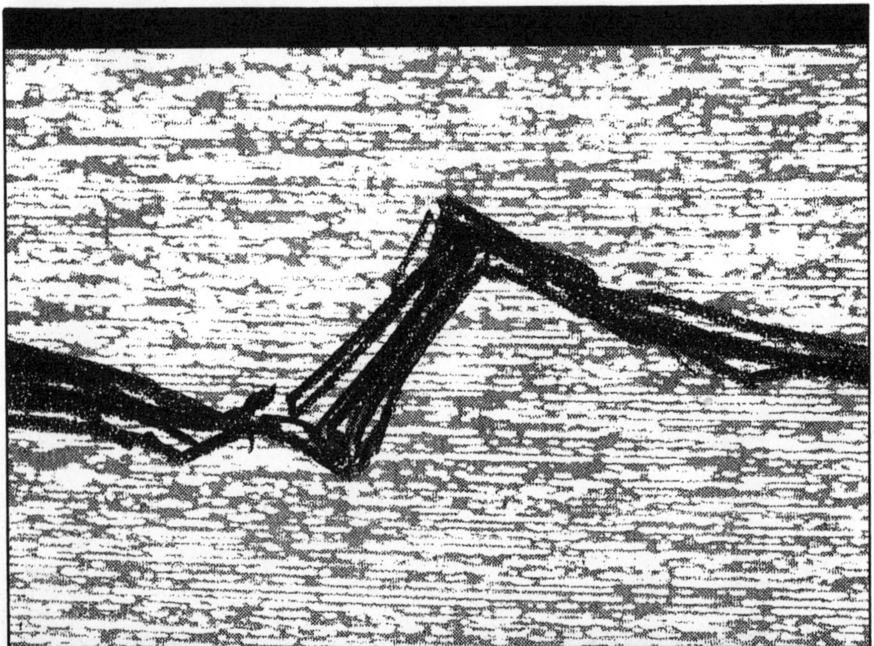

Act 13 FALSE MEMORY

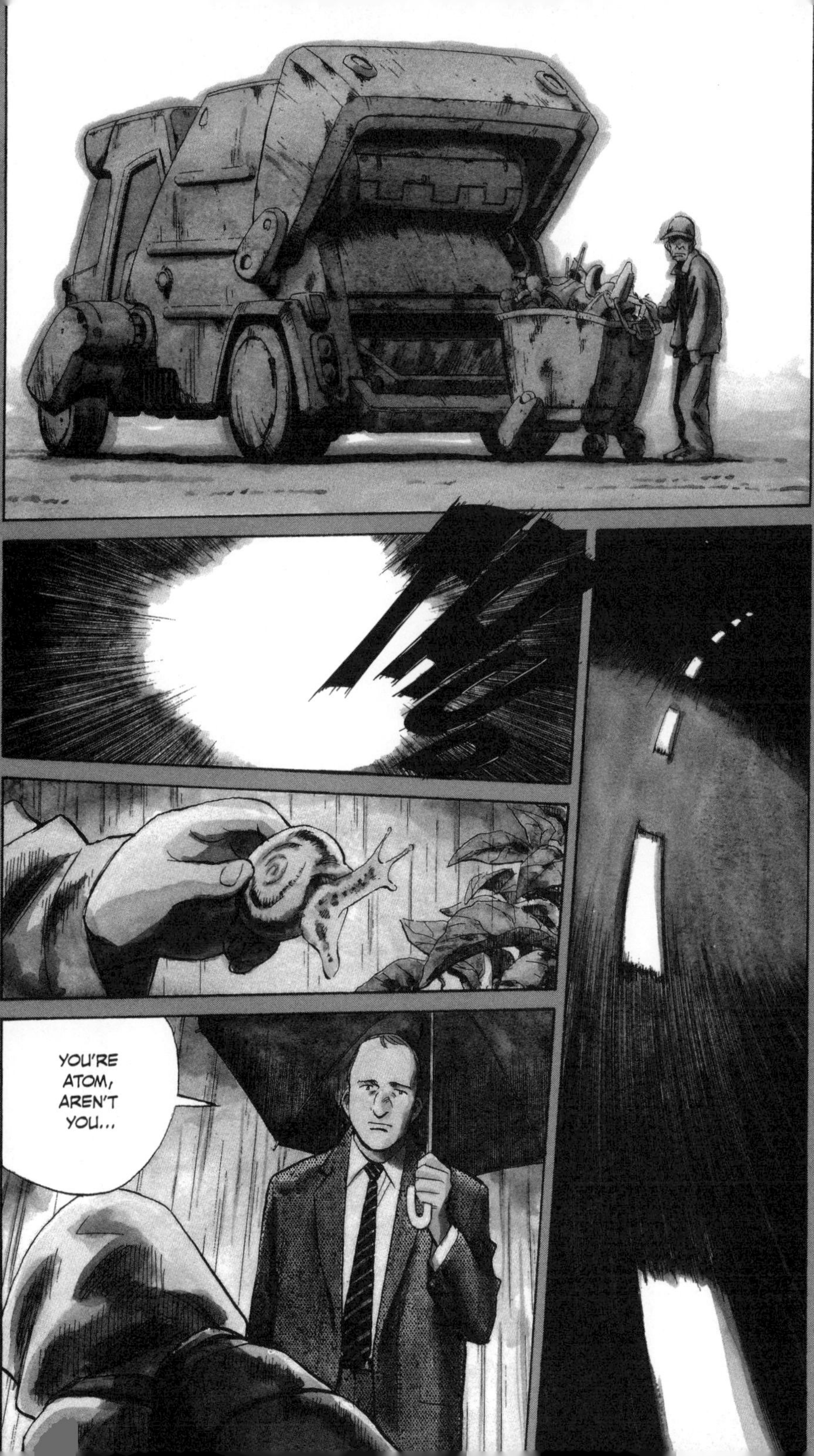
YOU'RE ATOM, AREN'T YOU...

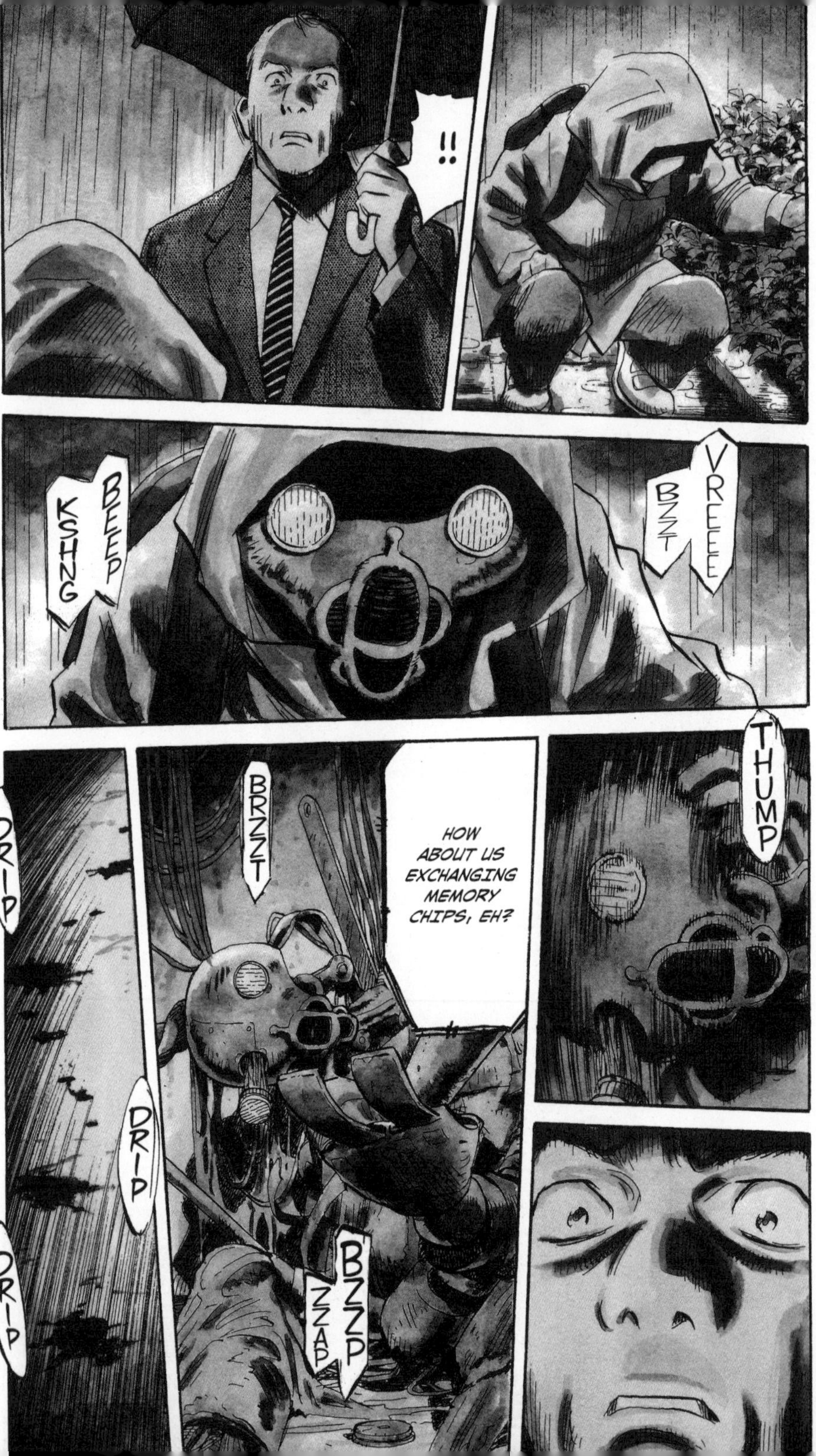
!!
VREEEE
BZZT
BEEP
KSHNG
THUMP
HOW ABOUT US EXCHANGING MEMORY CHIPS, EH?
BRZZT
BZZP
ZZAP
DRIP
DRIP
DRIP

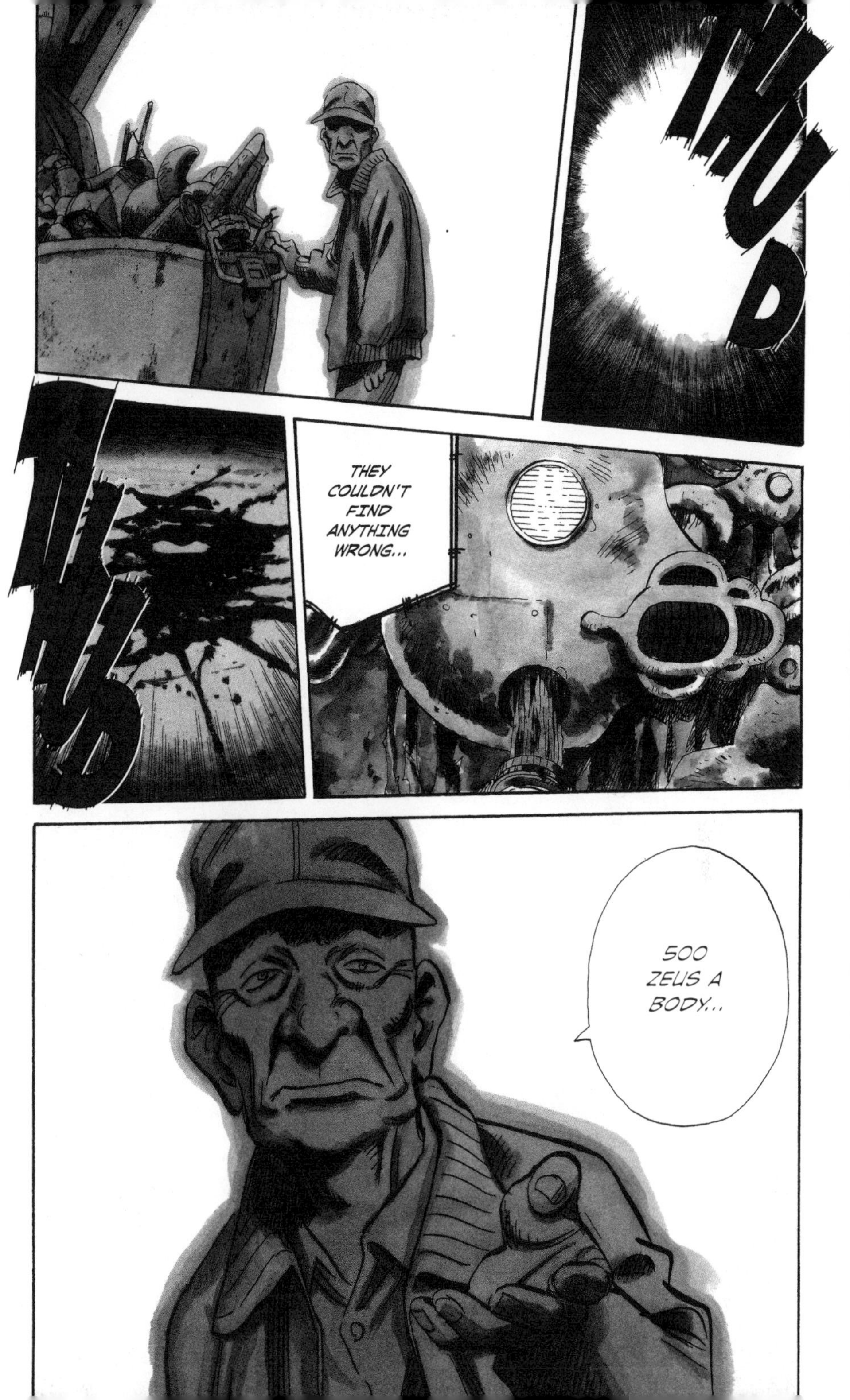
THUD
THEY COULDN'T FIND ANYTHING WRONG...
500 ZEUS A BODY...

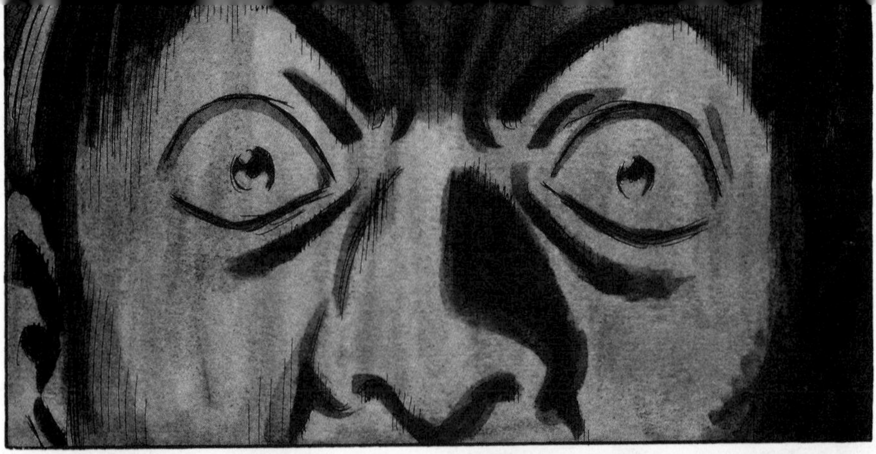

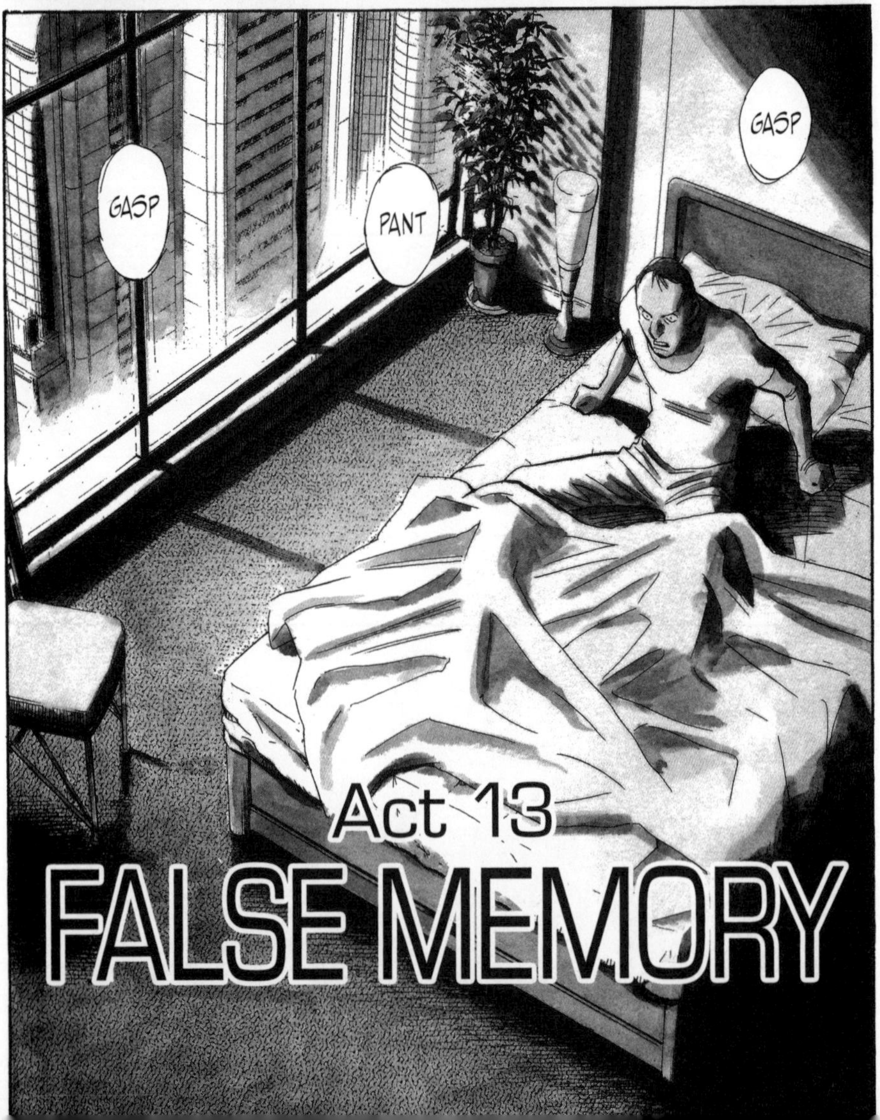
GASP
PANT
GASP
Act 13
FALSE MEMORY

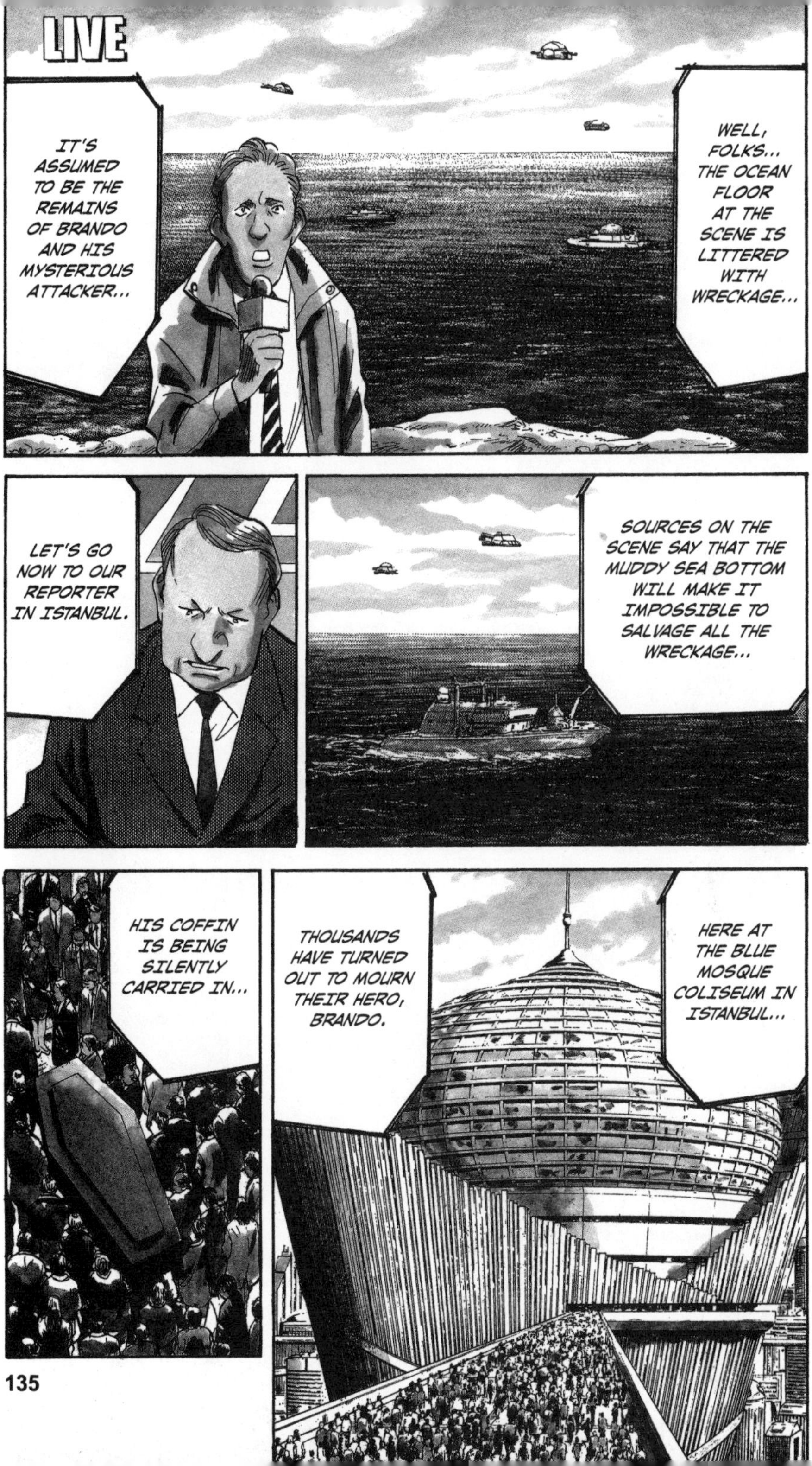
LIVE
WELL, FOLKS... THE OCEAN FLOOR AT THE SCENE IS LITTERED WITH WRECKAGE...
IT'S ASSUMED TO BE THE REMAINS OF BRANDO AND HIS MYSTERIOUS ATTACKER...
SOURCES ON THE SCENE SAY THAT THE MUDDY SEA BOTTOM WILL MAKE IT IMPOSSIBLE TO SALVAGE ALL THE WRECKAGE...
LET'S GO NOW TO OUR REPORTER IN ISTANBUL.
HERE AT THE BLUE MOSQUE COLISEUM IN ISTANBUL...
THOUSANDS HAVE TURNED OUT TO MOURN THEIR HERO, BRANDO.
HIS COFFIN IS BEING SILENTLY CARRIED IN...

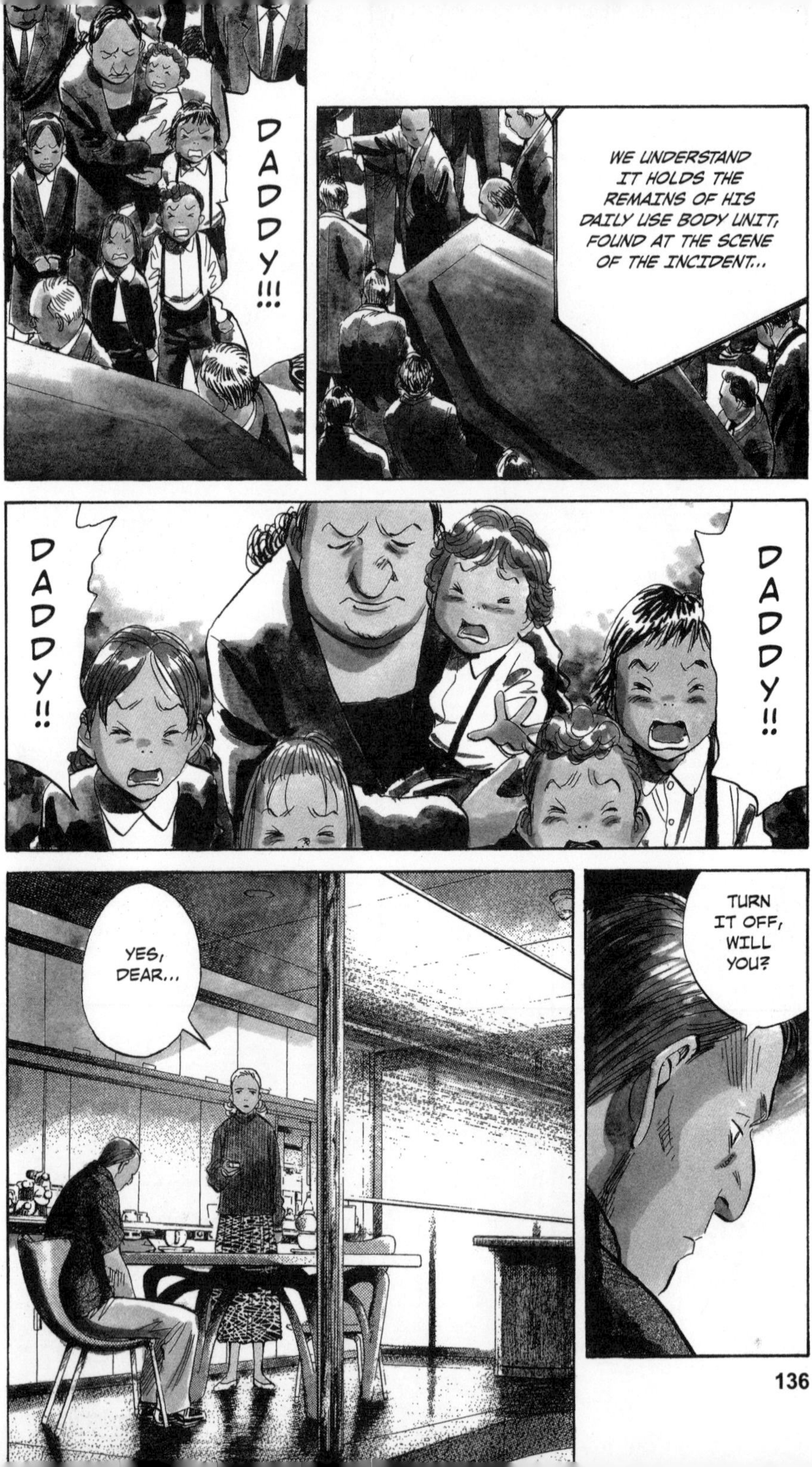
WE UNDERSTAND IT HOLDS THE REMAINS OF HIS DAILY USE BODY UNIT, FOUND AT THE SCENE OF THE INCIDENT...
DADDY!!!
DADDY!!
DADDY!!
TURN IT OFF, WILL YOU?
YES, DEAR...

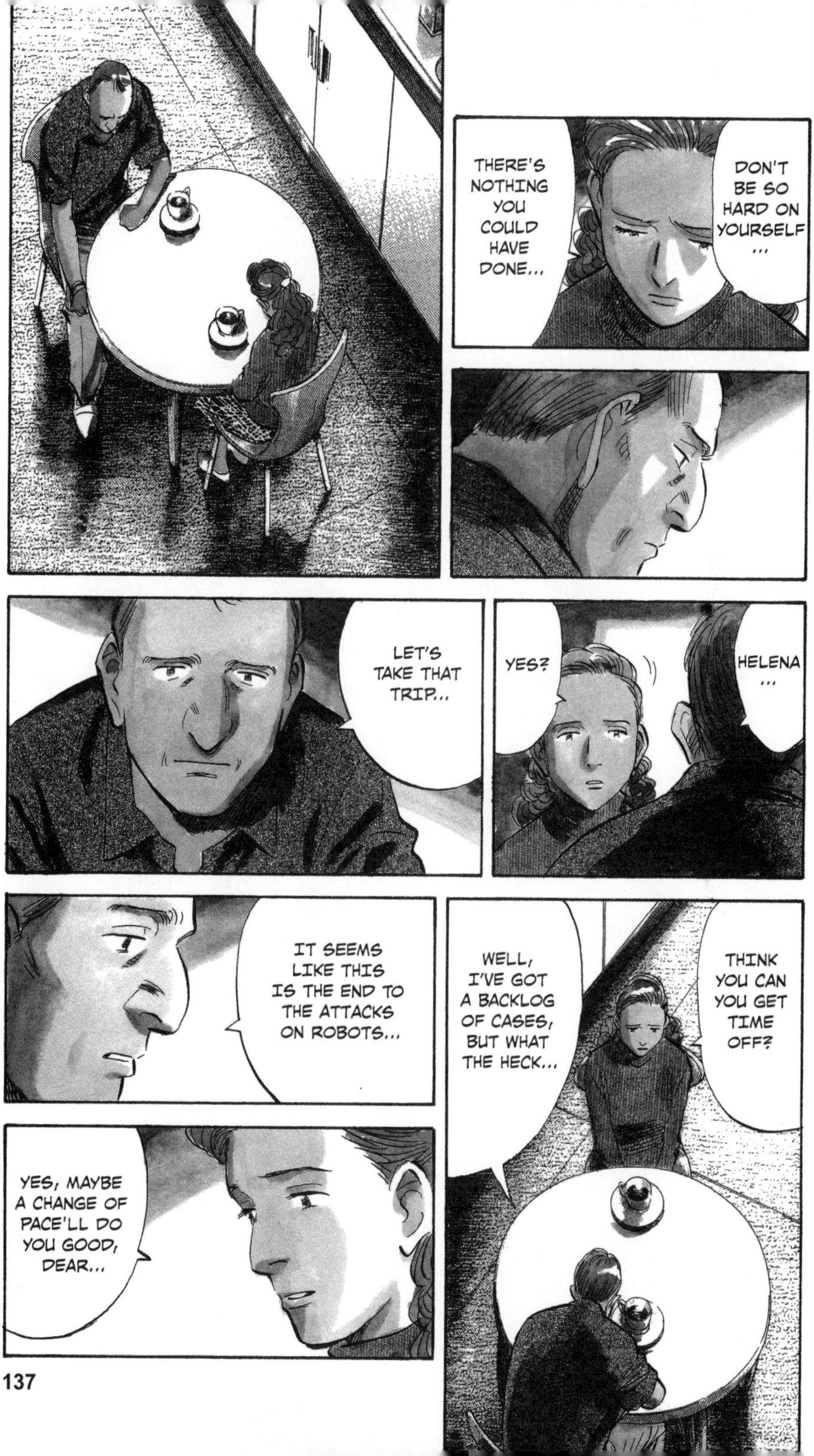
DON'T BE SO HARD ON YOURSELF ...
THERE'S NOTHING YOU COULD HAVE DONE...
HELENA ...
YES?
LET'S TAKE THAT TRIP...
THINK YOU CAN YOU GET TIME OFF?
WELL, I'VE GOT A BACKLOG OF CASES, BUT WHAT THE HECK...
IT SEEMS LIKE THIS IS THE END TO THE ATTACKS ON ROBOTS...
YES, MAYBE A CHANGE OF PACE'LL DO YOU GOOD, DEAR...

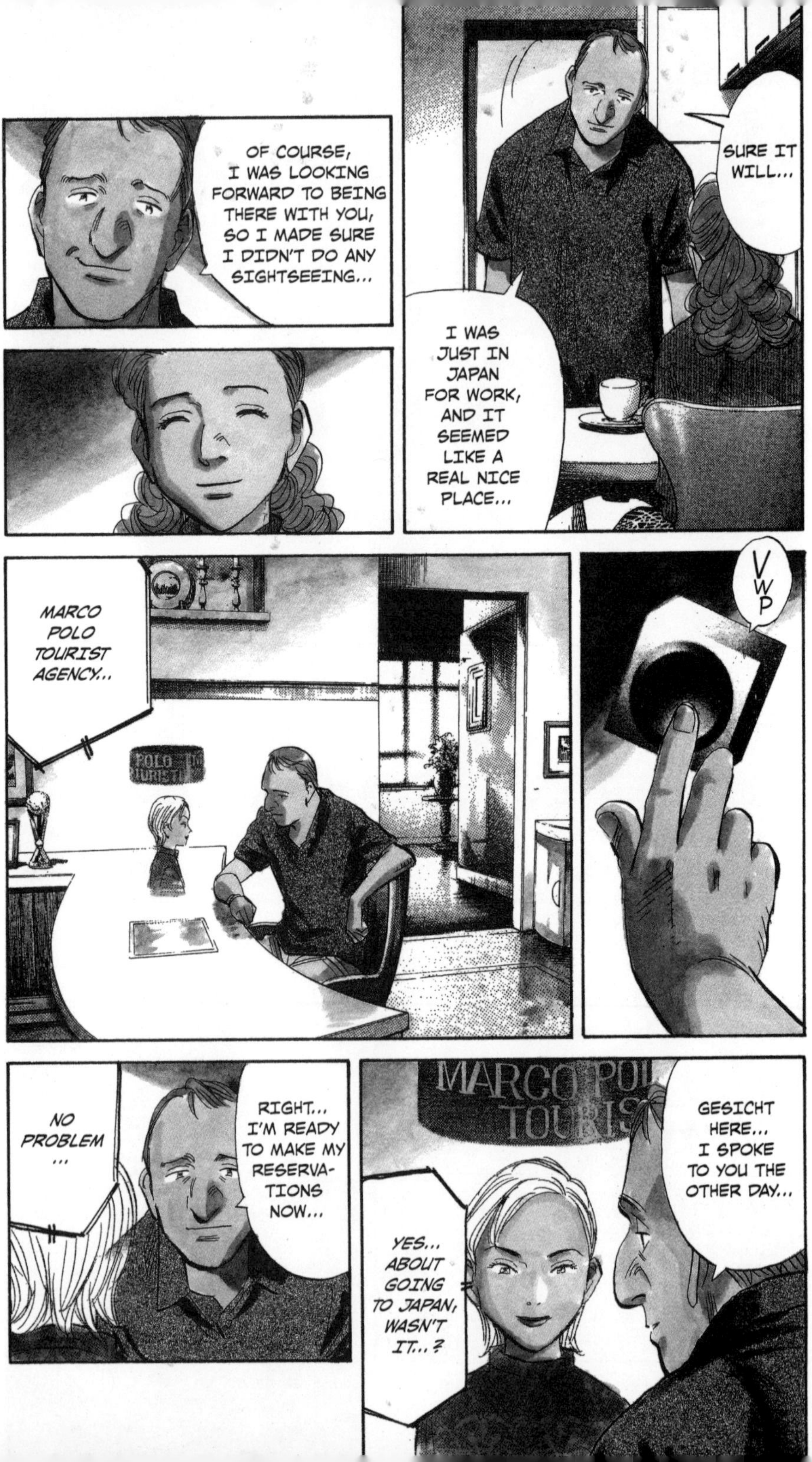
SURE IT WILL...
I WAS JUST IN JAPAN FOR WORK, AND IT SEEMED LIKE A REAL NICE PLACE...
OF COURSE, I WAS LOOKING FORWARD TO BEING THERE WITH YOU, SO I MADE SURE I DIDN'T DO ANY SIGHTSEEING...
VWP
MARCO POLO TOURIST AGENCY...
GESICHT HERE... I SPOKE TO YOU THE OTHER DAY...
YES... ABOUT GOING TO JAPAN, WASN'T IT...?
RIGHT... I'M READY TO MAKE MY RESERVATIONS NOW...
NO PROBLEM...

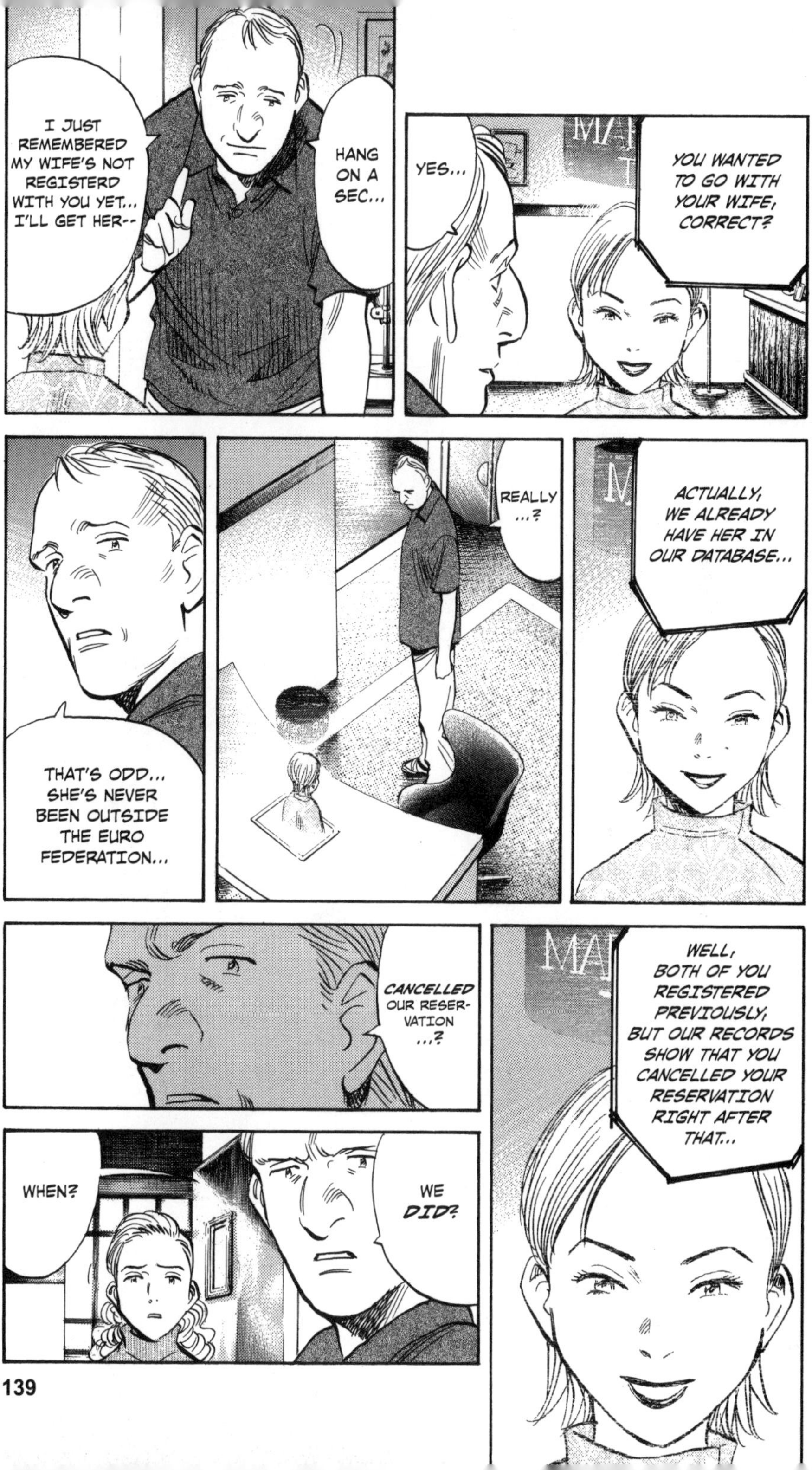
YOU WANTED TO GO WITH YOUR WIFE, CORRECT?
YES...
HANG ON A SEC...
I JUST REMEMBERED MY WIFE'S NOT REGISTERD WITH YOU YET... I'LL GET HER--
ACTUALLY, WE ALREADY HAVE HER IN OUR DATABASE...
REALLY ...?
THAT'S ODD... SHE'S NEVER BEEN OUTSIDE THE EURO FEDERATION...
WELL, BOTH OF YOU REGISTERED PREVIOUSLY, BUT OUR RECORDS SHOW THAT YOU CANCELLED YOUR RESERVATION RIGHT AFTER THAT...
CANCELLED OUR RESERVATION ...?
WE DID?
WHEN?

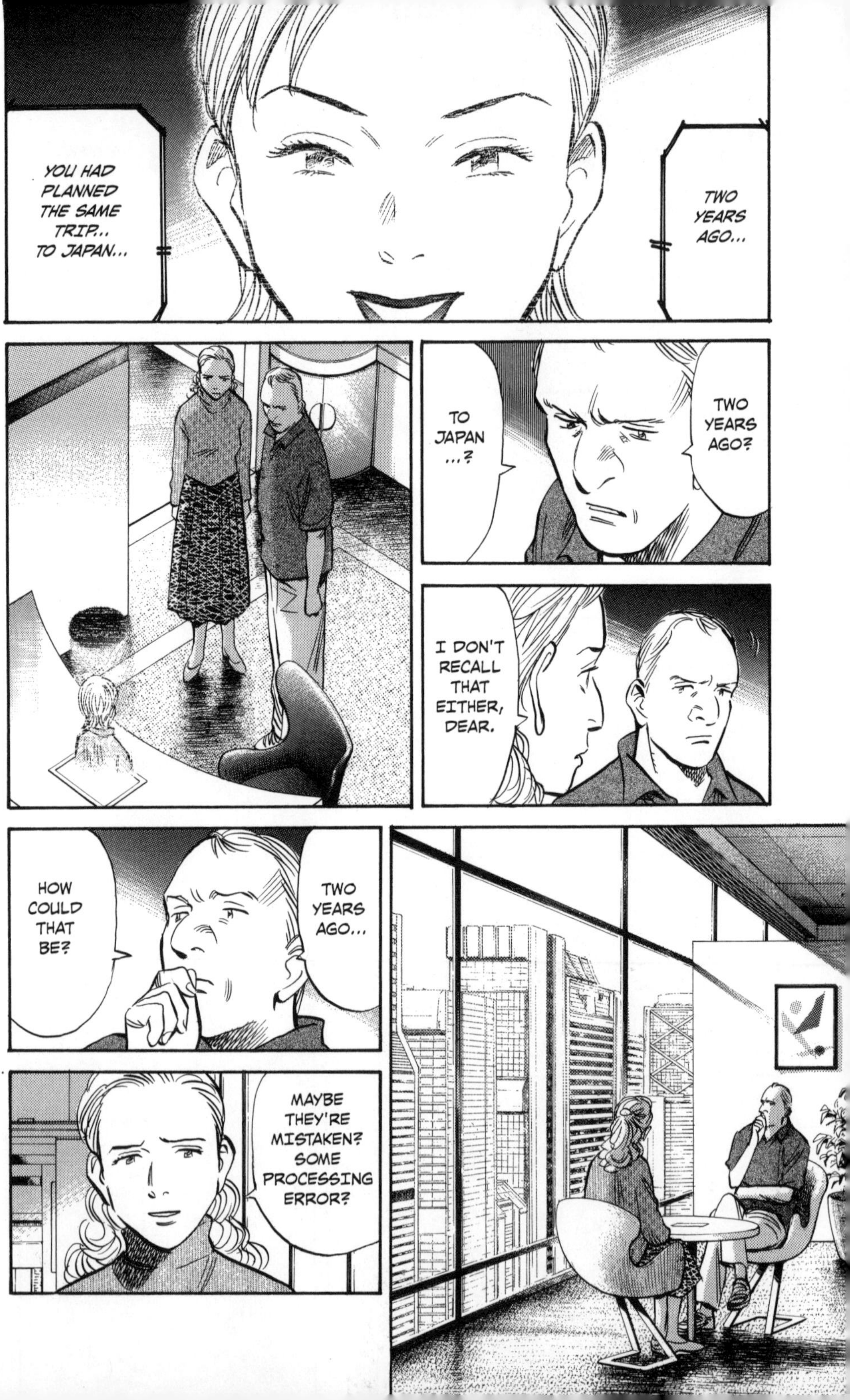
TWO YEARS AGO...
YOU HAD PLANNED THE SAME TRIP... TO JAPAN...
TWO YEARS AGO?
TO JAPAN ...?
I DON'T RECALL THAT EITHER, DEAR.
TWO YEARS AGO...
HOW COULD THAT BE?
MAYBE THEY'RE MISTAKEN? SOME PROCESSING ERROR?

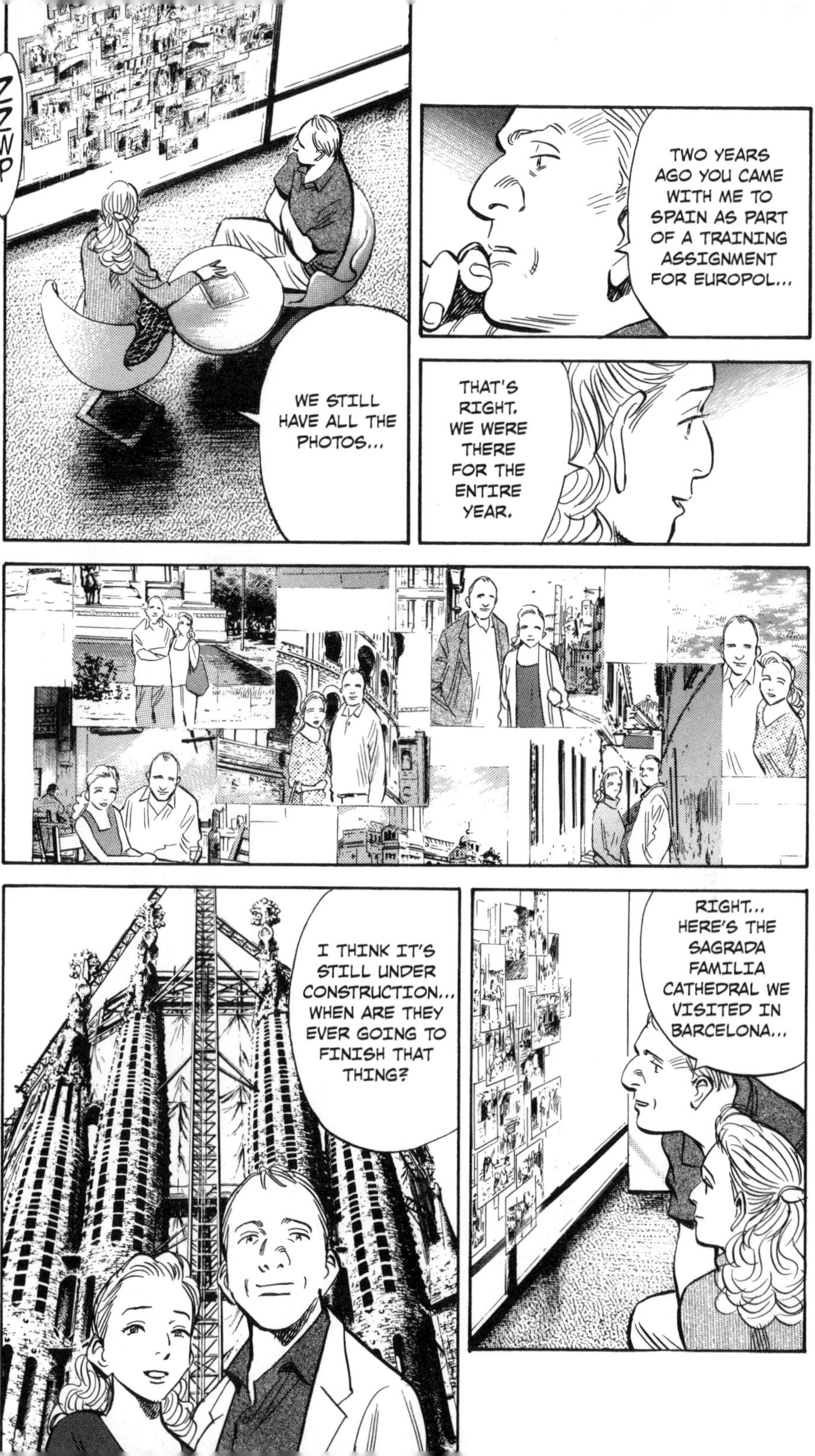
TWO YEARS AGO YOU CAME WITH ME TO SPAIN AS PART OF A TRAINING ASSIGNMENT FOR EUROPOL...
THAT'S RIGHT. WE WERE THERE FOR THE ENTIRE YEAR.
ZZWP
WE STILL HAVE ALL THE PHOTOS...
RIGHT... HERE'S THE SAGRADA FAMILIA CATHEDRAL WE VISITED IN BARCELONA...
I THINK IT'S STILL UNDER CONSTRUCTION... WHEN ARE THEY EVER GOING TO FINISH THAT THING?

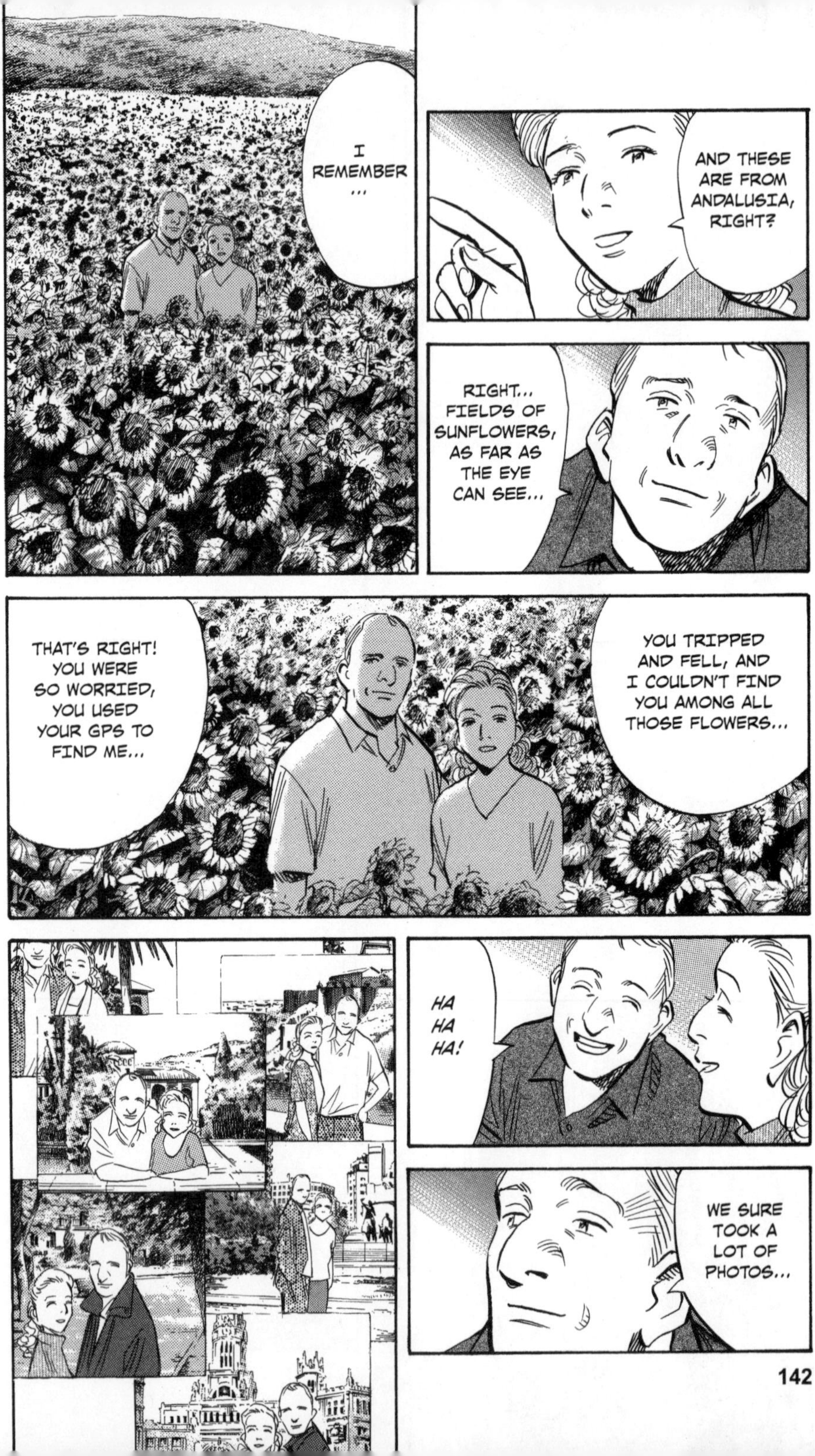
AND THESE ARE FROM ANDALUSIA, RIGHT?
RIGHT... FIELDS OF SUNFLOWERS, AS FAR AS THE EYE CAN SEE...
I REMEMBER ...
YOU TRIPPED AND FELL, AND I COULDN'T FIND YOU AMONG ALL THOSE FLOWERS...
THAT'S RIGHT! YOU WERE SO WORRIED, YOU USED YOUR GPS TO FIND ME...
HA HA HA!
WE SURE TOOK A LOT OF PHOTOS...

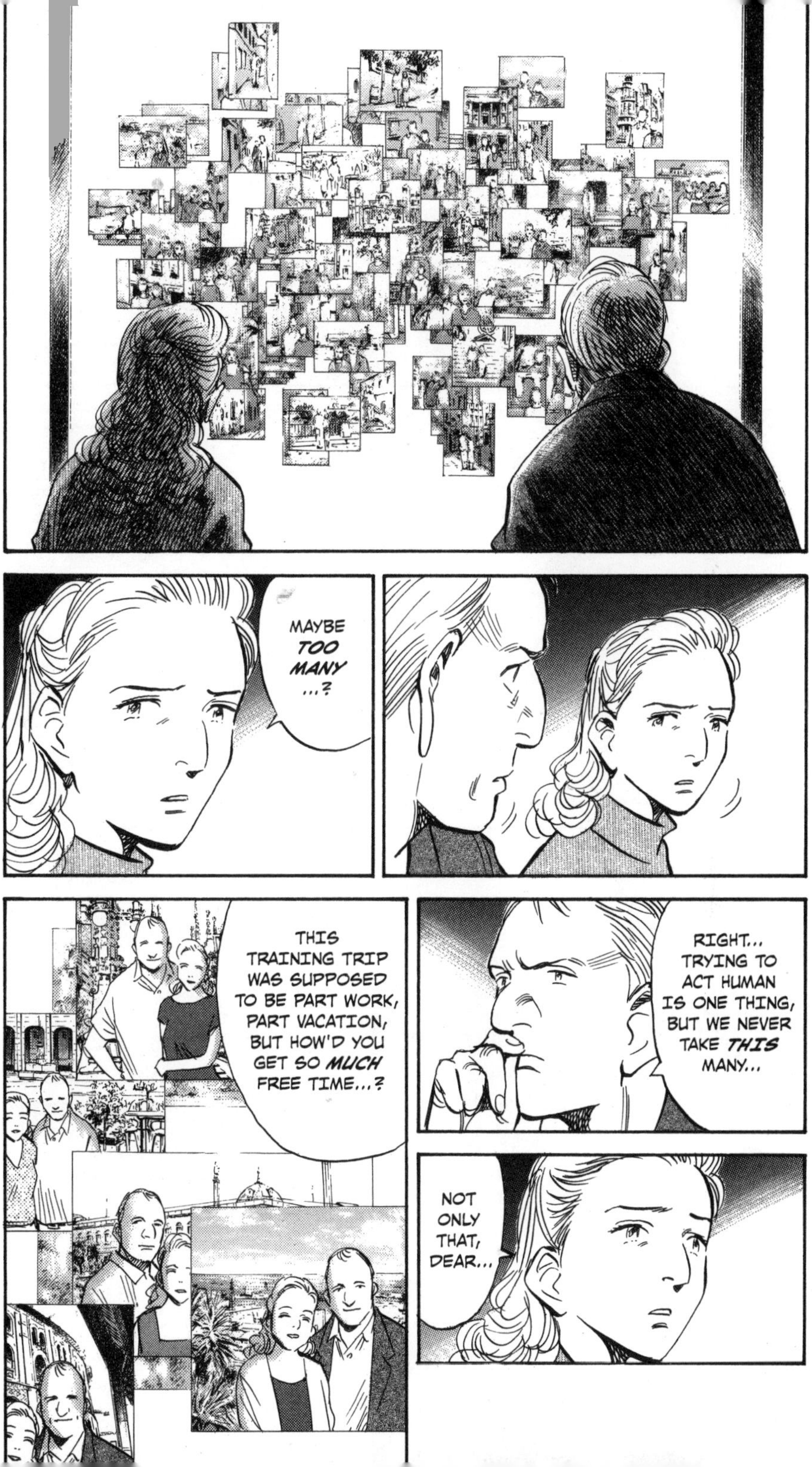
MAYBE *TOO MANY*...?
RIGHT... TRYING TO ACT HUMAN IS ONE THING, BUT WE NEVER TAKE *THIS* MANY...
NOT ONLY THAT, DEAR...
THIS TRAINING TRIP WAS SUPPOSED TO BE PART WORK, PART VACATION, BUT HOW'D YOU GET SO *MUCH* FREE TIME...?

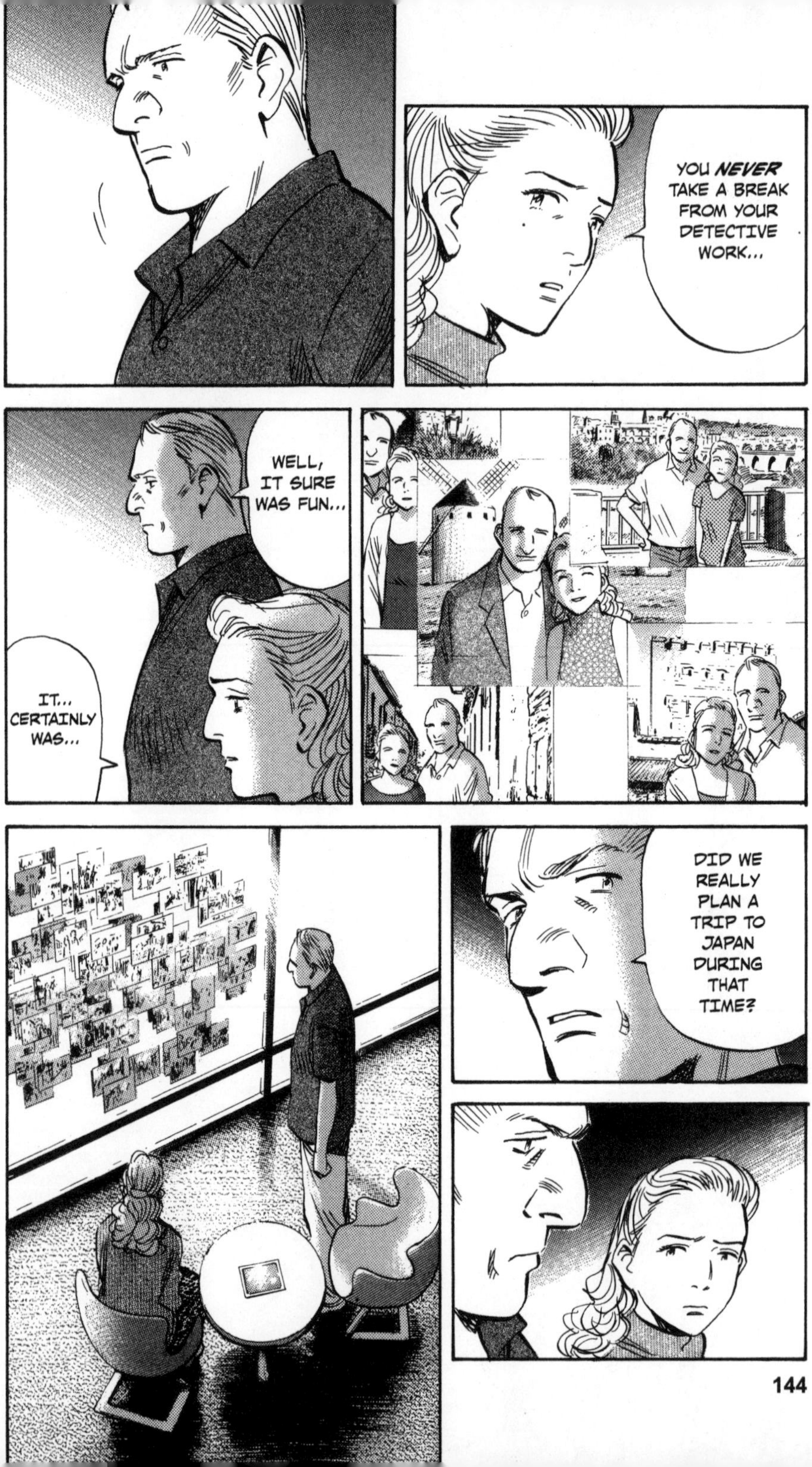
YOU *NEVER* TAKE A BREAK FROM YOUR DETECTIVE WORK...
WELL, IT SURE WAS FUN...
IT... CERTAINLY WAS...
DID WE REALLY PLAN A TRIP TO JAPAN DURING THAT TIME?

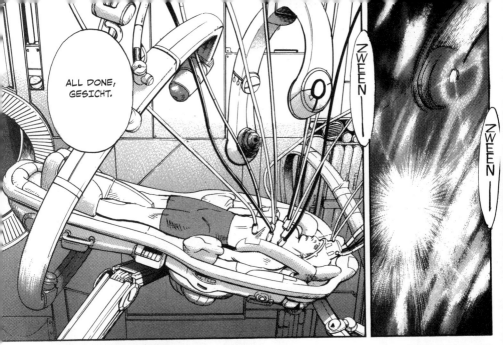

ZWEEN—
ZWEEN—
ALL DONE, GESICHT.
A CLEAN BILL OF HEALTH.
THANKS, PROFESSOR HOFFMAN...
YOU WEREN'T DUE FOR ANY MAINTENANCE YET, YOU KNOW...
SINCE YOU INSISTED ON COMING IN, I FIGURED THERE MUST BE A ***PROBLEM*** SOMEWHERE...
BUT ACCORDING TO THE DATA, EVERYTHING CHECKS OUT JUST FINE.

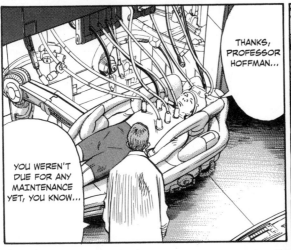

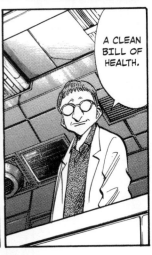

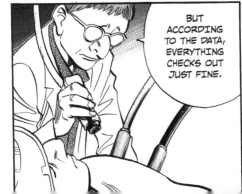

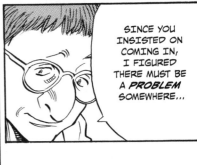

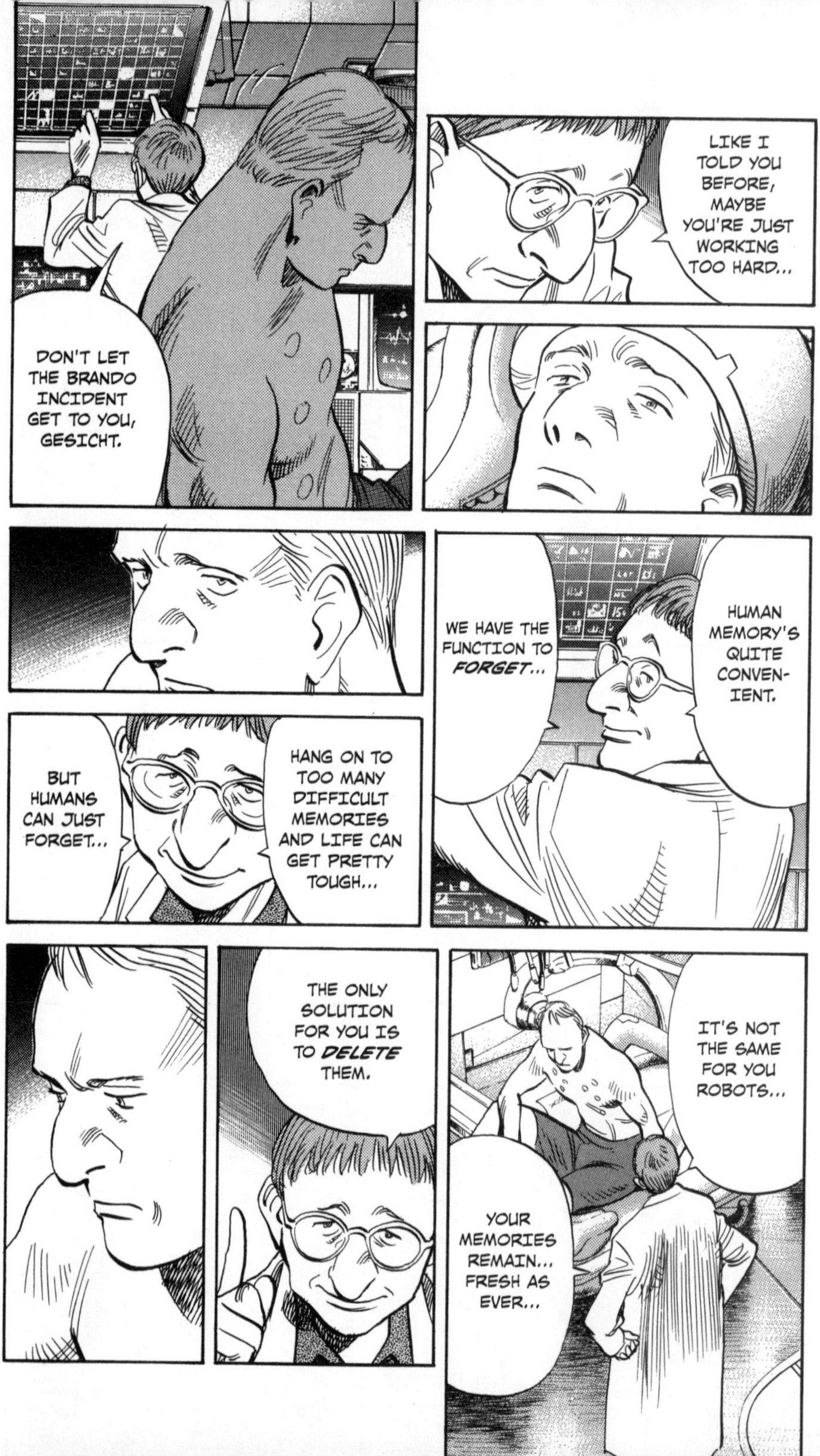
LIKE I TOLD YOU BEFORE, MAYBE YOU'RE JUST WORKING TOO HARD...
DON'T LET THE BRANDO INCIDENT GET TO YOU, GESICHT.
HUMAN MEMORY'S QUITE CONVEN-IENT.
WE HAVE THE FUNCTION TO *FORGET*...
HANG ON TO TOO MANY DIFFICULT MEMORIES AND LIFE CAN GET PRETTY TOUGH...
BUT HUMANS CAN JUST FORGET...
IT'S NOT THE SAME FOR YOU ROBOTS...
YOUR MEMORIES REMAIN... FRESH AS EVER...
THE ONLY SOLUTION FOR YOU IS TO *DELETE* THEM.

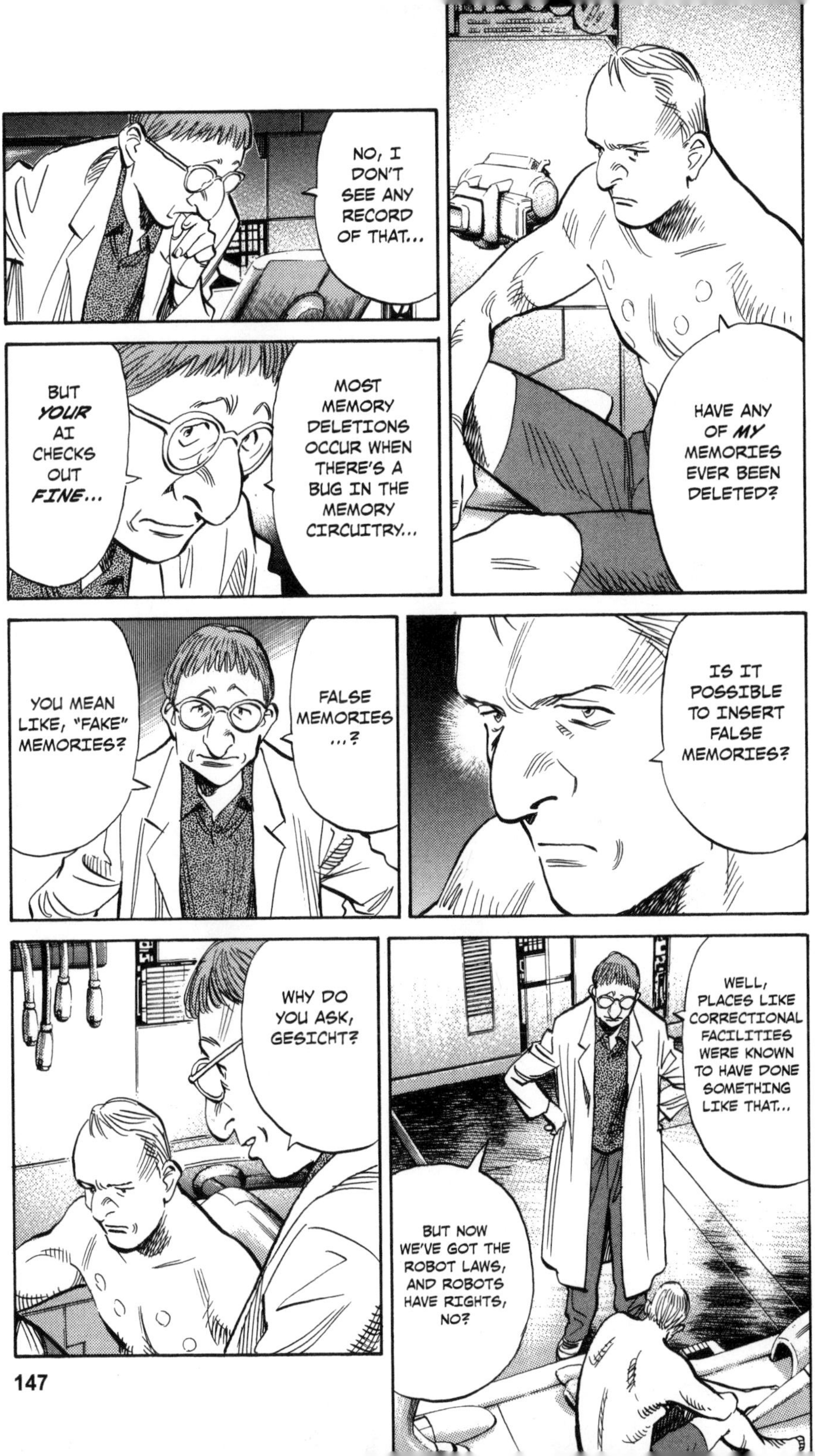
HAVE ANY OF *MY* MEMORIES EVER BEEN DELETED?
NO, I DON'T SEE ANY RECORD OF THAT...
MOST MEMORY DELETIONS OCCUR WHEN THERE'S A BUG IN THE MEMORY CIRCUITRY...
BUT *YOUR* AI CHECKS OUT *FINE*...
IS IT POSSIBLE TO INSERT FALSE MEMORIES?
FALSE MEMORIES ...?
YOU MEAN LIKE, "FAKE" MEMORIES?
WELL, PLACES LIKE CORRECTIONAL FACILITIES WERE KNOWN TO HAVE DONE SOMETHING LIKE THAT...
BUT NOW WE'VE GOT THE ROBOT LAWS, AND ROBOTS HAVE RIGHTS, NO?
WHY DO YOU ASK, GESICHT?

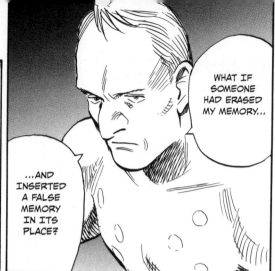

WHAT IF SOMEONE HAD ERASED MY MEMORY...

...AND INSERTED A FALSE MEMORY IN ITS PLACE?

COULD THAT BE THE REASON I KEEP HAVING NIGHTMARES?

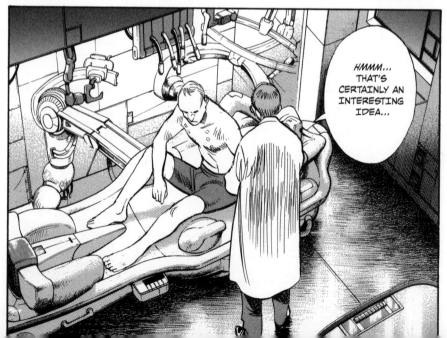

HMMM... THAT'S CERTAINLY AN INTERESTING IDEA...

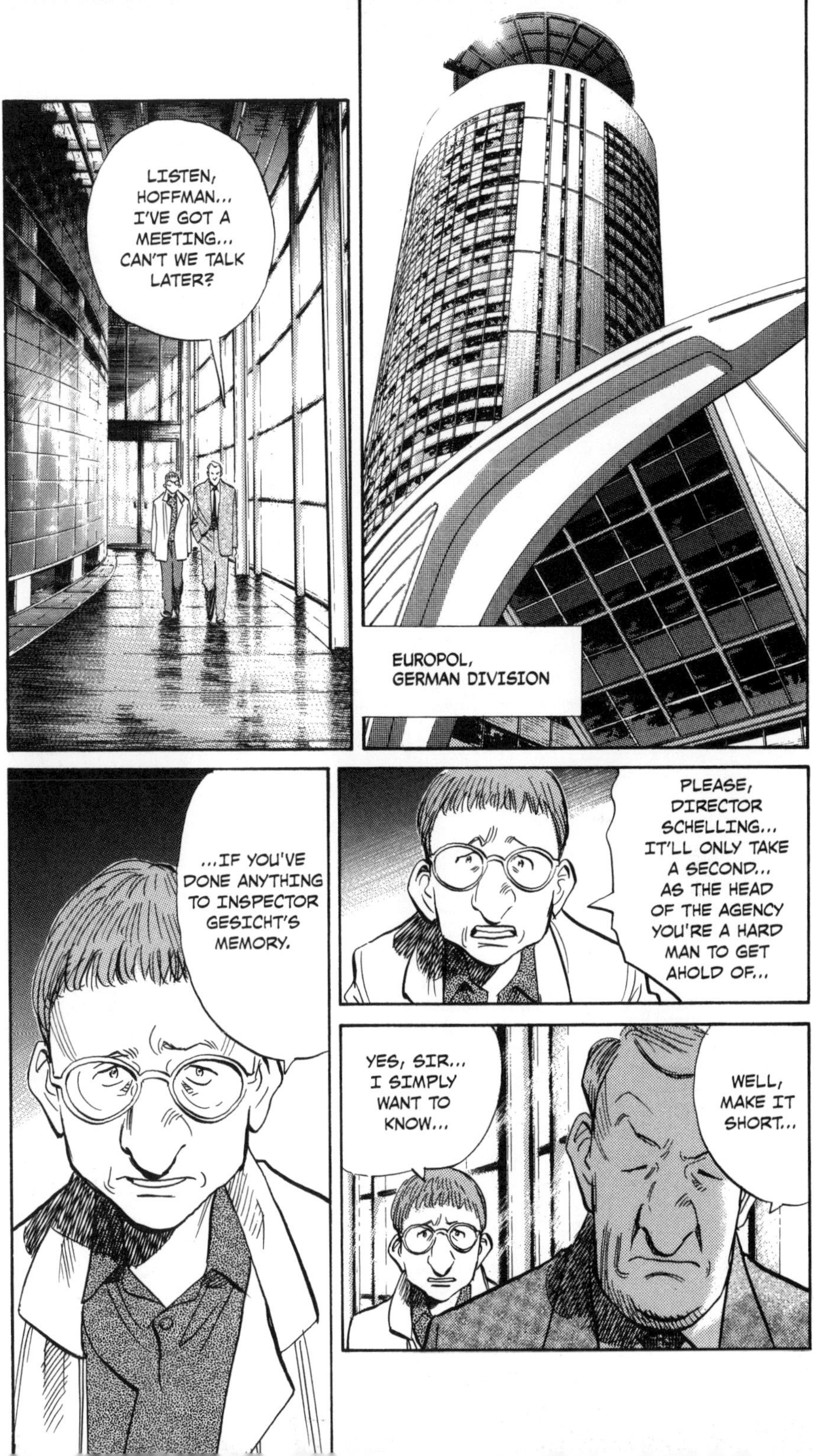
EUROPOL, GERMAN DIVISION
LISTEN, HOFFMAN... I'VE GOT A MEETING... CAN'T WE TALK LATER?
PLEASE, DIRECTOR SCHELLING... IT'LL ONLY TAKE A SECOND... AS THE HEAD OF THE AGENCY YOU'RE A HARD MAN TO GET AHOLD OF...
WELL, MAKE IT SHORT...
YES, SIR... I SIMPLY WANT TO KNOW...
...IF YOU'VE DONE ANYTHING TO INSPECTOR GESICHT'S MEMORY.

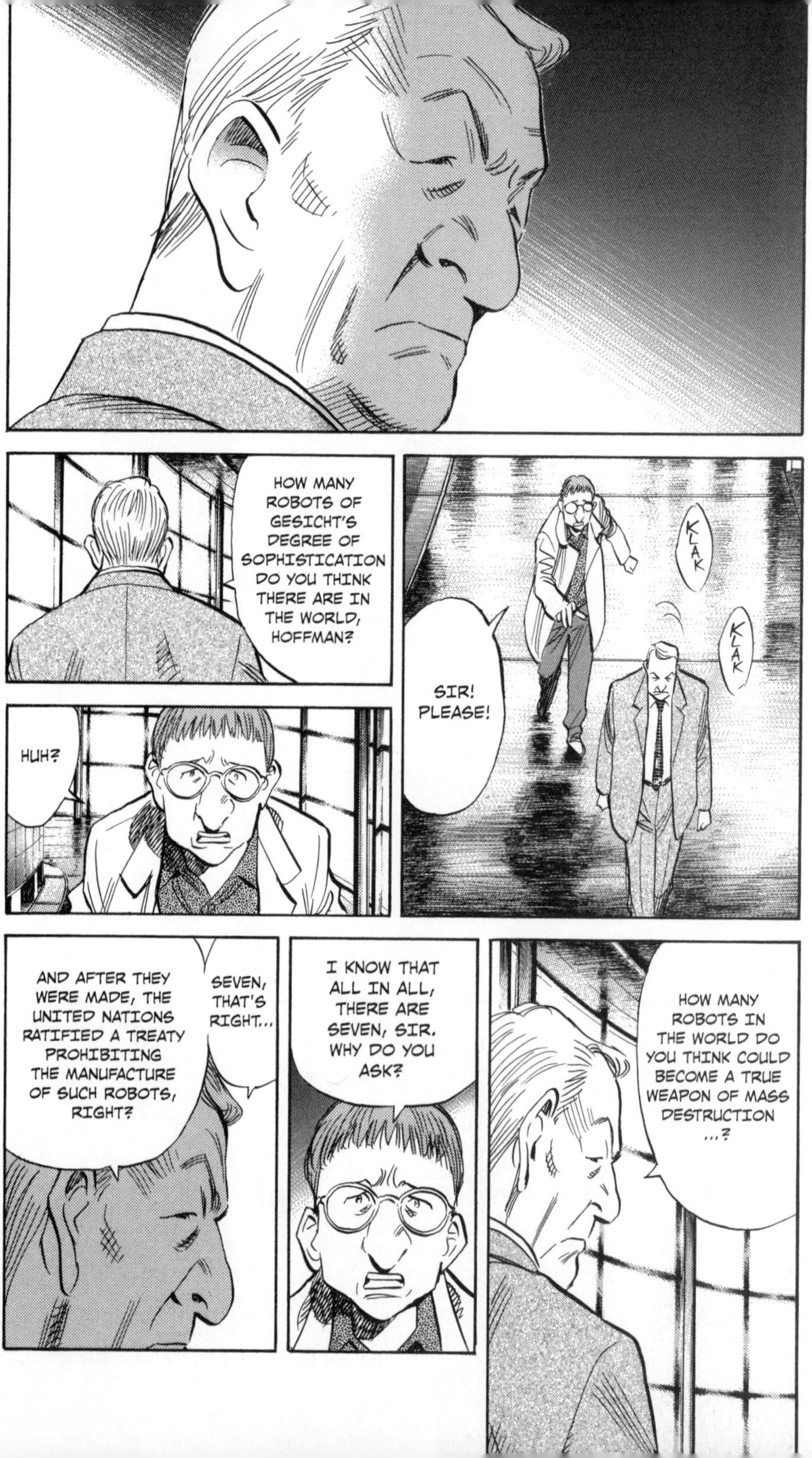
KLAK
KLAK
SIR! PLEASE!
HOW MANY ROBOTS OF GESICHT'S DEGREE OF SOPHISTICATION DO YOU THINK THERE ARE IN THE WORLD, HOFFMAN?
HUH?
HOW MANY ROBOTS IN THE WORLD DO YOU THINK COULD BECOME A TRUE WEAPON OF MASS DESTRUCTION ...?
I KNOW THAT ALL IN ALL, THERE ARE SEVEN, SIR. WHY DO YOU ASK?
SEVEN, THAT'S RIGHT...
AND AFTER THEY WERE MADE, THE UNITED NATIONS RATIFIED A TREATY PROHIBITING THE MANUFACTURE OF SUCH ROBOTS, RIGHT?

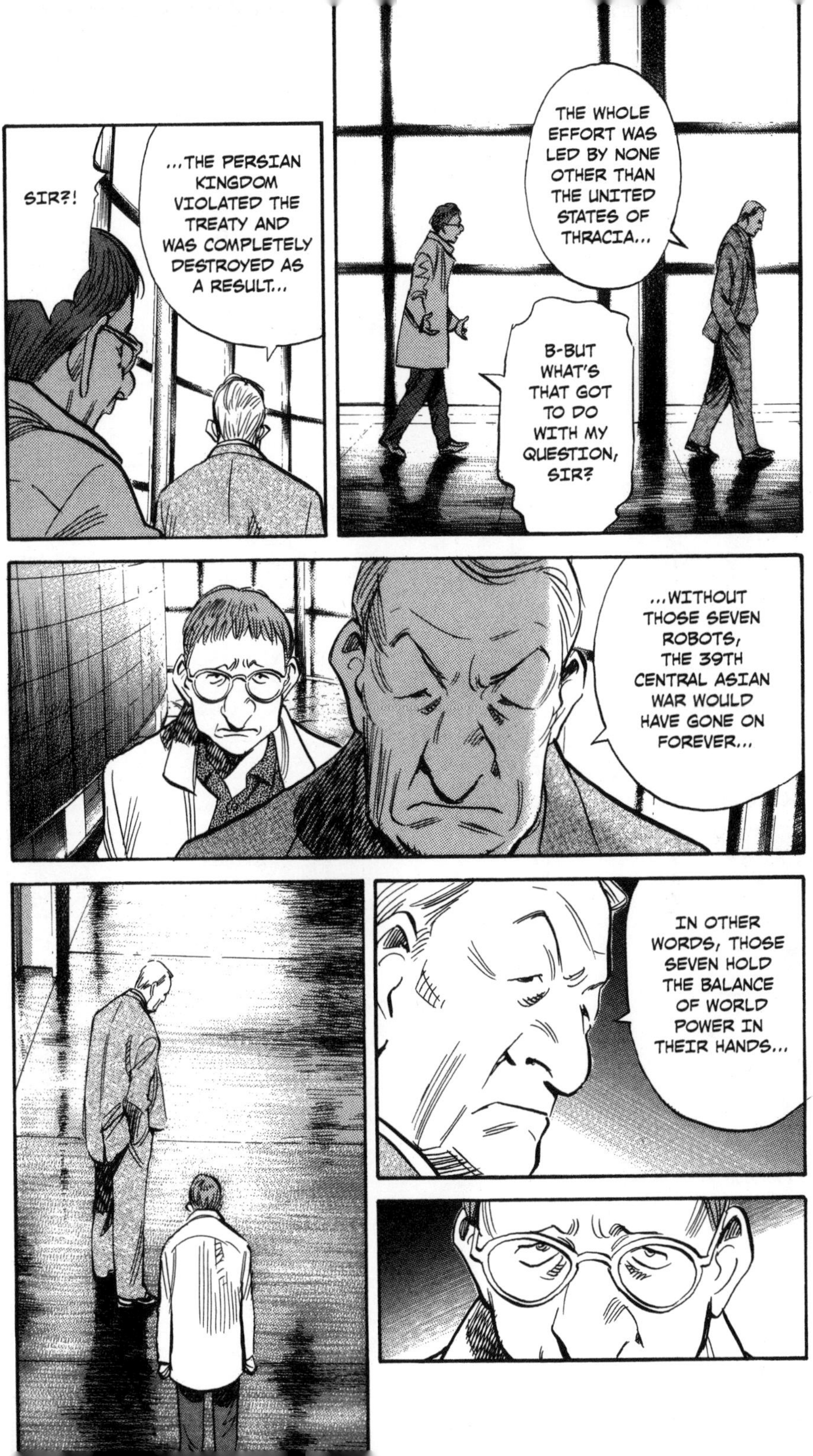
SIR?!
...THE PERSIAN KINGDOM VIOLATED THE TREATY AND WAS COMPLETELY DESTROYED AS A RESULT...
THE WHOLE EFFORT WAS LED BY NONE OTHER THAN THE UNITED STATES OF THRACIA...
B-BUT WHAT'S THAT GOT TO DO WITH MY QUESTION, SIR?
...WITHOUT THOSE SEVEN ROBOTS, THE 39TH CENTRAL ASIAN WAR WOULD HAVE GONE ON FOREVER...
IN OTHER WORDS, THOSE SEVEN HOLD THE BALANCE OF WORLD POWER IN THEIR HANDS...

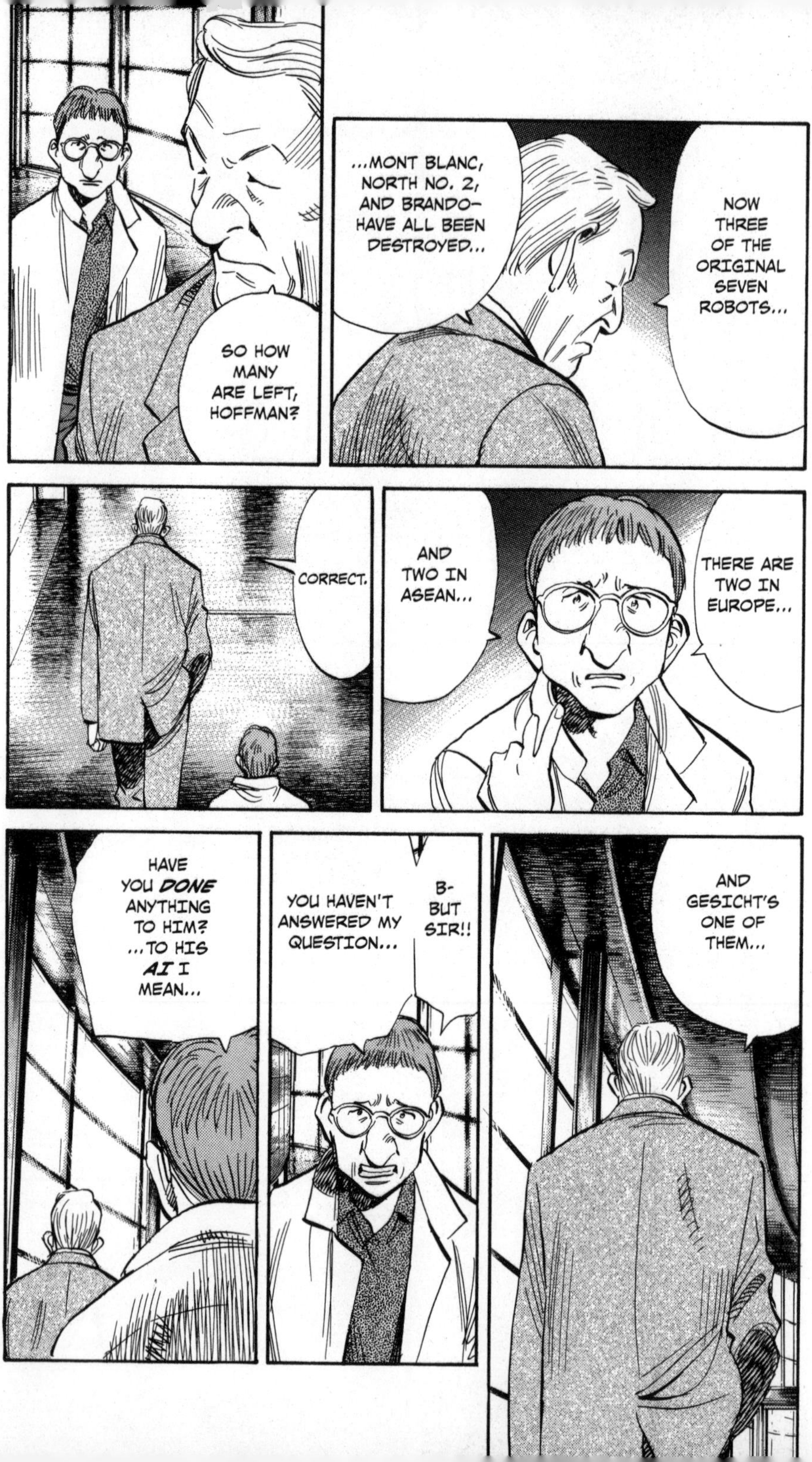
NOW THREE OF THE ORIGINAL SEVEN ROBOTS...
...MONT BLANC, NORTH NO. 2, AND BRANDO—HAVE ALL BEEN DESTROYED...
SO HOW MANY ARE LEFT, HOFFMAN?
THERE ARE TWO IN EUROPE...
AND TWO IN ASEAN...
CORRECT.
AND GESICHT'S ONE OF THEM...
B-BUT SIR!!
YOU HAVEN'T ANSWERED MY QUESTION...
HAVE YOU DONE ANYTHING TO HIM? ...TO HIS AI I MEAN...

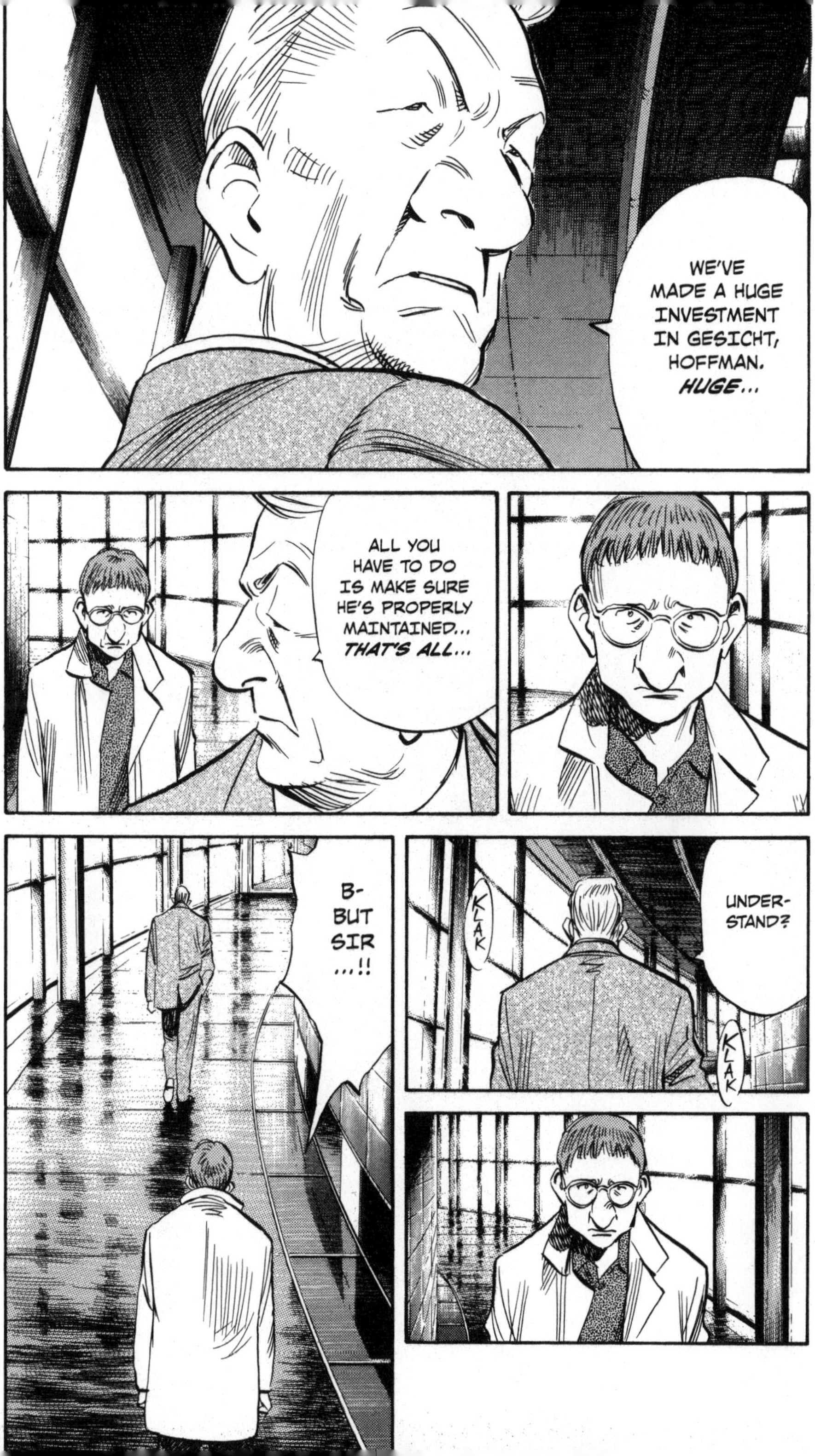
WE'VE MADE A HUGE INVESTMENT IN GESICHT, HOFFMAN. *HUGE...*
ALL YOU HAVE TO DO IS MAKE SURE HE'S PROPERLY MAINTAINED... *THAT'S ALL...*
UNDER-STAND?
KLAK
KLAK
B-BUT SIR ...!!

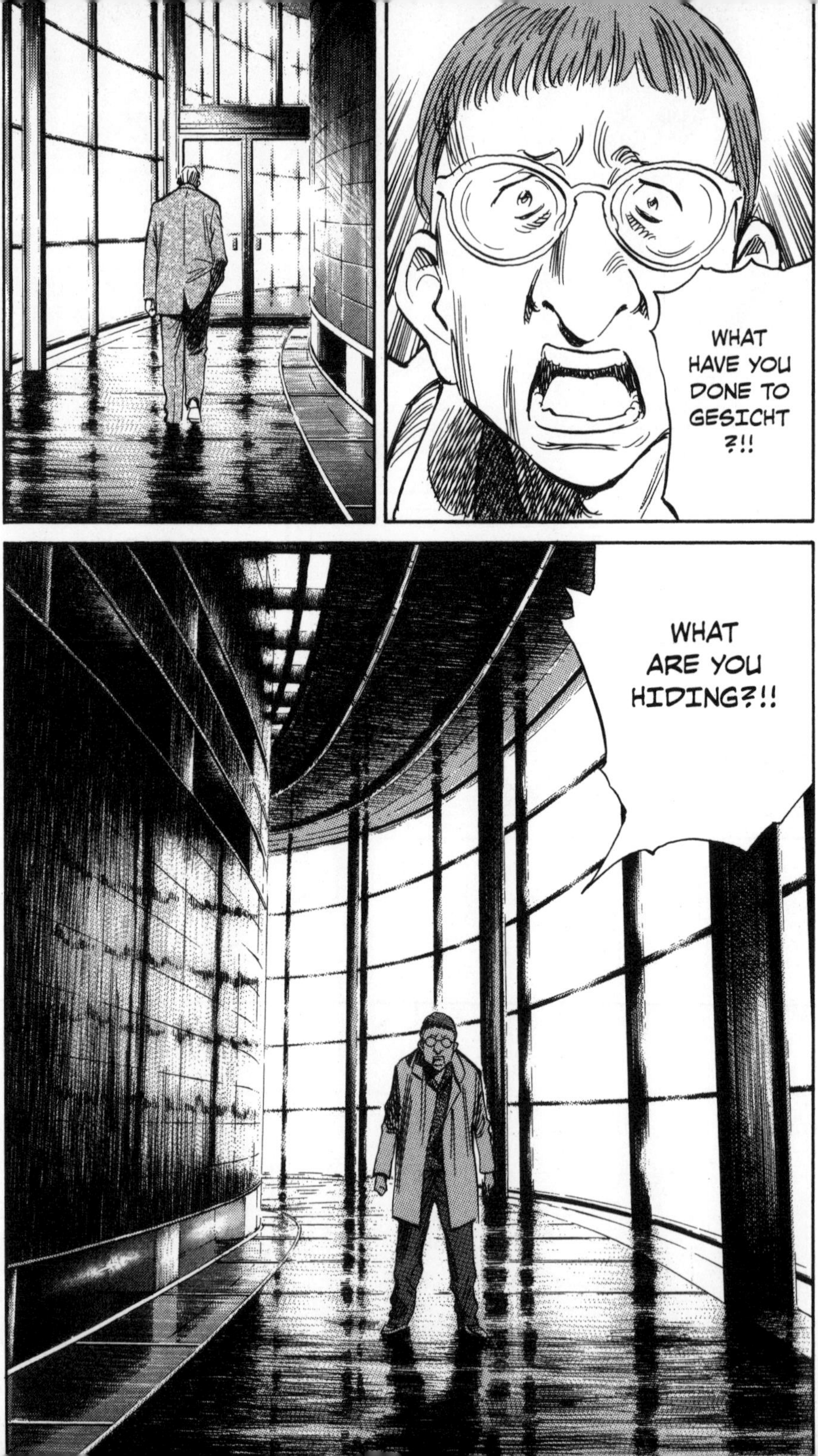
WHAT HAVE YOU DONE TO GESICHT ?!!
WHAT ARE YOU HIDING?!!

Act 14 Dr. Roosevelt

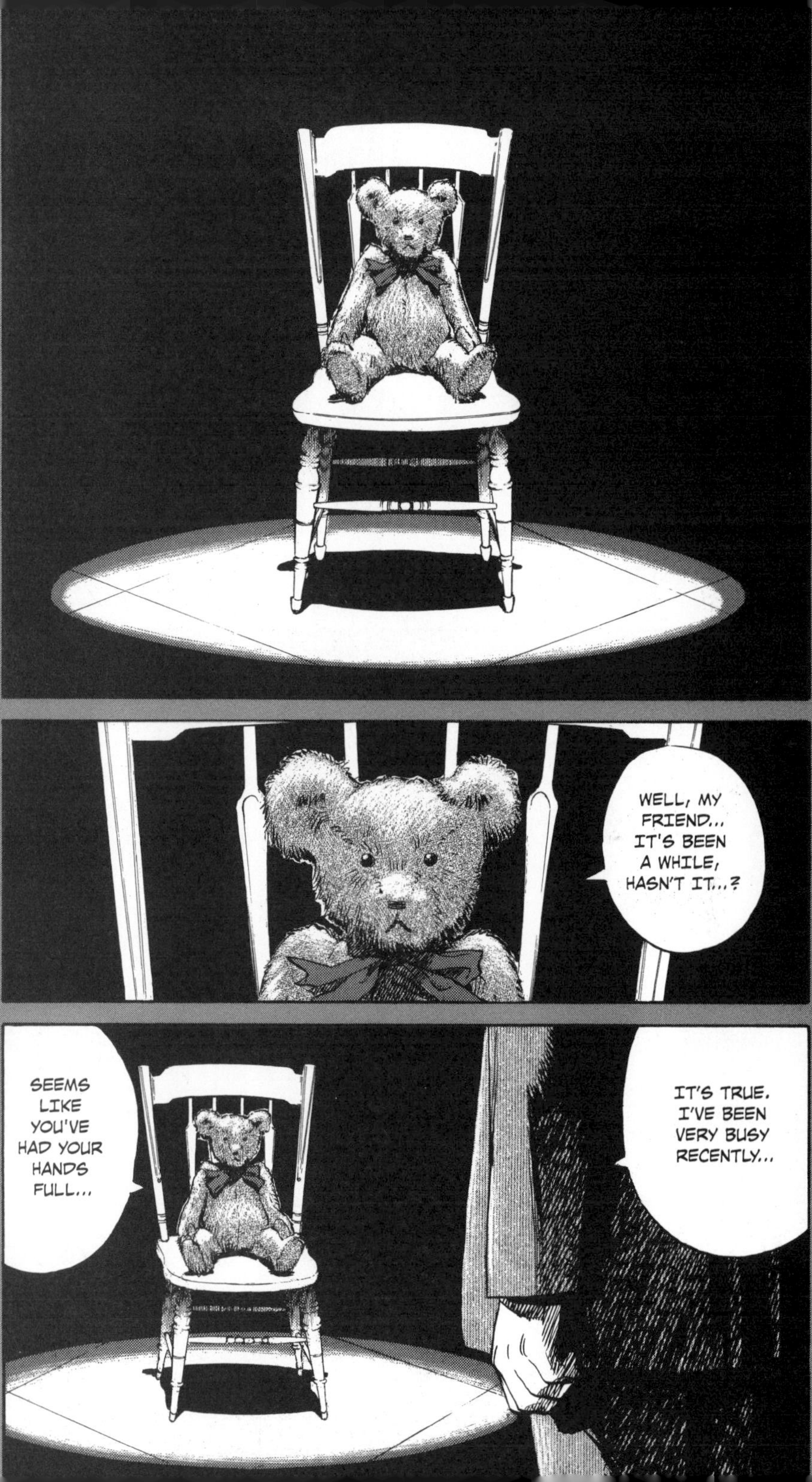
WELL, MY FRIEND... IT'S BEEN A WHILE, HASN'T IT...?
SEEMS LIKE YOU'VE HAD YOUR HANDS FULL...
IT'S TRUE. I'VE BEEN VERY BUSY RECENTLY...

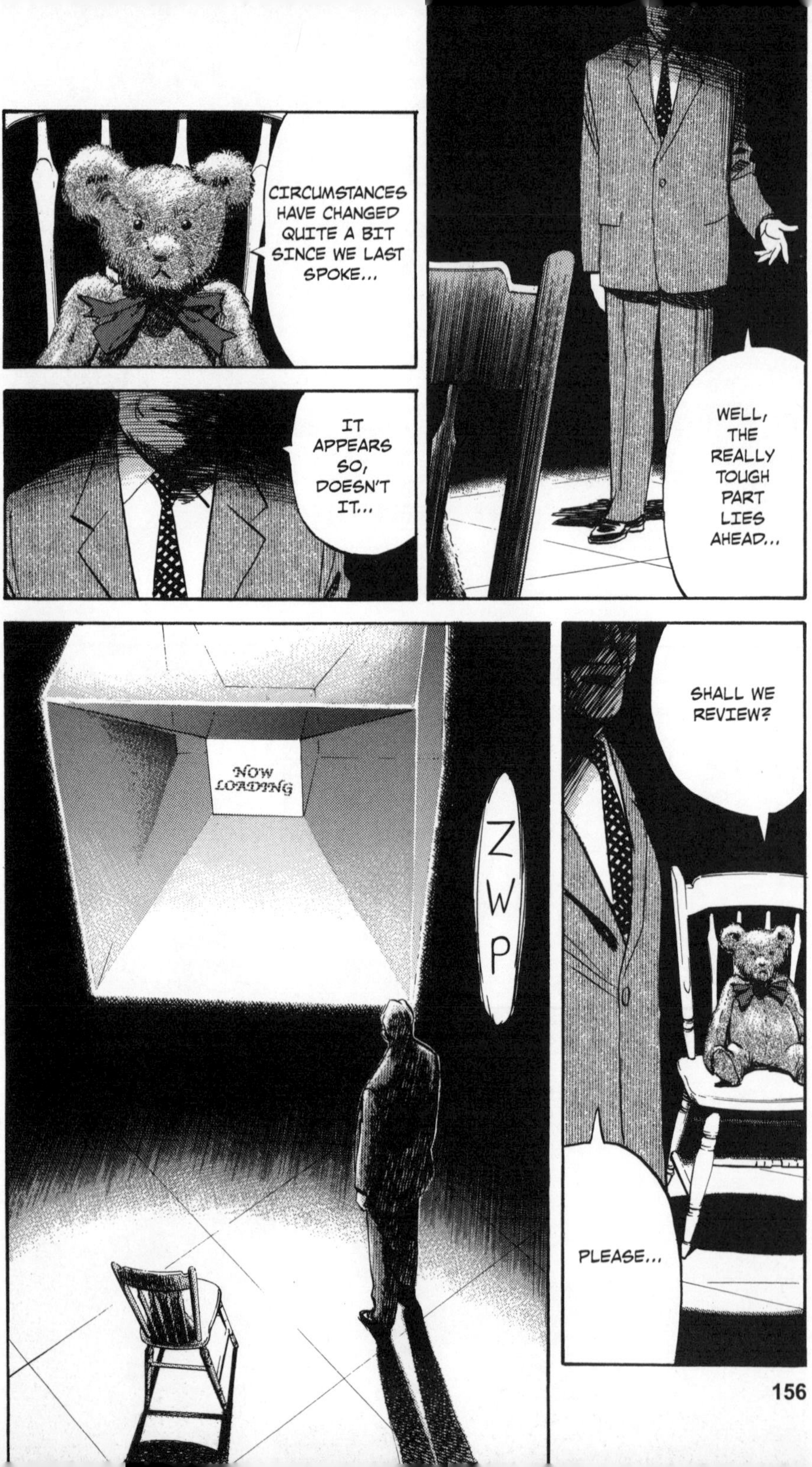
WELL, THE REALLY TOUGH PART LIES AHEAD...
CIRCUMSTANCES HAVE CHANGED QUITE A BIT SINCE WE LAST SPOKE...
IT APPEARS SO, DOESN'T IT...
SHALL WE REVIEW?
PLEASE...
ZWP
NOW LOADING

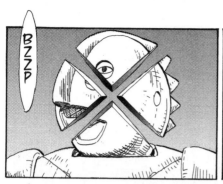

BZZP

SWITZER-
LAND'S
MONT
BLANC.

BZZP

ENGLAND'S
NORTH
NO. 2.

BZZP

BRANDO
OF TURKEY.

MEANING?

EVERYTHING'S
GONE WELL...
UP TO THIS
POINT...

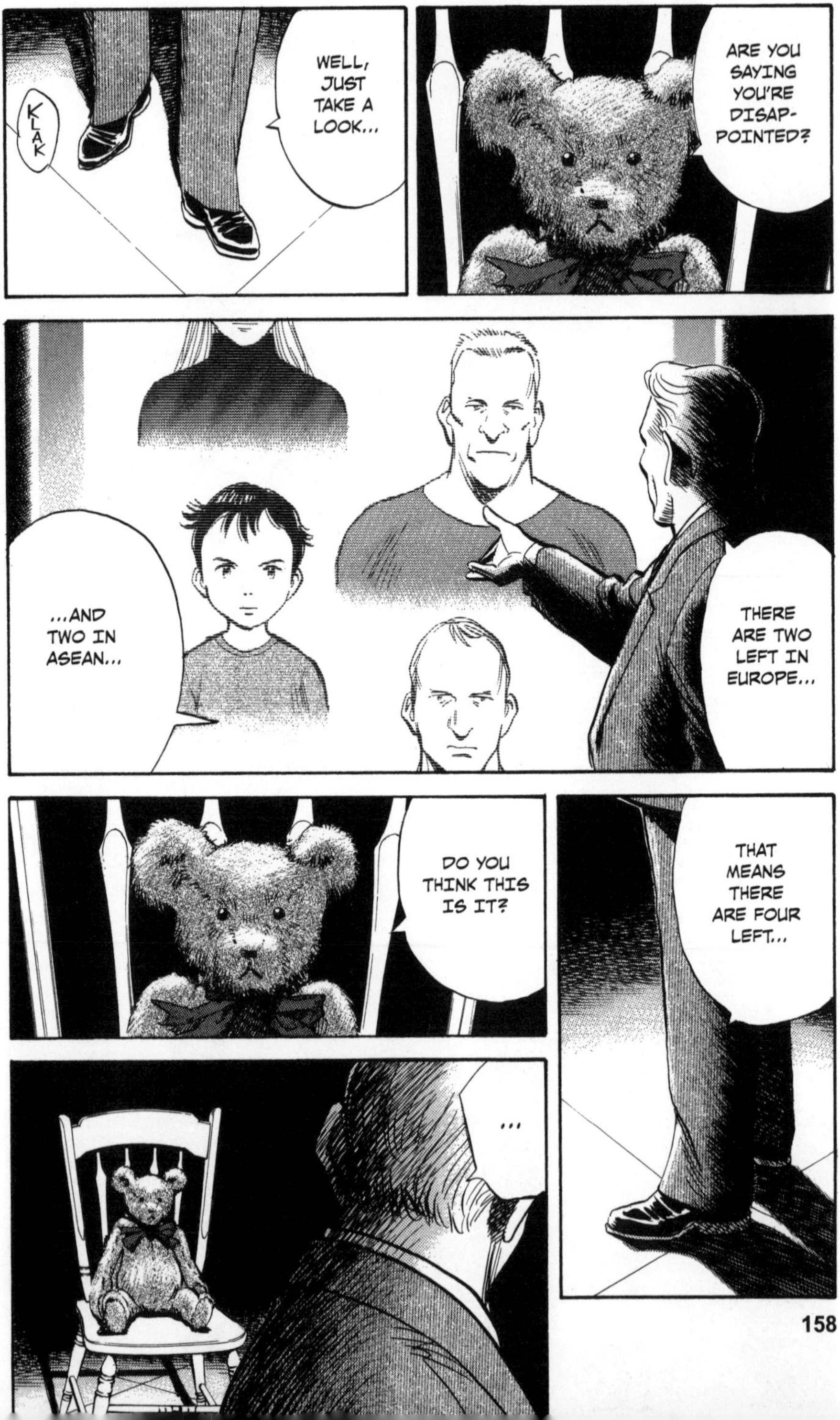
ARE YOU SAYING YOU'RE DISAP-POINTED?
WELL, JUST TAKE A LOOK...
KLAK
THERE ARE TWO LEFT IN EUROPE...
...AND TWO IN ASEAN...
THAT MEANS THERE ARE FOUR LEFT...
DO YOU THINK THIS IS IT?
...

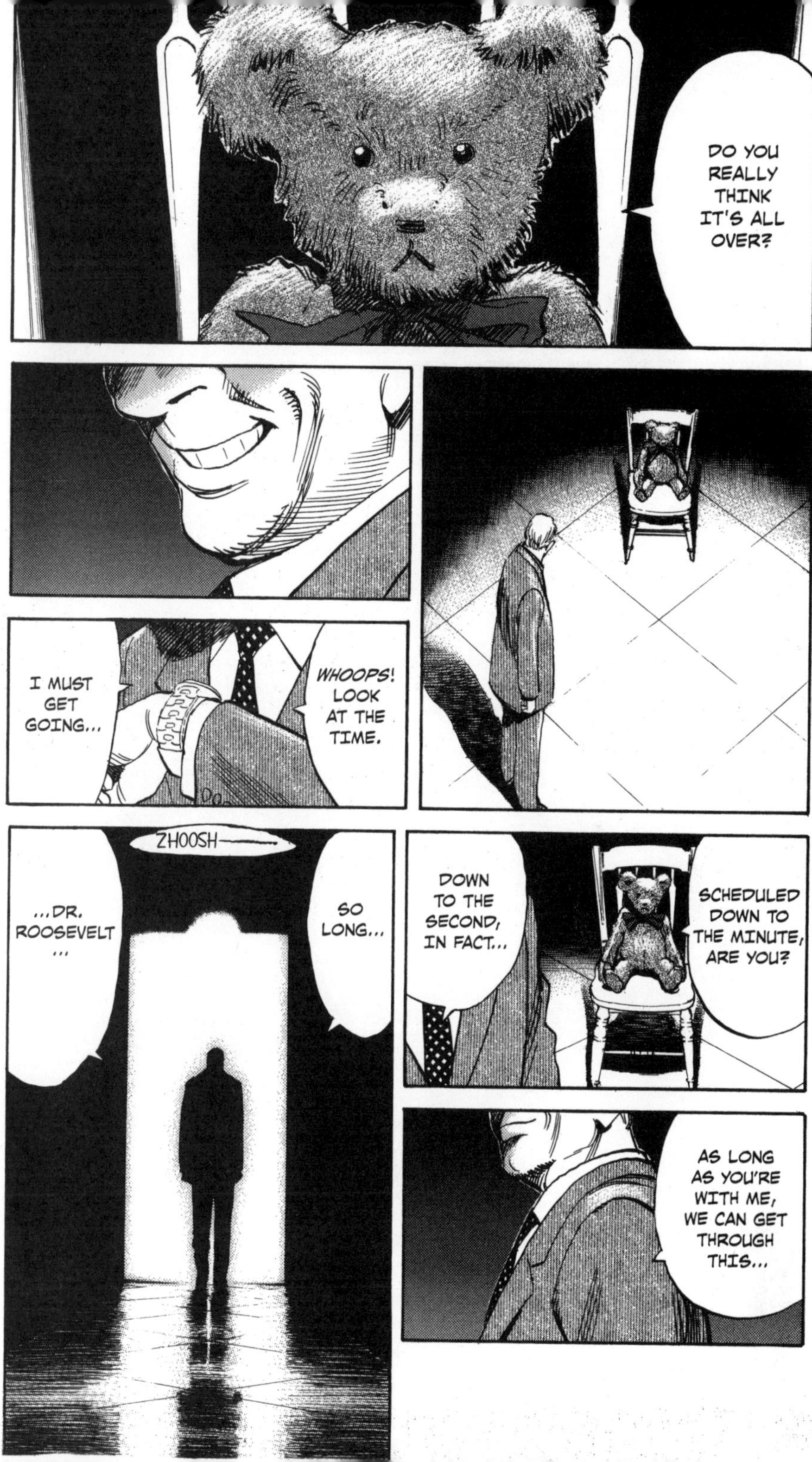
DO YOU REALLY THINK IT'S ALL OVER?
WHOOPS! LOOK AT THE TIME.
I MUST GET GOING...
SCHEDULED DOWN TO THE MINUTE, ARE YOU?
DOWN TO THE SECOND, IN FACT...
AS LONG AS YOU'RE WITH ME, WE CAN GET THROUGH THIS...
ZHOOSH
SO LONG...
...DR. ROOSEVELT ...

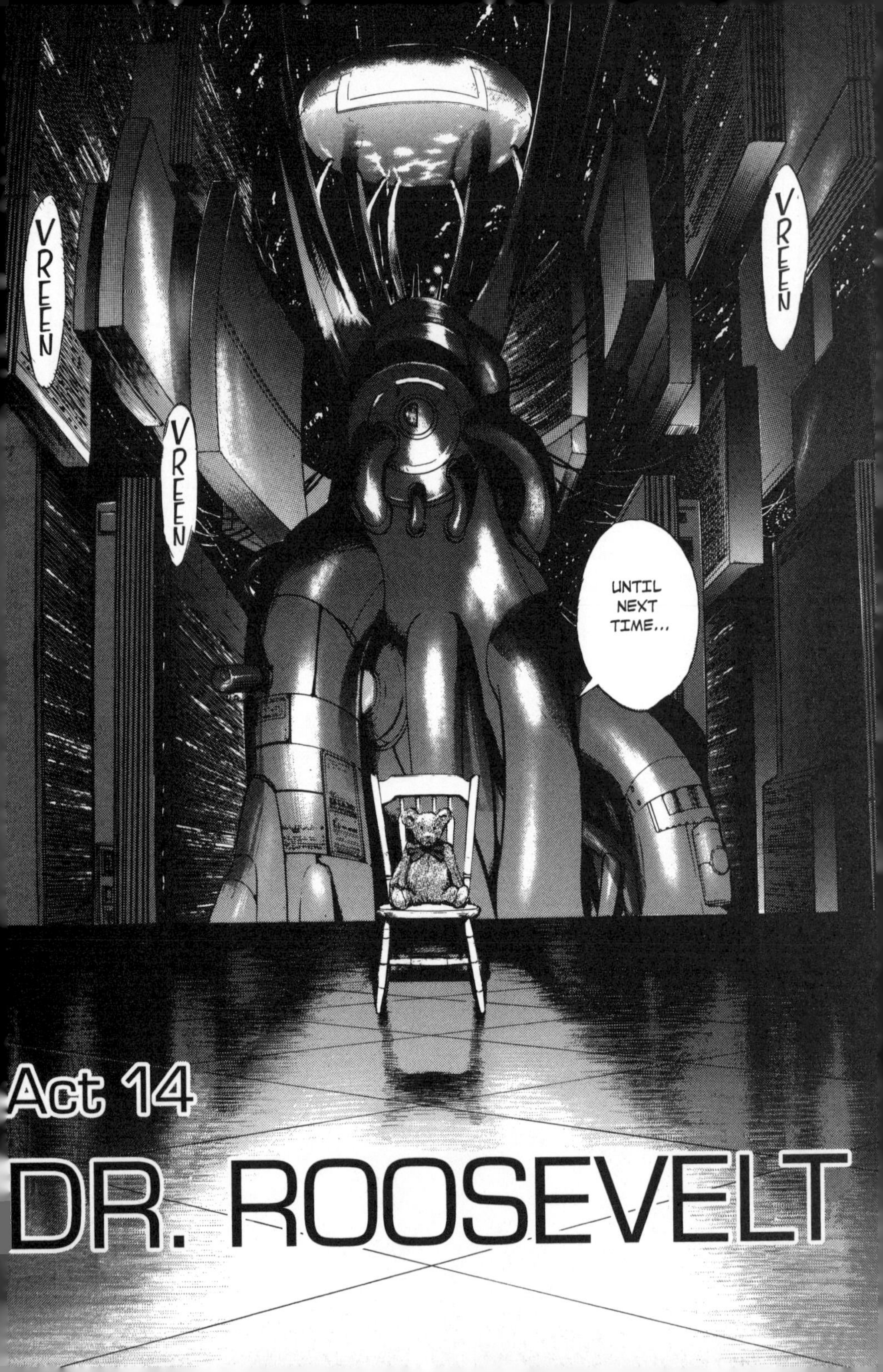
VREEN
VREEN
VREEN
UNTIL NEXT TIME...

Act 14 DR. ROOSEVELT

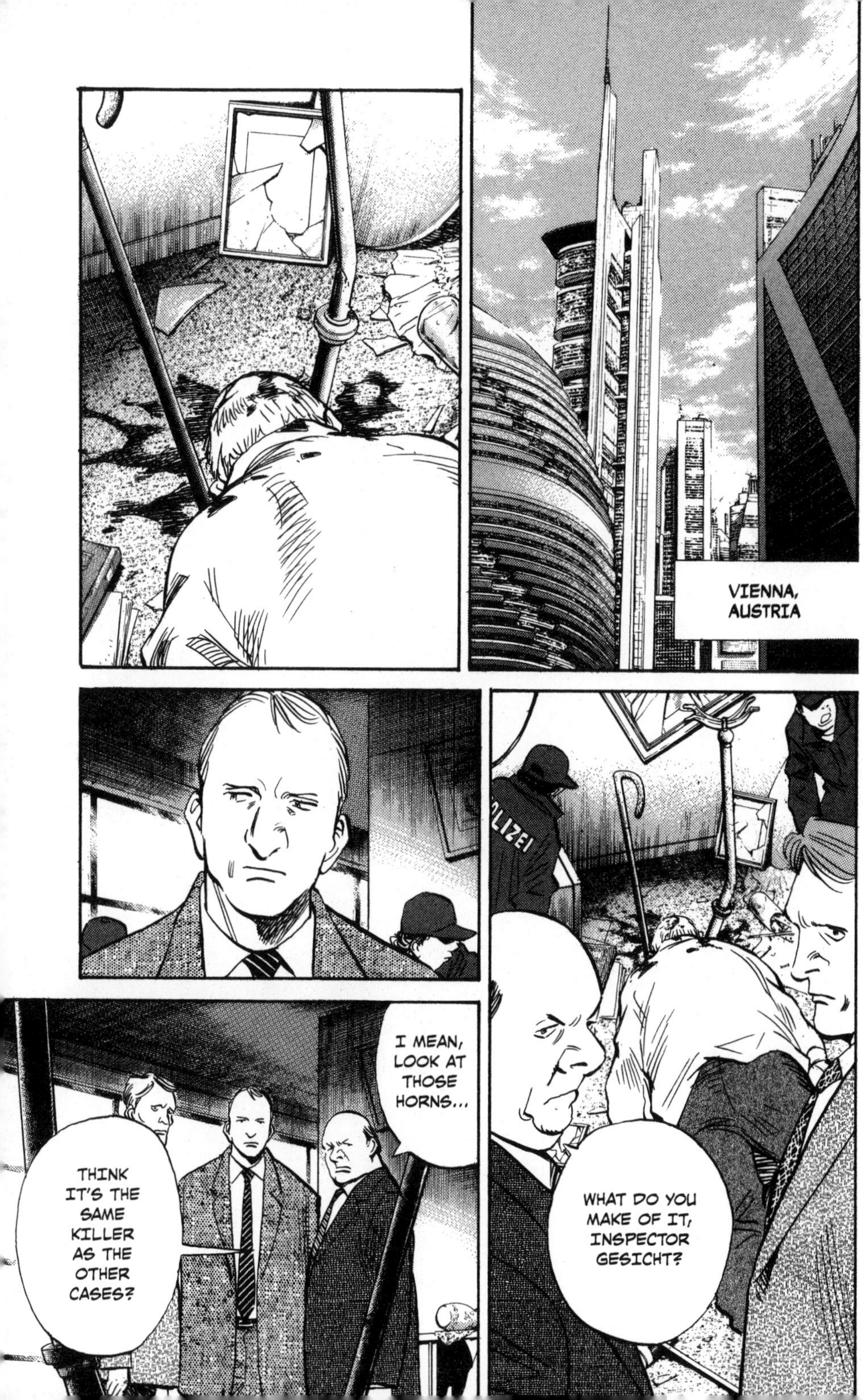
VIENNA, AUSTRIA
WHAT DO YOU MAKE OF IT, INSPECTOR GESICHT?
I MEAN, LOOK AT THOSE HORNS...
THINK IT'S THE SAME KILLER AS THE OTHER CASES?

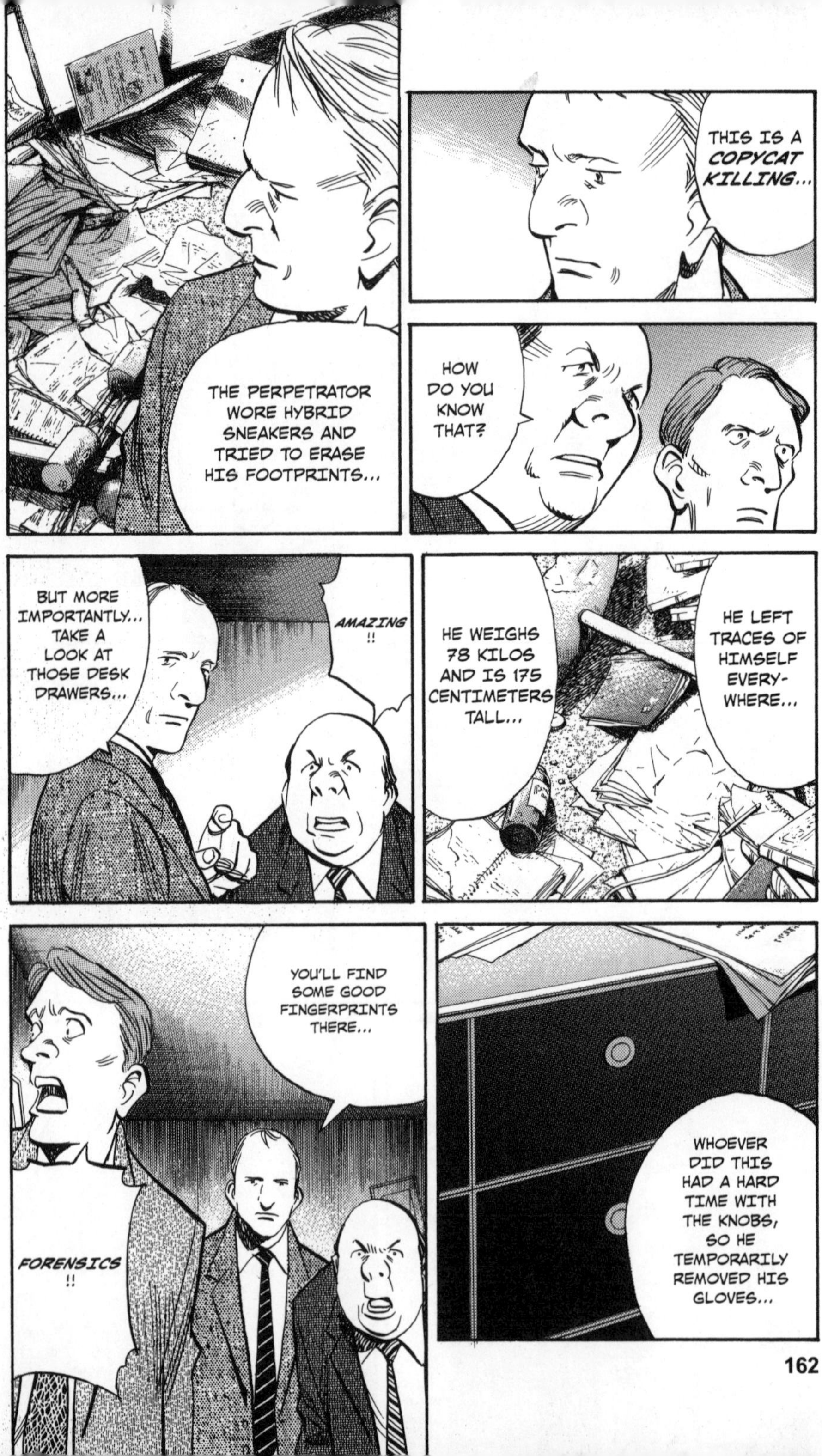
THIS IS A COPYCAT KILLING...
HOW DO YOU KNOW THAT?
THE PERPETRATOR WORE HYBRID SNEAKERS AND TRIED TO ERASE HIS FOOTPRINTS...
HE LEFT TRACES OF HIMSELF EVERYWHERE...
HE WEIGHS 78 KILOS AND IS 175 CENTIMETERS TALL...
AMAZING !!
BUT MORE IMPORTANTLY... TAKE A LOOK AT THOSE DESK DRAWERS...
WHOEVER DID THIS HAD A HARD TIME WITH THE KNOBS, SO HE TEMPORARILY REMOVED HIS GLOVES...
YOU'LL FIND SOME GOOD FINGERPRINTS THERE...
FORENSICS !!

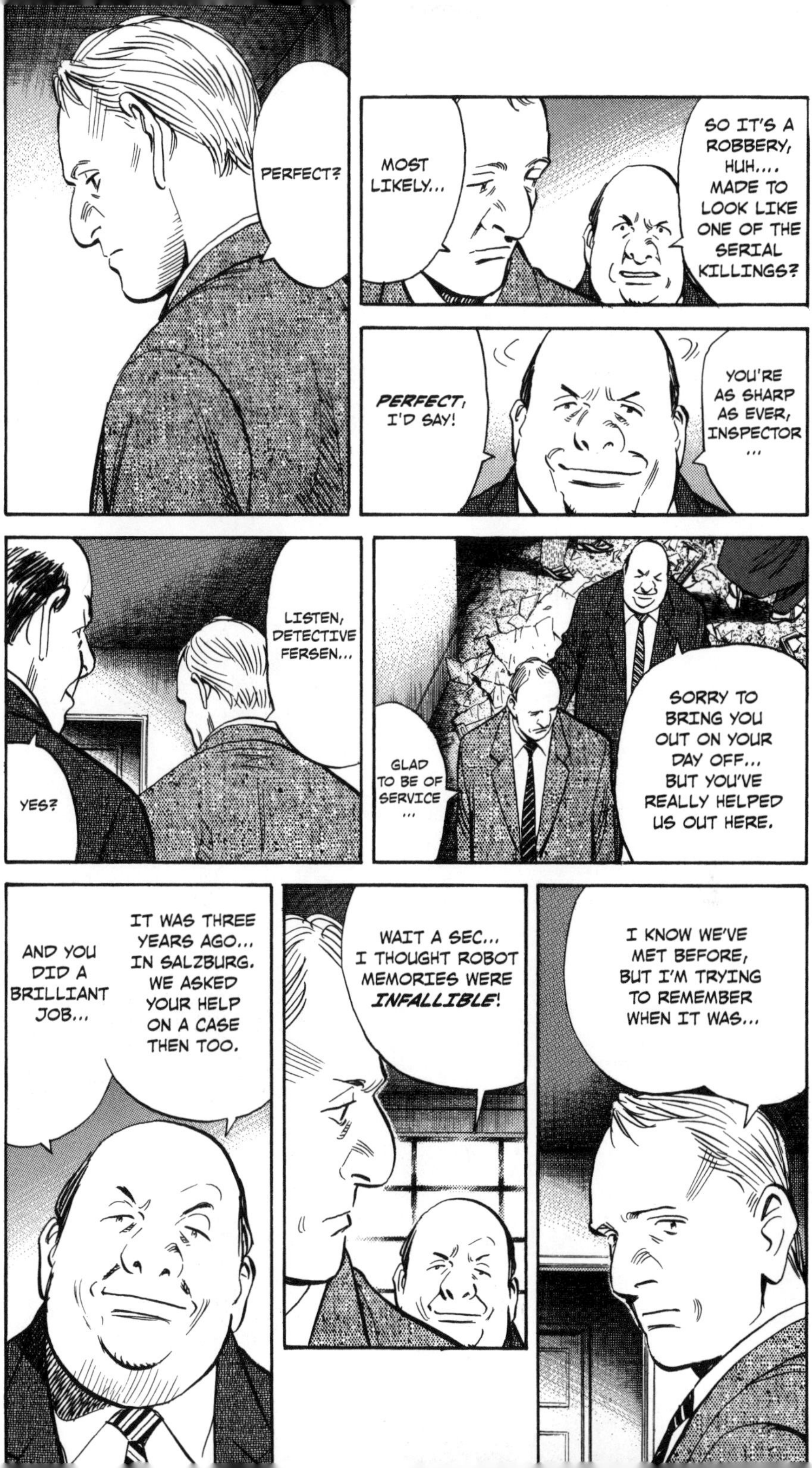
SO IT'S A ROBBERY, HUH.... MADE TO LOOK LIKE ONE OF THE SERIAL KILLINGS?
MOST LIKELY...
YOU'RE AS SHARP AS EVER, INSPECTOR ...
PERFECT, I'D SAY!
PERFECT?
SORRY TO BRING YOU OUT ON YOUR DAY OFF... BUT YOU'VE REALLY HELPED US OUT HERE.
GLAD TO BE OF SERVICE ...
LISTEN, DETECTIVE FERSEN...
YES?
I KNOW WE'VE MET BEFORE, BUT I'M TRYING TO REMEMBER WHEN IT WAS...
WAIT A SEC... I THOUGHT ROBOT MEMORIES WERE *INFALLIBLE*!
IT WAS THREE YEARS AGO... IN SALZBURG. WE ASKED YOUR HELP ON A CASE THEN TOO.
AND YOU DID A BRILLIANT JOB...

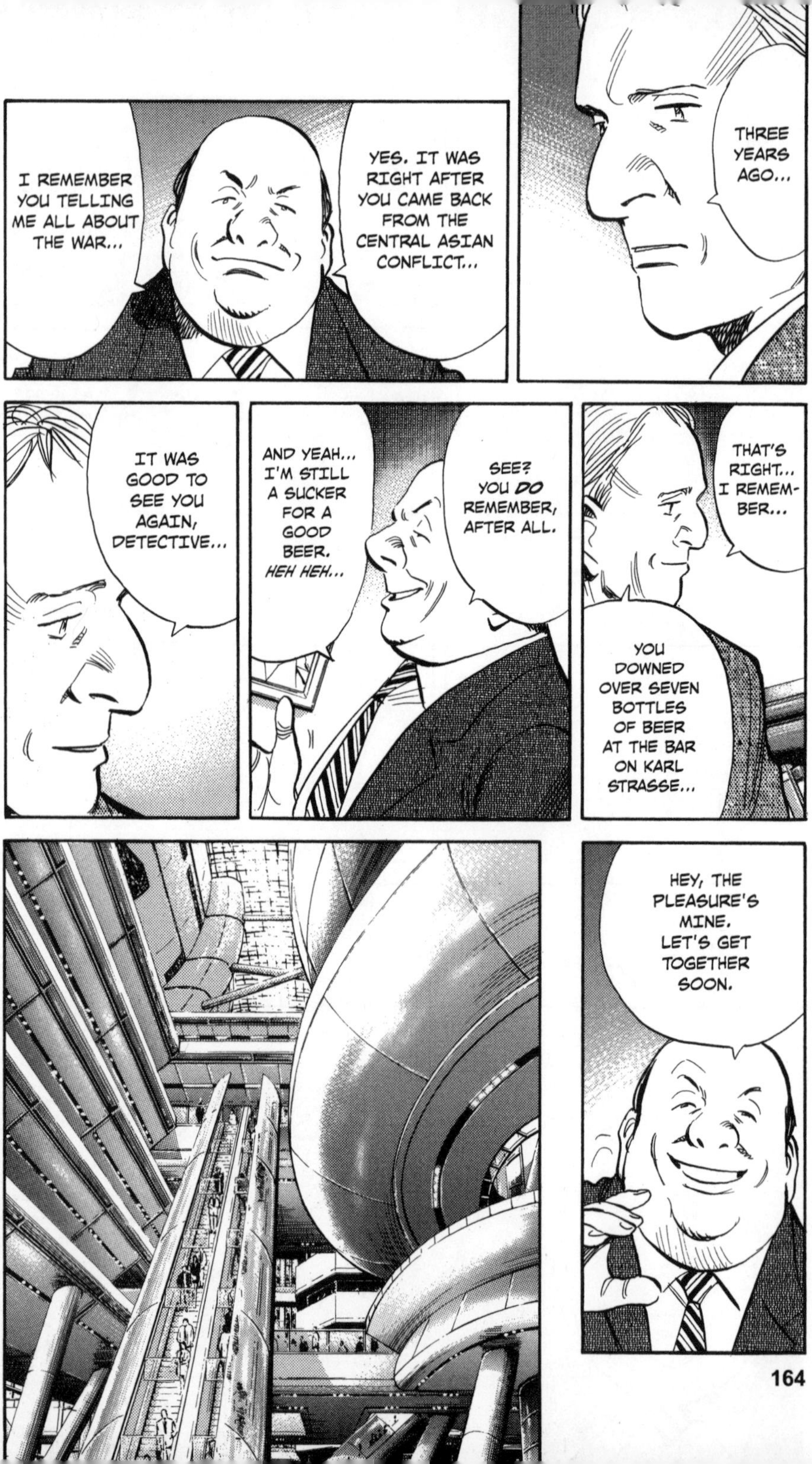
THREE YEARS AGO...
YES. IT WAS RIGHT AFTER YOU CAME BACK FROM THE CENTRAL ASIAN CONFLICT...
I REMEMBER YOU TELLING ME ALL ABOUT THE WAR...
THAT'S RIGHT... I REMEMBER...
YOU DOWNED OVER SEVEN BOTTLES OF BEER AT THE BAR ON KARL STRASSE...
SEE? YOU *DO* REMEMBER, AFTER ALL.
AND YEAH... I'M STILL A SUCKER FOR A GOOD BEER. *HEH HEH...*
IT WAS GOOD TO SEE YOU AGAIN, DETECTIVE...
HEY, THE PLEASURE'S MINE. LET'S GET TOGETHER SOON.

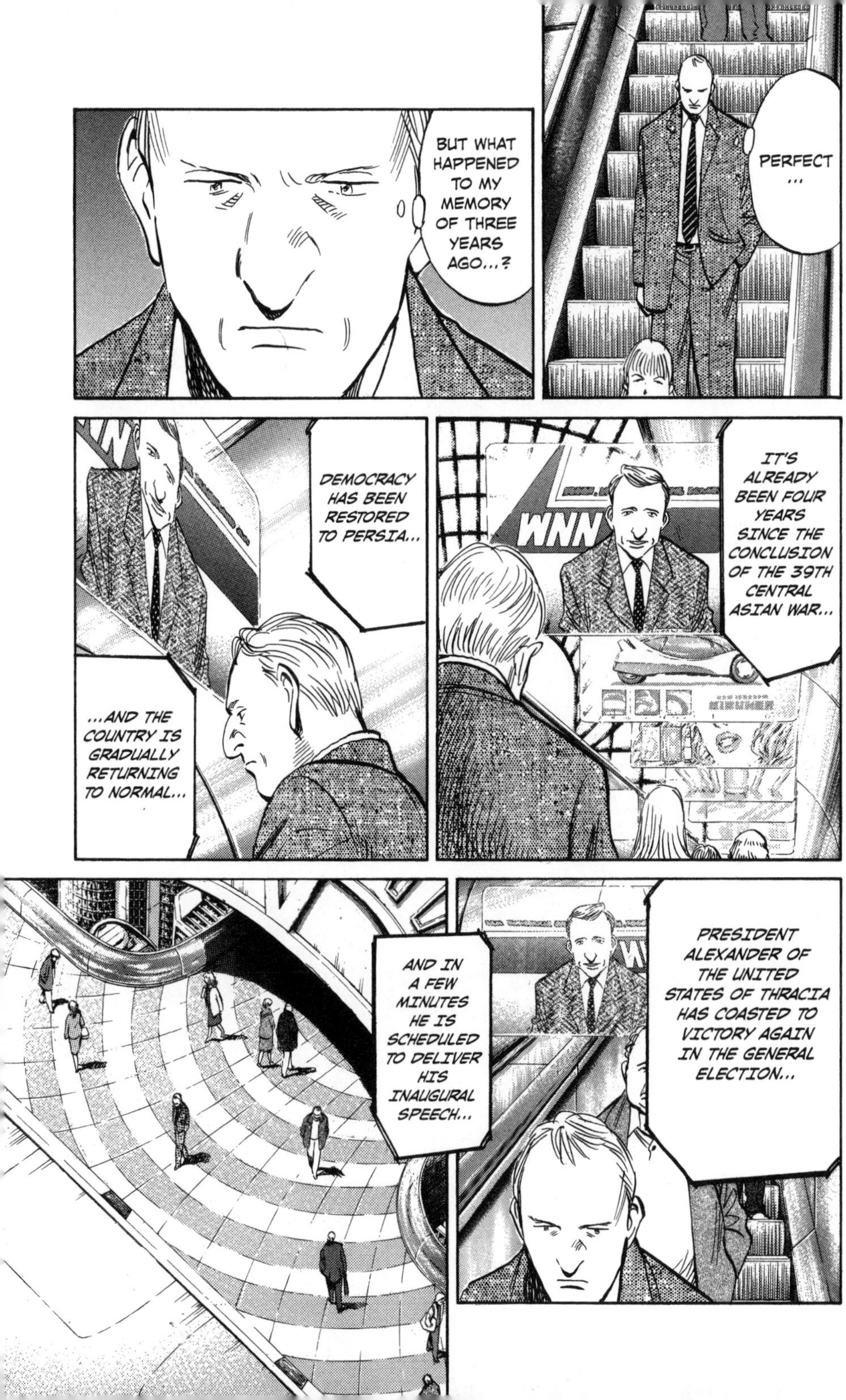
PERFECT...
BUT WHAT HAPPENED TO MY MEMORY OF THREE YEARS AGO...?
IT'S ALREADY BEEN FOUR YEARS SINCE THE CONCLUSION OF THE 39TH CENTRAL ASIAN WAR...
WNN
DEMOCRACY HAS BEEN RESTORED TO PERSIA...
...AND THE COUNTRY IS GRADUALLY RETURNING TO NORMAL...
PRESIDENT ALEXANDER OF THE UNITED STATES OF THRACIA HAS COASTED TO VICTORY AGAIN IN THE GENERAL ELECTION...
AND IN A FEW MINUTES HE IS SCHEDULED TO DELIVER HIS INAUGURAL SPEECH...

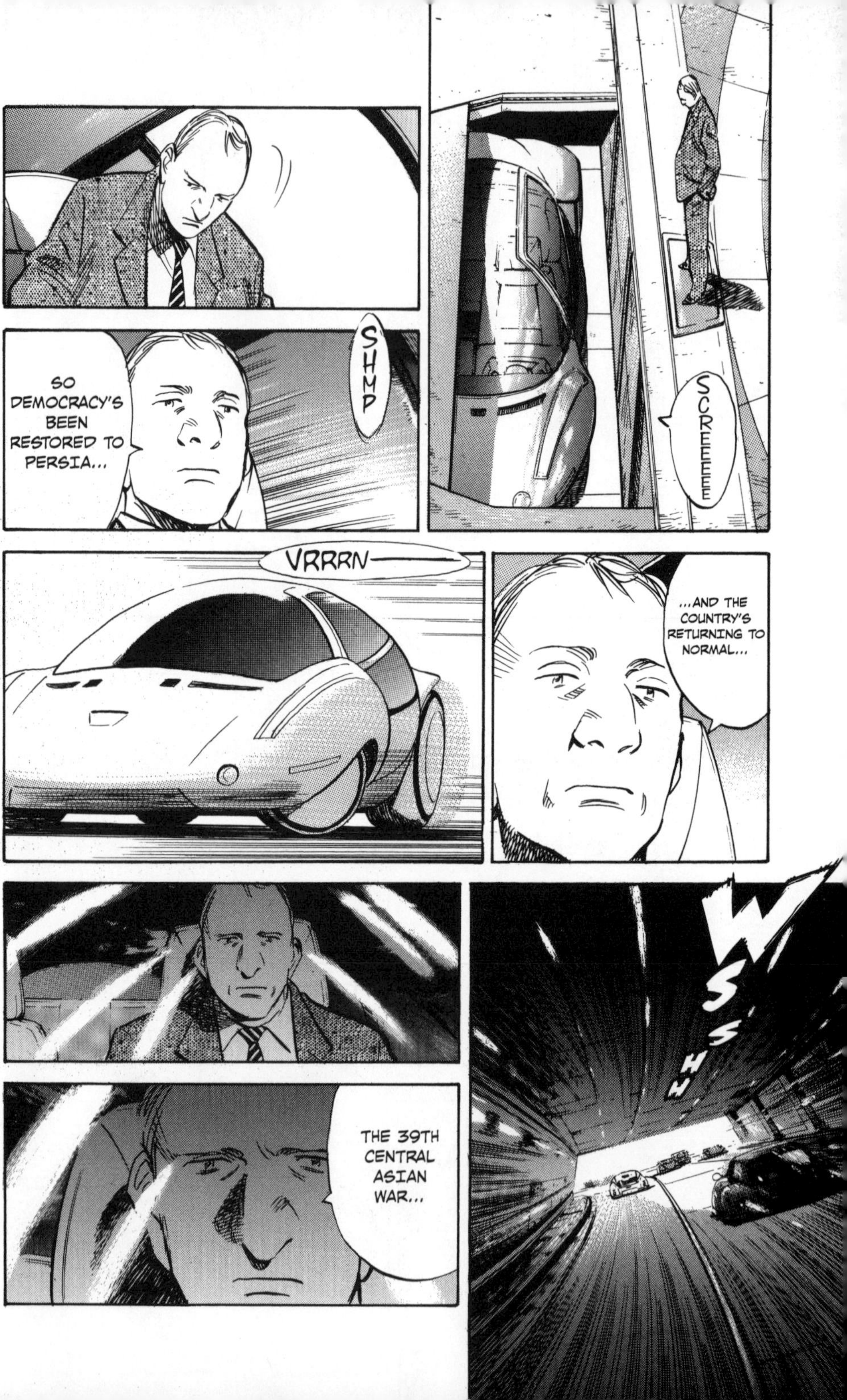
SCREEEEE
SHMP
SO DEMOCRACY'S BEEN RESTORED TO PERSIA...
...AND THE COUNTRY'S RETURNING TO NORMAL...
VRRRN
WSSHH
THE 39TH CENTRAL ASIAN WAR...

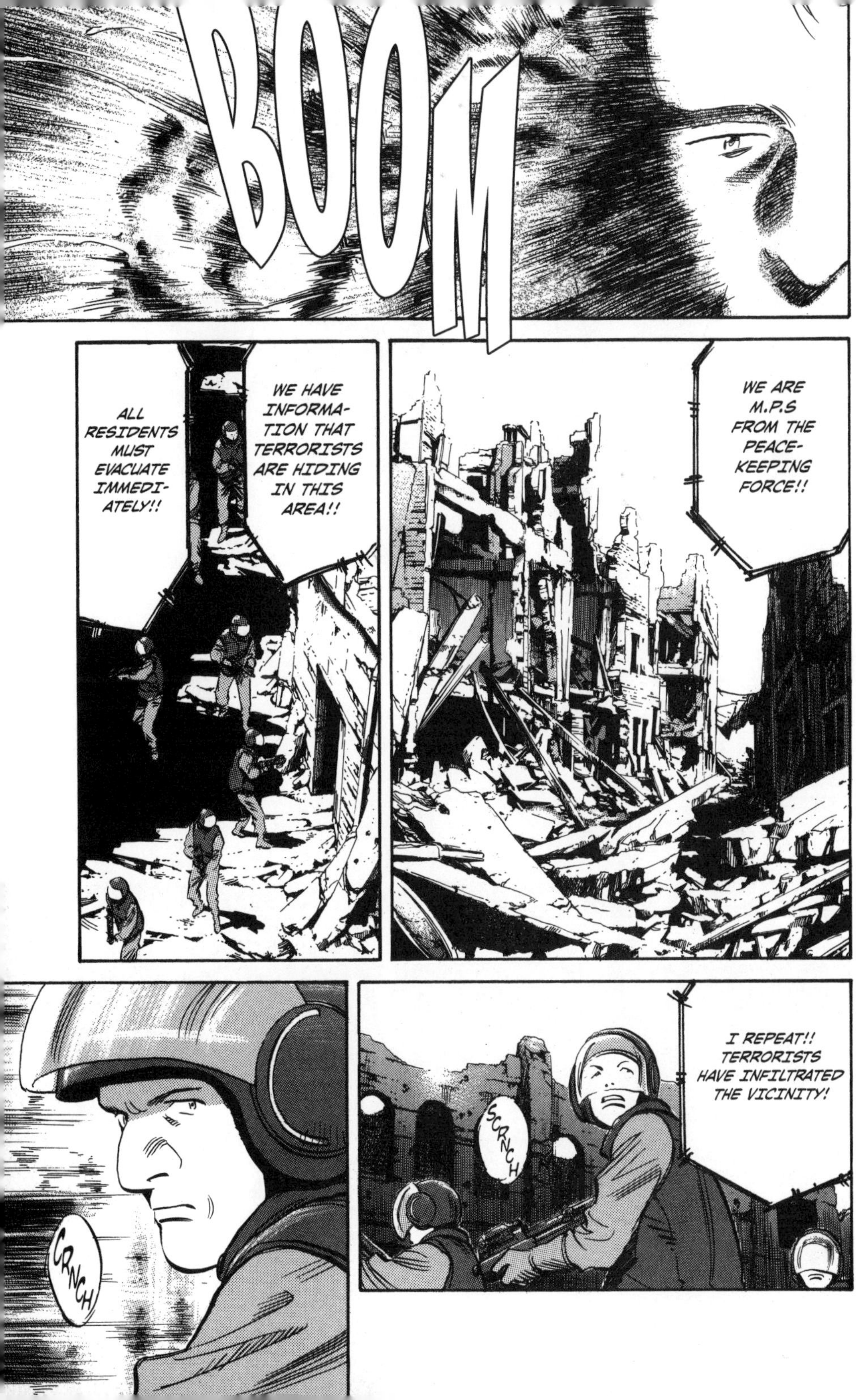
BOOM
WE ARE M.P.S FROM THE PEACE-KEEPING FORCE!!
WE HAVE INFORMATION THAT TERRORISTS ARE HIDING IN THIS AREA!!
ALL RESIDENTS MUST EVACUATE IMMEDIATELY!!
I REPEAT!! TERRORISTS HAVE INFILTRATED THE VICINITY!
SCRNCH
CRNCH

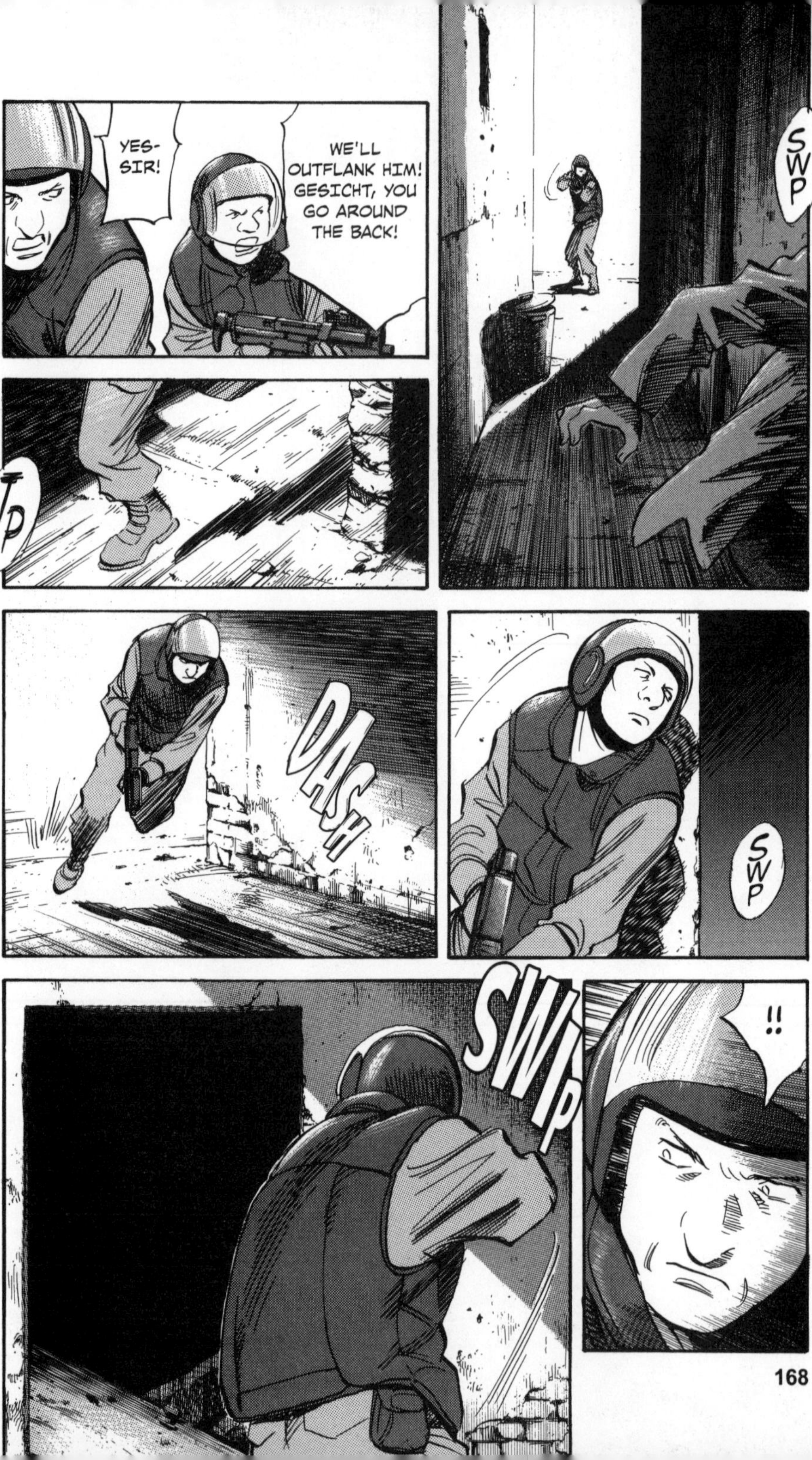
SWP
WE'LL OUTFLANK HIM! GESICHT, YOU GO AROUND THE BACK!
YES-SIR!
TP
SWP
DASH
!!
SWIP

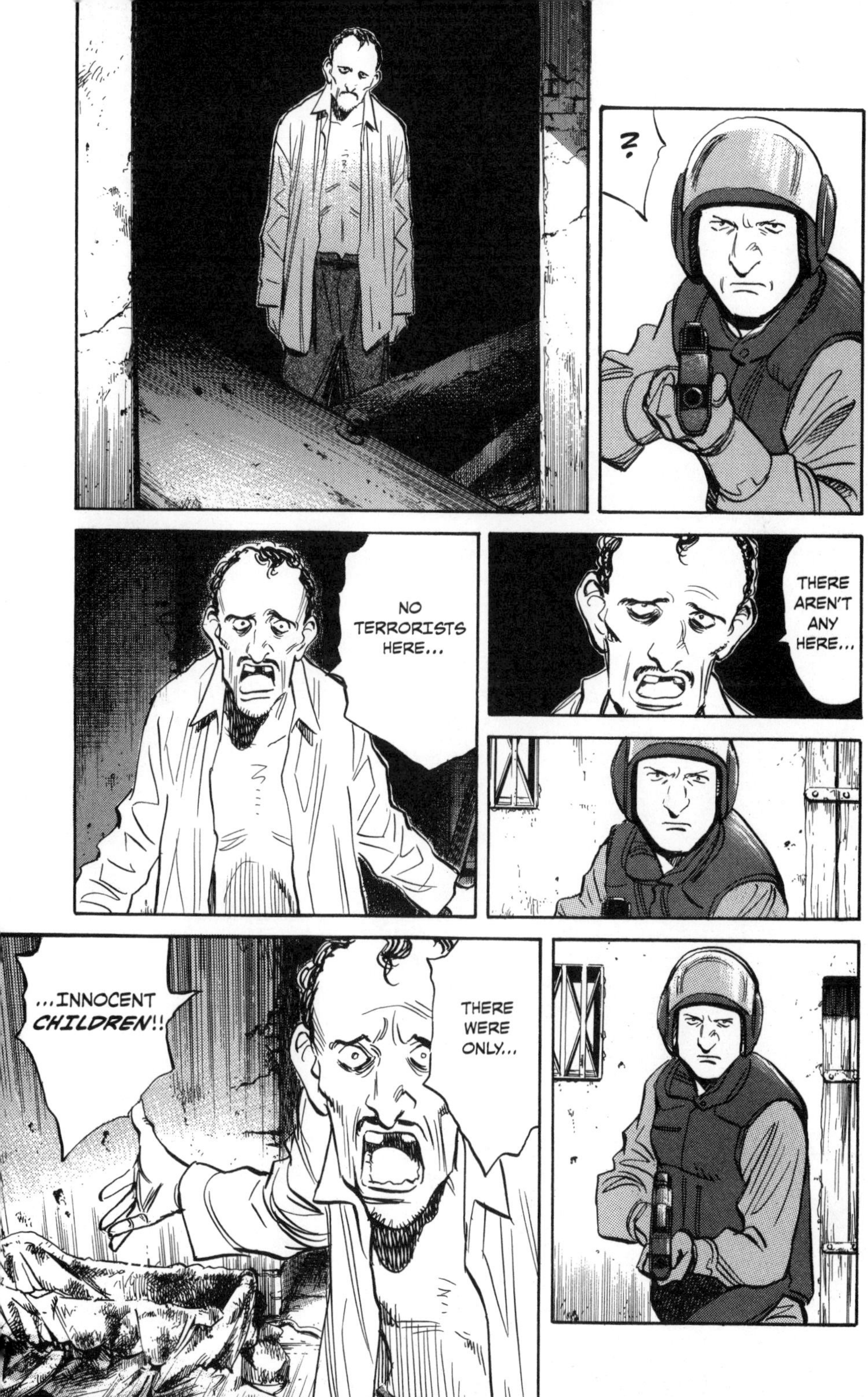
?
THERE AREN'T ANY HERE...
NO TERRORISTS HERE...
THERE WERE ONLY...
...INNOCENT CHILDREN!!

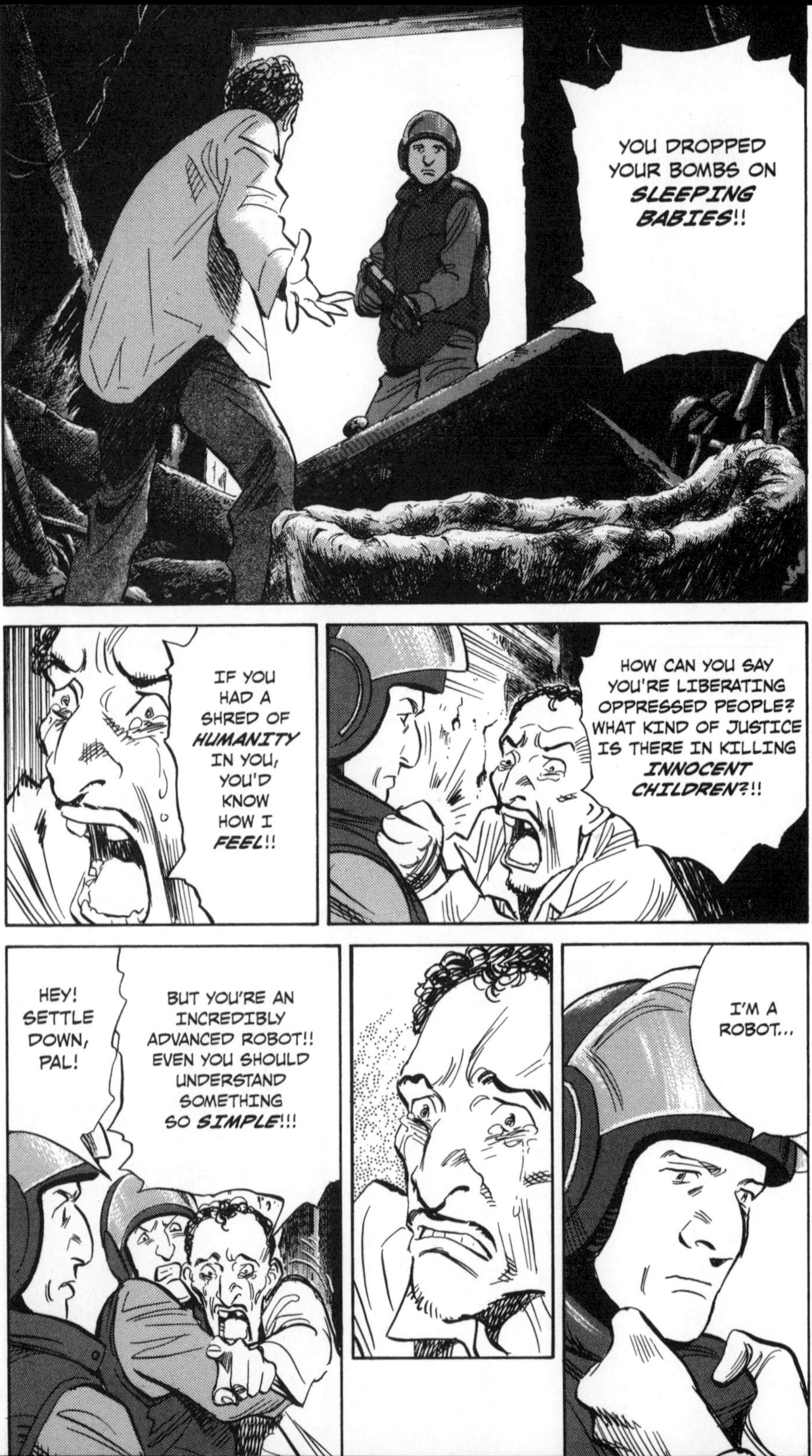
YOU DROPPED YOUR BOMBS ON *SLEEPING BABIES*!!
HOW CAN YOU SAY YOU'RE LIBERATING OPPRESSED PEOPLE? WHAT KIND OF JUSTICE IS THERE IN KILLING *INNOCENT CHILDREN*?!!
IF YOU HAD A SHRED OF *HUMANITY* IN YOU, YOU'D KNOW HOW I *FEEL*!!
I'M A ROBOT...
BUT YOU'RE AN INCREDIBLY ADVANCED ROBOT!! EVEN YOU SHOULD UNDERSTAND SOMETHING SO *SIMPLE*!!!
HEY! SETTLE DOWN, PAL!

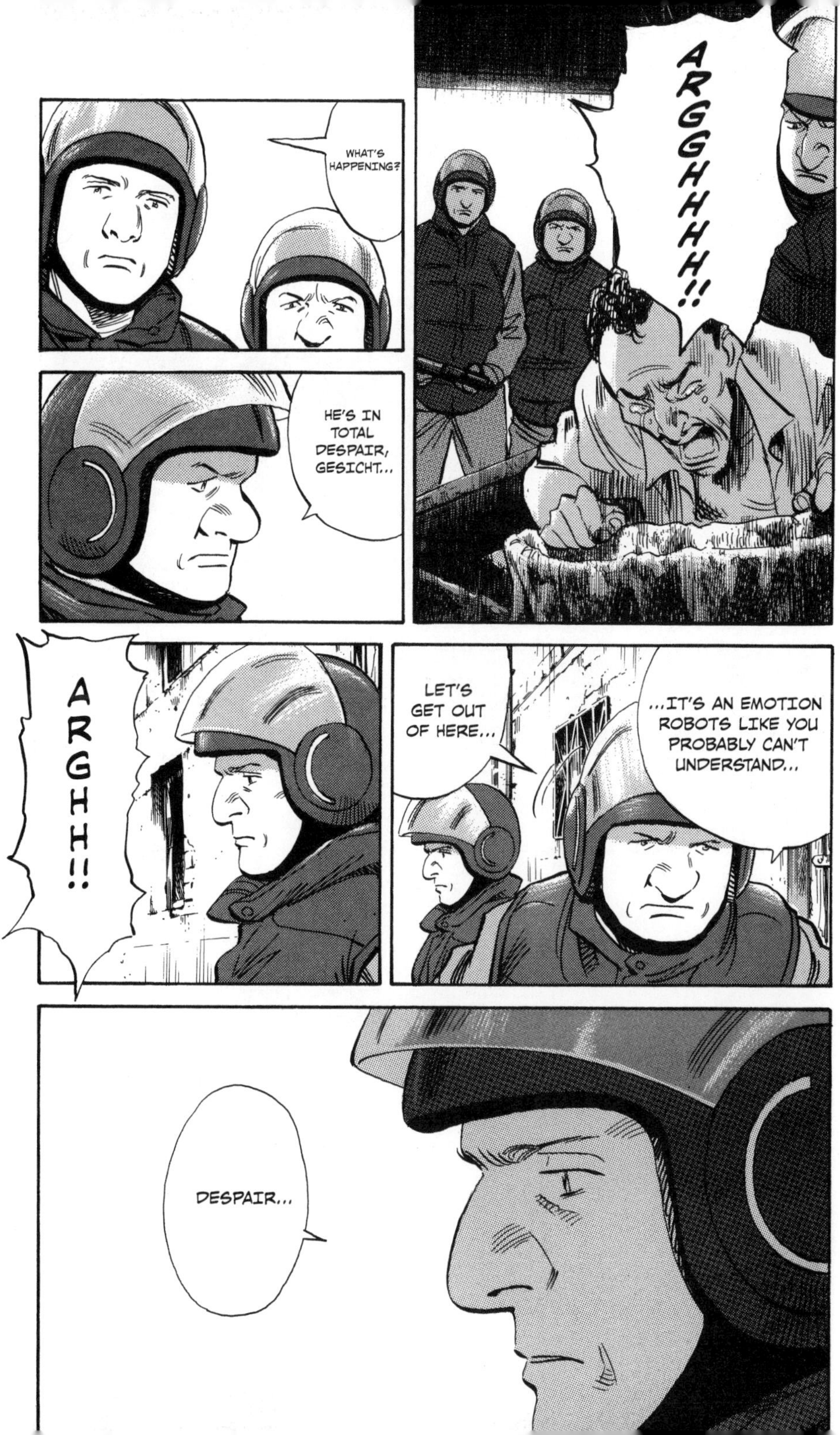
ARGGHHHH!!
WHAT'S HAPPENING?
HE'S IN TOTAL DESPAIR, GESICHT...
...IT'S AN EMOTION ROBOTS LIKE YOU PROBABLY CAN'T UNDERSTAND...
LET'S GET OUT OF HERE...
ARGHH!!
DESPAIR...

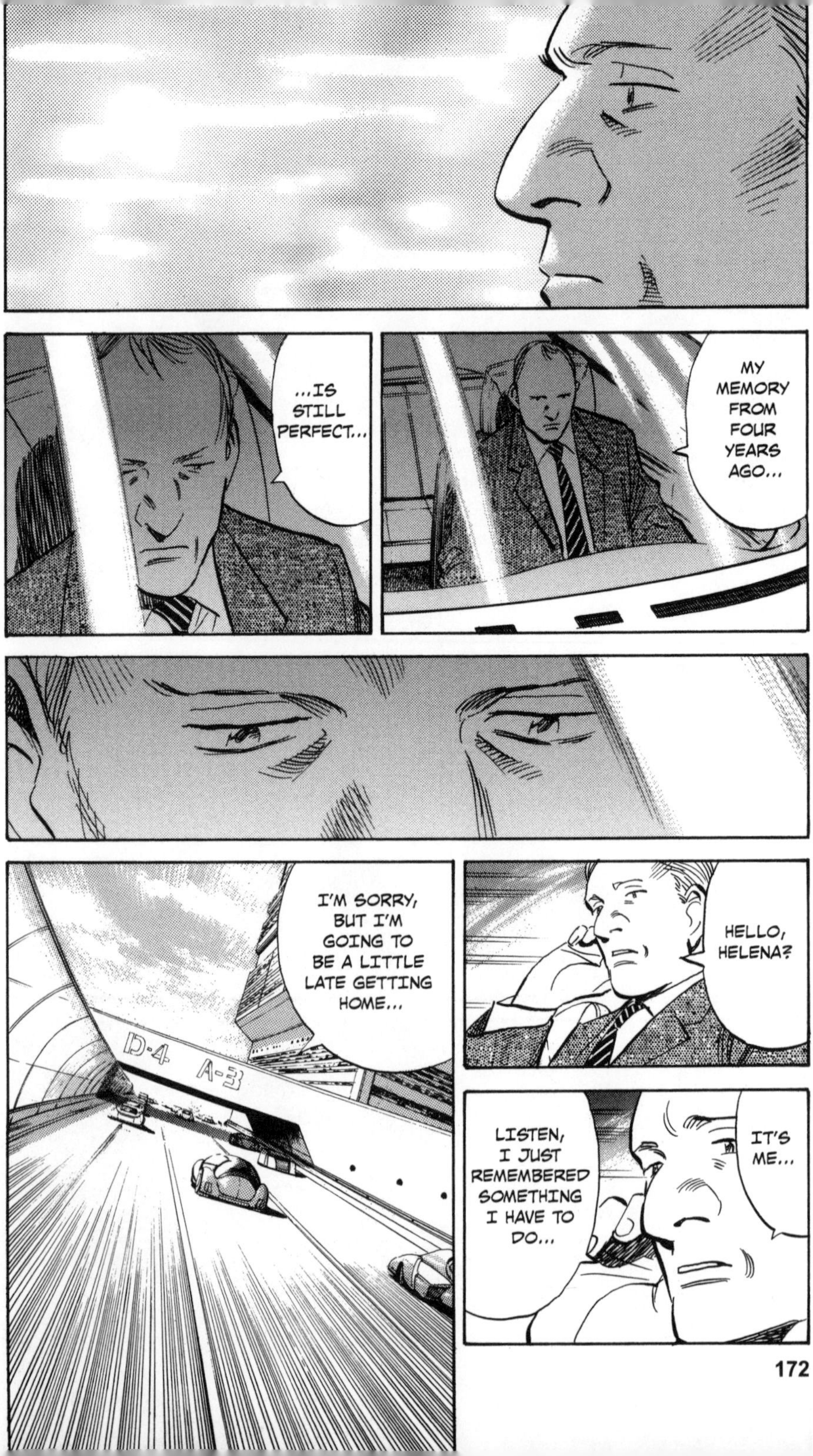
MY MEMORY FROM FOUR YEARS AGO...
...IS STILL PERFECT...
HELLO, HELENA?
IT'S ME...
LISTEN, I JUST REMEMBERED SOMETHING I HAVE TO DO...
I'M SORRY, BUT I'M GOING TO BE A LITTLE LATE GETTING HOME...
D-4
A-3

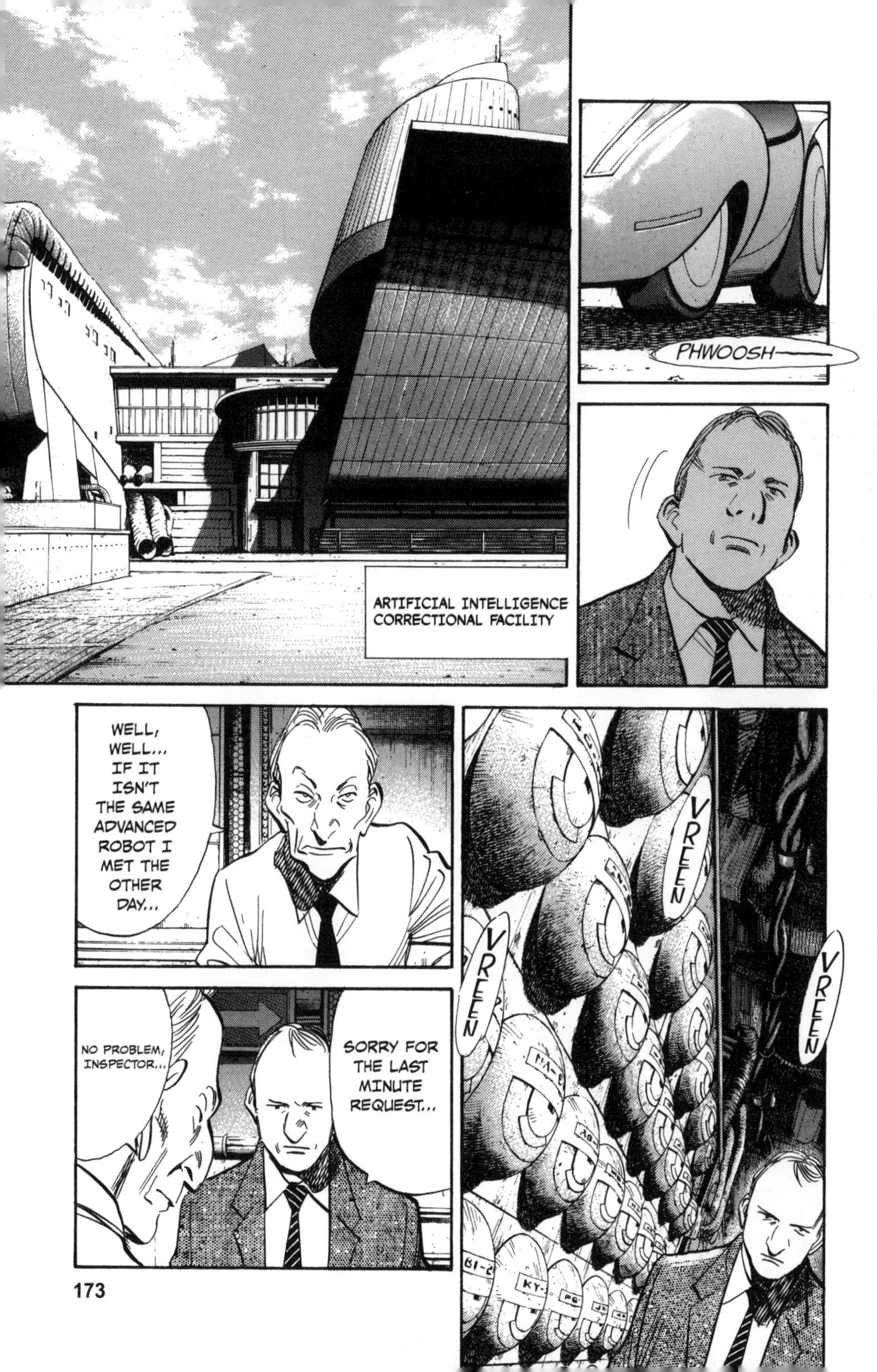
PHWOOSH
ARTIFICIAL INTELLIGENCE CORRECTIONAL FACILITY
VREEN
VREEN
VREEN
WELL, WELL... IF IT ISN'T THE SAME ADVANCED ROBOT I MET THE OTHER DAY...
SORRY FOR THE LAST MINUTE REQUEST...
NO PROBLEM, INSPECTOR...

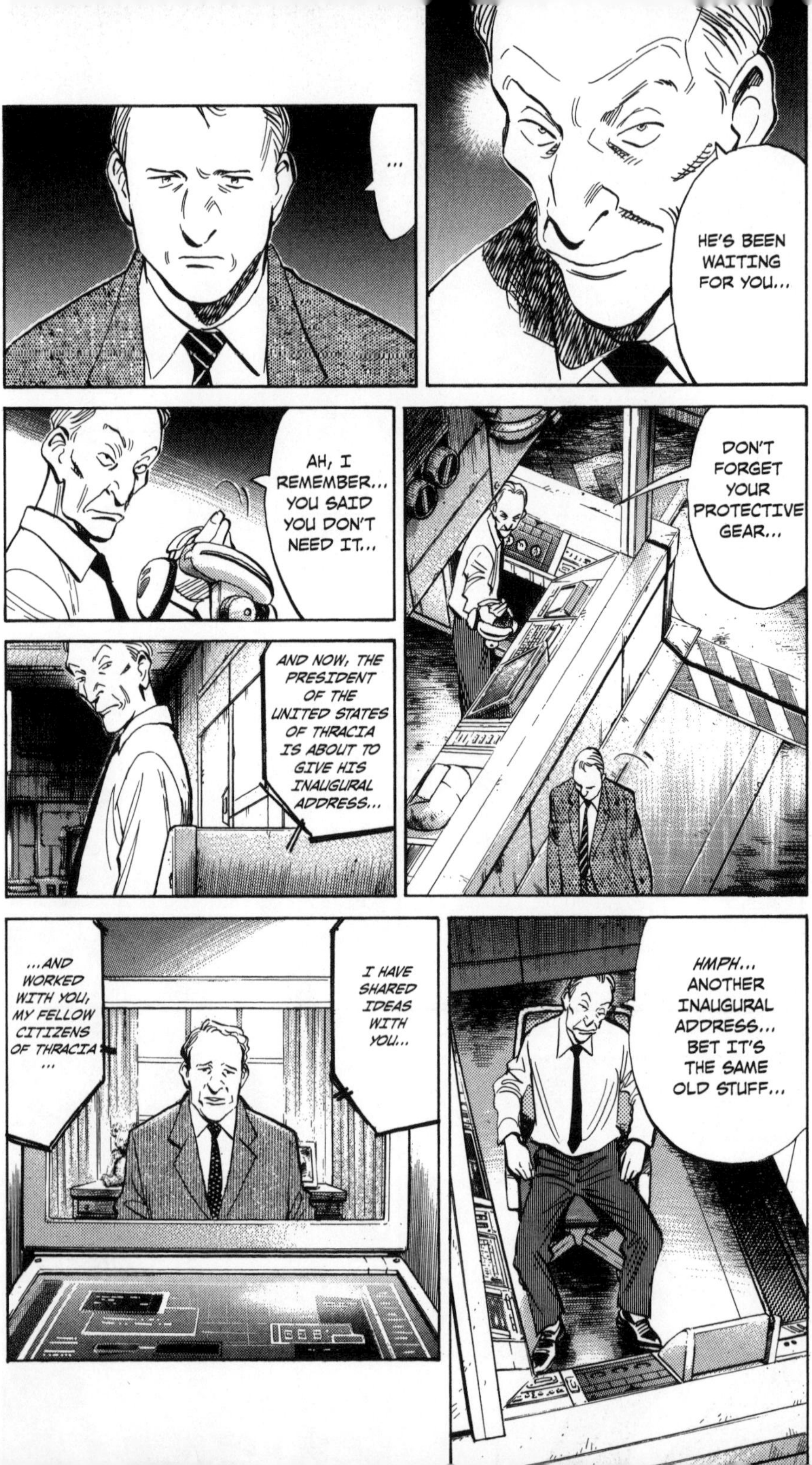
HE'S BEEN WAITING FOR YOU...
...
DON'T FORGET YOUR PROTECTIVE GEAR...
AH, I REMEMBER... YOU SAID YOU DON'T NEED IT...
AND NOW, THE PRESIDENT OF THE UNITED STATES OF THRACIA IS ABOUT TO GIVE HIS INAUGURAL ADDRESS...
HMPH... ANOTHER INAUGURAL ADDRESS... BET IT'S THE SAME OLD STUFF...
I HAVE SHARED IDEAS WITH YOU...
...AND WORKED WITH YOU, MY FELLOW CITIZENS OF THRACIA...

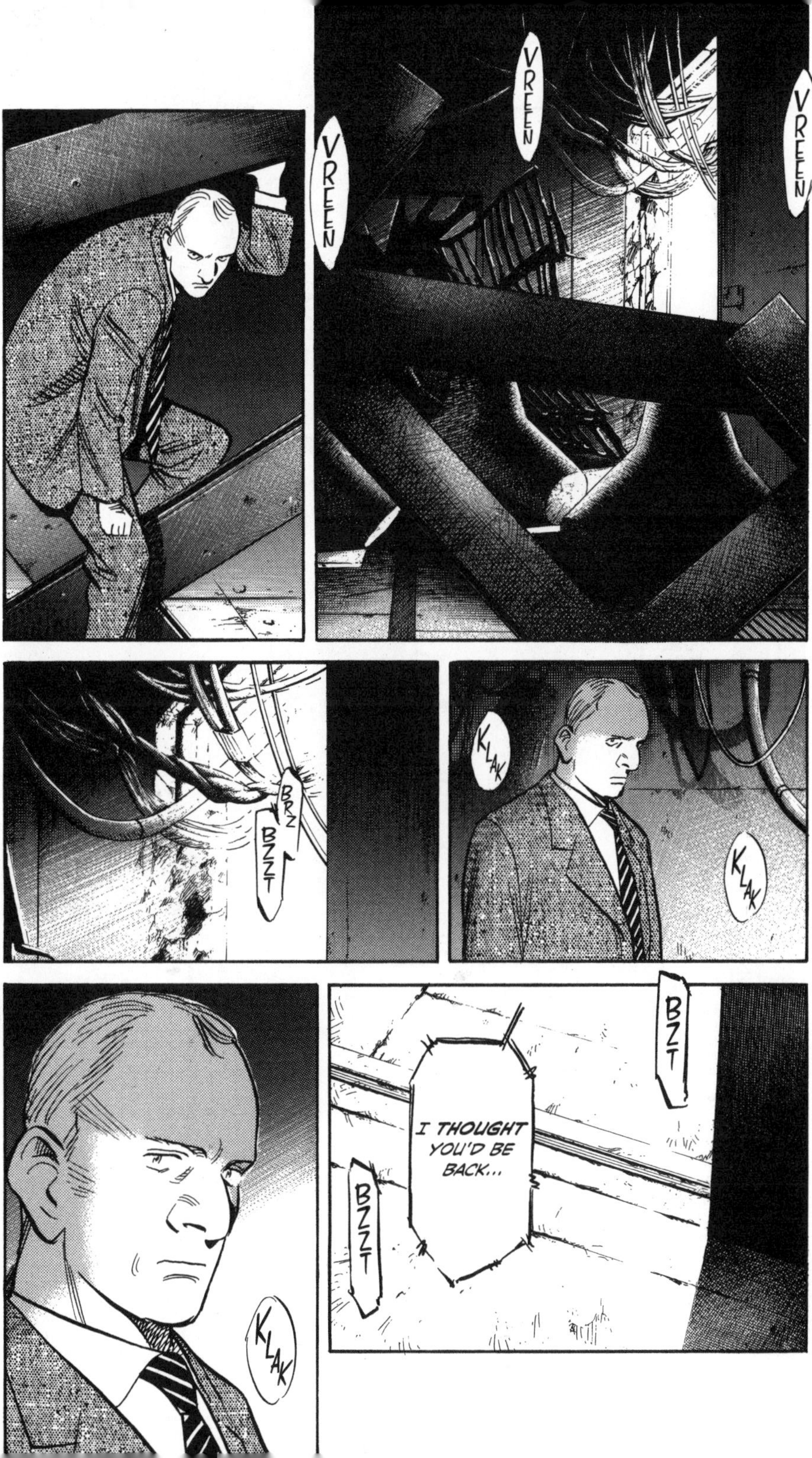
VREEN
VREEN
VREEN
KLAK
KLAK
BRZ
BZZT
BZT
I THOUGHT YOU'D BE BACK...
BZZT
KLAK

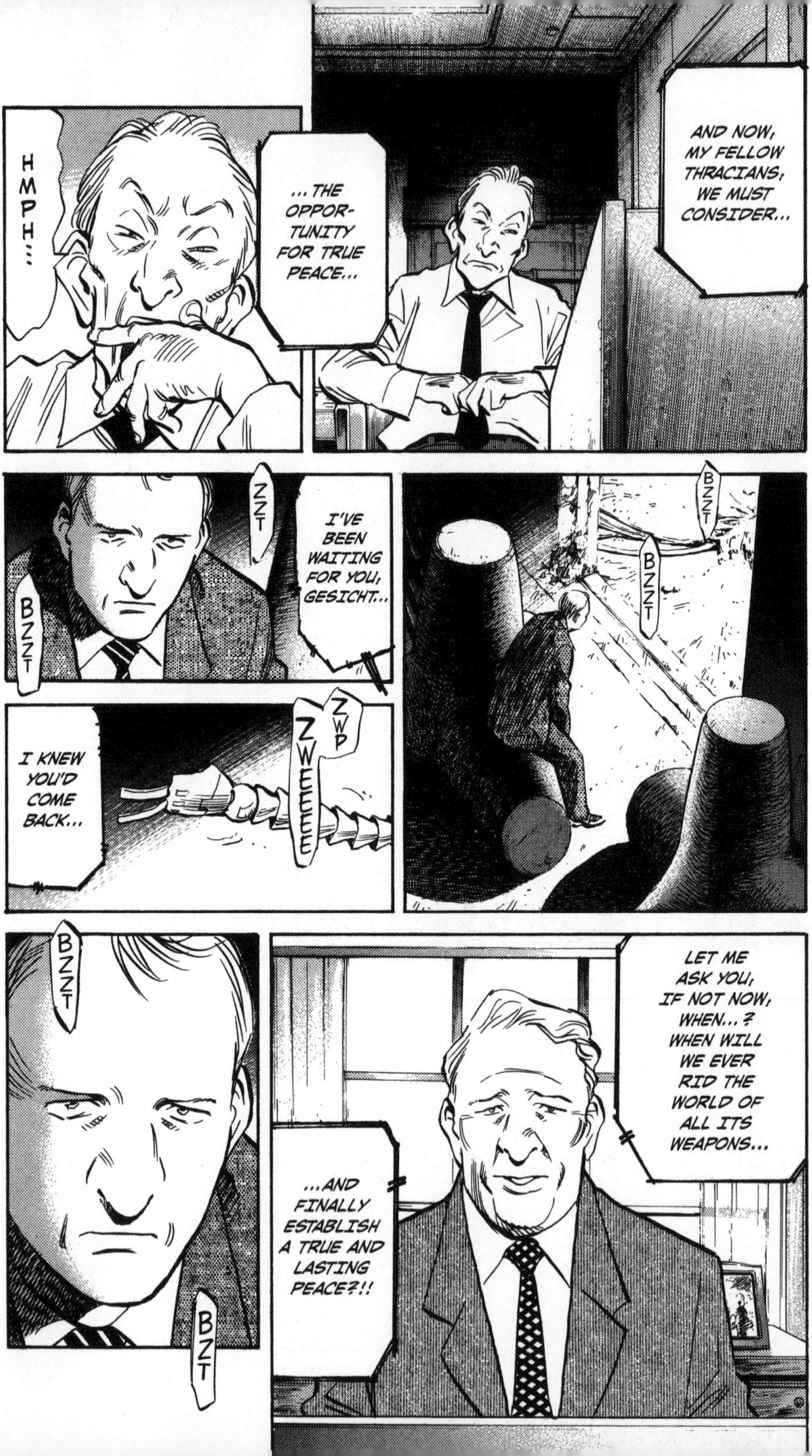
AND NOW, MY FELLOW THRACIANS, WE MUST CONSIDER...
...THE OPPORTUNITY FOR TRUE PEACE...
HMPH...
BZZT
BZZT
ZZT
I'VE BEEN WAITING FOR YOU, GESICHT...
BZZT
ZWP
ZWEEEEE
I KNEW YOU'D COME BACK...
LET ME ASK YOU, IF NOT NOW, WHEN...? WHEN WILL WE EVER RID THE WORLD OF ALL ITS WEAPONS...
...AND FINALLY ESTABLISH A TRUE AND LASTING PEACE?!!
BZZT
BZT

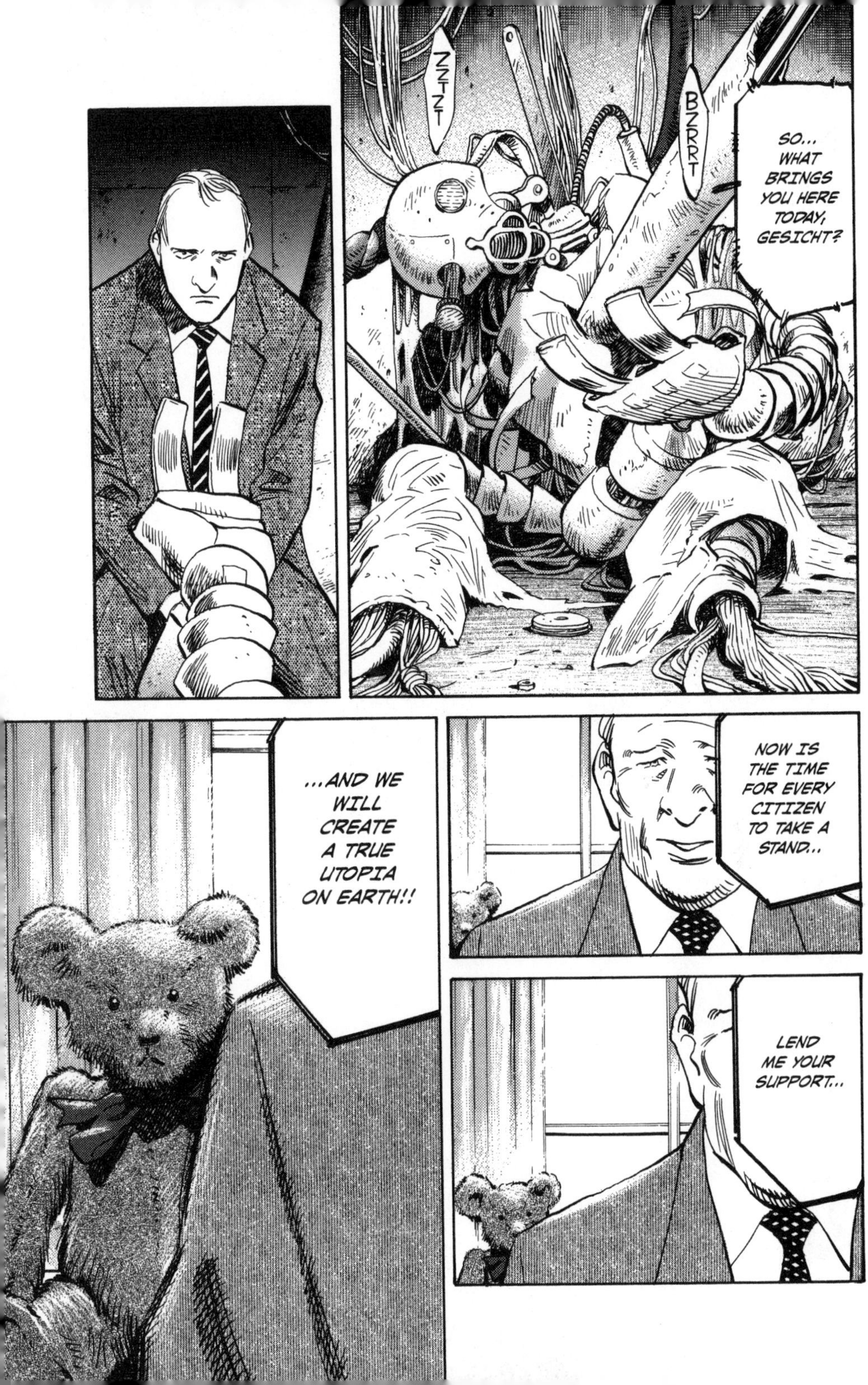
SO... WHAT BRINGS YOU HERE TODAY, GESICHT?
BZRRT
ZZTZT
NOW IS THE TIME FOR EVERY CITIZEN TO TAKE A STAND...
LEND ME YOUR SUPPORT...
...AND WE WILL CREATE A TRUE UTOPIA ON EARTH!!

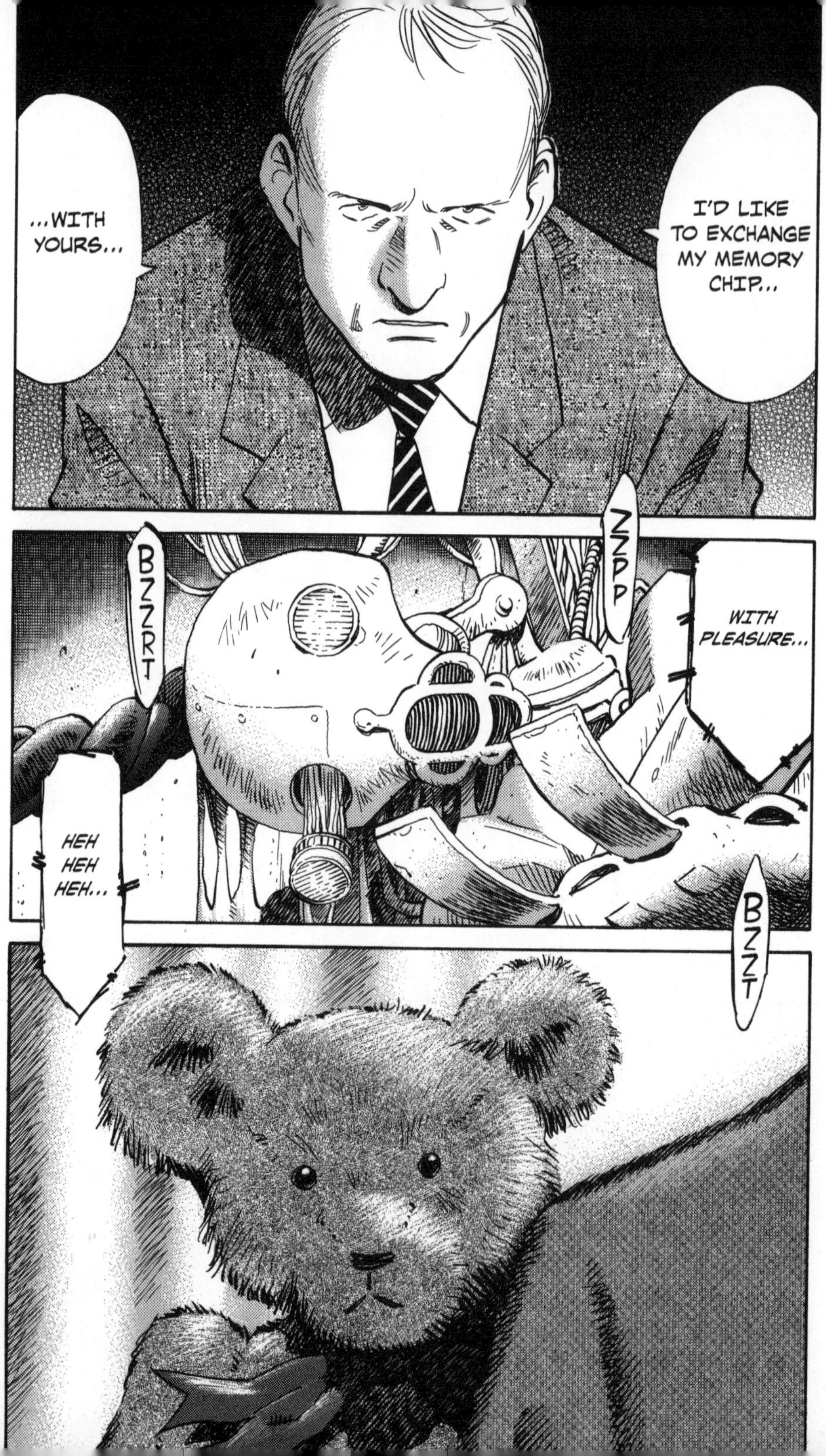
I'D LIKE TO EXCHANGE MY MEMORY CHIP...
...WITH YOURS...
ZZPP
WITH PLEASURE...
BZZRT
HEH HEH HEH...
BZZT

Act 15 ENEMY PARTS

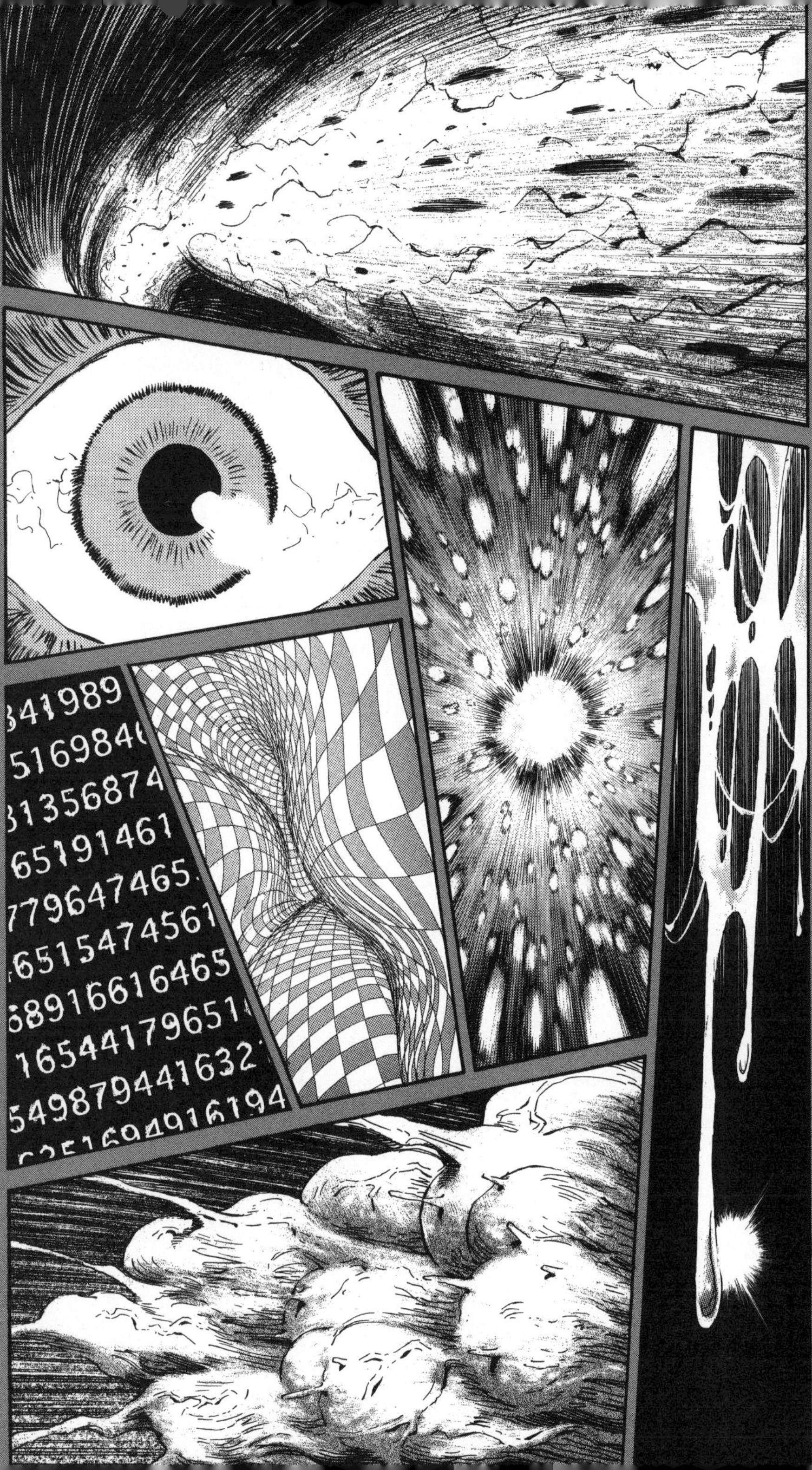

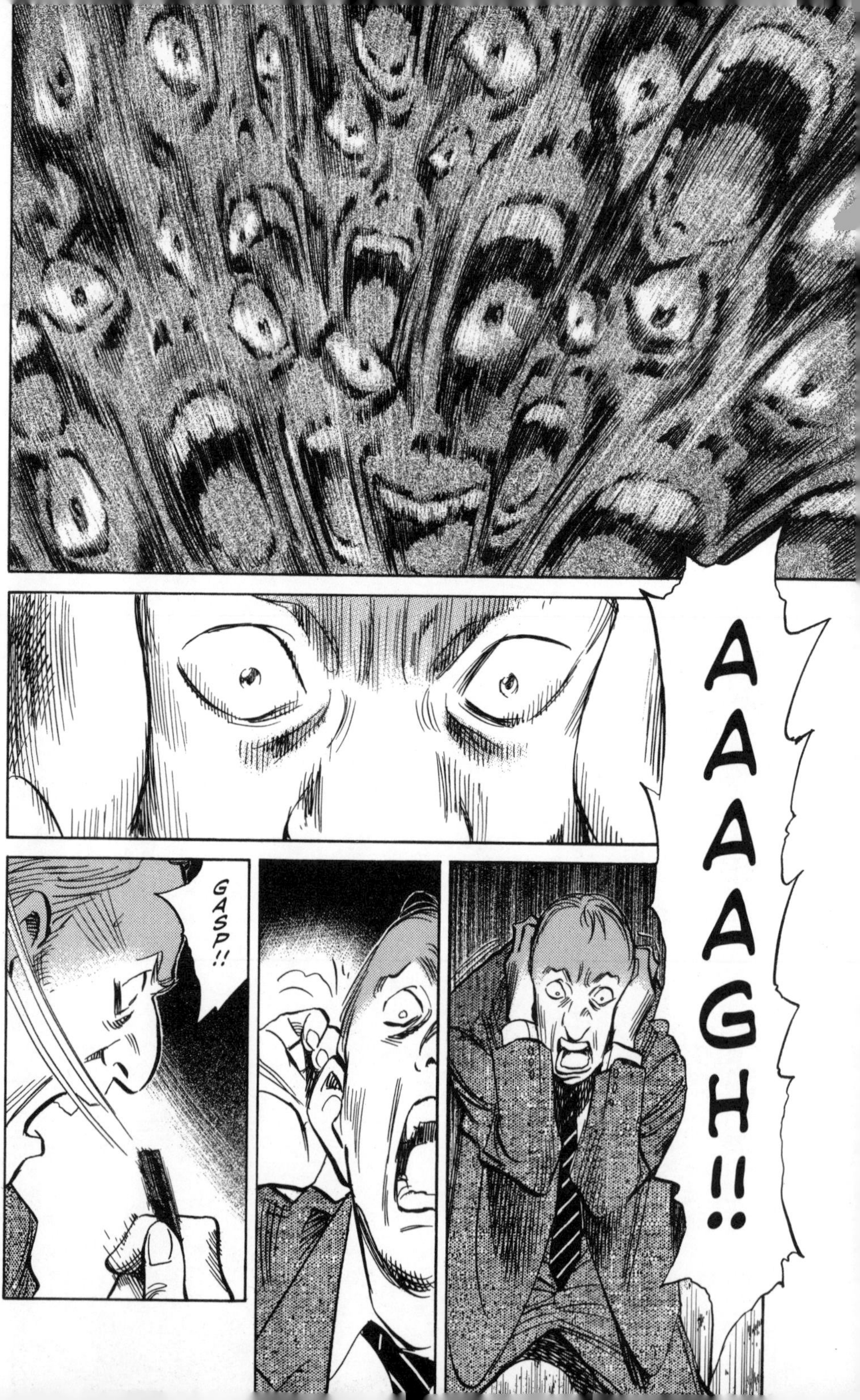
AAAAGH!!
GASP!!

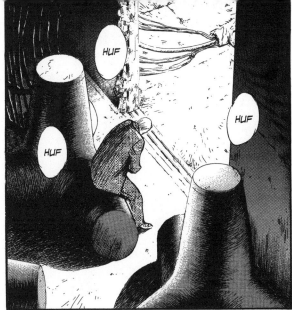

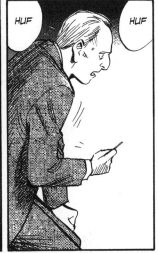

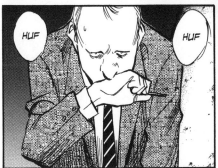

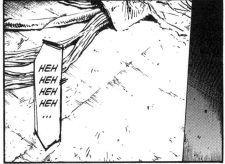

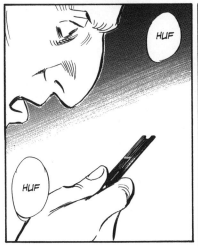

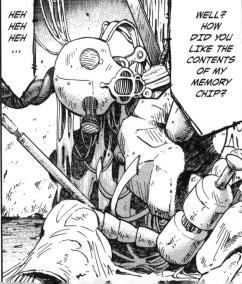

HUF
HUF
HUF
HUF
HUF
HEH HEH HEH HEH ...
HUF
HUF
WELL? HOW DID YOU LIKE THE CONTENTS OF MY MEMORY CHIP?
HEH HEH HEH ...
HUF
HUF

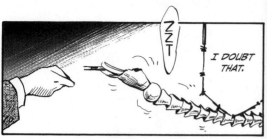

I...
I COULDN'T READ THE DATA...
ZZT
I DOUBT THAT.
BZZRT
A HIGHLY DEVELOPED ROBOT LIKE YOURSELF...?
HEH HEH HEH ...
THEN AGAIN, HIGHLY DEVELOPED COULD MEAN MANY THINGS...
FORGET ABOUT THAT... WHAT ABOUT MY MEMORY CHIP...?
I SEE THE PRESIDENT WAS RE-ELECTED ...
THE PRESIDENT?
YES. THE PRESIDENT OF THE UNITED STATES OF THRACIA...
HE HAS A BRAIN BEHIND HIM, YOU KNOW...

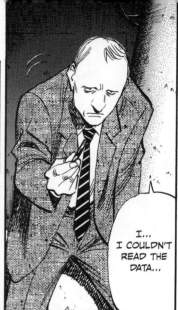

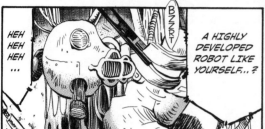

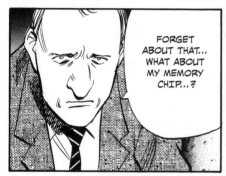

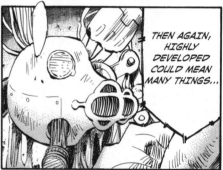

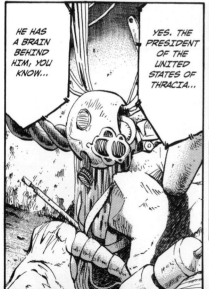

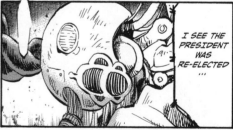

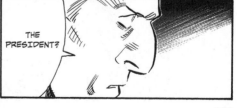

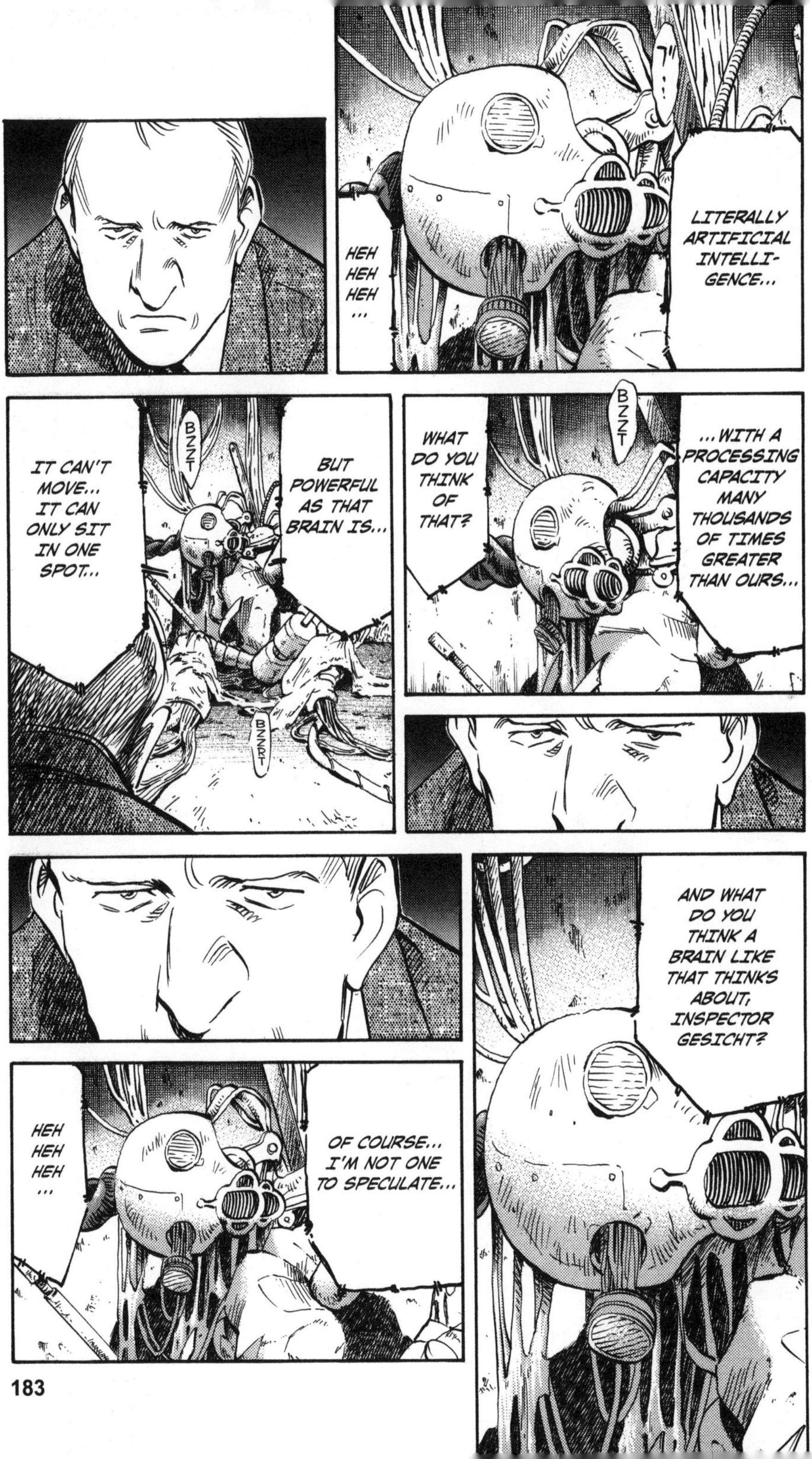
LITERALLY ARTIFICIAL INTELLIGENCE...
HEH HEH HEH ...
...WITH A PROCESSING CAPACITY MANY THOUSANDS OF TIMES GREATER THAN OURS...
BZZT
WHAT DO YOU THINK OF THAT?
BUT POWERFUL AS THAT BRAIN IS...
BZZT
IT CAN'T MOVE... IT CAN ONLY SIT IN ONE SPOT...
BZZRT
AND WHAT DO YOU THINK A BRAIN LIKE THAT THINKS ABOUT, INSPECTOR GESICHT?
OF COURSE... I'M NOT ONE TO SPECULATE...
HEH HEH HEH ...

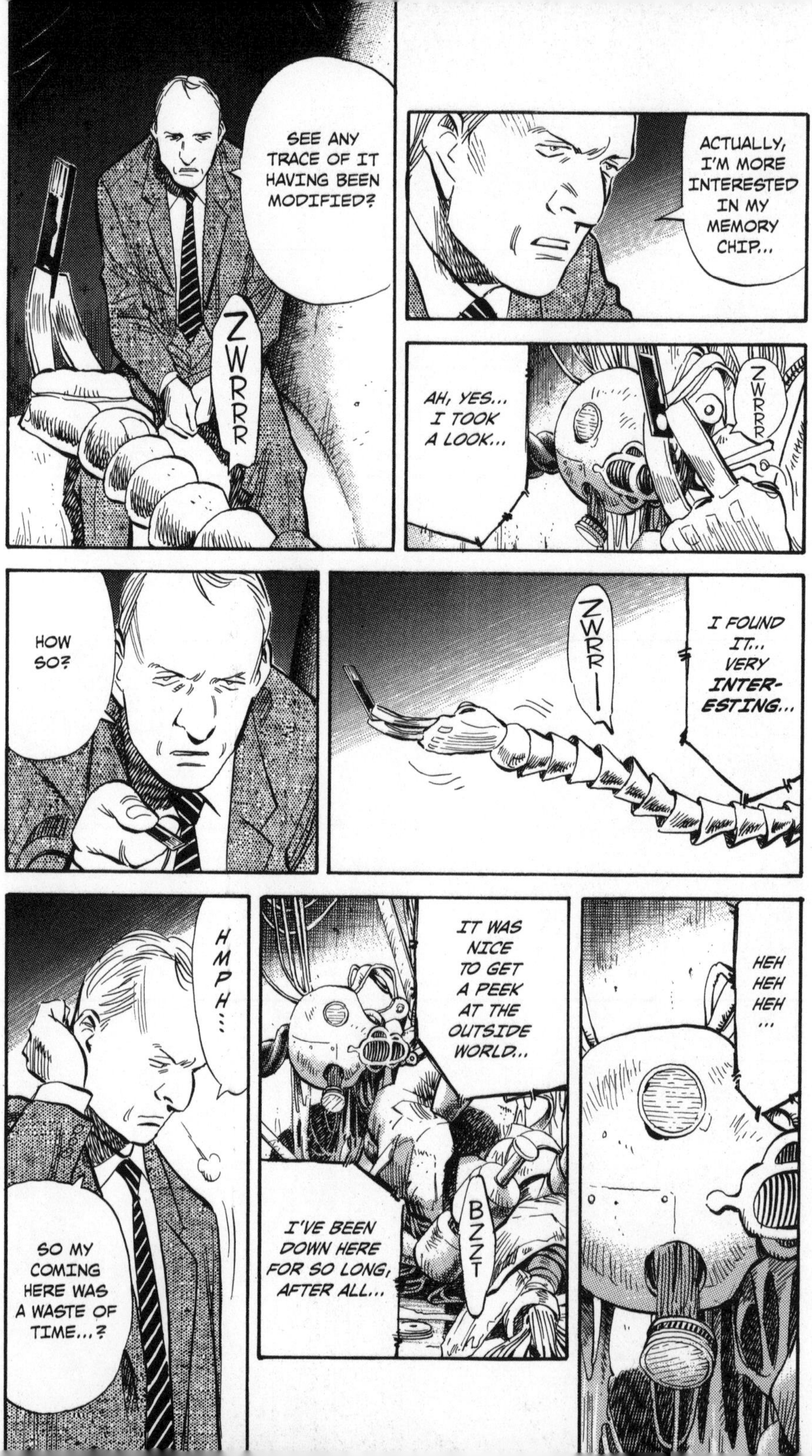
ACTUALLY, I'M MORE INTERESTED IN MY MEMORY CHIP...
AH, YES... I TOOK A LOOK...
ZWRRR
SEE ANY TRACE OF IT HAVING BEEN MODIFIED?
ZWRRR
I FOUND IT... VERY INTER-ESTING...
ZWRR
HOW SO?
HEH HEH HEH...
IT WAS NICE TO GET A PEEK AT THE OUTSIDE WORLD...
I'VE BEEN DOWN HERE FOR SO LONG, AFTER ALL...
BZZT
HMPH...
SO MY COMING HERE WAS A WASTE OF TIME...?

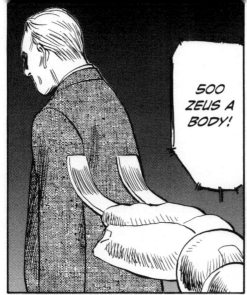

500 ZEUS A BODY!

BZZZT

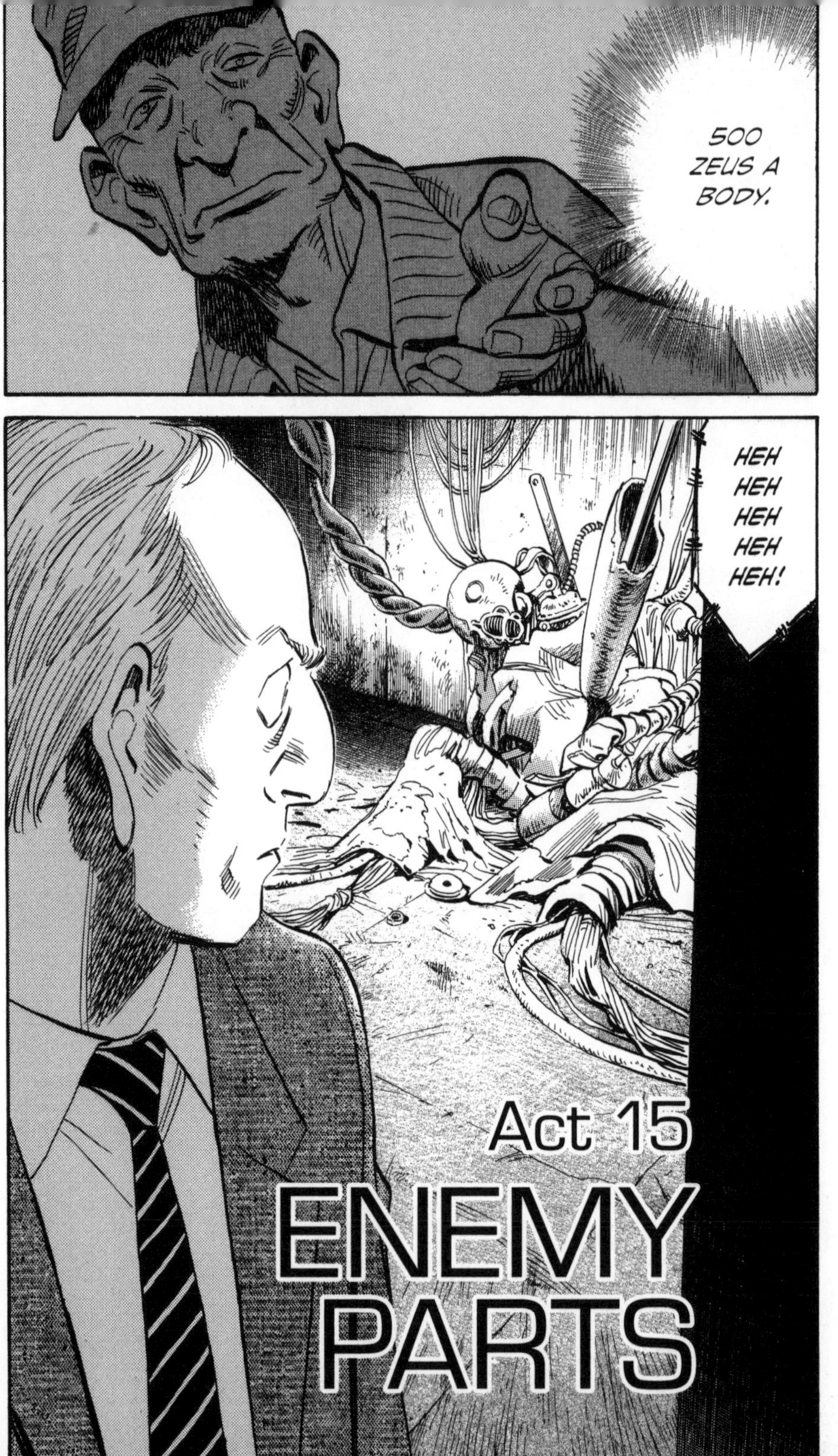
500 ZEUS A BODY.
HEH HEH HEH HEH HEH!
Act 15
ENEMY PARTS

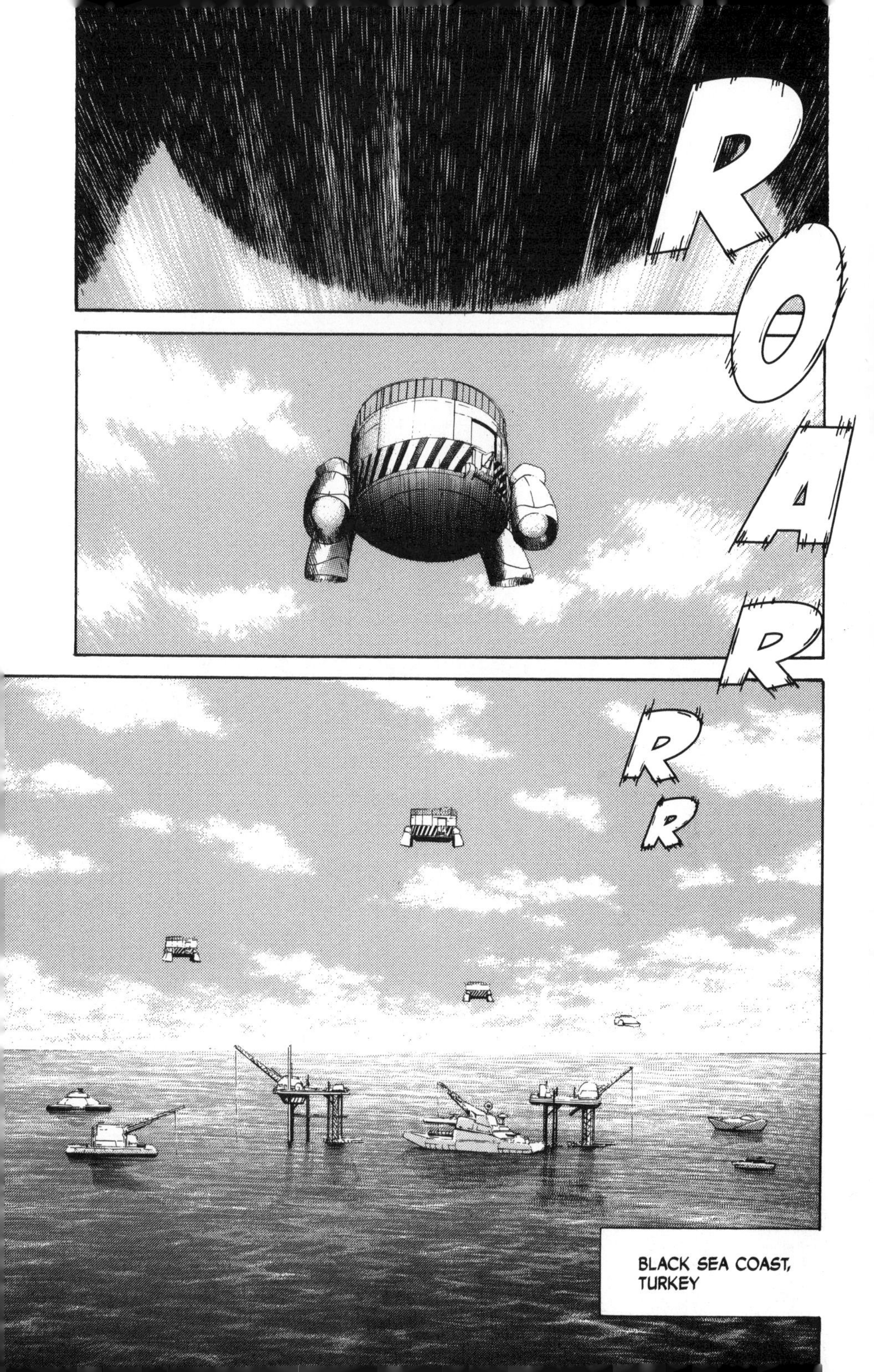
ROAARRR
BLACK SEA COAST, TURKEY

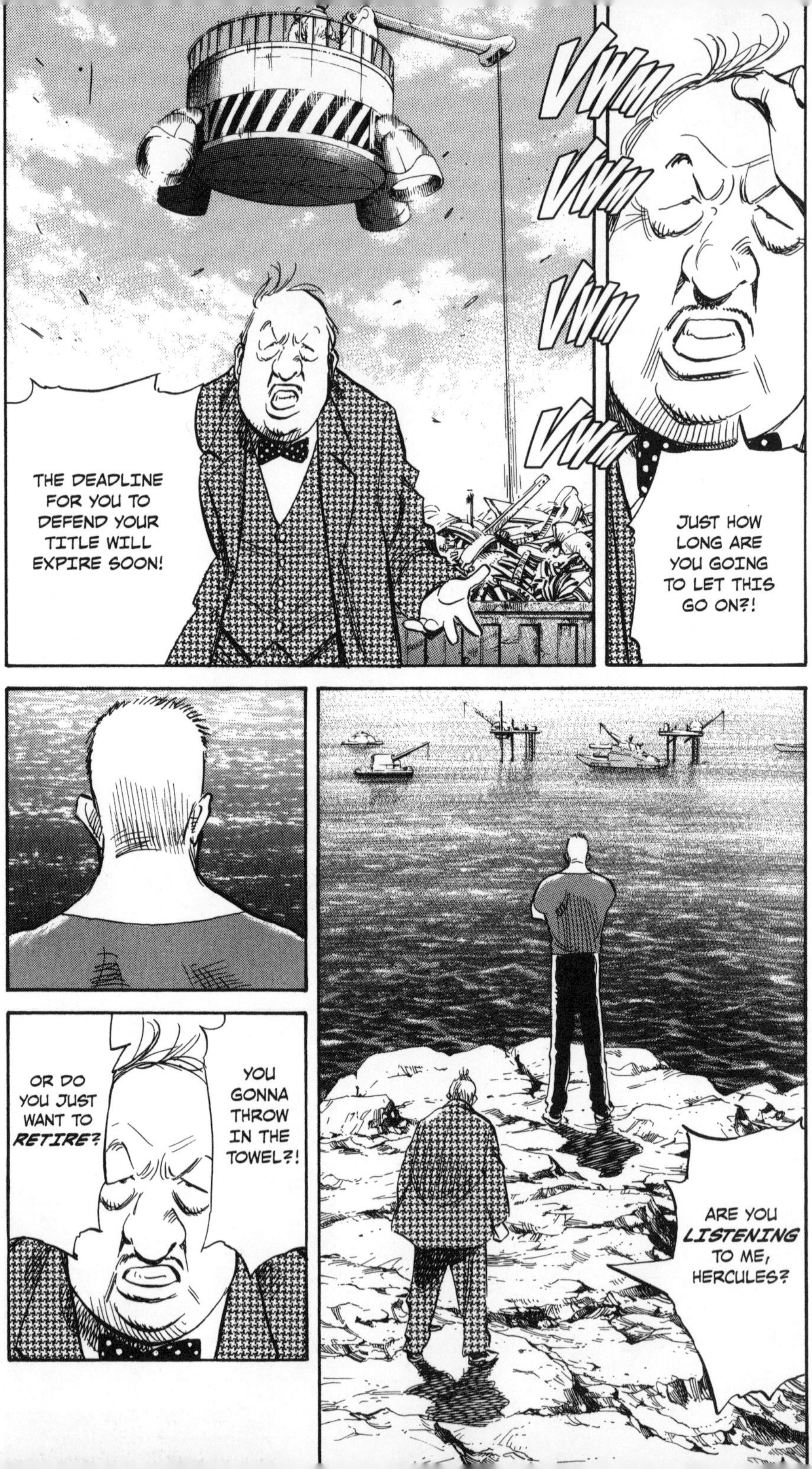
VWWW
VWWW
VWWW
VWWW
JUST HOW LONG ARE YOU GOING TO LET THIS GO ON?!
THE DEADLINE FOR YOU TO DEFEND YOUR TITLE WILL EXPIRE SOON!
ARE YOU *LISTENING* TO ME, HERCULES?
YOU GONNA THROW IN THE TOWEL?!
OR DO YOU JUST WANT TO *RETIRE*?

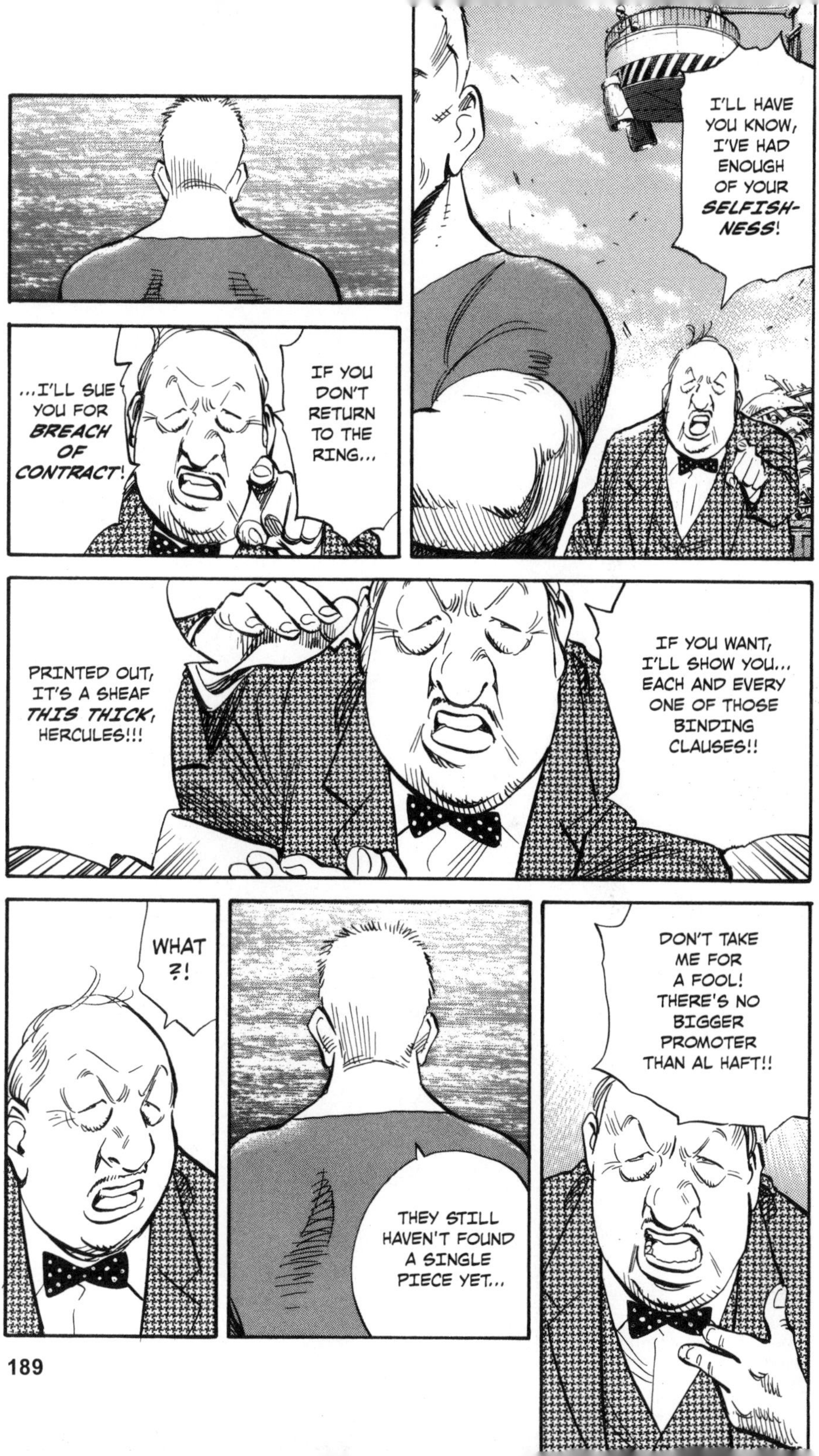
I'LL HAVE YOU KNOW, I'VE HAD ENOUGH OF YOUR *SELFISHNESS*!
IF YOU DON'T RETURN TO THE RING...
...I'LL SUE YOU FOR *BREACH OF CONTRACT*!
IF YOU WANT, I'LL SHOW YOU... EACH AND EVERY ONE OF THOSE BINDING CLAUSES!!
PRINTED OUT, IT'S A SHEAF *THIS THICK*, HERCULES!!!
DON'T TAKE ME FOR A FOOL! THERE'S NO BIGGER PROMOTER THAN AL HAFT!!
THEY STILL HAVEN'T FOUND A SINGLE PIECE YET...
WHAT?!

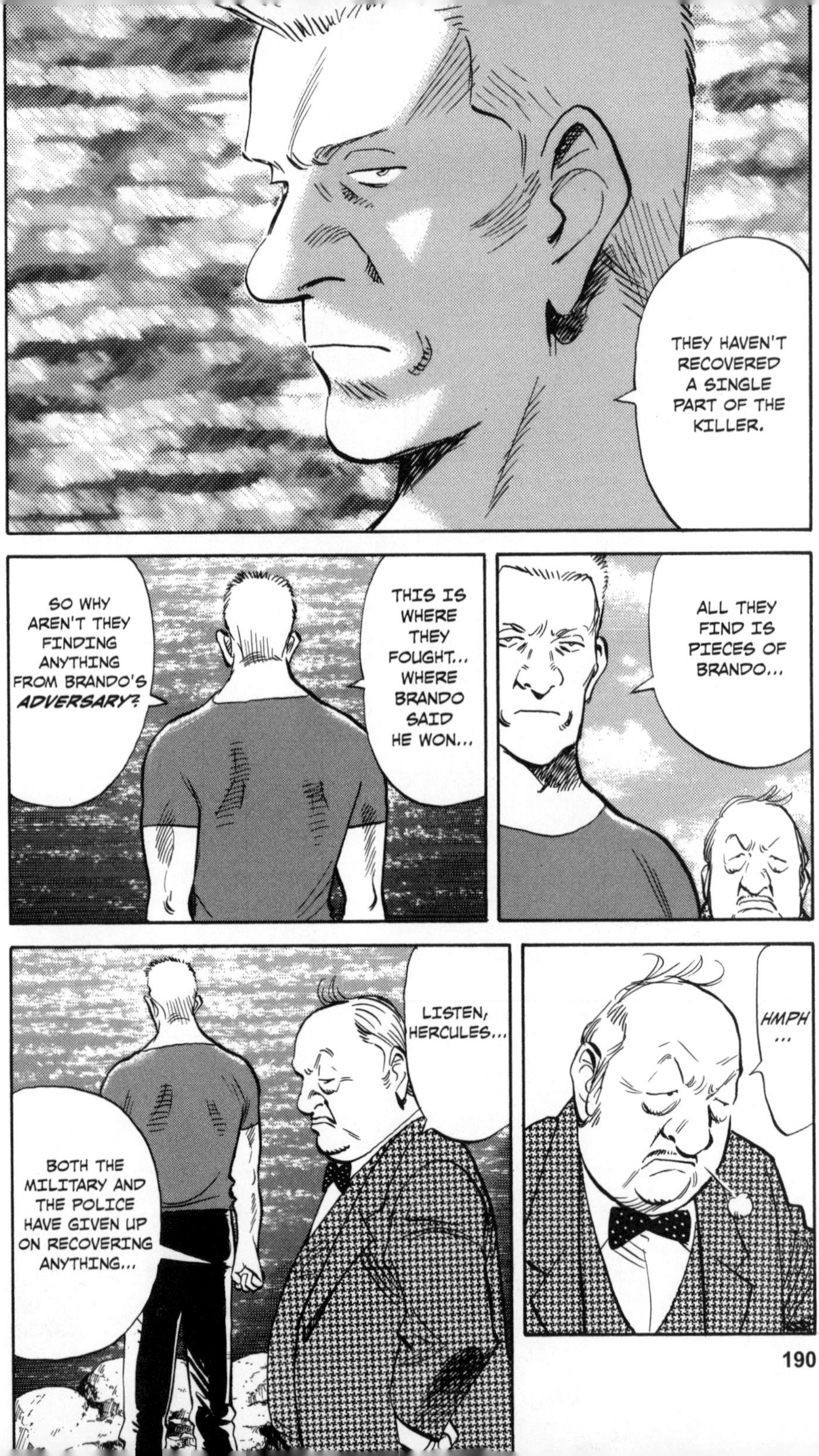
THEY HAVEN'T RECOVERED A SINGLE PART OF THE KILLER.
ALL THEY FIND IS PIECES OF BRANDO...
THIS IS WHERE THEY FOUGHT... WHERE BRANDO SAID HE WON...
SO WHY AREN'T THEY FINDING ANYTHING FROM BRANDO'S *ADVERSARY*?
HMPH ...
LISTEN, HERCULES...
BOTH THE MILITARY AND THE POLICE HAVE GIVEN UP ON RECOVERING ANYTHING...

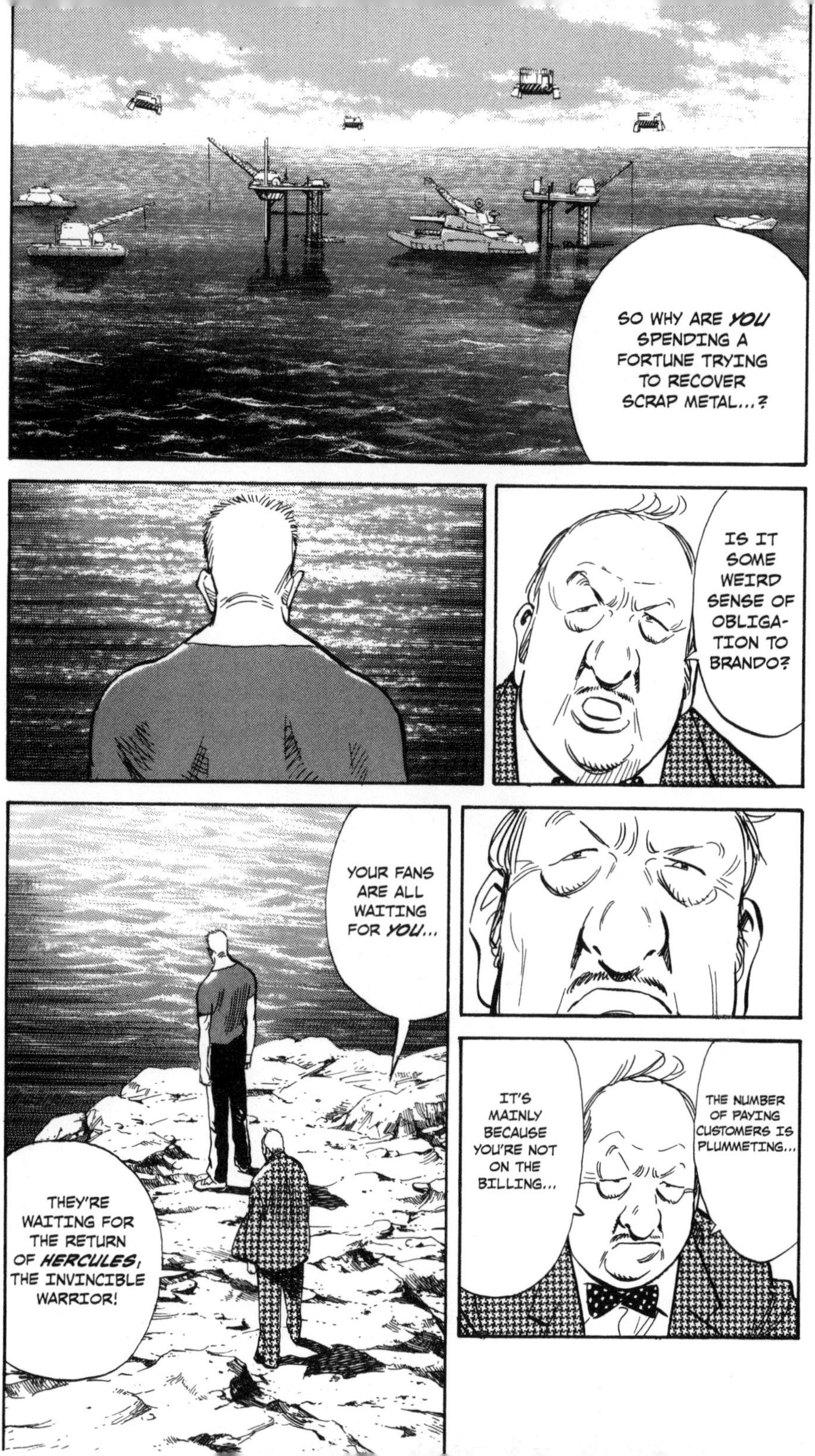
SO WHY ARE *YOU* SPENDING A FORTUNE TRYING TO RECOVER SCRAP METAL...?
IS IT SOME WEIRD SENSE OF OBLIGATION TO BRANDO?
THE NUMBER OF PAYING CUSTOMERS IS PLUMMETING...
IT'S MAINLY BECAUSE YOU'RE NOT ON THE BILLING...
YOUR FANS ARE ALL WAITING FOR *YOU*...
THEY'RE WAITING FOR THE RETURN OF ***HERCULES***, THE INVINCIBLE WARRIOR!

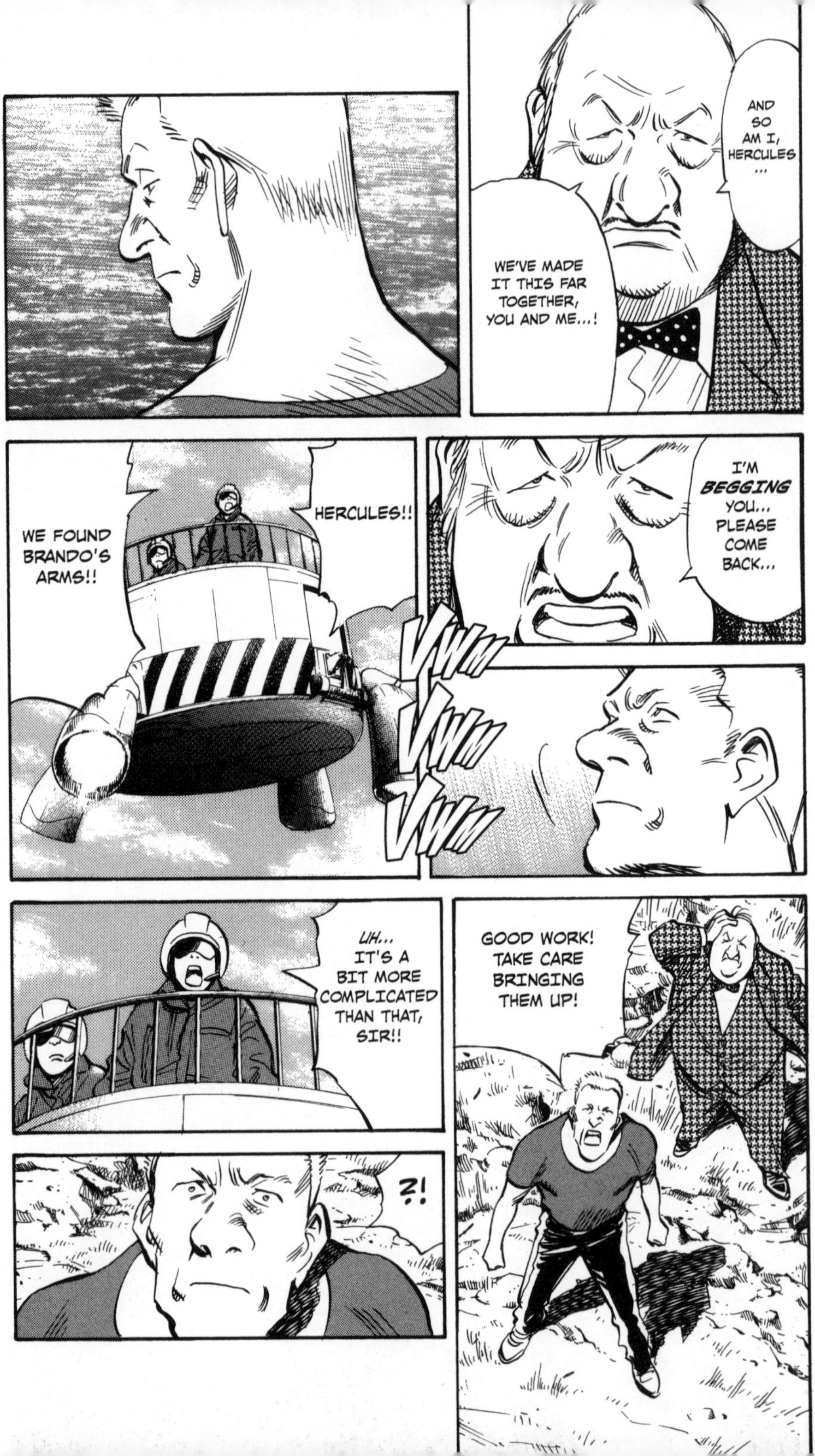
AND SO AM I, HERCULES ...
WE'VE MADE IT THIS FAR TOGETHER, YOU AND ME...!
I'M *BEGGING* YOU... PLEASE COME BACK...
VWM VWM VWM
HERCULES!!
WE FOUND BRANDO'S ARMS!!
GOOD WORK! TAKE CARE BRINGING THEM UP!
UH... IT'S A BIT MORE COMPLICATED THAN THAT, SIR!!
?!

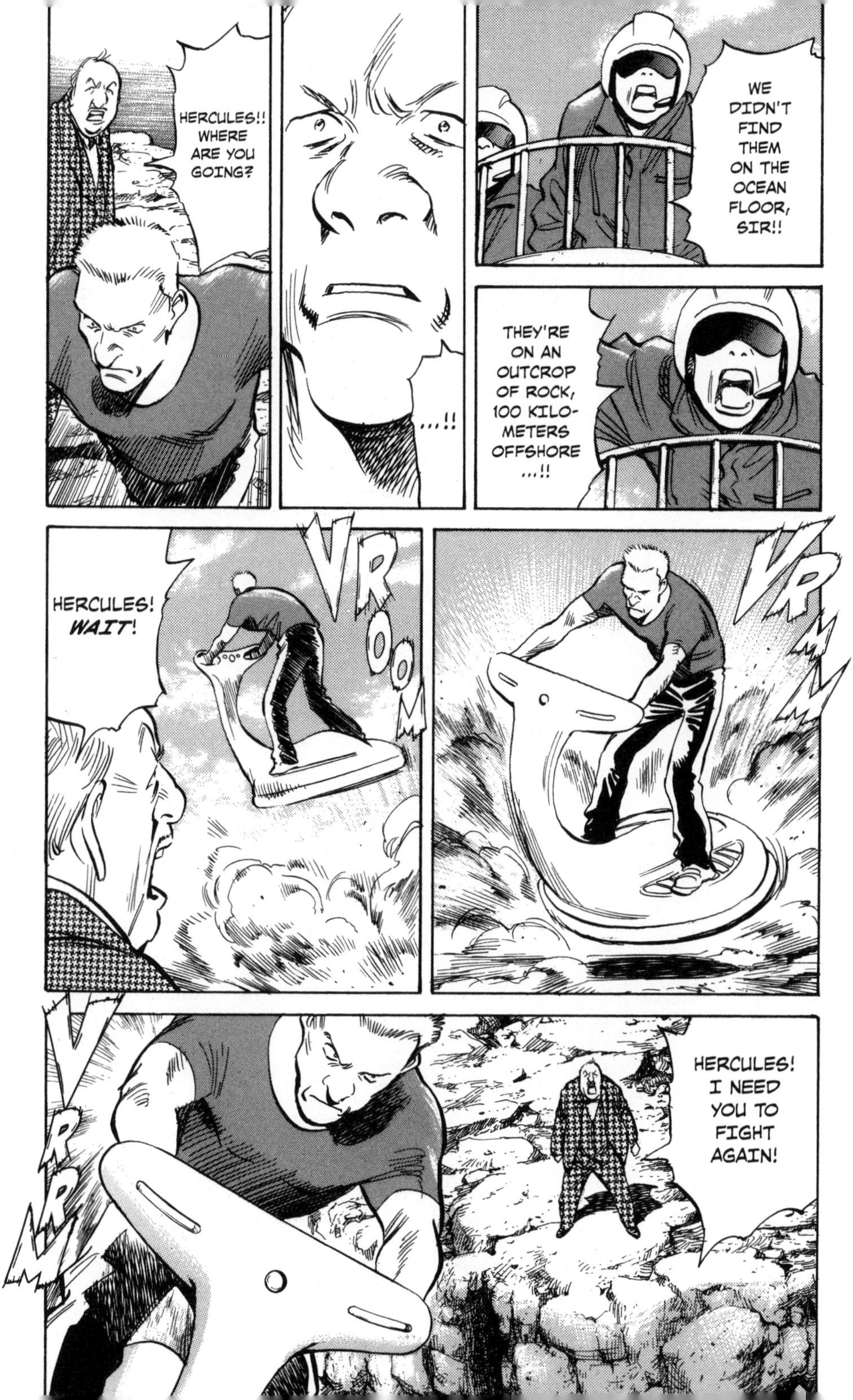
WE DIDN'T FIND THEM ON THE OCEAN FLOOR, SIR!!
THEY'RE ON AN OUTCROP OF ROCK, 100 KILOMETERS OFFSHORE ...!!
...!!
HERCULES!! WHERE ARE YOU GOING?
VROOM
HERCULES! *WAIT*!
HERCULES! I NEED YOU TO FIGHT AGAIN!

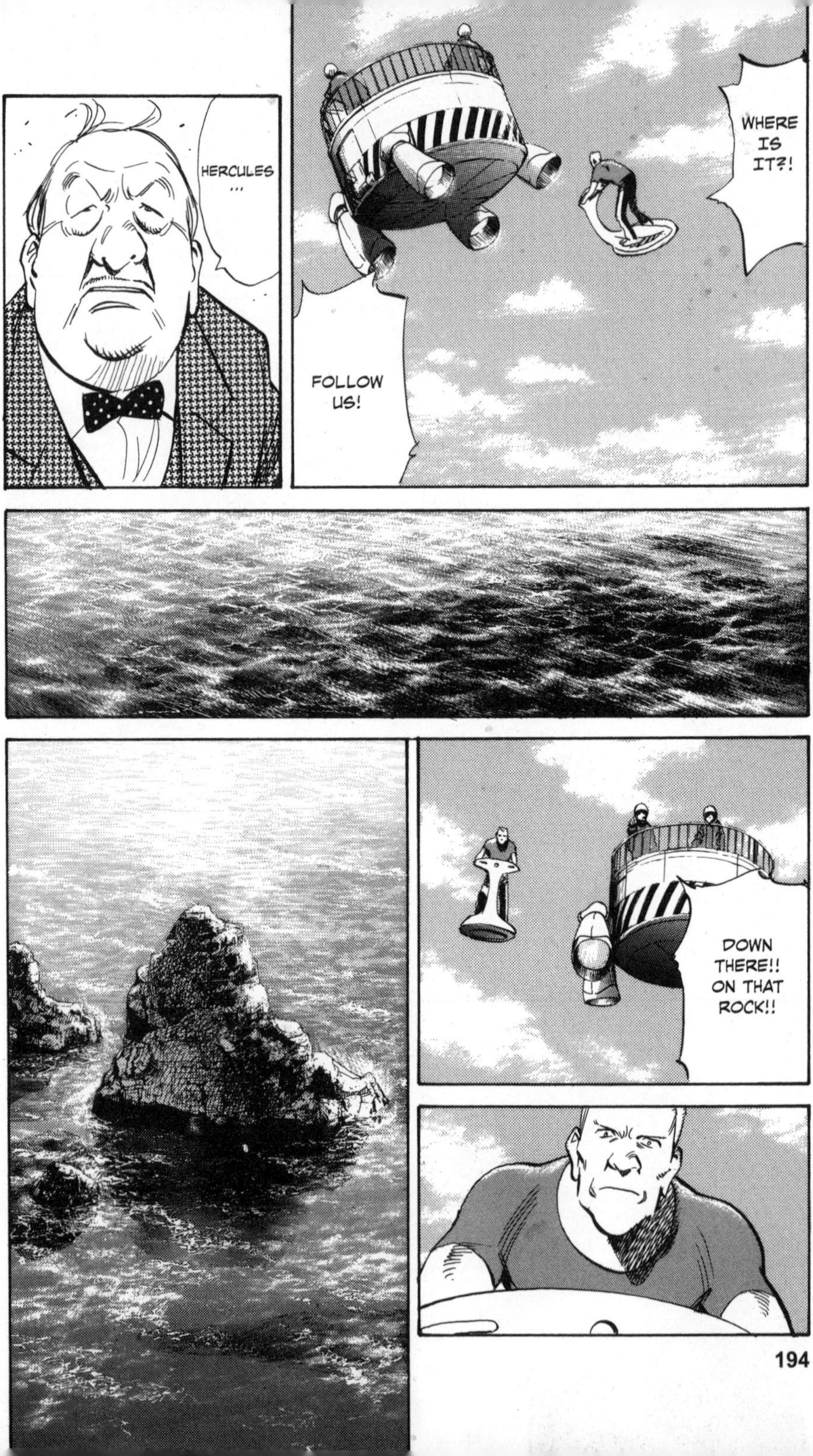
WHERE IS IT?!
FOLLOW US!
HERCULES ...
DOWN THERE!! ON THAT ROCK!!

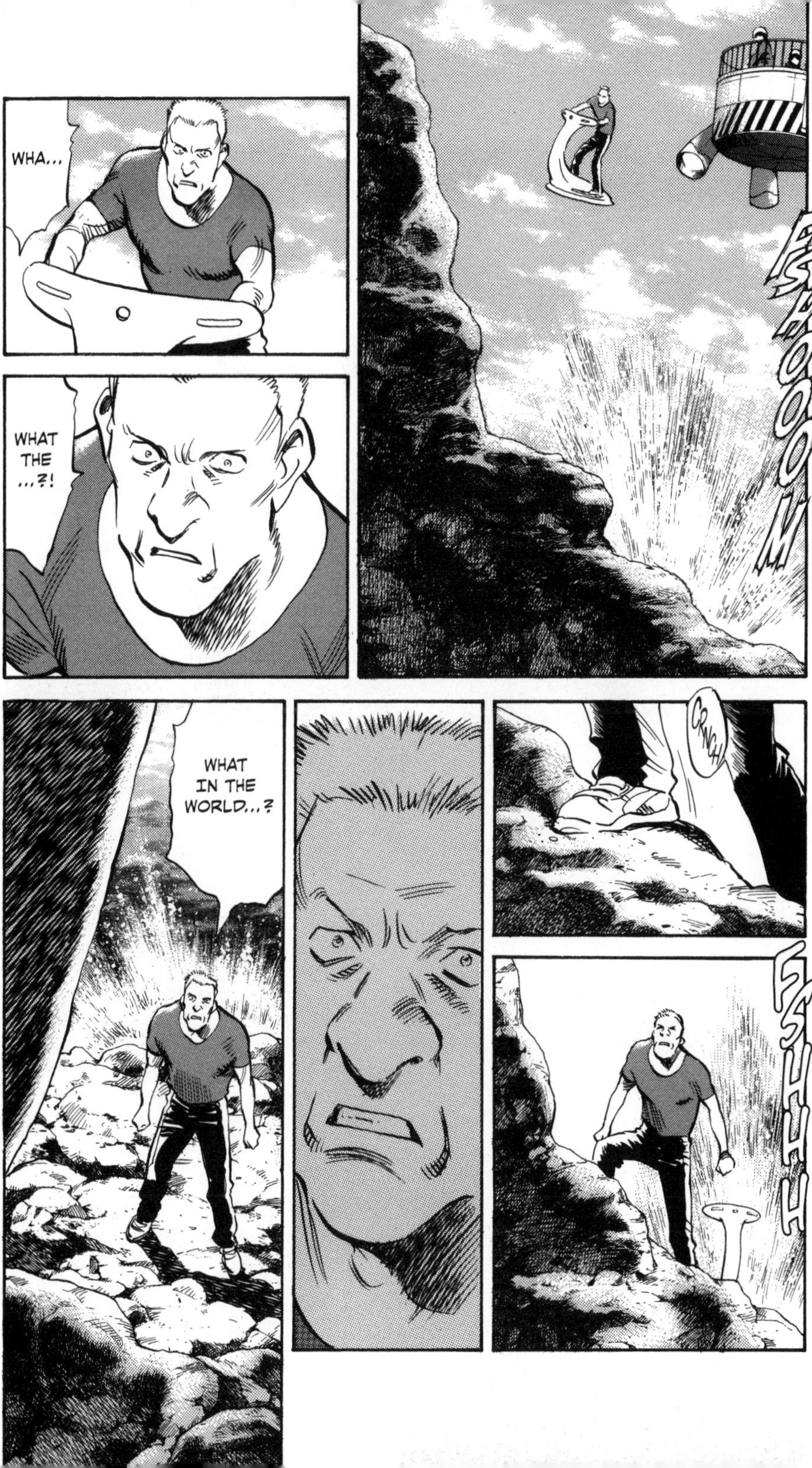
FSHOOOOM
WHA...
WHAT THE ...?!
CRNCH
FSHHHHH
WHAT IN THE WORLD...?

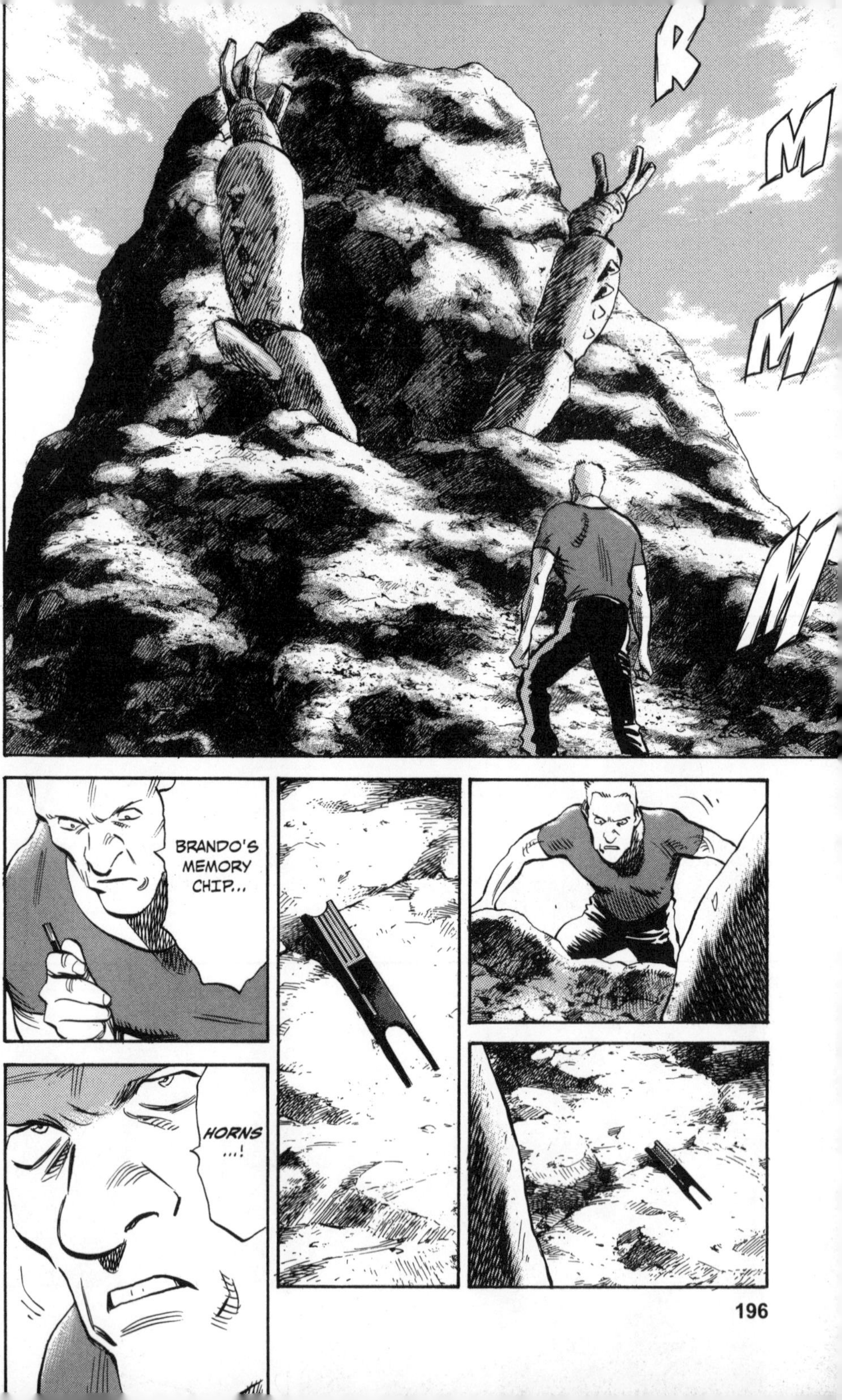
RMMM
BRANDO'S MEMORY CHIP...
HORNS ...!

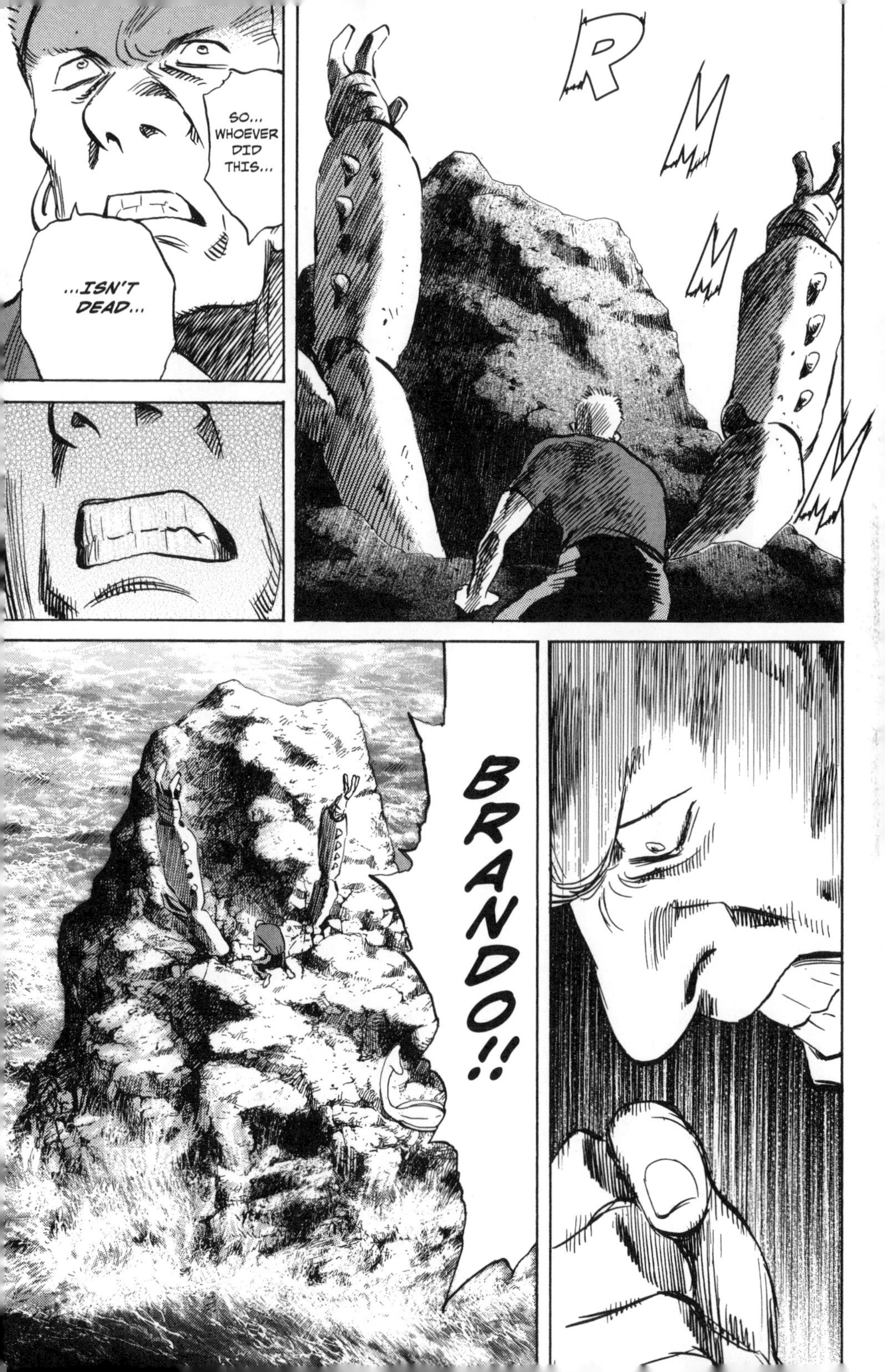
RMMM
SO... WHOEVER DID THIS...
...ISN'T DEAD...
BRANDO!!

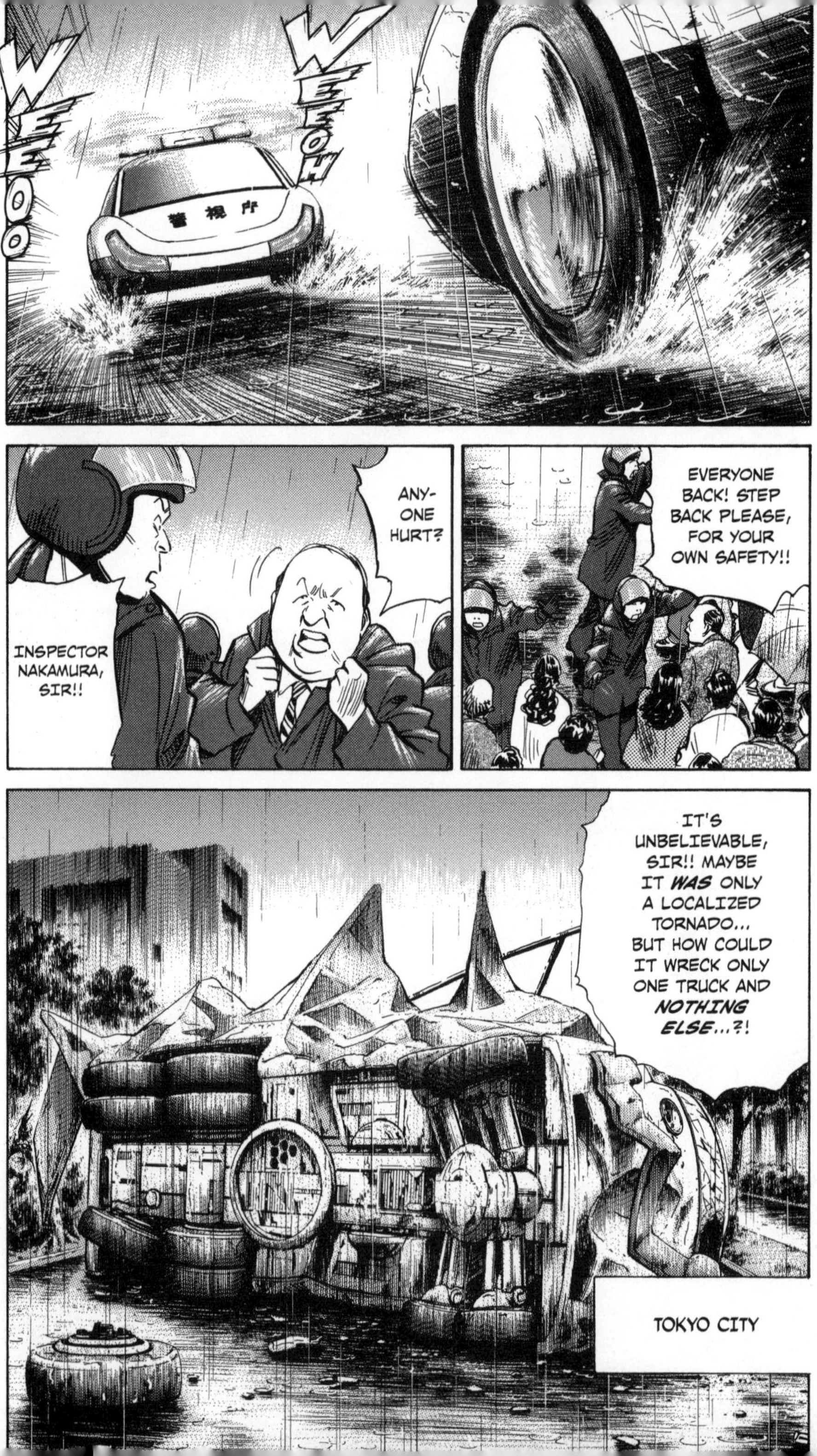
WEEEOH
WEEEOO
警視庁
EVERYONE BACK! STEP BACK PLEASE, FOR YOUR OWN SAFETY!!
ANY-ONE HURT?
INSPECTOR NAKAMURA, SIR!!
IT'S UNBELIEVABLE, SIR!! MAYBE IT ***WAS*** ONLY A LOCALIZED TORNADO... BUT HOW COULD IT WRECK ONLY ONE TRUCK AND ***NOTHING ELSE***...?!
TOKYO CITY

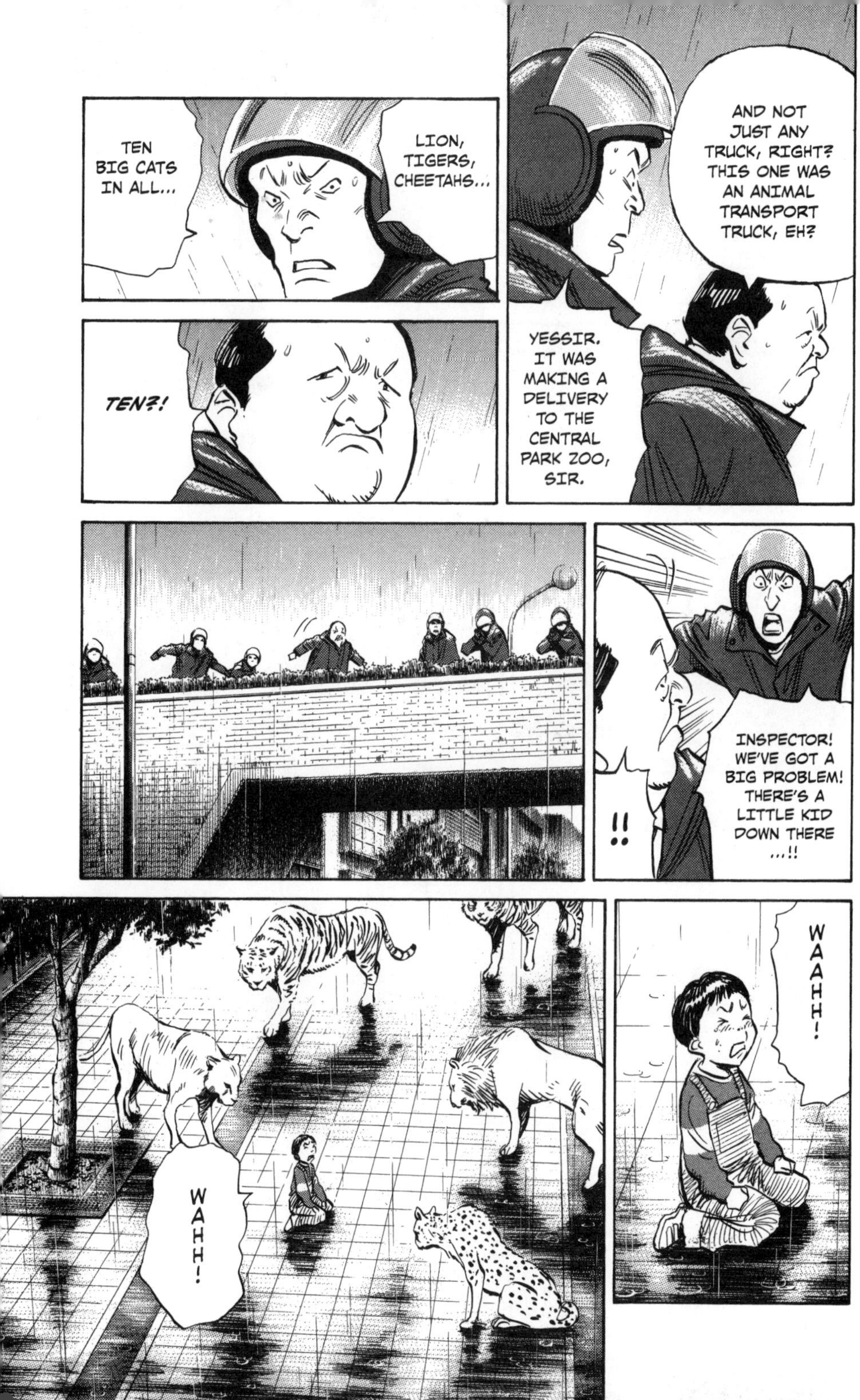
AND NOT JUST ANY TRUCK, RIGHT? THIS ONE WAS AN ANIMAL TRANSPORT TRUCK, EH?
YESSIR. IT WAS MAKING A DELIVERY TO THE CENTRAL PARK ZOO, SIR.
LION, TIGERS, CHEETAHS...
TEN BIG CATS IN ALL...
TEN?!
INSPECTOR! WE'VE GOT A BIG PROBLEM! THERE'S A LITTLE KID DOWN THERE ...!!
!!
WAAHH!
WAHH!

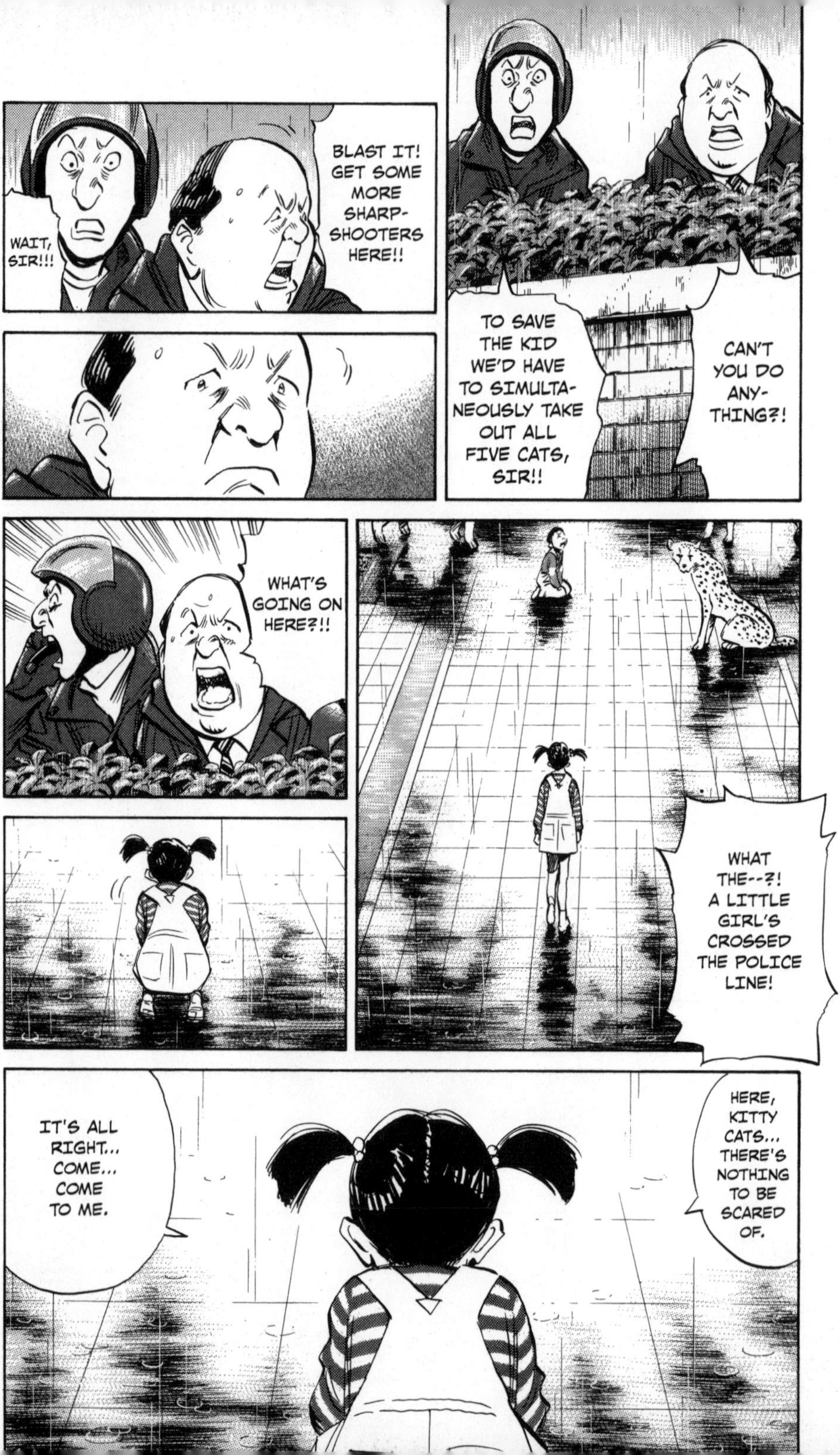
CAN'T YOU DO ANY-THING?!
TO SAVE THE KID WE'D HAVE TO SIMULTA-NEOUSLY TAKE OUT ALL FIVE CATS, SIR!!
BLAST IT! GET SOME MORE SHARP-SHOOTERS HERE!!
WAIT, SIR!!!
WHAT THE--?! A LITTLE GIRL'S CROSSED THE POLICE LINE!
WHAT'S GOING ON HERE?!!
HERE, KITTY CATS... THERE'S NOTHING TO BE SCARED OF.
IT'S ALL RIGHT... COME... COME TO ME.

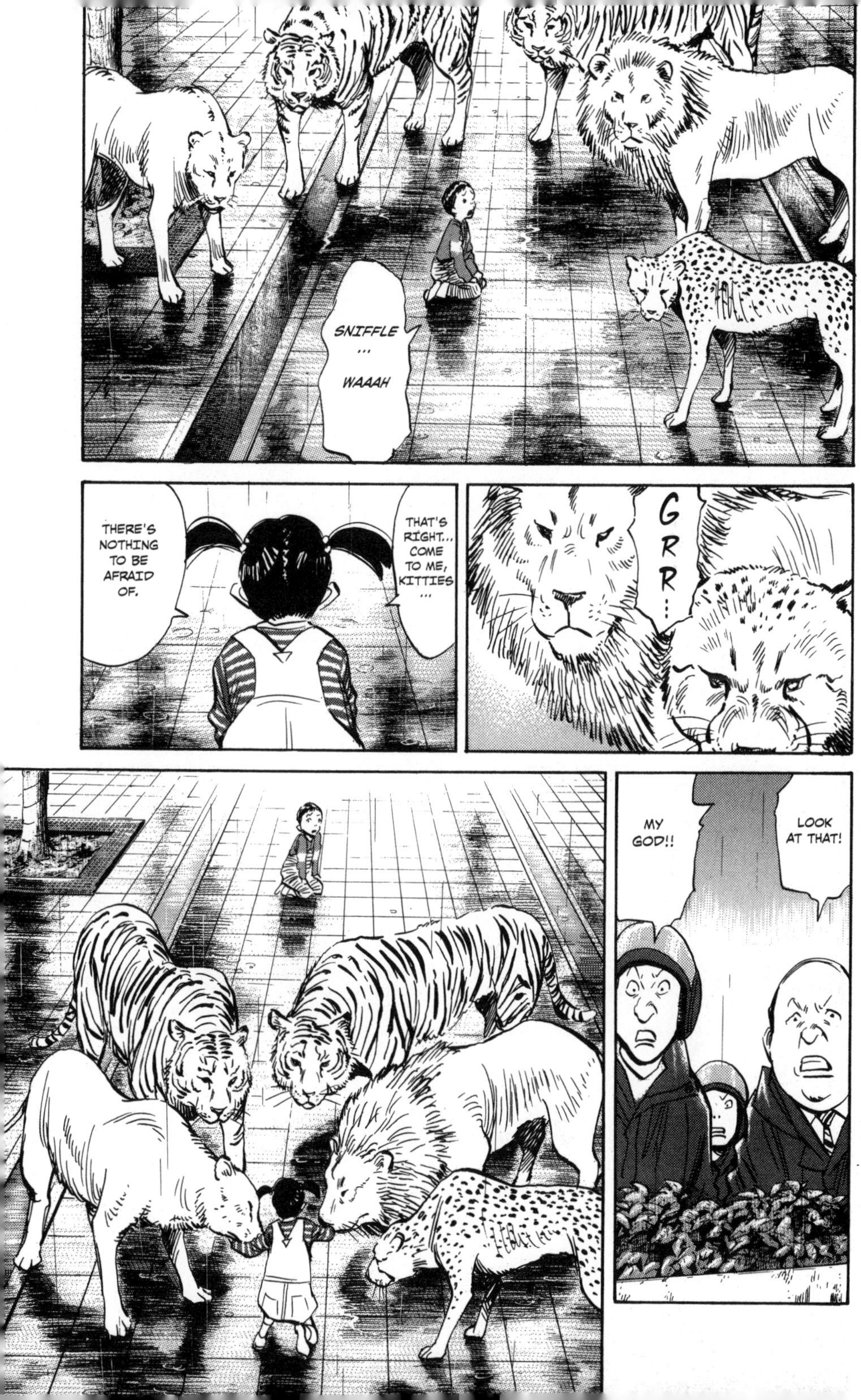
SNIFFLE ... WAAAH
GRR...
THAT'S RIGHT... COME TO ME, KITTIES ...
THERE'S NOTHING TO BE AFRAID OF.
LOOK AT THAT!
MY GOD!!

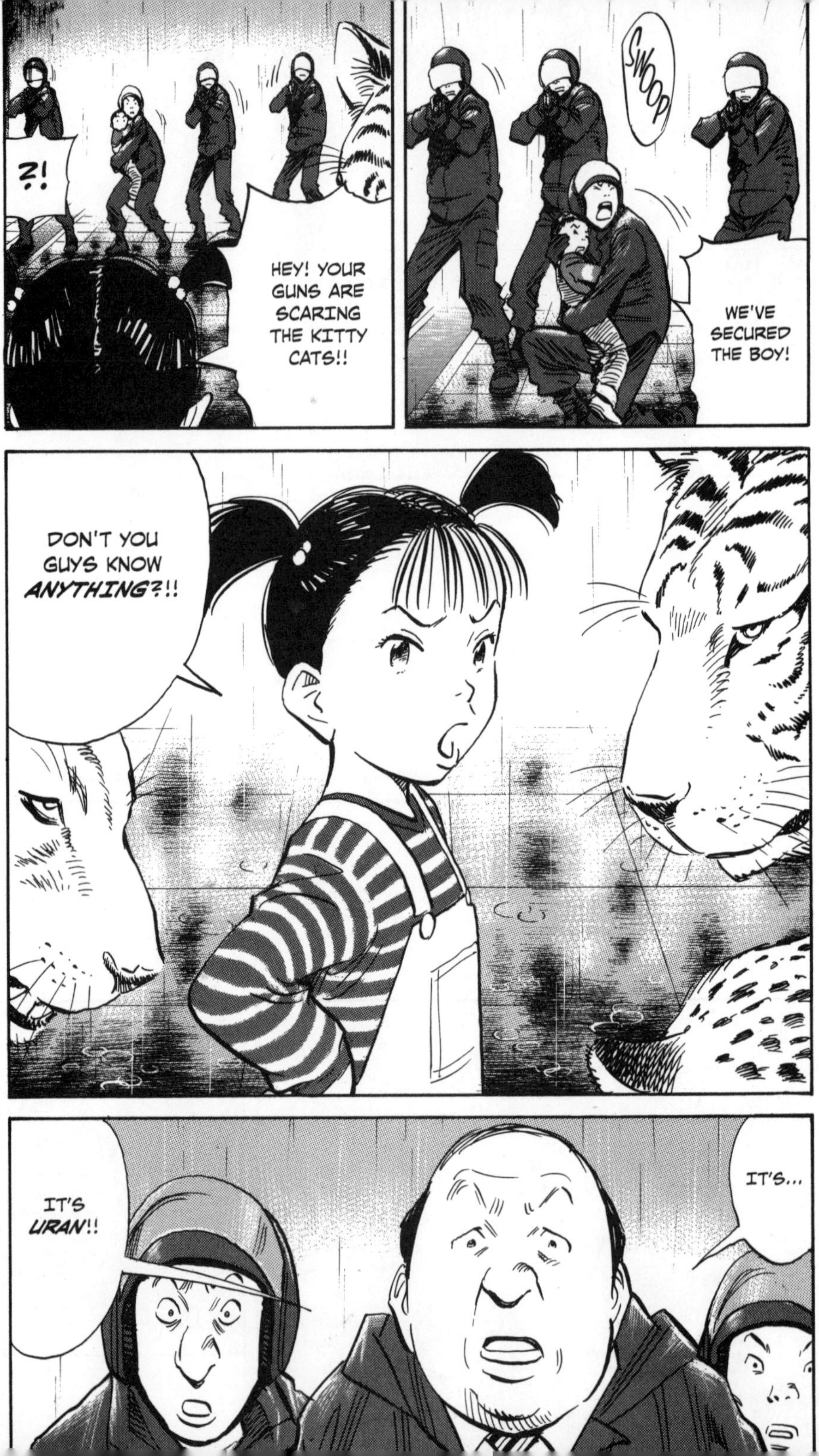
SWOOP
WE'VE SECURED THE BOY!
HEY! YOUR GUNS ARE SCARING THE KITTY CATS!!
?!
DON'T YOU GUYS KNOW *ANYTHING*?!!
IT'S...
IT'S *URAN*!!

POSTSCRIPT

Macoto Tezka, Visualist

I t was the winter of 2002. Someone came to me saying, "Naoki Urasawa wants to draw 'The Greatest Robot on Earth' story arc from the *Astro Boy* series."

"Really?" I said, "An artist as popular as Mr. Urasawa wants to make a new manga out of an already classic manga?"

With apologies to Mr. Urasawa, I was slightly taken aback. But it wasn't as bad as I first feared. April 7, 2003 was the birthday of Astro in the original manga series, so when I heard that this project was intended to commemorate that fact, it made a certain sense to me.

I don't want my father's works to always be treated as something overly precious. No matter how much time passes, I want them to be read and enjoyed by as many people as possible. And for that to happen, I do believe they need to be reborn in a variety of different media using different modes of expression.

And Mr. Urasawa certainly wouldn't have been the first artist to turn my father's work into his or her own manga. In fact, at an exhibition titled *My Atom*, over one hundred artists had already rendered their own interpretation of *Astro Boy*. But almost all of the works created then had been either an homage or a parody, and while the exhibit itself was interesting, I would be hard put to say that the individual works stood on their own very well.

So when I heard of Mr. Urasawa's idea, I thought, "Here we go again," and never expected that it might be more than that.

Then I was told that Mr. Urasawa hoped to serialize his interpretation in a major manga magazine and that he even wanted to eventually compile it into paperback books. When asked my opinion, I recall replying that the timing was probably a bit premature. In my mind, I thought that there would be plenty of opportunity at a future date to have other artists do a remake of *Astro Boy*, and that there really was no particular need to specifically link it to the upcoming birthday events. We had already created a new *Astro Boy* TV anime series, and there were a large number of other commemorative events already being planned. If we really went ahead with a project such as the one Mr. Urasawa was suggesting, I worried that it might seem to be too blatant an attempt to capitalize on the *Astro* "boom" then occurring in Japan. So I answered him to that effect.

In other words, as a representative of the Tezuka family, I gently turned Mr. Urasawa down.

My thinking then was that if Mr. Urasawa were to be put off by my suggestion of pursuing the project at another time, and if he were to decide to simply give up, well, that would settle things.

But he did not give up. He said that he wanted to have a chance to talk with me so he could show me some rough sketches and explain what sort of story he planned to create, and how he wanted to configure it. He said he would give me a full presentation.

Given that he was so serious about this project, I felt that I was left with few alternatives. I made sure that I had lots of time to get back to him, and after thinking the matter over thoroughly, I eventually agreed to meet him. Mr. Urasawa, for his part, probably thought that he didn't stand a chance, but he wanted to have me hear him out and understand how enthusiastic he was about the project.

I, on the other hand, have to be careful because actually meeting with artists can be construed as tantamount to giving my seal of approval to their ideas. And ultimately I am the one who has to take responsibility for the act of sending a project like this out into the world. I knew some of my father's fans would probably react extremely negatively to a project like Urasawa's. And if this happened I knew we'd both have to take the heat.

On March 28, 2003, I met with Mr. Urasawa, his producer, Mr. Nagasaki, and others at a place in the Ginza and heard them out until late at night. With great passion, Mr. Urasawa explained that "The Greatest Robot on Earth" in the *Astro Boy* series had been the first manga that deeply impressed him, and that it had been the inspiration for all of his subsequent creative work.

I had no intention of gleefully giving him the go-ahead right then and there, no matter what he said, so I insisted on one condition. I made him promise that he would create the work in his own style and make it his own work. I said this because the initial character designs and sketches Mr. Urasawa showed me betrayed a certain deference to Tezuka's work and looked more like an imitation. Atom would be immediately recognizable by anyone as Atom, and Gesicht had the same face that Tezuka had used in his original manga.

I told Mr. Urasawa then that if he were going to go ahead with a project like this, that he shouldn't just imitate Tezuka; I wanted to see something that was really his—Urasawa's—own work. I even took it upon myself to ask him to rethink his character designs. Having downed a few drinks by then, I probably was starting to sound rather rude. I told him that up to that point everyone else had merely offered up homages to my father, and that if he would only get truly serious and really go to the mat on this one to compete head-on with my father, I would be the referee.

That's probably when Mr. Urasawa's real agonies began. In retrospect, I feel bad for having acted in such an immature fashion.

While this certainly won't serve as an apology, since I am serving as the referee for this competition, I have to say that the first round definitely goes to Mr. Urasawa. I'm not suggesting that his manga, or even my father's, is best. What I am saying is that Mr. Urasawa has challenged my father head on, and he has not lost. That alone deserves a great deal of praise. But of course this is only the first round, and the match continues.

I hope that you, the readers, will enjoy watching—with sweaty palms—as this thrilling contest unfolds. The participants—Osamu Tezuka and Naoki Urasawa—are both world-class entertainers, fully capable of enchanting us all.

The late Osamu Tezuka, a manga artist for whom I have the utmost respect, created the series *Astro Boy*. This timeless classic has been read by countless numbers of fans from when it was first created in the fifties to now. As a child, "The Greatest Robot on Earth" story arc from *Astro Boy* was the first manga I ever read that really moved me and inspired me to become a manga artist. With *Pluto* I've attempted to infuse that story with a fresh new spirit. I hope you enjoy it.

NAOKI URASAWA

Manga wouldn't exist without Tezuka Osamu. He is the Leonardo da Vinci, the Goethe, the Dostoevsky of the manga world. Naoki Urasawa and I have always felt that his achievements and work must not be allowed to fade away. Tezuka wrote that Atom, the main character of his most representative work *Astro Boy*, was born in 2003. This was the same year that we re-made "The Greatest Robot on Earth" story arc from the *Astro Boy* series. Who was Osamu Tezuka and what was his message? For those of you readers who are interested in *Pluto*, I highly recommend you read it alongside Tezuka's original work.

TAKASHI NAGASAKI

PLUTO: URASAWA × TEZUKA
VOLUME 2
VIZ SIGNATURE EDITION

BY **Naoki Urasawa & Osamu Tezuka**
CO-AUTHORED WITH **Takashi Nagasaki**
WITH THE COOPERATION OF **Tezuka Productions**

TRANSLATION **Jared Cook & Frederick L. Schodt**
TOUCH-UP & LETTERING **James Gaubatz**
COVER ART DIRECTION **Kazuo Umino**
LOGO & COVER DESIGN **Mikiyo Kobayashi & Bay Bridge Studio**
VIZ SIGNATURE EDITION DESIGNER **Courtney Utt**
EDITOR **Andy Nakatani**

EDITOR IN CHIEF, BOOKS **Alvin Lu**
EDITOR IN CHIEF, MAGAZINES **Marc Weidenbaum**
VP, PUBLISHING LICENSING **Rika Inouye**
VP, SALES & PRODUCT MARKETING **Gonzalo Ferreyra**
VP, CREATIVE **Linda Espinosa**
PUBLISHER **Hyoe Narita**

Printed in the U.S.A.

Published by VIZ Media, LLC
P.O. Box 77010
San Francisco, CA 94107

10 9 8 7 6 5 4 3 2 1
First printing, March 2009

‹ www.viz.com store.viz.com ›

ASTRO BOY

Osamu Tezuka's iconic *Astro Boy* series was a truly groundbreaking work about a loveable boy robot that would pave the way for all manga and anime to follow. Tezuka created the manga in 1951 and in January of 1963 adapted it to become the first weekly animated TV series ever to be broadcast in Japan. In September of that same year, it became the first animated TV series from Japan to hit the airwaves in the United States. The series and its title character were originally known in Japan as *Tetsuwan Atom*, which translates to "mighty Atom" – or for the more literally minded, "iron-arm Atom" – but was released in the U.S. as *Astro Boy*. Decades later, in 2000, Dark Horse Comics brought the manga for the first time to English readers, also under the title *Astro Boy*.

Within the context of the story for this English edition of *Pluto: Urasawa × Tezuka*, the precocious boy robot will be referred to as "Atom" in the manner in which he has been known and loved in Japan for over fifty years. Elsewhere, such as in the end matter, the series will be referred to as *Astro Boy* as it has been known outside of Japan since 1963.